WHOOPI GOLDBERG

Also by James Robert Parish

Rosie: Rosie O'Donnell's Biography
The Unofficial "Murder, She Wrote" Casebook
Today's Black Hollywood
Let's Talk! America's Favorite Talk Show Hosts
Hollywood Celebrity Death Book
Prostitution in Hollywood Films
Great Cop Pictures
The Slapstick Queens
The RKO Gals
Great Western Stars
The Jeanette MacDonald Story
Vincent Price Unmasked
Black Action Pictures
Elvis Presley Scrapbook

Among those he has cowritten are:

Hollywood Baby Boomer
Complete Actors TV Credits
Hollywood Songsters
Great Detective Pictures
The George Raft File
The MGM Stock Company
Liza!: The Liza Minnelli Story
The Funsters
Hollywood on Hollywood
Great Science Fiction Pictures

WHOOPI GOLDBERG

Her Journey From Poverty to Megastardom

James Robert Parish

A Birch Lane Press Book
Published by Carol Publishing Group

A Birch Lane Press Book
Published by Carol Publishing Group
Birch Lane Press is a registered trademark of Carol Communications, Inc.

Editorial, sales and distribution, and rights and permissions inquiries should be addressed to Carol Publishing Group, 120 Enterprise Avenue, Secaucus, N.J. 07094.

In Canada: Canadian Manda Group, One Atlantic Avenue, Suite 105, Toronto, Ontario M6K 3E7.

Carol Publishing Group books may be purchased in bulk at special discounts for sales promotion, fund-raising, or educational purposes. Special editions can be created to specifications. For details, contact Special Sales Department, Carol Publishing Group, 120 Enterprise Avenue, Secaucus, N.J. 07094.

Manufactured in the United States of America
10 9 8 7 6 5 4 3 2 1

Library of Congress Cataloging-in-Publication Data
Parish, James Robert.
    Whoopi Goldberg : her journey from poverty to megastardom / James Robert Parish.
        p.   cm.
    "A Birch Lane Press book."
    Filmography: p.
    Includes bibliographical references and index.
    ISBN 1–55972–431–5 (hc)
    1. Goldberg, Whoopi, 1955- . 2. Comedians—United States—Biography.   3. Afro-American comedians—United States—Biography.   4. Motion picture actors and actresses—United States—Biography.   5. Afro-American motion picture actors and actresses—United States—Biography.
I. Title.
    PN2287.G578P37   1997
    791.43′028′092—dc21
    [B]   97–27808
                                                                                                          CIP

Contents

Acknowledgments

Academy of Motion Picture Arts and Sciences: Margaret Herrick Library, Acme Whoopi Goldberg Internet Home Page (Patrick Spreng), Michael Gene Ankerich, Archive Photos (Michael Shulman), Kathy Bartels, Dave Bell, Louise Bianco, John Cocchi, John Cork, Ernest Cunningham, Annette D'Agostino, George Fergus, Friars Club of New York (Jean-Pierre L. Trebot), Mary Alice Fry, Charlene George, Alex Gildzen, Bruce Gold, Pierre Guinle, James S. Harris, David Hofstede, Matt Kennedy, Jani Klain, Steve Klain, Steven Lance, John Lavalie, Randi Miller Levine, Retta Lewis, Sandy Levy, Jennifer Liao, Jerry London, Alvin H. Marill, Lee Mattson, Peter McCarron, Meredith McMinn, Mrs. Earl Meisinger, Jim Meyer, Eric Monder, Museum of Television and Radio (Jonathan Schwartz—Research Department), *New York Observer* (Garnet Shaw), New York Public Library at Lincoln Center (the Billy Rose Theater Collection), Dr. Martin Norden, Photofest (Howard Mandelbaum), Prof. Robert Potter, Barry Rivadue, Jerry Roberts, Margie Schultz, Brenda Scott Royce, San Diego Repertory Theatre, Arleen Schwartz, Les Schwartz, Seth Poppel's Yearbook Archives, Les Spindle, Lara Starcevich, Dot Stenning, Charlie Stumpf, Jerry Vermilye, Tom Walsh, Rev. Wyatt Tee Walker, Don Wigal, Bernice Wynn.

I also wish to thank my agent, Robert G. Diforio, and my editor, Hillel Black, without whom this book would not have come to be.

Editorial consultant: Allan Taylor.

PART I

The Way She Was

CHAPTER ONE

A Night at the Friars

What has happened to this country's sense of humor
that once was a strength: It is disappearing.
Disappearing. Disappearing. It is really scary because
what looks like the result of this lost humor is really
ugly. It is coming from everywhere. People are slowly
losing their ability to listen and make judgments for
themselves. It is sad.

—WHOOPI GOLDBERG, DECEMBER 1993

On October 7, 1993, Toni Morrison became the eighth woman to win a Nobel Prize in Literature and the first African-American woman to do so. Morrison acknowledged: "Regardless of what we all say and truly believe about the irrelevance of prizes and their relationship to the real work, nevertheless this is a signal honor for me."

The next day, another African-American woman was to be honored. On that Friday, Whoopi Goldberg would be feted by the Friars Club in New York City, the bastion of show-business greats. She was to be "roasted" by this venerable organization at their famous annual celebrity luncheon, scheduled to be held at the New York Hilton, located on the Avenue of the Americas at Fifty-third Street.

The much-celebrated Friars Club traces its origins back to the early 1900s. Early on, the club inaugurated a tradition of honoring noteworthy personalities in the entertainment field with a special dinner. The first such awardee was Victor Herbert, the king of American operetta composers. Several decades later, in 1953, torch singer Sophie Tucker was the first woman to be honored at a Friars' celebrity roast. Other notables

3

celebrated at these get-togethers include Humphrey Bogart (1955), Lucille Ball (1961), Neil Simon (1978), Phyllis Diller (1985), Bruce Willis (1989), and Billy Crystal (1992). Over the years the house rule was that anything and everything was fair game at these fund-raisers. Depending on who was the guest of "honor," speakers (especially veteran comedians) pulled no punches whatsoever in toasting and roasting the celebrity "victim."

That sunny day in October 1993, the Friars celebrity luncheon was sold out. No one seemed to care that the main course would be the typical banquet-room rubbery chicken or that ten or more people would be crowded together at each of the many tables in the huge dining room. Everyone agreed that the roast would be great fun. Its featured guest was a New York success story, a still relatively young woman who had gone from high school dropout to Broadway fame and on to Hollywood superstardom and an Academy Award. With her trademark dreadlocks, wide-mouth grin, and distinctive looks this talented performer was universally regarded as a great comedian, a fine dramatic actor, and a determined humanitarian.

Adding to Whoopi Goldberg's allure as a top celebrity and, at the time, Hollywood's highest-paid actor was her yearlong romance with Emmy Award–winning actor Ted Danson, the beloved Sam Malone of the hugely popular TV sitcom *Cheers*. In the summer of 1992, African-American Goldberg and Caucasian Danson—he was married and the father of two daughters—had costarred in the screen comedy *Made in America*. The costars' rapport on the set led to a hot off-camera romance. At first, the surprising—some insisted improbable—relationship had remained hidden. However, the resourceful supermarket tabloids broke the titillating story despite the couple's persistent denials.

Once the media uncovered the love match, the two stars enjoyed few moments of real privacy. The public apparently could not get enough information on what the world's master playboy, at least on TV, found so enticing about "plain Jane" Goldberg, who, because of her string of asexual screen roles and unusual looks, many thought to be a wallflower offscreen. It didn't matter to the public that Goldberg was already twice divorced, the mother of a grown daughter who now had her own child, or that Whoopi had enjoyed a series of other romantic liaisons over the years.

Throughout late 1992 and much of 1993, the supposed incongruity of the Whoopi-Ted romance had been explored, dissected, and joked about endlessly by the media. Just as in 1963, three decades earlier, the world had avidly consumed every detail of the romantic shenanigans of Elizabeth Taylor and Richard Burton on and off the set of *Cleopatra,* now they devoured every tidbit and innuendo about the latest change in romantic status of thirty-eight-year-old Goldberg, now considered sexy by the tabloids, and forty-six-year-old Danson. And just when there finally seemed to be no more to say about this amorous union, the couple would have a spat, divulged by the media, which was, in turn, followed by a reconciliation that restored the duo to the top of the media watch list.

It was certainly known by the Friars and many others that Danson would be Goldberg's escort to the club's big annual bash. Far more enticing was that Danson was scheduled to be the master of ceremonies and, as such, would be one of those prime guests on the dais lined up to "really" dish Whoopi during the luncheon. The consensus was that this event was not to be missed!

In recent years, just as women had become part of the celebrity audience at the Friars' get-togethers, it was now customary to indulge the media before the roast luncheon actually began. The press was permitted a comprehensive photo opportunity, especially with the guest of honor and others of the forty to fifty celebrities who would be seated at the head table. As the stream of notables began to arrive at the Hilton that noontime, accredited network journalists as well as freelancing paparazzi were able to interview famous attendees, snap photos, roll their video camcorders, or transcribe overheard gossip as the rich and famous dished one another.

Thus, while the invitees rushed to the Hilton's Grand Ballroom that Friday afternoon, celebrity attendees were questioned about the forthcoming event of the day. Actor Michael Douglas, who had produced Whoopi's movie *Made in America,* said: "Any opportunity to trash Whoopi I couldn't resist." *Saturday Night Live* regular Mike Myers rhapsodized: "She's absolutely like butter. She's to die for. She's one of our people." And comedian-actor Robin Williams, a longtime Goldberg chum exclaimed, "To roast her, wow!"

The guest of honor certainly did not escape the press as she made her way through the crowded hotel lobby. "I'm well dressed; I'm wearing

Armani," she enthused. But such comments were not sufficient for Jill Rappaport of NBC-TV's *Today Show*. She persuaded a determinedly gracious and very tastefully dressed Whoopi to say a few words for the video cameras about America's favorite topic—her relationship with Danson:

> It's tough if you have to explain to somebody about a friendship when they're determined to make your friendship into something else. . . . Photographs can be taken, and people put their captions under it, and you're stuck, you know, you're stuck. He is my best friend and has been for a while. And that's what it is. . . . I think friendship is the key to everything. Without that, I mean, you know, why bother. So that's what we've got. We've got—as I said, my best buddy, you know. And—and to say, "Do you love him?" Yeah, I do. This is my friend. If you ask me if we're running off to get married, no, no. I don't want to be married to anybody. I don't want to be in love with anybody.

The nattily groomed Danson—wearing a dark suit and sporting sunglasses—offered a terse but congenial response to a similar question: "We're—we're happily, wonderfully private, thank you." After posing for photos, he and a beaming Whoopi walked briskly into the Grand Ballroom.

Such celebrity fests have tight security to protect the famous guests from harm. So everyone had to pass through obligatory metal detectors similar to those found at every airport. Once inside, the invited mingled at the bar or submitted to photo sessions with the eager press. As one o'clock neared, everyone headed to assigned tables both in the main ballroom and in the mezzanine area, where a video and still camera crew stood ready to record the event for the Friars' private archives.

Before long, the entire assemblage—more than twenty-two hundred guests—was served food and drink. In bygone years, once dessert was consumed, the waiters, photographers, and reporters were asked to leave the room so that the raunchy roast could begin. Now it is customary to allow such outsiders to remain. This latest change to the once-traditional celebrity stag affair was one that the elders of the Friars would come to bemoan in the next frantic hours, when all hell broke loose in the Hilton Ballroom.

Seated at the ballroom dais were, of course, Whoopi Goldberg and the master of ceremonies, Ted Danson. Other members of the eclectic group at the head table included Jasmine Guy, Sugar Ray Leonard, Alan King, Shari Belafonte, RuPaul, Chris Rock, Prof. Irwin Corey, Vanessa Williams, Malcolm-Jamal Warner, Anita Baker, Beverly Johnson, Michael Spinks, and that refugee from *The A-Team* television series, Mr. T. The Big Apple's current civic head, Mayor David Dinkins, who was scheduled to make remarks at the get-together, was late in arriving from a prior engagement, and his chair remained empty for the time being. Another at the head table was the Friars' "dean," a position then held by Jack L. Green. It was he who signaled the start of the roast and recited the usual banal opening remarks and perfunctory introductions that were the necessary foreplay to the fun to come.

Only later did attendees recall that during Green's introductory remarks and thank-yous Ted Danson had quietly left the dais and disappeared from sight. When Green's matter-of-fact discourse concluded, he signaled for the stage curtains to open. Even those who had been discourteously whispering to one another during Green's preamble were struck speechless by the vision that greeted them. There—seemingly floating alone on the stage—was the six-foot-two Danson, now costumed in formal white tie, black tails, and top hat. He stood there frozen in position, his legs planted far apart on the stage floor and his long arms raised wide. That in itself was not the shocker. What was amazing was that he was made up in full blackface, with huge white lips painted on his face, a bizarre sight accentuated by his broad, beaming smile.

For many this "Sambo" tableau was sufficiently astounding to leave them dumbstruck. All eyes were fixed on Goldberg, who seemed to be vastly amused by her lover's "shocking" behavior. Danson then went over to where she sat and said, "I wanted to dress elegantly for you—my woman." Next, he kissed her fully on the lips and then gave her a hug that she reciprocated with obvious enthusiasm.

Hardly had the roomful of mirth makers recovered when Danson launched into a barrage of outrageous, X-rated one-liners that left the listeners gasping.

Although no one on hand that day—except the Friars' video team in the mezzanine—was recording the astonishing event verbatim, one reporter present made his detailed notes of what transpired available to the *New York Observer*. This weekly publication, in turn, published a full account of the flabbergasting episode in "The Transom" column of their October 18, 1993, issue. Their summary of this incredible escapade ran with the following caveat: "Because the ceremony was not recorded by the reporter, the jokes may not be verbatim, and some of their setups have been paraphrased." They also noted: " 'The Transom' attempted to run the jokes by Ms. Goldberg, who claimed authorship of most of them, but the comedian did not return phone calls. 'The Transom's' conclusion: I guess you had to be there."

According to the *Observer,* the blackfaced "Mr. Danson began his remarks by saying that as he was shaving that morning and thinking about what he'd say at the Friars Roast, he looked down and saw that Ms. Goldberg was performing oral sex on him. His response to her: "Come on, Whoop, don't nigger-lip it." With the nonplused audience gaping in disbelief, Ted continued his shocking riff: "Black chicks sure do know their way around a dick. But, in all fairness, white girls get toys for Christmas."

In the course of his routine, no subject was sacred. Regarding Whoopi, Danson offered, "We've been so busy we haven't seen each other in a coon's age." He also offered anatomical reportage about her vagina: "[It's] wider than South Africa and twice as inflamed." As to their personal rapport, he insisted, "Our first fight was over a Disney picture called *The Nigger Lover*. Miss Diva insisted on being the nigger. But I told her, You always play the nigger."

The "highlight" of Danson's routine focused on the supposed occasion when he took Whoopi to his family's home to meet his parents *and* where she "cleaned the house." According to the *New York Observer*'s account, Danson next said, "I took her up to the bedroom and fucked the shit out of her. She gave me some of that monkey love she's so famous for. In the throes of passion . . . Ms. Goldberg screamed, 'Yes, you lily-white motherfucker, fuck me good.' "

According to the *Observer,* Danson next quipped that "his mother walked in on them and proceeded to lecture him and 'Miss Goldfarb' on the supposed realities of having mulatto children. Among them: 'Who will convince the children if they have diarrhea that they're not melting? . . . If the children go to the beach, cats will try to bury them.' Mr. Danson's reply: 'I told her, Mom, relax. I'm fucking her in the ass.' "

Other anecdotal "details" provided by Danson included the observation that when he and Whoopi had made love at his parents' home, her screaming "opened the garage door." Ted's witticisms reportedly also included: "My mother got along with Whoopi beautifully—because my mother's a dyke!" As to his dad's reaction to Goldberg's supposed visit to the Dansons' home, Ted noted, "After Whoopi had done the laundry and dusted and finished cleaning up, I could tell my dad had warmed up to her because he offered to drop her off at the bus stop."

Near the end of his "act," according to the *Observer,* a waiter brought a watermelon out onstage for Danson. Ted took a bite and then remarked gleefully, "That really hits the spot." He then glanced in Whoopi's direction and joked, "I do think I remember you saying, 'I dare you.' "

By this time, Whoopi was rolling with laughter, even if polite, strained chuckles were the most a few others on the dais or in the audience could muster for Danson's weirdly tasteless remarks. By now, a breathless Mayor Dinkins had rushed into the ballroom, making his apologies for being detained by prior commitments. A city-hall aide quickly apprised His Honor of what had just happened, including Ted's earlier statement to the crowd that he (Danson) had been advised that because African-American Dinkins was to be on hand, "Don't do any political jokes. Just do nigger jokes."

When the obviously flustered and embarrassed Mayor Dinkins was handed a live microphone, he admitted he didn't know what to say next, given what had apparently gone before. At that juncture, comedian Robin Williams shouted from the dais: "Tell a blow-job joke!" Trying to recover his dignity, Dinkins cracked a few weak jokes concerning his forthcoming mayoral battle against Rudy Giuliani, quickly read a city proclamation in Goldberg's honor, and beat a hasty retreat.

Among the other speakers that tumultuous day was oddball stand-up comedian Bobcat Goldthwait, who had worked with Goldberg in the film *Burglar* in 1987. Unconventional at best and downright outrageous and annoyingly eccentric at worst, even he was dumbstruck by the scene in the ballroom. Uniquely at a loss for words, Goldthwait regained sufficient poise to chide master of ceremonies Danson: "Did you really think black people would think this is funny in 1993?" He added, "I'm sure Mayor Dinkins is really glad he's here."

Following Mayor Dinkins, a Bill Clinton lookalike joined the mounting chaos onstage. He turned to Whoopi and, unzipping his fly, began pulling out an endless American flag. "See," he told the amused guest of honor, "I'm built like a black guy."

The climax came with the closing remarks by the guest of honor. As if it were possible to stun the audience any further, she opened with: "Nigger, nigger, nigger. Whitey, whitey, whitey." Launching into a minidiatribe, she insisted, "It takes a whole lot of #$%& courage to come out in blackface in front of three thousand #$%& people." After adding, "I don't care if you don't like it. I do," she launched into a graphic description of how Ted Danson pleased her sexually. The luncheon soon came to a close. Or so it seemed.

CHAPTER TWO

The World Reacts

Whoopi's been on the warpath defending this thing;
I just think she's confused. There's just no way she
can defend what transpired.
—SPIKE LEE, OCTOBER 1993

Ted Danson had not yet wrapped up his astounding appearance when talk-show host Montel Williams, an African American, charged out of the Hilton's main ballroom with his distressed white wife in tow. Only a small number of the attendees actually paid attention to Williams's exit. Before leaving the Hilton, Montel charged over to the hotel's hospitality desk and dashed off a telegram to Bob Saks, chairman of the Friars' still-in-progress roast. The missive, delivered to Saks in the ballroom, read:

As a new member of the Friars Club I attended my first celebrity roast 15 minutes ago. And after the 7 minutes that I stayed I was confused as to whether or not I was at a Friars event or at a rally for the KKK and Aryan Nation. I understand what humor is, I understand what comedy is, and what good and bad taste is, but I am shocked that an organization that I held with such high regard and always wanted to be a member of could sponsor an event that was as disgusting and tasteless as this one.

My dues are paid in full, so therefore you have no reason to contact me ever again in the future.

Montel Williams

11

Later, Montel detailed what had prompted his strong reaction to Danson's comedy misfire: "When Ted made the jokes about the racially mixed kids—and everyone knows my wife is white and just gave birth to our child—I could see my wife start to cry. If that's what Whoopi and Ted find funny in their bedroom, it's not funny to the outside world."

The mushrooming disaster still might have been contained with immediate damage control. However, en route home, Montel, still steaming, called Terrie Williams, a high-profile public-relations expert. He asked her for the addresses of all the black women who had been seated at the roast's main table. He explained that he wanted to send each of them roses and to apologize for Danson's insensitive behavior. To fulfill his request, Williams's office quickly began networking to locate the celebrity addresses Montel required.

One of the persons contacted was *New York Daily News* gossip columnist Linda Stasi, who had been at the Whoopi roast. The journalist was already formulating her newspaper coverage of the debacle. However, the new twist regarding Montel's Friars Club resignation made the event even more newsworthy. Later, when she was a guest on the October 28, 1993, edition of Geraldo Rivera's TV talk show, Stasi would recollect the opportune phone call she had received from her publicist friend: " 'You know. Montel just called me. He's really upset. Do you have the address of so-and-so?' And I said, 'What is—what's going on?' She said—and then she explained it to me. I said, 'Well, listen, I'm writing the story. Maybe he [Montel] wants to talk to me.' She said, 'I don't think so.' Anyway, we negotiated back and forth."

In short order, Stasi obtained Montel's telegram, which would become a pivotal part of her account in the next day's *New York Daily News*. Her reportage in the Saturday, October 9, 1993, issue, a major piece, was headlined "Few Whoops for Roast: Blackface and Race Jokes at Goldberg Fete." Stasi's article also included quotes from Mayor Dinkins: "As you know, Friars Club roasts can be raucous affairs with jokes close to, and sometimes even crossing, the line between good humor and bad taste. Frankly, that is why I approach its roasts with some trepidation. Had my friend Whoopi not been the honoree, I might have skipped today's event. . . . Regrettably, the jokes today were pretty vulgar and many were way, way over the line. I was embarrassed for Whoopi and the audience and felt a tremendous sense of relief when it was over." Dinkins concluded: "Today is not a day any of its [i.e., the Friars Club's] members is likely to recall fondly. Nor will I."

For her *Daily News* report, Stasi also interviewed Bob Saks. The beleaguered chairman of the Friars Club celebrity luncheon admitted, for the record, that he was shocked that anyone had taken umbrage at Danson's routine: "Whoopi knew and so did all the black performers what was going to happen. It's always way over the line—it's supposed to be. It's the industry honoring itself and the industry honoring the person they love the most. This has been going on for eighty-nine years and will go on for another eighty-nine years." Another in agreement with Saks was African-American fashion model Beverly Johnson, who had been at the head table. She reasoned, "If you can't see the humor at a place where there's supposed to be over-the-line jokes, then there's something really wrong."

Stasi's piece in the *Daily News* set torch to tinder. (Another edition of the same newspaper that day reprinted the story with larger photos of the event, including two of Danson in blackface.) Once the paper reached the newsstands, the expected blaze roared through New York City and, in short order, the United States. It proved to be another of many instances of the always-on-the-edge Whoopi Goldberg finding herself at the center of a storm of controversy.

That same Saturday, Jack L. Green, the harassed dean of the Friars Club, issued a statement on behalf of the Friars, who were "saddened by the racially offensive nature of some of the material" used by Danson during the evening. He added, "While raucous and X-rated humor are usually the tradition of these annual events, they are never intended to ridicule or disparage any segment of our society. . . . In a time when we are all concerned about healing and not dividing the races, we at the New York Friars Club apologize to Mayor Dinkins, Montel Williams, and all others who were discomforted and offended by the racial remarks. They are not in the spirit of the Friars Club."

As this affair drew attention, many of the celebrities who had attended the roast were contacted. Robert De Niro insisted: "That was the most disgusting display of racism I've ever seen. It made me sick." Another actor, Matthew Modine, a longtime acquaintance of Whoopi's, declared, "It was totally offensive. I've never been to something like this." Screen beauty Halle Berry, who had called Whoopi Goldberg her idol before the event, now swore she would never attend another roast. "It blew my mind. Whether it was racial jokes or crude comments about women's body parts, the whole thing upset me because I had no idea what it was going to be like. I said to myself, I flew all this way for this? It was lewd and crude. What good is coming out of it?"

Over the weekend, Ted and Whoopi returned to Los Angeles. A deeply disturbed Danson went into seclusion, even canceling an upcoming scheduled appearance on Chevy Chase's TV talk show on the Fox network. Buffered by his public-relations task force, Ted became incommunicado with the press. Only later would it be revealed that Danson was trying desperately to explain to his wife, Casey, from whom he was separated, why, as reports had it, he and Whoopi had been so intimate at the Friars roast. By now, word had gotten back to Casey about Danson and Goldberg's very affectionate weekend back east. Casey once again was convinced that Danson could not have been serious about his recent pledge to make a fresh domestic start with her and their two daughters.

Whoopi, never fearful of meeting any controversy head-on, hastily called a Sunday press conference in Beverly Hills. From her perspective, everyone, including the African-American community, was making a mountain out of a molehill. "We knocked Somalia off the cover of the New York newspapers. This is insane to me." In her typically direct, confrontational style, she suggested that Montel Williams's resigning from the Friars via telegram and his conversation with a *New York Daily News* reporter might have been motivated by his desire for free publicity. "Perhaps Montel's show is not doing as well as it could be and this was his way of drawing attention."

During the course of her well-attended news briefing, Whoopi read a prepared statement from Ted Danson in which he declared: "There was too much love behind my words to ever be misconstrued as racist." His official explanation also included: "Words by themselves are—are not racist. Racism is a matter of intent. My intent was to amuse my dear friend Whoopi in what I thought was the privacy of the Friars Club. Those people who are making this public and a matter of the press are, I'm afraid, turning this into a matter of racism."

To a somewhat disbelieving group of reporters Goldberg revealed that she had written much of Danson's luncheon material. It was she who had found the makeup artist for Ted's blackface routine. Many wondered if this wasn't a last-minute attempt on her part to cover up Ted's tremendous bad judgment.

Getting back to the heart of Danson's minstrel-show routine, Goldberg insisted, "Anyone coming into that room who didn't know what they were coming into, you know, is—is crazy—and that it is okay for them to sit and talk to—talk to Billy [Crystal who was roasted in 1992] and deal with Billy as a Jew, you know, or Joan Rivers as a Jew, you know. It's amazing to me that they wouldn't think somebody was going to deal with the word 'nigger.' " Goldberg further explained, "We were not trying to be politically correct. We were trying to be funny for ourselves."

By Monday, October 11, three days after the disastrous tribute, the matter still refused to die. Fueling the controversy, the press sought additional celebrity reaction to the mishap. Needing fresh material, they now turned to notables who had not even been present at the event but who nevertheless had opinions about the roast.

Filmmaker Spike Lee, never a Whoopi Goldberg booster in the best of times, contended, "It wasn't funny. African Americans have been through too much for this kind of thing to be seen as funny." He laid the blame on Goldberg: "The Friars didn't tell Whoopi to do what she did." Gloria Allred, an attorney who became the first female member of the Beverly Hills Friars in 1987, agreed: "These are the old boys sitting around chuckling about their prejudices. It's not just offensive but harmful to the rights of the people they're attacking." Kathie Lee Gifford, cohost with Regis Philbin of a New York–based TV talk show, observed on the air that she "personally was offended" by Danson's antics at the Hilton.

Anne Marie Johnson, African-American costar of *In Living Color,* offered a sharp analogy: "I'm very upset with Whoopi. She said she helped write it. That [blackface Sambo] image has caused death. It would be like my showing up to a Jewish function dressed like Hitler. Just because it's a Friars roast doesn't mean you can insult a whole race."

Among those who had not been at the Hilton that Friday but had a positive reaction to the Danson-Goldberg performance was veteran Friar and African-American comedian Slappy White. He rejoined that he never regarded the humor at the roasts to be in bad taste or filled with real prejudice: "Hell, I was a Friar before I got off the back of the bus."

Another comedian, Jackie Mason, who himself had quit the Friars over its cancellation of a planned roast in his honor, felt that the Whoopi Goldberg roast "was no worse than any of the others. . . . It's the spirit that counts, not the words. Everybody knows that the whole thing is a labor of love." He added: "Somehow political correctness has gone to such an extreme that we have to live in fear—we're not allowed to tell a joke anymore about certain subjects." Soupy Sales, who, like Mason, was white, Jewish, over sixty, and male, pointed out, "Those roasts are the raunchiest things, and it's always been that way. No barriers. It's not racist or anything; it's a Friars roast. I did a *This Is Your Life* on Della Reese, and I said, 'Here's the guy who gave you your first big break,' and a guy comes out dressed as Abraham Lincoln. And that was on TV!"

In circulating a new "official" statement on Monday, the Friars inadvertently jumped back into the frying pan. The statement was signed by Jack L. Green, who explained the need to reiterate the Friars' position in light of the deluge of calls he had received. (Possibly his statement was also prompted by Goldberg's remark at her Sunday press conference, when she had chastised the Friars for buckling under to the pressure to publicly apologize for the event.) Now the club offered a new view: "Although we are saddened that some people felt that remarks directed at Whoopi Goldberg were done in a seemingly racist manner, we stand by our roast format. . . . Sometimes the language is the bluest, the insults the basest and the jokes the most embarrassing, but they are all said with great love and affection and gracefully accepted by our Roastee, in this case, Whoopi Goldberg. Ted Danson and Whoopi Goldberg had every reason to believe that all of the guests were fully aware of this tradition and prepared their material accordingly, which they deemed suitable for this event and this event only."

This changed view would also appear in the entertainment industry's trade papers the *Hollywood Reporter* and *Daily Variety* in the form of full-page ads, which also noted that the money raised by such roasts "go to many deserving charities serving people of all races and creeds."

On Thursday, October 21, Whoopi and Ted gave their first joint interview since the Friars mess. Their forum of choice was *Screen Scene,* a program aired over BET (Black Entertainment Television, a cable network). On the show, a very composed Whoopi mostly reiterated what she'd offered before: "People were somehow surprised that there was racial, sexual, feminist, antifeminist, all kinds of over-the-top kind of stuff. As far as roasts, eighty-nine years they've been doing this. Doesn't matter who you are, you are there for your friends to tear you to shreds for the entertainment of you and for the entertainment of the people who have been invited to this roast."

Ted Danson was more revealing in his explanations. Decidedly nervous, this white man in an African-American setting admitted that while he was proud of his part in the roast, he had been scared about giving a monologue replete with the word *nigger* before a huge crowd—and while wearing blackface. "I picked jokes and racial jokes, and sexual jokes, that were so over-the-top that there would be no way, I thought, that anyone could construe this as serious, you know? It was like a bad joke, and a bad joke, and a—so far [out] that you could not help but go [whistles]. "He added, "We are a racist nation. It's time maybe we started talking." These last remarks by Danson prompted *US* magazine in its January 1994 issue to assess this latest rhubarb: "The really nutty part came a couple of days later when Ted Danson said he was proud of starting a national discussion about race. Actually, it was a national discussion about the lack of celebrity common sense."

During the *Screen Scene* TV outing, Whoopi confided that Ted's routine had *not* been an overnight, last-minute inspiration performed off-the-cuff. "This was done over a long period of time and checking and double-checking and quadruple-checking; are we within our forum to do this? Everybody said yes. It led us to believe everybody was expecting what they didn't know what they were going to get, but they knew it was going to be out there."

Both Whoopi and Ted apologized on the air to anyone at the event who had been offended. However, they attacked the news media for what they termed as very biased, slanted coverage. Further explaining what had inspired his blackface appearance, Danson noted that the couple had endured vicious racial attacks since they had begun dating eighteen months before. A visibly emotional Danson said, "I've had people call me nigger lover. Now I have people who call me a racist." The more stoic Whoopi acknowledged that since dating Ted she had been getting "mail that says, 'I hope if you and Ted Danson have babies, I hope they die.'" (On another occasion, Goldberg would say, "We are a zebra couple. . . . That's what we live with, and it's the context for the jokes and black-face.")

On another tack, Whoopi insisted that blacks should not permit themselves to be upset by the word *nigger*. According to Goldberg's emphatic reasoning, that word "means nothing to me. Because if every time I hear it I have to choke and clench, I would be dead."

As Whoopi remarked to *Jet,* the American public has known for a long time she is no saint. "I'm the woman who made m.f. a household word. . . . I've always been known as the other side of tasteful." She also reasoned aloud that some of the onslaught of criticism must be coming from those "who are trying to get back at Ted's and my relationship. I told him that if he was going to be in a friendship with me he would have to expect this [vicious mail]." One of her final and most cogent points to the *Jet* interviewer was "The X-rated stuff is a Friars Club tradition. Should the roasters have to tiptoe around me because I'm a black woman?"

Some months later, African-American writer Karen Grisby Bates, writing for the December 1993/January 1994 issue of *Emerge,* would sum up one of the strong contending points of views regarding Whoopi and the Friars muddle.

> [I]ts okay for her [Whoopi] to put her bags on the platform and jump aboard the train of progressive racial humor if she wants to. But not everyone will wish to relieve themselves of that load at the same time Goldberg does, and they may not share her interest in hopping on her particular train. Our destinations as African Americans may be mutual, but we may not all get there at once, and our routes and means of transportation may vary greatly.
>
> Goldberg's decision to shock her audience into a new, enlightened consciousness using racial humor was a long shot. . . . And in this case, it didn't pay off. Danson wrongfully bore the brunt of African-American anger. Goldberg convinced Danson to appear in blackface; he assumed that because she was black, she knew what she was talking about. She assumed that enough time had passed, enough progress had been made, that blackface would not be the red flag it still is. They both assumed that America had grown enough to begin to laugh at its own racist fears. . . . Wrong on all counts.

On a personal level, the October 1993 blackface misadventure would have dramatic, lasting affects on Goldberg's future relationship with Ted Danson. In the bigger picture, it demonstrated yet again how the talented, bright Goldberg, because of her celebrity status as well as her position as role model for the African-American community and her unrelenting, in-your-face personality, often found herself at the center of a maelstrom. The Friars Club nightmare was one more illustration of how so much in Whoopi's life would be frequently expanded from a personal experience into a national cause célèbre.

CHAPTER THREE

Modest Beginnings

I couldn't know how tough it is raising kids until I had mine. One day I called my mom up and said, "Shit. I'm sorry for being such an asshole." For my mother to have done what she did—she was a nurse and then a Head Start teacher—is phenomenal.

—WHOOPI GOLDBERG, JUNE 1987

She was born Caryn Elaine Johnson on November 13, 1955, in New York City. Or at least that date is the one the future Whoopi Goldberg has insisted on for the past decade. The issue of Goldberg's age discrepancy arose in the late 1970s when she was jump-starting her professional career as both an actor and an improvisational performer. At that time, her playbill biographies and information provided for her media interviews suggest she was actually born on November 13, 1949.

Whoopi would provide one of her first explanations for the discrepancy while talking with David Rensin for a 1987 *Playboy* interview: "I lied about my age for a long time, because nobody would hire me to act. Everyone said I was too young. So, when I was twenty, I put six years on my life. I also said I'd studied with Lee Strasberg. I'd already done a lot of acting. But for some reason people don't give you credit for learning anything in a short amount of time. I grew up in New York and knew stuff that people growing up other places just didn't."

The Local History Genealogy Division of the New York Public Library at Forty-second Street has long maintained ledgers of all recorded births in the five boroughs of New York City. A division listing indicates that one "Caren Johnson" (birth record number B44886) was born in the borough of Manhattan on Sunday, November 13, 1955. This birth year is corroborated by Goldberg's first husband, who was interviewed on Joan Rivers's TV talk show in the fall of 1993. He was forty-one and mentioned that when he met and married Caryn, she was three years his junior. The math obviously works in favor of her statements about her true age.

The future Whoopi Goldberg has said, "The story my mother tells is that when I came out—you know, babies come out with the head, then their shoulder, and then their arm—I came out, pulled my arm out, put my thumb in my mouth, like 'Wait. Stop. Look at this.' I was ready."

Very little is known of the background of the star-to-be's parents other than the fact that Robert James Johnson, her father, was born in 1930 in South Carolina. As a young man he came north to New York City, where he worked at odd jobs. He met and married Emma Harris. Their first child, Clyde K., was born in 1949. By this point, the Johnsons' marriage was fast disintegrating. Emma had to take charge as the family's breadwinner and decision maker. It was left to her to bring up their son with the sense of responsibility that Robert so lacked at the time. Not long after Caryn was born, her father left the family. However, Mrs. Johnson, who remains tight-lipped about the reasons for and the details of the split-up, never sought a divorce. Only years later—in the late 1980s—would Whoopi, who never forgave her dad for walking out on the family, learn the sad details of what had happened to him in the interim.

The Johnsons' home was a small sixth-floor apartment on Twenty-sixth Street and Tenth Avenue in what is known as the Chelsea-Clinton projects in Manhattan. Today this low-cost housing complex is in a depressing section of New York City, with no parks and only concrete playgrounds and walkways to separate the collection of eleven-story buildings.

Chelsea was a multicultural section of New York when Caryn Johnson grew up in the late 1950s and throughout the 1960s. It was also home to many of the city's beatniks in the fifties and hippies in the sixties. As Whoopi would recall years later, "[I]t was a great microcosm of the world. We had people from Puerto Rico and Greece and Italy and Africa and Indonesia. . . . It had everybody. And nobody ever knew they were poor."

As an adult, Whoopi would look back and assess her home life under the strict guidance of her refined, ambitious mother, who had always dreamed of becoming a doctor. Because of economics and the strictures of the time, her mother had to settle for becoming a nurse at French Hospital. (Emma would later abandon nursing to become a Head Start teacher but never got to fulfill another ambition—to become an actor.) "We never wanted for anything. We were always clean, and Christmas was always fun. I'm realizing now, as we're talking, that maybe what I thought was her distance was simply her taking needed space for her time and private thoughts."

Compared to many of her low-income housing neighbors, Emma Johnson was sophisticated, cultured, and talked in a precise, distinctive manner. She would pass these characteristics on to her two children, especially young Caryn. Whoopi has described her mother as "a very formidable woman. Very. There wasn't a lot of testing the waters with her. She had a death-ray look that could melt concrete, that could burn through walls. She didn't have to say a word, nothing. Just the look was enough to tear you apart." If Mrs. Johnson was very strict, especially with her daughter, she was also very loving and generous in trying to provide the best she could for her children. Emma might not have been openly affectionate or verbal about her strong feelings about the importance of family, but she made her two offspring feel very loved.

Because of the six-year age difference between young Caryn and her brother, they did not spend much time together. When Clyde rushed out of the apartment to play baseball or engage in other activities with neighborhood pals, the last thing he or his friends wanted was his little sister tagging along. Mealtimes were one of the few occasions of the day when Caryn could spend any time with Clyde.

As a result, little Caryn would amuse herself while her mother was out working and her brother was at school or out playing. Being a very imaginative youngster, she would sit for hours playing fantasy games that she either invented or were derived from whatever she happened to be watching on television. It was often the Johnsons' neighbors who watched over Caryn, at least keeping tabs on her when she was playing outside. In those days it did not seem dangerous to allow a little girl to play in the streets or in nearby parks.

Despite everything, the Whoopi Goldberg of today says she enjoyed her childhood. "I was never miserable. I was left with one parent, but she loved me a ton. And we had our grandpa. . . . My brother, Clyde, and I never knew at the time that we were poor. In our neighborhood everybody was poor, so we all looked rich to each other. We had wonderful summers when we went to Coney Island and took trips on the Circle Line around Manhattan." (To this day, Whoopi still recalls with relish the wonderful picnic meals that her mother would prepare for such excursions.)

As an observant, curious youngster, Caryn learned useful life lessons from her strict, emotionally restrained, but loving single parent: "My mom taught me to share. She said that would be the best way to go through life, because you'll always find somebody that you have more than. You have one crust of bread; somebody has none. So you slice your crust of bread, and you give some away. Make sure you keep some for you, because you can't be a saint."

Whoopi recalls proudly that Emma taught her and Clyde that they could make any and all of their dreams come true if they invested the necessary time and energy. More so than Clyde, who was more content to accept life as it was, Caryn took this belief to heart, and it became a guiding influence in her later life.

Reflecting on the basic rules of her very blue collar neighborhood, Whoopi noted, "I grew up in a place where people said, 'Do whatever you can do and do it well, because it's going to be tough, you know? Not because you're a woman, not because you're black, but because it's a motherfucker out there.' I didn't know about women's rights or men's rights. As far as I knew, I had all the rights that I needed. Then, suddenly, in the sixties, we had middle-class women who decided that the PTA wasn't enough, that being a cuff link on their husband's arm was not enough. So they called themselves women's liberators. But they weren't liberating people in *my neighborhood,* because the mothers were *always* working mothers. Single parents often raised their children."

While economic survival was important, little Caryn's home turf was a place where people looked out for their neighbors. "I grew up in a neighborhood where if you messed up, your mother knew before you got home, because in the neighborhood . . . all those neighbors looking out the window and the whole village knew."

She also has observed that, "color was never an issue. My mother would say, 'Look, you're black. You woke up black this morning, you'll go to bed black tonight. But it doesn't make any difference.'" What impressionable Caryn didn't realize at the time was that the color of her skin would prove to be an obstacle she would have to overcome.

CHAPTER FOUR

School Days

I grew up in a time of great hope, coming through
the sixties. I never grew up with racism in New York.
I didn't find racism until I came here to California.
Back then, kids had hope. . . . I was a kid. The
government believed in me. Private enterprise
believed in me. The Helena Rubinstein Foundation
had a children's theater for kids like me.
—WHOOPI GOLDBERG, NOVEMBER 1992

B y the time Caryn turned six, in 1961, she had entered the first
grade at St. Columba, the parish school attached to the Catholic
church at 343 West Twenty-fifth Street. The choice of a parochial
institution was not based on the fact that the Johnsons were especially
drawn to organized religion. Rather, Emma Johnson had other reasons.
For one, the school was located only a few blocks from their apartment.
The future Whoopi Goldberg explained years later: "My mother sent me
to Catholic school for a better education, I guess. They considered me
Catholic, but I only considered myself Catholic because I went to Catholic school. I didn't believe a lot of the things they said. An angry God was
not the one I felt I knew. I believed in a kinder God than the one they
were talking about."

Each weekday Caryn trudged to classes at St. Columba. Surrounded
by bright red brick apartment structures twenty-two-stories high, the
school was one of three buildings connected to the church itself. St.
Columba stood out in the neighborhood, for it was four stories high and
was faced with tan and cream bricks with cream and pink ledges and

lintels. Each day, as Caryn approached the building, she could look up at
the windows facing the street and wonder what the school day would be
like.

Having come from a loosely structured household, the youngster
found it difficult to adjust to the strict discipline of the forbidding nuns.
Years later she would describe her memories of the teaching sisters:
"Well, I went to Catholic school, and they did float. They did float. They
had no feet, you know. And there was some— I mean, when you think
about it, it's— They're just like *Whoo-whoo. Whack! Whoo-whoo.*"

Her teachers and classmates realized that Caryn was slow to learn.
They thought that this restless little girl was backward mentally. That she
spoke in a very precise manner, as did her brother, Clyde, did not help.
They were duplicating their mother's cultured diction and formal way of
expressing herself. (Much later, Whoopi would describe the situation:
"When people spoke to us, we spoke like this [using a very refined, well-
modulated voice]. Kids would say, 'Wanna do sumpin'?' and we'd say,
'No, thank you.'") As the years passed, Caryn learned to "double-talk."
At school or with her neighborhood pals she would talk fast, in slang,
while at home she would use a more genteel way of speaking. This ability
to mimic and to adapt her voice would prove to be very useful in later
life.

Another aspect of Emma Johnson's refined ways that young Caryn
did not appreciate was her penchant for serving only healthy, name-
brand foods. Caryn preferred the deep-fried, starchy foods and snacks
that her friends were fed by their mothers. And although Mrs. Johnson
was a diligent cook, there were some recipes that she could not master,
such as chocolate cake. To this day, Whoopi recalls how she and her
brother would pretend to eat the funny-tasting dessert but instead would
find ways to secretly toss slice after slice into the garbage. Not aware of
her children's machinations, Mrs. Johnson assumed they liked the special
pastry so much that she would treat them by baking yet another.

Once through with classes for the day, Caryn would hurry home,
for this is where she felt that her real schooling began. No sooner was the
youngster back in her sixth-floor apartment than she would turn on the
television. She would sit entranced for hours in front of the flickering
images, intently watching vintage movies on the black-and-white set. "I
didn't even know these movies were old or that they were all in black and
white. I figured they were in color—only to discover I was wrong when I
[later] got a color TV. But ultimately the absence of color made it easier

to fantasize along with the movies. Like *Psycho* [1960]. All the color you see is nonexistent. But it was perfect for me, because I love to live in my head. I love to pretend."

Already Caryn had her favorite movie stars: Bette Davis, John Garfield, Claudette Colbert, and Carole Lombard. At the time, it never occurred to her that these screen images were of films made many years before and that some of the leading players (e.g., Carole Lombard and John Garfield) had been dead for years.

As Whoopi has said, "On TV, they had the Early and the Late and Late, Late Show and the Million Dollar Movie, and WPIX had all these great movies. I'd watch three or four a day—the Three Stooges or Abbott and Costello. But what I loved most was watching movies from the thirties, forties, and fifties with John Garfield, Carole Lombard, Norma Shearer, Joan Crawford. And because I grew up in an environment that never denied anything to me that I wanted to be, the world of pretend was so great."

She also liked the notion of seeing Clark Gable in World War II and then switching to another TV channel where he would be riding a horse. She said, "I wanted to come down staircases like Carole Lombard; I wanted to do scenes with John Garfield."

Whenever Emma Johnson had free time and spare money, she would take her daughter to local movie theaters. These excursions into the world of celluloid make-believe became, along with her TV watching, a crucial part of Caryn's childhood. It gave her stability, escape, and hope. She vividly recalls: "I went to the theater and watched movies all the time. I always thought of myself as the fantasy character with them. They didn't know I was there, but I could hear and see everything they were saying and doing. So I didn't have imaginary friends; I had John Garfield."

When Caryn was eight, she came to several conclusions. She sensed, then realized, that she was different from the other little girls she knew at school or in the neighborhood. With her wide eyes, prominent nose, big mouth, and full lips, she had a plain appearance. She did not look like any of her acquaintances no matter what their ethnic background. With this realization fixed in her mind, part of her wanted to believe it was okay to look different, that it made her unique in a positive way. Another part of her wanted to conform and be more like the others. When she allowed herself to focus on being different, she felt left out in the classroom. It seemed she could not learn the academic basics. Indeed, some of her teachers were convinced that she was a "slow" child and were already suggesting to Mrs. Johnson that her offspring might be mentally retarded.

The role models all around her made her feel different, even as a child. Both in the old movies on TV and in the new films at the movie theaters, her idols were all beautiful, sophisticated, and white. With rare exception, Hollywood relegated blacks to playing maids and handymen on-camera. They were never the stars or enviable leading players in the movies that Caryn saw as a child.

With these appealing white female images firmly in mind, Caryn would stare into the mirror and wonder what she might do to transform herself into one of these glamorous Hollywood stars. When watching TV or flipping through magazines, she studied the alluring ads filled with beguiling models—attractive young Caucasian women—all of whom seemed to be part of a wonderful, enviable lifestyle.

Decades later, Caryn would still remember a particularly telling childhood episode. "When I was growing up, you looked at the back of a magazine and saw the Breck girl. And you just knew it wasn't going to happen. You'd take the magazine to your mother, and she would just say, 'Ain't going to happen.'" This realistic statement from her strong, practical mother shocked Caryn, who bridled at rules and restrictions.

Although Emma Johnson was pragmatic about the bitter realities of racial discrimination, she encouraged her daughter to exercise her creative imagination and artistic bent. This certainly was true when Caryn began taking advantage of the Hudson Guild at 441 West Twenty-sixth Street, where her mother was now a Head Start teacher. Located near the projects, the Hudson Guild was one of the original settlement houses founded in late-nineteenth-century New York City to help low-income families and the poor enjoy a fuller life. It provided a variety of community services for participants of all ages. For children, there were preschool and school-age activities, which also included supervised after-school programs. In addition, the Hudson Guild offered organized sports as well as day camps. And, most wondrous of all, it owned a five-hundred-acre farm in New Jersey, which, among other features, had a petting zoo, nature studies, and arts and crafts.

The Hudson Guild began its performing-arts activities in 1896 with the founding of the Shakespearean Club. By 1926 it became the headquarters of a year-round community theater company—one of the first in the country. Its productions took place in the basement of the building.

Caryn recalled her days at the settlement house thusly: "You went there after school to do whatever you were interested in—until your parents got off work and came for you. For me, it was like being in a candy store and being able to have any piece of candy I wanted. I knew right away that I liked it."

From the start, the Hudson Guild's acting program for youngsters—sponsored by the Helena Rubinstein Performing Workshops—intrigued her. "Here was a place where I could go and be Eleanor of Aquitaine. I could be Peter Pan and fly, and it was cool. This to me was an amazing thing. Because there were lots of things in my head, characters and stories, I thought this was the place for me. I wanted to come down a set of stairs in satin and be a grand broad with a cigarette holder. When you're seven years old, that looks great. And my mother said, 'There's no reason you can't do that.' I said, 'What? You mean that I could pretend that I was a princess?' She said, 'Yes, you can be anything you want when you act.' And I thought, Well, then, I'm getting into this!"

As Caryn approached her teen years, she became more involved in the Hudson Guild's activities, which reinforced her childhood dreams of one day becoming a professional performer. She could still enthuse years later about her theater sanctuary: "I could be a princess, a teapot, a rabbit. . . . And in a way it's been children's theater ever since." Best of all, when onstage she was part of a group—where she belonged. She could shine, and people would respond to her special qualities.

Caryn's mother reinforced her child's growing love of the performing arts: "Mom took me to movies. She made me go to Leonard Bernstein's Young People's Concerts. She'd send me to see Broadway shows. I remember watching Diana Sands play *Joan of Arc* [1968] and James Earl Jones in *The Great White Hope* [1968] and Carol Channing in *Hello, Dolly!* [1964]. . . . My mother would tell me, 'I know you want to be a performer. Don't be afraid even if things don't work out the way you have them planned. Anything is possible for you.'" The Whoopi of today reflects: "It has never occurred to me that there was anything I couldn't do if I set my mind to it. Mom never hinted that the world wasn't my oyster."

Caryn's strong passion for show business separated her even more from her classmates and neighborhood acquaintances. In a telling, terse commentary, the Whoopi Goldberg of the 1990s recalls childhood peers: "They were all dancing to Motown. And I'd be singing a tune from *State Fair* [1945]. Sometimes you end up getting lonely if the rest of the kids think you a little bit odd." On another occasion, she reminisced: "I was a very quiet and very dull child. I liked things other kids weren't into at the time—movies, theater, ballet, opera. When you grow up in Manhattan, all these things are accessible."

Meanwhile, she continued her regimented school days at St. Columba, where all the girls wore plaid skirts, little white socks, and a red blazer. Unlike many who have been educated in a demanding Catholic-school environment, very little of the strict scholastic discipline and the "fear-of-God" training affected Caryn. She became insulated, for she had created her own world with different goals and interests. Unlike many other youngsters over the decades, she did not find that attending Catholic school was scary or led to any guilt-induced emotions regarding religion and the proper way of life.

"Well," Whoopi said, "I didn't have a whole lot invested in it. Because I've always sort of had my own concept of who God is and was. And it never fit any of the sort of group religion. So it [school] was cool." (Later, as an adult, she would admit she was no longer a practicing Catholic, but would add: "I still believe in God. I don't agree with everything the Catholics are into, but I also don't agree with everything the Jews are into or the Buddhists and all the other religions I encompass and embrace. I'm kinda formulating my own.")

Caryn's teachers at St. Columba immediately recognized the importance to her of performing. It was Caryn's *raison d'être*. Sister Jeanne Fielder, who taught both seventh- and eighth-grade classes at St. Columba, said: "The Hudson Guild was Caryn's first love. Acting was in her genes. She was a performer. You couldn't miss it. She had the lead in several plays; she played the lead in every play she was in. She was Maria in *The Sound of Music*." Sister Jeanne also said, Caryn was "full of the devil, an average student. . . . She would pull a prank and look at you with those great big eyes and you couldn't stay mad. She smiled at you so innocently that you just melted."

In a similar vein, Sister Marie Cafferty, who was then the principal at St. Columba, depicted Caryn as "frisky, friendly, outgoing, and full of fun. . . . [S]he was the center of attention when she walked into a group. Our school was racially mixed, and she got along with everyone."

Similar observations of the young Caryn were made by Don Sledge, a longtime worker at the Hudson Guild who knew Caryn from her earliest days performing there. He would tell authors Rose Blue and Corinne J. Naden for their book *Whoopi Goldberg: Entertainer*, "She was funny, and when you're funny, kids like you. She was an outgoing kid, always talented. She seemed cut out to be an actor or comedian even then. And she was determined. You just knew that. She had a goal. . . . She wasn't ashamed to ask anything she needed to know. I remember one time that a neighborhood program was in trouble. . . . Well, the funds ran out and . . . the whole program . . . [was] in danger. So Caryn took over. She ran right out in the street, yelling and performing. She even started pulling out water hoses, anything to get anyone's attention. Wanted to get the neighborhood people and politicians to hear the problem. And she did."

Caryn had difficulty in her studies, and her attention wandered. She constantly was daydreaming about her future in show business. In her fantasies, which preoccupied her, she was always imagining how, once she had become a star, she would magically become the center of interest and no longer be viewed as an outsider. Caryn already knew how to be self-contained, having learned that trait from her mother. As even Don Sledge would emphasize, there were two sides to the complex Caryn Johnson. "She kept her [private] business to herself. What she couldn't hide, she couldn't. But she tried to keep her private business out of sight."

Being different because of her fixation with show business was one matter, but being excluded by her neighborhood peers was another. Years later, when interviewed by Barbara Walters, Whoopi would speak of her childhood years as "kinda lonesome in a way. I had different interests from most of the people I grew up with. Kinda odd." Then, pointing to her face, Goldberg offered, "Because I've always looked like this. Except now I'm taller. But this was always the face." By her own admission, she said she was "not particularly very hip" and that the kids of the Chelsea district "could dupe me really easy."

Decades thereafter, the wounds from her isolated childhood still bothered her. She confided to David Rensin in the June 1987 issue of *Playboy* magazine:

> I was just not a popular girl. I couldn't get a boyfriend. I couldn't get into a clique. I felt I wasn't hip enough or smart enough or fast enough or funny enough or cute enough. I couldn't even dance well. The people who were those things were the people who were going places. I am an overly sensitive person. It's very easy to hurt me. Only I know that,

though. People can say things to me and I'll just respond, "Hey, fuck you!" But inside, it hurts, because I'm still this kid. The best way to explain it is I wanted so much to be accepted that I'd hang out in the park with some of the girls and guys, and when they'd say, "Well, we want to get some candy," I'd run and I'd get some candy. But I'd come back and they'd have gone. And I'd sit and I'd wait. What hurts so much about things like that is that I didn't learn. I'd get the candy again. But it contributed something to me, because I don't let myself do that to people. [*pause*] Sometimes, I get so busy, I get callous. I forget stuff. But that memory has made me concerned about how I treat other people, because it's painful, still.

Caryn graduated from St. Columba on June 15, 1969. Academically, her first eight years in school had proved a struggle for her, with no signs of improvement lying ahead. That fall, she entered high school. It was not at the "glamorous" High School for Performing Arts (made popular by the film and TV series *Fame*) that Caryn claimed in her early playbill biographies, press releases, and interviews—all in a bid to give her background more professional distinction and polish. Instead, she enrolled at a very public institution, Washington Irving High School.

Her new school was several blocks from the projects. The big, imposing building, which is some seventy feet tall, takes up almost the entire block from Sixteenth to Seventeenth Street and from Irving Place to Third Avenue. It is a big boxlike structure faced with dirty pink and tan bricks. (Nowadays there are iron grilles on all the windows.)

But Caryn and Washington Irving High School were not destined for a long association. Barely two weeks into her freshman year, she quit. She now explains: "I was gone. I mean, I know I'm not supposed to be saying that now, because we're supposed to encourage kids to stay in school. But I can say that when I left school, there was a lot more out there. You could go to the Museum of Natural History for classes, and you could go hear, as I said, [Leonard] Bernstein or any number of opera singers. There was information out there that you could gather without having to be in a closed situation."

Severing her ties with the educational system had been far more complicated than she sometimes acknowledged. It was not even a matter that "I just wasn't cut out for it." Nor was it merely that she quit "because it was boring. You couldn't ask questions. People would tell you what they thought you should know." Closer to the truth was her later admission: "I couldn't understand what they were doing." She was even franker when, years after the fact, she disclosed the tremendous frustration and hurt generated by being unable to keep up academically with her classmates. She also stressed the effects of being branded a reject by the educational system. "You don't want to be *retarded* all your life. I was *retarded* for a good part of mine, according to all the paperwork, and I just couldn't handle it." Feeling totally defeated, she gave up, cleaned out her school locker, and, "hit the streets."

The saddest part of it all was that no one at the time had discovered the true cause of Caryn's academic difficulties. In actuality, she suffered from what would now be diagnosed as the reading disorder dyslexia—for which there is often successful treatment. Years later, Whoopi Goldberg would be able to say, "I learned how to deal with dyslexia through a lot of hard work and the help of a lot of different people." However, at the time, this failure to pinpoint her learning disability proved a painful setback in her young life.

CHAPTER FIVE

Hippie Daze

Sex was never mentioned in school, God no. My
mom—who was a nurse—was pretty up-front. She
said, "This is how babies were made." Period. Very
clinical. Nothing about the fun stuff. I didn't know
about birth control when I was a kid. I didn't learn
about it until well into my teens.
                                    —WHOOPI GOLDBERG, 1991

O n November 13, 1969, Caryn Johnson turned fourteen, and her
life seemed to be spinning out of control. While she respected
and loved her strong-willed mother, Emma Johnson was too
much of an authority figure for her daughter to accept her "suggestions"
for getting her life in order by working constructively toward a future
that would revolve around a job and a stable home life. As for her low-
keyed twenty-year-old brother, Clyde, he was out of reach, preoccupied
by his own rough-and-tumble lifestyle. Then, too, for a time, he was
away from home, in Alabama, living with relatives.

A few months earlier, much against her mother's wishes, Caryn
ended her ninth-grade studies at Washington Irving High School. To
appease her distressed mom, she would occasionally attend various cultural events: young people's concerts, museums, the planetarium. However, Caryn much preferred to wander around Central Park. She would
stop to examine the latest happening—a political rally, an impromptu
washtub drum concert—look at the zoo animals, or just people-watch as
New Yorkers meandered by in the park. There were also trips to Coney
Island's amusement park.

In her mid-teens, Caryn worked as a junior counselor at the Ethnic Culture Camp in Peekskill, New York. She also continued to perform sporadically at the Hudson Guild. She later became very involved in student protests against the Vietnam War staged at Columbia University as well as civil-rights marches and what she would later term "hippie politics."

On occasion, Whoopi would later glibly reconstruct her traumatic teen years: "It's tough to be a kid now. I wouldn't even want to try it. When I was kid, it was easy: You were a kid; you knew what your duties as a kid were. Peer pressure was to do things like smoke a cigarette. Now it's a little different. Who shoots who first? How much crack can you sell?"

At other times, she would recall with poignancy the deep pain of her adolescent years, when she thought herself to be the odd duck. "It was sad. I look at that little girl [herself as a youngster]. She's very cute, that kid, you know—when I think of her. She was cute and she was nice and they just didn't get it." In a more expansive moment, she would describe herself as being "incredibly insecure about me as a person, because I was kind of a weird kid. All I wanted to do was have some way to communicate with people and be friends with people, but my interests were always very different."

In her desperate campaign to persuade people to like her, Caryn would say "things that I didn't mean and try to be ways that I wasn't. See, I'm a hippie. I was born a hippie and will be one till I die. . . . When I say hippie, I mean humanist, environmentalist. Someone who wants world peace. Zen politics. Sunshine and rainbows. God. It all appeals to me. But that was not cool in my neighborhood.

"[But] one also had to be hip and black. And I wasn't hip. I was just this kid who liked theater and music and guys. It didn't matter to me what color people were. But then I'd be with a white guy and we'd get hit with eggs. . . . I tried really hard to get into it [dating black men], and I couldn't, because it was bullshit to me. Why the fuck should I be worried about whether or not the guy's white. If he's an ax murderer, then I'm concerned. My instinct was always to just go one on one and see how it went."

Because of Caryn's shyness and her plain looks, dating was more difficult for her than for other girls her age in the Chelsea projects. Already suffering from low self-esteem, Caryn's sense of self-worth dropped even further as she tried to prove her desirability by making herself socially accessible to anyone of the opposite sex. Later, she would admit that as a teen she applied very few standards to her choice of escorts: "Yeah. I went out with anybody who wanted to go out with me. Guys were so hard to find." That her succession of dates included whites achieved the opposite results in her quest for peer approval. It made her suspect in the neighborhood for crossing the unstated color line. This pattern of interracial dating would continue into her adult life and cause her a good deal of grief as she sometimes became the object of hostility from *both* blacks and whites.

It was almost inevitable in the pre-AIDS era of the 1960s, when free love epitomized the "Age of Aquarius," that free-spirited Caryn would experiment with sex on her succession of dates. She lost her virginity when she was thirteen. The next year, one of her dating adventures resulted in her becoming pregnant. She candidly details the hysteria she experienced: "I talked to nobody. I panicked. I sat in hot baths. I drank these strange concoctions girls told me about—something like Johnny Walker Red with a little bit of Clorox, alcohol, baking soda, which probably saved my stomach, and some sort of cream. You mixed it all up. I got violently ill."

However, the "home remedies" did not solve her pregnancy problem. Years later, in *The Choices We Made* (1991), edited by Angela Bonavoglia, Goldberg would be one of the several celebrities who each wrote a chapter on their personal experience with an abortion. At that point she was more concerned with having to explain to anybody what was wrong. "Probably I was afraid to admit that I had had sex, because, remember, the Catholics said you only did it when you were married, and then only in the dark, and here I'd done it in the light in some hallway. But I also didn't grow up around young unmarried girls having kids."

Determined to rid herself of this unwanted child, the fourteen-year-old Caryn went to the local dry cleaners and asked for a wire hanger: "I took it to the park in Chelsea because it was close and had a bathroom. There wasn't a lot of traffic in and out. I didn't do it at home because parents are funny—when you want them to go away, they go, and then they come right back. It was just a private thing, something I needed to do. I never thought I was going to die; young people never think they're going to die. It seemed very simple at the time. You just do that and it goes away."

The deed done, Whoopi recalled: "I didn't bleed a ton, but some, so

I cleaned up a little and rinsed out my underwear like a good girl. Afterwards, I was in a lot of pain. I think the hanger worked, 'cause I then had a period several days later. God was with me—knock on wood. I punctured nothing. I didn't completely destroy my body. But I have a bad body; I have a sensitive body. Whenever I go to the gynecologist, any probing is very painful; it's always been that way."

After the successful self-abortion, Goldberg confessed, "I cried a little bit at the time of that abortion, but not much. I was not a crier. . . . I cry now sometimes when I think of it, when I think that I could have gone to my mother, as I discovered the following year. I could have saved myself a trip to the park with a hanger." Goldberg's searing emotional experience and physical pain while coping with this awful episode in her young life would find its way into her one-woman show— *The Spook Show,* a.k.a *The Whoopi Goldberg Show*—several years later, in which one of her characters, the teenage California Valley Girl, undertakes a self-abortion.

Caught up in the present moment and frequently unmindful of her past experiences, Caryn underwent another abortion when she fifteen. By then such a procedure was legal in New York State. "That decision was harder because I wasn't exactly sure I didn't want to have a baby, but my mother knew I didn't want to have a baby. She was great. She said, 'Look. You can't do this now. There's too much you have to do.' She was right. I knew I was not ready for a child." She explains further: "I hadn't been using birth control at that time. For one thing, I still didn't know where to go for it. And it was the late sixties; everybody was having sex. You had sex in Central Park; it was that free. Those were the good times. Cream was at the Fillmore; the Doors were at the Fillmore; all those cats. It was peace on earth and balloons and flowers and a place for everybody, so people were having children left and right. I hate to call them the good times, because I know they really weren't."

As a coda to this latest difficult episode in her life, Caryn tried something different. She went to Planned Parenthood to have her abortion. To help her avoid becoming pregnant again, staff members there gave Caryn birth-control pills. However, she was one of those individuals who did not respond to the contraceptive pill and, while using this birth-control method, became pregnant three more times over subsequent years.

All through this transitional period, even before she dropped out of Washington Irving High School in 1969, Caryn had experimented with drugs. As she has reasoned (or rationalized) since: "My mother was not a drug addict and not on welfare. But I was a drug addict in my early, early years, back in the sixties. There was a time when you could eat acid and walk down the street. You were high, the cops were high, everybody was loaded. We could sleep in Central Park. You could take a toke off somebody else's joint and not be worried. It was a time of drugs and expansion. That's when I used drugs."

Through this amazing, reckless, and self-absorbed phase, Caryn was at loggerheads with her high-principled mother, who, she admits in a considerable understatement, "was not pleased" by her daughter's antiestablishment behavior. Rather than upset her mother further or be subjected to parental scrutiny, the teenager took to the streets of New York City. Don Sledge, the veteran Hudson Guild worker who was acquainted with Caryn since she began to participate with its theater group, has recalled to interviewers: "The drug problem hit. Emma [Johnson] wouldn't speak of it. Caryn just dropped out of sight. She was heard of from time to time, but she was gone from the community."

How young Caryn survived day to day, month to month, and year to year in the early 1970s remains undocumented but can certainly be hypothesized: a hand-to-mouth existence dependent on the generosity of here-today, gone-tomorrow pals as she drifted about New York. Her experimental passage through the city's wilder underside would provide observations and revelations that would stand her in good stead when years later she returned to the performing arts.

Years after the fact, in 1987, Whoopi would divulge to *Playboy*'s David Rensin that her druggie life cycle was "interesting." However, she refused to provide graphic specifics regarding these hand-to-mouth years on the street when she could easily have been a flower-child poster girl: filled with hallucinatory drugs, a disciple of free love, inner peace, and the cosmic affect of the Zodiac. She also had a glow inside, not only from drugs but because she was a part of the "now" generation. She also insisted to Rensin of *Playboy* that these "lost years" were not "a mystery. It's just something I don't want to talk about for public consumption, you know? I am a little gun-shy. . . . And so I just keep this stuff to myself. I lived. I survived. I grew up." What she will concede, though, is that she never went to jail for any of her unbridled, free-spirited activities.

As to exactly when her attraction to recreational drugs began, to this day she remains vague. However, she does says, "Acid, pills, and heroin were in vogue. I did everything. And large quantities of everything." As to why she did drugs, she has often claimed that it was because everyone seemed to be doing them in the sixties and that it "was almost normal" to be a social user. "You could be real open and do good stuff when you were loaded." Besides marijuana, says Goldberg, "I did heroin. Yeah. . . . Shooting it. At the time it was just another drug [and this in a time before there was concern about contracting AIDS from a dirty needle]. . . . Look, strychnine, rat poison, and Clorox will all kill you. They're all fucked. Acid will get you killed. Opium. Pills. For me it was just another drug. I did lots of drugs. I was a junkie. I was chemically dependent on many things for many years."

From the safety of survival and megasuccess, the Whoopi Goldberg of recent years can afford to reflect: "Those times were not tragic and terrible for me because it was part of the whole picture of what was going on. Of course, I would not recommend anyone go through that, because the safety nets are gone."

As recently as early 1997, Whoopi Goldberg would suggest that reportage exaggerated her teenage lifestyle, which she admitted she used to overstate to make herself newsworthy to interviewers. She believes these exaggerations on her part were expanded by both the white and black media, which, with typical bias, assumed that any black woman from the ghetto (which Goldberg was not) must have been under the influence of hard drugs most of the time (which she insists she was not) and would have certainly fallen upon very hard times (which she today asserts was not true). As Whoopi now sums it up, "People seem to want me to have come from the dregs and dragged myself up, but that's just not the way it was."

CHAPTER SIX

A Little Love and Marriage

Maybe I just got tired of it. I just knew it was
necessary. I decided to go into a program. They took
me—and yelled at me a lot and I yelled at them, and
they put me through this Gestalt therapy, and it
straightened me out.

—WHOOPI GOLDBERG, JUNE 1987

Somehow during her life in the streets, Caryn started to comprehend that she was on a potentially fast road to death. Many people around her—both from her crowd and those in the celebrity limelight—were dying as a result of their drug habits. She must have realized that substance-abuse on a long-term basis was a lot harsher than the psychedelic, mind-expanding journey depicted in such feature films as Peter Fonda's 1967 movie *The Trip*. This realization eventually led her to understand that "there ain't no joy in a high—none. You *think* there's a joy in a high because it feels good temporarily. But it feels good less and less often, so you've got to do it more and more often. It ain't your friend."

Looking back on this crucial fork in her life, Goldberg would admit in the mid-1990s: "It just got to be too much, yeah. I knew: 'This is gonna become really dangerous.' By that time, people were dropping dead. [Jimi] Hendrix [died in 1969] and [Janis] Joplin [died in 1970] and all of these people. People around me were just disappearing. Either their minds would just kind of go 'Zip!' and they'd be gone, or they'd OD."

As more friends and acquaintances in Caryn's circle began suc-
cumbing to drug overdoses, it became clear to her that being part of the
heavy-duty drug culture had too many liabilities. For example, as she
later explained: "The junkie's attitude is 'I hope I don't [die from an
overdose].' But if you do, you're on your own. No one wants to go to jail
as an accessory to murder [from supplying drugs or helping someone
feed his habit]. But a lot of the drugs started doing that—killing people.
Little mousetraps. Little mousetraps." Such assessments led her to the
next step, breaking her life-threatening habit: "Because, wow, you know.
I had to just, like, shake those drugs off. Because the world had started
getting real dark real fast. So I hooked up with a group of people at a
place called Horizon House, which was on Fifth [Avenue], between, like,
Sixteenth and Seventeenth."

Manhattan's Horizon House in the early 1970s was certainly not a
fancy drug-rehab facility like today's Betty Ford Center in Palm Springs,
California. Nevertheless, it was a functional haven for people, like Caryn,
who had determined by themselves, or been helped to decide by friends
and relatives, to kick their habits. There was also another incentive for
joining the Horizon House program which particularly appealed to
Caryn. It was a way to get off the tough streets and away from the
pressures of daily survival as a homeless person.

Whoopi's intensive four-week therapy program was very strict, with
the participants regimented by a timetable and assigned chores. "There's
a group. You have confrontations, heavy talks, people going, 'Fuck! What
am I? Why am I? Drugs didn't work. What do you have to offer to make
me feel better about myself as a person?' " As the treatment progressed,
Goldberg came to appreciate that her drug binges only gave her a short,
false high and that, inevitably, within a short time, she would need more
drugs to get back that feeling of exhilaration. It led her to question:
"What's the worse evil? Trying to make friends and keep them or trying
to get high and keep the feeling? At some point I had to decide what I
really wanted."

During the course of the rugged Horizon House program, the future
film star had tremendous emotional ups and downs in fighting her powerful drug habit. As she would come to accept, "Junkies never know they
have to stop, and I don't know now how I did." Years later, in retrospect,
she would realize: "All the people who stopped me [from using drugs]
are dead now. I'm the living legacy of this group of talented, wonderful
dope fiends who cleaned me up and made a lasting impression."

Both during and after her participation in the Horizon House treatment program, Caryn was *not* able to kick her habit entirely. She admits, "I didn't stop altogether at once. It took many, many tries. You fall a lot because it's *hard*." Getting permanently clean would be a long and painful procedure for young Caryn.

Later, more than a decade after participating in the Horizon House treatment regimen, Caryn began downplaying this earlier phase of her life. As she gained national prominence in the mid-1980s, she would glibly summarize the tortuous process of her drug rehabilitation: "I got bored with drugs, and I went into a drug program called Horizon House on Fifth Avenue in New York. Which was really great. I stayed with them for a little while and got myself together."

More recently, she has insisted repeatedly that the media accounts of her having had a horrendous time both in and out of drug addiction were highly exaggerated. Regardless of the actual degree and length of Caryn's drug addiction, Whoopi Goldberg became a staunch antidrug advocate. By then, the "born again" entertainer would crusade. "Drugs are cut with rat poison and shit. I could never do now what I did then. Today's drugs are too powerful." She says, "I tell kids, 'Save the money and just kill yourself, because that's what you're doing.'"

Caryn was still only seventeen when she was weaned off drugs at Horizon House. Part of that institution's help program involved the buddy system, with members providing support for one another. There was also a core group of staff helpers at the facility. One of them was Alvin Martin, a tall, thin, light-skinned African American three years her senior. As Caryn's drug counselor, he saw a good deal of the teenager. Years later, in reassessing her degree of addiction in the early 1970s, he decided she had *not* been a junkie. "It was more a phase she was going through, just doing a little bit of everything. She was never hooked on one drug."

Alvin recalls that one of the first things that struck him about the newcomer to the treatment center was her atypical looks: "She was very different from all the other people there. She always wore this huge Afro wig, which made her stand out; she was just like a black hippie." He also said, "She certainly was no conventional beauty; she didn't fit into any mold, and that's what attracted me to her. I had this curiosity about what made her tick, and once we started talking, I got to like her more and more."

For Caryn, at a very vulnerable point in her life, Alvin was a bless-ing—or so it appeared. As she began to put her druggie way of life behind her, her mind started to clear of the chemical fog, and her earlier career ambitions began to resurface. Once again, she thought enthusiasti-cally about the acting profession and how expressing herself onstage had always satisfied so many of her emotional needs. It was something she had missed in her hippie and substance-abuse period.

However, Caryn must have reasoned that to pursue the actor's life realistically, she needed a far more stable living environment. She cer-tainly had had enough of the rootlessness of the past four years, but she had no desire to stay at her mother's apartment in the Chelsea projects. Even though she was tempted, she knew that to do so would entail being trapped once more under that staunch lady's ever-watchful eyes. Once again, Caryn would be squarely in the line of vision of everyone in the projects who had ever known her and who would consider it their duty to report to Mrs. Johnson all of the young woman's activities. While returning home was out of the question, so was a job. Caryn was un-trained for any real task. Moreover, the thought of working in a struc-tured atmosphere was repugnant to her.

With such unpromising options in sight, Caryn chose to allow Alvin Martin to court her. It was not long after they began dating that she moved into his small Greenwich Village apartment. When Alvin took her to visit his mother, Caryn responded to Irma Martin's warmth, and the two became friends, just as she sought to do with Alvin's other relatives. In contrast, Caryn's reserved mother, Emma, was wary of her daughter's boyfriend, for Caryn and Alvin were living together *without* the blessing of the clergy. The very morally upright Emma urged her daughter to do the proper thing and marry this man. In 1973 they wed.

The groom was initially content with his love match. In those early romantic days, he found everything about her charming, including the fact that (as he would detail years later, when she had become famous) she was as eccentric as her wacky screen characters in *Ghost* and *Sister Act.*

In contrast, Caryn was filled with mixed emotions. The new bride would admit later, "It seemed like the thing to do at the time. He was bored with what he was doing and wanted to try something else. I fig-ured nobody was ever going to marry me so I might as well do it just in case." On another occasion, she phrased her rationale for marrying Mar-tin thusly: "I felt I had better do something, because I didn't know what was coming. I got married, but it wasn't particularly right for either of us."

By now, stable, responsible Alvin had quit his Horizon House job and was working as a clerk at Chase Manhattan Bank. After repeatedly pointing out to his bride that they needed a double income to get by financially, she allowed him to help her get a clerical job with the large banking institution. But it was wishful thinking on his part to hope that Caryn could or would remain in such a formal environment for very long. For example, her repeated refusal to dress professionally instead of wearing jeans and a frayed old shirt to the office prompted some of their more heated, early arguments. He recalls, "I'd buy her dresses and try to make her wear them, but she refused to conform. She just didn't fit in."

Caryn's constant battles with Alvin and with herself about whether or not she would go to work on a particular day, and if she did how she would comport herself, had a temporary suecase when she got pregnant. Some later chroniclers would infer that her pregnancy occurred *before* Caryn's marriage to Martin, but she has long insisted it was in the proper sequence of events. As to the contention that she got pregnant on purpose to have a "legitimate" excuse to quit her odious bank job, she counters, "My daughter, who I had when I was eighteen and married, was a Pill baby. I had taken the Pill religiously, religiously. Then I didn't get pregnant for a long time."

Alvin's recollections of becoming a father-to-be were: "It was nothing planned, but we decided to go ahead with it. . . . I know her main concern was that it meant she wouldn't have to go back to the bank. She just wanted to be available to check out new [acting] roles that were coming along."

In this *Rashomon*-like phase of Goldberg's chronology where many variations and points of views exist about events in the performer's hectic life, actor-singer Jenifer Lewis had her own take on what happened in Caryn's life at this time. Lewis appeared in *Corrina, Corrina* in the mid-1990s with Goldberg. In an August 1994 interview for *LA Weekly,* she mentioned to reporter Kristal Brent Zook: "People seem to forget that Whoopi was a junkie from twelve to nineteen years of age, [with] heroin running through her veins. They seem to forget that when she went for help, she was raped by her counselor and had to have an abortion." How much of these remarks are reality or repeated hearsay or an honest account of what are actually erroneous facts remains unknown.

While Caryn was on maternity leave from her bank job, she and

Martin moved from their modest Greenwich Village apartment to a better place in lower Manhattan and then, later, to one in Queens. The latter was an especially good location for the expectant Caryn, because she did not know how to cook, nor did she want to learn. As Alvin recalls, their new apartment was "underneath . . . a row of food shops—pasta, Chinese . . . and they delivered, so, of course, we lived on take-outs."

By the time Alexandrea (named after Alexander the Great) was born in May 1974, the Martins' marriage had reached a crucial turning point. Alvin was stressed out from working two jobs to support the household. Meanwhile, Caryn refused to return to the dead-end bank position. As he has explained, they now were having constant arguments over money: "She wanted to be a movie star, and I wanted to pay bills. The two things don't mix."

According to Martin, Caryn, the new mother, was getting bit acting roles here and there—none of which paid much money. It put a heavier burden on Alvin not only to be the family's breadwinner but also to be, increasingly, a baby-sitter for their infant daughter. Martin explained that they were at odds about her choice of priorities. The bottom line was that Caryn was determined to be a star. "Once the maternity benefit stopped," Alvin said, "we were short of money. But she wouldn't go back to work. That's when we really started to argue. We used to have screaming matches."

Whoopi Goldberg now depicts her domestic life in the early 1970s as fun. "I was married and very happy to have a kid." Earlier she would contend that she had made a terrible mistake "because the man I was married to wasn't really supportive of art. And I have to have that or I will die." She concluded about her faulty union: "It wasn't right. You get married because you love someone, and for no other reason. It can only last if you're deeply in love, and we weren't. It was mutual."

At loose ends, Caryn had no choice but to fall back on her mother's help. So she and tiny Alexandrea moved into her mother's place in Manhattan. Caryn was now back in the Chelsea projects, wondering what to do next. Within a month she had her answer.

PART II

Life on the Wicked Stage

CHAPTER SEVEN

What's in a Name

. . . a friend who had been working in the theater
called to ask if I wanted to go to California. Bingo!
We drove a barf-green car to San Diego via Lubbock,
Texas. I was appalled. I thought we were going to
Hollywood. But it was okay, because I was going to
be acting.
—WHOOPI GOLDBERG, JUNE 1987

W hen Caryn and Alvin Martin separated in 1974, their marriage
was less than two years old. The breakup was emotionally
charged on both sides, and for a time the couple remained on
bad terms. Alvin was still unable to fathom the degree of his wife's show-
business ambitions. As he would relate to Joan Rivers on her TV talk
show in October 1993, while Alvin and Caryn were married, and even
thereafter, Alvin had been unable to appreciate fully her determination to
become a professional performer. Moreover, he never suspected that
within his intense, sensitive wife lurked a budding comedian. After all, he
explained to Rivers, her aim in those days was to achieve fame as a
dramatic actor. According to Martin, during their short-circuited union,
neither she nor their life together had been particularly funny at all.

As the weeks passed, there was no hint of a possible reconciliation.
Alvin and Caryn each went their separate ways. In time, Martin would
put his failed marriage behind him, and in the late 1970s, he and Caryn
would divorce. By then, she was living three thousand miles away, in
California, and there was little opportunity for him to see his daughter.
Nevertheless, he stayed in touch with his ex-wife because of their child.

As time passed, Caryn and Martin came to terms with their once-volatile alliance, and their relationship eventually evolved from acrimonious to passably friendly. ("It's hard to fight long-distance," Martin would explain.)

More than a decade later, Alvin received a call from his brother, who also lived in the New York City area. He told Alvin to go out and buy a copy of Sunday's *New York Daily News* and that he'd be very surprised. A puzzled Martin hurried to a local newsstand. There, on the magazine section's cover, was a photo of a beaming Caryn. By this point, she had adopted an unusual new professional name. The article went on to detail that this highly talented, insightful comedian was about to open in a one-woman show. Alvin was equally taken off guard when Caryn sent him tickets to see her show. He recalls: "She wanted to keep in touch with my mother and went to see my family."

More years passed, and Martin's former wife became not only a Broadway star but also a Grammy and Oscar winner. During this period she never referred to Martin by name in any of her media interviews. Seeing his ex-mate achieve the success she had so desired, Alvin could only admit, belatedly, "Caryn has worked very hard for what she has and was very single-minded about getting it. Perhaps she was right to have been going after the roles while I was worrying about money [during their abortive marriage]."

Eventually, Martin and his famous ex-spouse lost touch with one another. Martin places some of the blame on Caryn's mother, Emma. "She never did like me." Then, when Alexandrea was in her mid-teens and living in California, she underwent a personal crisis. Alvin made it his business to call and speak with his daughter. Once he realized she was firm in her decision as to how to handle the tough situation confronting her, he gave his offspring all he could offer at the time—his emotional support. After that, Alvin and his former family drifted apart even further. He explains: "I stopped calling Caryn because I'd have to go through her people and they'd contact her so she could get back to me. . . . It was all so much of a hassle." (In contrast, Caryn's take on the situation, as recorded in mid-1987, was to suggest that although she and Martin were no longer in communication, he apparently was making no real effort to see their teenaged child. As Whoopi put it: "His loss.")

As to his ex-wife's subsequent marriages, Martin would observe: "Of course, her second husband, David Claessen, was white. And I'm very light-skinned. But I think I was a bit of a detour for her." Later, when

Goldberg was having her romantic fling with Ted Danson, the tabloids asked Alvin what he thought of the highly publicized interracial relationship. He called the romance "cute" and then added, "When I saw them together in *Made in America* [1993], I could see there was more in it than just acting."

Looking back on Caryn's grand success, Martin remembers that he used to tease his now-prominent former wife that "if it wasn't for me, she wouldn't be where she is now. If I hadn't been there to fight with her as much as I was, she would never have gone to California." And he still refers to her by her given name, because "somehow Whoopi doesn't fit. I identify with Caryn." On a more serious note, Alvin, now a New York City Medicaid worker, said, "I can't look back and say I should have hung there with her and reaped some of her rewards. It would still have ended the way it did."

Caryn remained with her mother in the Chelsea projects for approximately a month. It all seemed such a dead end to the restless young woman who craved to make something of her life, especially in the performing arts. Then, by chance, a friend who worked in show business mentioned that soon she was driving out to California. Caryn asked her whether she and baby Alexandrea might tag along. The answer was yes. In short order, Caryn and her infant were heading to the West Coast. Maybe, Caryn reasoned, in the warm climate of Los Angeles she could pursue her acting career and, just maybe, break into the movies.

The trio in the beat-up car took the southern route westward, which eventually found them driving through Texas and then into California. When they reached San Diego, Caryn's friend decided to remain there, so the young mother and her baby also stayed on in that expansive port city, 130 miles southeast of Los Angeles.

Stranded in a strange city, Caryn could only wonder at the wisdom of her impromptu, dramatic decision to distance herself from her family and friends back in New York. She was bewildered by the rash act that had led her to relocate so far from home. Even though she was happy to have left her drug past far behind her, the young woman panicked. She told herself: "I made a mistake. I made a terrible mistake. I don't know how to drive. I don't know how to do any of this stuff. There are . . . lots and lots of stuff out here I've never seen . . . palm trees."

As she would recall for TV journalist Ed Bradley on the June 6,

1993, edition of *60 Minutes*: "You know I'm from . . . New York . . . and everything [in California] moved really slow." For Bradley, Goldberg recollected how she had pondered, "Hey, so what do I do now, you know? Somebody said, 'Maybe you need to find a job.' And I tried, but what could I do? I didn't know how to do much."

At one point in her desperate search for work—of any type—before her limited funds ran out, Caryn arranged to take care of her would-be employer's children. However, that position fell through. Instead, she scrounged for odd jobs and became, for a time, a bricklayer's assistant and then a sheet-rock installer. However, her lack of real training disqualified her for any long-lasting position. Down and nearly out, for one brief juncture she worked in strip joints. However, she insists, "I never got my clothes off. People were screaming, 'Don't do it!' I have great legs, but once you get up near my butt, it's not good."

Financially, everything went from bad to worse. "Somebody said, 'While you're starving, you might want to consider the welfare system.' Now, I wasn't raised in a welfare household, so this was a rough thing to do. But I'm glad they were there, although it's a system I've come to see, in hindsight, that's devised for you not to get off. It's demeaning and dehumanizing." She noted, "It only takes one person coming to your house looking at you like you're dog mess and going through your cupboards to see if you're eating more than your allotted share." Expanding on this subject, today's Whoopi said about her decision to accept welfare, "[W]hen you are trying to raise a child and you have no job or a chance of a job, there aren't many alternatives."

Being on the public dole was not only emotionally debilitating for the young woman; it also required a radical lifestyle adjustment. "The welfare workers used to make these surprise visits, because you weren't allowed to have friends, especially not friends to whom you might want to be polite and *feed* something. If a welfare worker did surprise you and you happened to have a friend in the house with a plate of food in front of them, it would be deducted from your money the next month." Making the situation even worse, the ex-New Yorker had a "caseworker who was nasty as hell."

At one point, in order to develop much-needed workforce skills, Caryn, who had already done occasional hair modeling, took cosmetology courses, which, surprisingly, led her to part-time employment at a San Diego mortuary. Years later, when asked if she didn't find this unusual occupation particularly weird, she responded, "No. Life is weird.

Death seems to be very easy." She also explained why she had not utilized her cosmetology skills in a more conventional setting in San Diego,
such as a hair salon: "When you work in a beauty parlor, you can't talk
back, and you can't talk mean. Dead folks—you can have conversations
with 'em and tell 'em how you really feel: 'I'm glad you're dead. I think
you're a bitch.' You can grab their head and go, 'Hey, come on. Sit up
here. Let's try the Joan Crawford look on you. Nah, that doesn't work.
Let's try Lucille Ball.' "

On yet another occasion, she further described her mortuary post:
"You play with the bodies. They're like big dolls. No one's around. You
put them in a chair, paint their lips, do eye shadow. Make them look
punk. Or very, very dead. . . . You can powder their face totally white.
Or make them look like a Raggedy Ann doll. And then you get to work.
It's good work." For the imaginative Caryn, this bizarre setting proved to
be another rich opportunity for her to play act.

Being full of pride, every time Caryn found work—such as at the
mortuary—she would declare the income to the welfare department,
which, of course, deducted a portion of it from her next paycheck. By
that point she might be out of work and badly in need of the full allot-
ment ($273 per month) to sustain herself and her child until the next job
or welfare check materialized. She says she was prompted to such hon-
esty "because I didn't want my daughter seeing Mom lying."

Over her nearly eight-year stay in San Diego, Caryn would bounce
back and forth between jobs and her reliance on welfare. Toward the end
of her San Diego period, she would work at the Big Kitchen Restaurant at
3003 Grape Street. It was located in the Golden Hill area, on the east and
south sides of the city's Balboa Park. The Big Kitchen was, and still is,
owned by Judy Foreman, whose business philosophy has been to cater to
the average person in the neighborhood. Caryn's signature still remains
on the cafe's kitchen wall, with the scribbled warning "Don't paint over
this."

One of Caryn's strangest jobs in these presuccess years would be
held in 1980, when she was part of a group—which included mostly
improvisational actors—that worked in nearby La Jolla. They had been
hired for a psychiatric think tank which was participating in a state-
funded PBS-TV documentary dealing with isolation and loneliness. Unlike the rest of the assemblage, who came from other parts of the country,
Caryn had been employed locally. Another member of the group was
Janet Coleman, a writer from New York. In a 1984 *Vanity Fair* profile of

Whoopi Goldberg, Coleman said, "She was not just the token black member of the cast. Like a seltzer bottle in the desert, she was the only black [improvisational] comedian in all of San Diego County."

Having led a very active dating life before her marriage and still a very young woman with healthy sexual appetites, nineteen-year-old Caryn began socializing once she was "settled" in San Diego. However, because she was existing mostly on welfare, she had to be circumspect about such dating, especially if she and the man became more than casually involved. She spelled out welfare's attitude on the subject: "You're a single woman with a child, you're not encouraged to develop a relationship with [a man]. Because maybe he's going to give you some money and help you out, you know. You start feeling, Well, s——, you don't want me to get off welfare. You don't want me to get off." Rightly so, she found it demeaning that welfare caseworkers should be "sniffing around" to determine if some man might be living on her allowance.

According to Whoopi, she had no trouble finding male companionship in San Diego when and if she so desired: "Well, shit! All you got to do is open your legs and you can get a guy. Pussy talks, you know? But then, what do you do when you're finished. If it's just about getting a guy, that's very easy to do. But I was not so interested in that. I really wanted someone I could spend time with if I was going to choose to do that. But if you're a single parent and you're a woman, you get these lines from guys: 'Oh, you know I don't want to get involved.' 'Well, I don't want to be a father.' It's like: Hey, we're only going to the movies, Jack! Cool the chill! What makes you think I want you to be a father to my kid? Cool out! They just assume you must be desperate."

At another point, discussing her apprentice years in San Diego, Whoopi would say, "I had a boyfriend for a little while, but otherwise I kept pretty much to myself. I didn't want a lot of guys in my house when my kid woke up."

Throughout this makeshift period of sustaining herself and Alexandrea, Caryn reached out in every possible direction to find theater work. Whenever time and her budget permitted, she auditioned with the various local stage outlets, which ranged from repertory groups to dinner theaters. Whatever her unfocused potential may have been at the time, she met with a great deal of resistance from casting people: (1) She lacked needed acting experience; (2) she was black, and it was hard to cast her in shows populated with white actors and supported by a predominantly white audience, which, it was assumed, had not yet come to grips with interracial story lines; and (3) her looks were distinctively different.

If onlookers had considered her features offbeat back in New York, there was even more reason to do so in San Diego, because by now Caryn had adopted a new hairstyle. She was wearing dreadlocks, which consisted of weaving her head of thick black hair into tightly knit braids, which she then allowed to cascade down her shoulders and back. Once set into place, it required very little grooming to maintain. Why did Caryn pick this unusual grooming style? Her answer was "because it's comfortable and I like it." Actually, she first got the notion for this hair fashion by watching rising African-American actor Rosalind Cash, who had appeared in such movies as *The Omega Man* (1971), *Hickey and Boggs* (1972), *Uptown Saturday Night* (1974), and *Dr. Black and Mr. Hyde* (1975). Cash wore dreads whenever film, TV, or stage producers would allow her to do so. At other times, she was forced to place wigs over her unique hair fashion.

Goldberg acknowledged in the late 1990s: "The first person I ever saw with dreads was Rosalind Cash, and I remember thinking she looked incredible, but I didn't consider it for me then. I was wearing my hair in a little natural [style], and I used to braid it. And then one day, much later, I just got tired and I said, 'You know, I'm never taking these braids out.' But for so long my particular package was alien to everybody. Today, when I see dread braids, plum lipstick, and women wearing flats and sneakers, I know part of that is because of me."

To make matters worse in her search for professional theater work, Caryn decided in the mid-1970s to change her name. By now she was having a bit of luck in finding acting work, mostly with the fledgling San Diego Repertory Company. One Christmas, the group was presenting their adaptation of Charles Dickens's *Christmas Carol*. She said, "We'd sit backstage and talk about names we'd never give our children, like Pork Pie or Independence. Of course, now people are walking around with those names. A woman said to me, 'If I was your mother, I would have called you Whoopi, because when you're unhappy you make a sound like a whoopee cushion. It sounds like a fart.' It was like 'Ha-ha-ha-ha— Whoopi!' "

Caryn, who was indeed prone to flatulism under the best of circumstances, thought it amusing and perceived that "Whoopi" would be a gimmicky new moniker for her that just might make casting directors and audiences remember her. With a bit more embellishment of the conceit, she became "Whoopi Cushion," and then, for a time, using the French variation of her surname, she called herself "Whoopi Coussin."

Supposedly, the star claims, it was at this point in her renaming process that her serious-minded mother back in New York could hold her silence no longer. She told her ever-experimenting daughter, "You won't be taken seriously if you call yourself Whoopi Cushion." Although the young actor remained firm about keeping her newly found first name Whoopi, she conceded to her mother's request that she adopt a more serious sounding last name. It was then, so legend has it, that either Emma Johnson or the future Whoopi drew upon their extended family tree and came up with a distant relative who was Jewish and named "Goldberg." Thus, the combination of Whoopi Goldberg was born. As she rightly surmised, it proved to be a distinctive gimmick. Audiences were forever surprised that the owner of this odd Jewish-sounding name turned out to be an African American who had a strange hairdo and a very special look.

Especially at the start of her breakthrough to stardom in the mid-1980s, Goldberg made a big thing about her unusual name, for it seemed that every reporter who interviewed her would ask about its origins. For a while, to make it sound more mysterious and inspired, she insisted that the surname Goldberg had come to her in a vision of a burning bush that talked like a little, old Jewish tailor with an accent and from that apparition emerged the unexpected appellation.

Only later would Whoopi admit publicly that yes, indeed, it was her mother who had thought of adding Goldberg to the Whoopi stage name. "She just thought it flowed better. Mothers, you know, they sit and think about shit like this. But you tell people the truth and they go, 'Oh, come on. It's not interesting enough.' So that's why I made up the burning-bush story. All I know is that when I tried it, the name worked. People said, 'What a great name! What a great fucking name!' Except critics. In a review, one said, 'Whoopi Goldberg was fantastic as *Mother Courage* [1981], but that name is ridiculous.' I wrote him a letter and said that a rose by any other name would still be an actor."

CHAPTER EIGHT

Mother Courage

There had not been anyone that looked like me anywhere in San Diego—and of course my name didn't hurt. You have to put together the look and the name and the weird characters to understand that I was a shock to the audiences. Nobody had seen it. Nobody was even looking for it. Nobody understood that what I did was like a play. Actors do monologues. That's all I was doing, but they made it seem like I was doing something amazing.

—WHOOPI GOLDBERG, FALL 1988

In the years since nineteen-year-old Caryn Johnson and her daughter came to San Diego, California, in 1974, Caryn worked at a variety of jobs, none of them well paying or permanent. Frequently, Whoopi's life was so precarious, it is a wonder that her frustrations and fears did not drive her back into becoming an active drug user. What emotionally sustained the confused young adult was her dream of acting. "Acting is the one thing I always knew I could do," she said. Her dream kept her focused and defined her as a person. However, its fulfillment did not come easily.

Now that she needed to concentrate totally on her career, her energy and direction were diluted by the responsibilities of motherhood. Her one-year-old girl needed attention and love, while Caryn needed money to keep the single-parent household going. Moreover, she was possessed by her ongoing craving for emotional and sexual rapport from a man, all of which combined to produce an exhausting physical and mental burden for the burgeoning actor. In the process, something had to give, and often this meant devoting less personal attention to her child.

As she made the rounds, Whoopi was smart enough to realize that she was too unseasoned to be accepted into the ranks of the professional regional theater companies. Nevertheless, she had enough faith in herself and blind ambition to audition for them. The frustrating rejections only made stronger her resolve to succeed—no matter what.

As time went on, Caryn expanded her career horizons and lessened her expectations. She began to audition for local dinner-theater companies. Years later she would describe her efforts: "It was much easier to find work in New York. Directors [in Manhattan] were more open to casting you in roles that weren't specifically white. In California they were not so willing to do that. You'd go for some role—say in *Moon for the Misbegotten*—and you'd give a perfectly wonderful reading, then they'd go, 'Well, you're great, but we're not quite ready to make that kind of statement.' "

She also got fed up with dinner-theater owners telling her, " 'We can't put you and a white guy together, because the folks from Texas can't handle it.' And: 'You *are* good, but our economy rides on people coming to see what they expect. And they're not expecting you.' "

So far her newly conceived name, Whoopi Goldberg, had not paid tangible dividends. But she remained undaunted and grew more cagey in anticipating what was required. As she continued to audition, she constantly refined her "image"—anything that might give her an edge in the essentially all-white theater community. Part of her gambit was to fabricate a more impressive academic past, one filled with appropriate theater credentials. In her early resumés (and, later, in playbill biographies) she would claim that she had attended the New York High School for the Performing Arts, matriculated at Boston College, and studied acting in New York City with famed coach Uta Hagen. Her biographies would also claim that at some unspecified time she had enjoyed small parts in several long-running Broadway musicals. According to the impression she fostered, she had appeared in *Hair* (the show's off-Broadway debut was October 17, 1967; its Broadway debut, April 29, 1968), *Jesus Christ Superstar* (its Broadway opening was October 12, 1971), and *Pippin* (its Broadway bow was October 23, 1972). Such chorus replacement jobs on the Broadway stage by Caryn Johnson have never been verified. In fact, years later, when Whoopi replaced the star of a big mainstream musical revival, she would comment repeatedly to the media that this engagement, in 1997, was her first Broadway musical.

Eventually, over the years in San Diego, she saved enough money to buy a beat-up, used Volkswagen. Having her own transportation was a great boon for tooling around San Diego as she tested for one stage role after another and, additionally, looked for income-generating jobs. Driving was very new to Goldberg, since there had never been a real need to be a licensed driver back in New York City. It proved to be a tough hurdle for the impatient, inexperienced Goldberg to become an adequate driver.

Finally, Whoopi enjoyed her first career break when she came across the San Diego Repertory Theater. For a change, when she insisted, "I can act, I really can," she was believed by the people in charge. This theatrical organization was the inspiration of Sam Woodhouse and Douglas Jacobs and was an outgrowth of Indian Magique, their street performance group. In 1976, Woodhouse and Jacobs—thanks to a core of actor friends—put together the San Diego Repertory Theater. As the group expanded, it began presenting mostly avant-garde works at San Diego City College, at the then-underused theater facilities. Later, a former San Diego mortuary was made available to the small acting company. It was converted into the two-hundred-seat Sixth Avenue Playhouse, which became the troupe's home for several years. The theater's physical structure was unglamorous, but it provided a forum for playwrights and actors. In seasons to come, the increasingly respected repertory group would present a series of innovative stage projects. In their first ten years, they gave nineteen San Diego premieres, twelve West Coast premieres, and ten world premieres.

The San Diego Repertory Theater was adventurous and liberal, especially compared to the norms and tastes of the average local residents. So it was not that surprising that they were open to inviting nonwhite performers to join their cast and crew. Whoopi would be one of the few black talents to participate in the predominantly white repertory group in its first years. This was primarily because in the mid-1970s relatively few blacks were considering careers in show business, which had so many racial limitations. Then, too, many of the small number of African Americans who did aspire to a show-business life assumed there would be no chance for them to participate in an integrated theater environment. They remained focused on nonmainstream black acting groups. Goldberg, who boasted a unique stage name and distinctive physical look, was an intriguing oddity in this newly formed stage organization.

For several reasons, being one of the few blacks in an essentially white theater company turned out to be both an advantage and a needed learning experience for the future star. It made her try all the harder to succeed in order to prove herself to the others. At the same time, her skin color and ethnic features made it easy for audiences to take note of her stage presence in the ensemble. To augment this peculiar notability she trained herself in the art of being—or at least seeming to be—very confident as a performer. This mask of exuberant self-faith was a cover-up both to the onlooker and to Whoopi, who generally appeared to "know"—as if by osmosis—what to do in front of the footlights.

In contrast, there were definite liabilities to being a different-looking black actor who insisted on wearing those unfashionable dreadlocks. Even in the progressive ambience of the San Diego Repertory Theater in the mid-1970s, there was a level of leading parts not considered "right" for her because they had been written for a comely white woman. Consequently, many potential acting assignments were denied this intuitive, talented apprentice no matter what the degree of her ever-improving acting talent. Sometimes the job turndowns were subconscious forms of racial discrimination. On other occasions it was because of Goldberg's offbeat physical appearance. As a result, the enthusiastic but unfulfilled player was often relegated to subordinate assignments for reasons having nothing or little to do with her acting talent.

The reality of being tracked into subordinate roles certainly must have irked her. After all, from childhood onward, she knew that she wanted to act and could handle acting roles and that only through the magical world of entertaining others could she find validation in her helter-skelter life. Whoopi badly needed the chance to express her ever-maturing observations on life's wonders and absurdities, especially as seen through the perspective of an offbeat black person.

In their fledgling years, the San Diego Repertory Theater performed local premieres of stage works by David Mamet, Sam Shepard, and many others. Some of their other productions included versions of Carlo Goldoni's *Servant of Two Masters* and Molière's *Scapin*. Most of the theater's offerings were by male playwrights, for this was still the era before women playwrights were considered the norm rather than the exception.

(Later, the group would perform stage works by such female playwrights as Caryl Churchill, Marsha Norman, and even improvisational work by Goldberg herself.)

One of the troupe's most successful early productions was Charles Dickens's *A Christmas Carol*, adapted by cofounder Douglas Jacobs. Their first offering of the holiday fare was in 1977 and began the day after Thanksgiving and ran through Christmas. It became a traditional seasonal offering by the company. Whoopi was part of the cast for this project and had five different characters to play.

The ongoing process of being a member of an established organization provided much-needed stability for the rootless Whoopi. For so long—by her own choices or circumstances—she had been an outsider. However, she now began to feel that she finally belonged somewhere, and the repertory's cast and crew became her extended family. She was no longer merely one individual against the world. At the same time, there was often little or no pay attached to her acting work. So, once again, she had to force herself to be grateful for the much-needed welfare checks she received and to make herself a harmonious part of the "system."

The novelty of merely being onstage in front of an audience, whether paying or not, eventually wore off. Moreover, there were periods when the repertory troupe was inactive or the roles assigned to Whoopi were of minimal consequence and left her with too many free hours. The ambitious Goldberg used the spare time to search out other performance gigs. Almost by default, when she looked for new places to seek acting work, she was forced to explore the improvisational arena. There she could occasionally find opportunities to work in ensemble sketches in which interracial casting seemed less of a problem. To give herself more stage exposure in these forums, she began devising little routines to showcase herself. One of these improv groups with which she became involved was called Spontaneous Combustion.

Eager to further expand her talents and demonstrate her abilities, Whoopi drifted into stand-up comedy. Ironically, when she began in the acting profession, the thought of eventually becoming a comedian was the furthest thing from her mind. She had always wanted to be a dramatic actor, one who would—she fantasized—become the toast of Broadway and, later, of the movies.

In the late 1970s, as she pursued new venues in the San Diego performers' community, Goldberg met comedian Don Victor. "Don is a very good stand-up, and I was sort of this weird actor type, and neither of us could get any work. I wanted to learn what he did, and he wanted to learn what I did, so we became 'Victor and Goldberg,' along the lines of Elaine May and Mike Nichols." The two eventually developed an act which they would perform at late-night theater venues around San Diego.

The Victor-Goldberg duo began just as the comedy industry was mushrooming, and it would have been easy for the team to get lost in the crowd of funster hopefuls. However, once again, the combination of Whoopi's unusual name and look—and of being black and one of the few women in the comedy arena—made her and Victor stand out from the pack.

Meanwhile, in the late 1970s, creator-producer Lorne Michaels and other executives of the New York–based *Saturday Night Live* (NBC-TV) let it be known that they were always looking for new talent to join their ensemble. (In 1979, Dan Aykroyd and John Belushi would defect from the troupe; in 1980, Gilda Radner would leave the lineup.) Whoopi and Don decided to give it a shot and sent an audition tape of their material to the *Saturday Night Live* decision makers. Goldberg said: "We didn't hear, didn't hear, didn't hear. Finally, the tape came back mangled. We called, and they said someone had accidentally smashed it. 'Sorry.' " Thus ended the duo's effort to join the ranks of America's prime TV comedy forum. It was a setback for them, but they, and Whoopi in particular, nevertheless kept looking for the next possible big break.

During her San Diego period, Whoopi, the young mother, was frequently on the edge of disaster as she tried to balance her priorities of survival, motherhood, and acting (not necessarily in that order). By the late 1970s, Goldberg had become fairly expert at this enervating juggling game, keeping the various aspects of her life going forward as best as she could. Very frequently, it was her welfare check that really sustained her and her daughter. Nevertheless, it continued to irk Whoopi to be a ward of a nonbenevolent, government-run system. When her pride overcame her reason, it required all her willpower to calm down. She had to constantly remind herself that the situation "was not forever." Meanwhile, she kept to her overall aim: to "know a lot more stuff than I knew."

During their 1979–80 season, the San Diego Repertory Theater offered the local premiere of Marsha Norman's drama *Getting Out,* the world premiere of John William See's *Lady Cries Murder,* a spoof of hard-boiled private-eye yarns, and in the spring of 1980, John Steinbeck's *Of Mice and Men.* Later in the year they mounted an elaborate musical version of Stud Turkel's *Working* (which also toured in the area). To wrap up 1980, the troupe presented its perennial favorite, *A Christmas Carol.*

By this point, there were twelve full-time administrative employees at the rep, which was still under the artistic direction of Sam Woodhouse and Douglas Jacobs. On a yearly basis, an average of forty thousand audience members now enjoyed the theater's productions. Some of the playgoers were repeat attendees who had season subscriptions. Bolstering the group's revenues to meet operational costs were federal funds from CETA (the Comprehensive Employment Training Act). However, when the newly installed president, Ronald Reagan, introduced cutbacks in federal programs, the CETA subsidy for the rep ended in mid-May 1981.

At this critical financial juncture, the troupe was operating at San Diego's old Lyceum Theatre. Unaware of the future, the board of directors had already put into preproduction their ambitious presentation of a new adaptation of *Mother Courage,* the epic comic drama written by German playwright Bertolt Brecht in 1933. The play traces the exodus of Bavarian Mother Courage and her children through a dozen years of the seventeenth century's holy wars in chaotic Europe. It depicts her life as she follows the armies with her wagon and wares, selling to both sides. As translated into English, it had been presented with some success on Broadway in 1963, with the talented Anne Bancroft in the lead role, and with a much less auspicious result in a short-lived off-Broadway version in 1980 with African-American actor Gloria Foster.

Meanwhile, in 1978, Prof. Robert Potter, the son of H. C. Potter, the Hollywood film director of several Golden Age movies, was commissioned by Tom Marcus, the artistic director of the Virginia Music Theatre, to write a new English-language adaptation of *Mother Courage.* It was Marcus's idea to make the classic drama with music pertinent to contemporary audiences by changing the setting to the United States during the Civil War and to cast a black actor as the lead performer.

Once Potter, then, as now, a member of the faculty at the University of California at Santa Barbara, was given the creative challenge, he found that "there's something that's instantly transferable about a woman heading a family, trying to keep it together, that relates directly to the black experience in America. It translates well from a sort of tough German peasant woman to a tough and canny black woman." Potter added, "The decision to cast Mother Courage and her family as blacks led me to a better understanding of the ironic position, well documented in Civil' War accounts, which black Americans occupied during the war—ostensibly its cause and too frequently its victim." As Potter further explained to this author, he replaced Brecht's 1930s German music with nineteenth-century American music. As much as possible, he kept Brecht's lyrics, rhyme, scheme, and meter intact while doing the complex translation.

The 1979 production of the new *Mother Courage* in Richmond, Virginia, met with mixed results. According to Potter, this was because the lead performer, a competent black character actor, did not bring the needed energy and drive to the pivotal role. A planned New York City presentation of the work evaporated in 1980 when Joseph Papp presented his own production of the famed drama (using a different adaptation) at the Circle in the Square. However, the next year, director Michael Addison, a teaching colleague of Potter's in California, brought Potter's *Mother Courage* project to the attention of the San Diego Repertory Theater. They agreed to remount the show. Potter made refinements in the script, including a decision to have the songs done a cappella so that the show would not be considered a musical.

During the time it took to complete the revised adaptation, Potter wondered whom the San Diego troupe would find to play the demanding key lead. One day, director Mike Addison called him in Santa Barbara to say he'd found the perfect Mother Courage, adding that the black actor's name was Whoopi Goldberg. Concerned about the talents of anyone with such a bizarre stage name, Potter was apprehensive about her abilities to tackle the demanding lead role.

In contrast, Whoopi was convinced she could handle this dream part. In fact, as she would describe later, she found that preparing for the mammoth performance was easy "because they let me play around with it. She was sort of 'Reggae Courage.' They put in all this wonderful reggae music because it was the only way I could keep the time. Singing is not my forte. They gave me that show so that they wouldn't have to put me in the musical *Working,* which has a *ton* of singing in it. I bugged them so badly, they said, 'Here, do *Mother Courage,* here, here!' It was perfect for me. It's a great role."

One hot afternoon during the Memorial Day weekend of 1981, Potter drove from Santa Barbara to San Diego to view a run-through of the play. The heat was stifling, and the actors were perspiring freely, but he found Goldberg riveting as Mother Courage. To save her voice for the marathon-role, they had cut out much of her singing. According to Potter, she managed the "humor, the guts, and energy of the character beautifully." His only qualification about her interpretation was that, at age twenty-six, she was physically too young for the part. (He still hopes that one day she will reprise the role *Mother Courage*—at the right age.)

With a cast of fifteen that included William Wright Graves and Philip E. Banks as her sons, Marvette Knight as the mute daughter, and Steve Pearson as a chaplain who knows the flesh rather than the spirits, *Mother Courage* debuted on Thursday, June 11, 1981.

Welton Jones, of the *San Diego Union*, reported that the rep's new show suffered from "the varied melodramatic acting styles" and that the costumes used were "so cheap and perfunctory that it's often impossible to tell the armies apart." However, he did say, approvingly: "The production does have a Mother Courage. The actor unfortunately called Whoopi Goldberg can play the part anywhere, so larger than life, so quick and deft physically and so infused with useful energy is she."

Christopher Schneider, of the *La Jolla Light*, observed: "Perhaps not surprisingly, it's the woman with the greatest training as a comedian who gives the most direct and memorable performance in *Mother Courage*: Whoopi Goldberg. . . . Hers is a strong, immediate presence. . . . [S]he's absolutely right for the part: playing each salty or ornery moment for all it's worth. Goldberg wipes virtually every other performer off the stage."

Jonathan Saville, of the *San Diego Reader*, agreed: "Her air of spontaneity and naturalness, familiar to San Diego audiences from her delightful comic improvisations in the team of Victor and Goldberg, makes her completely believable: a person of flesh and blood whose home is the real world or the naturalistic stage."

However, Saville pointed out one disappointing aspect of the overall production: "The problem is the singers—in particular, alas, Miss Goldberg herself. Her voice is all right, and though she evidently has not had training in vocal technique, not much is really needed for this kind of singing. But what Miss Goldberg does not seem to know is that in musical theater singing is a form of acting. She acts splendidly, bringing out the meaning and rhythm of each phrase; but when she comes to a song, all that emerges is a series of meaningless notes, unshaped and uninterpreted."

Mother Courage ran for a month at the San Diego Repertory Theater, closing on July 12, 1981. It proved to be the apex of Whoopi's acting career in the regional theater. She had no idea that she would soon be leaving the repertory group. Nor did she know that she and her daughter, Alexandrea, would be shortly relocating to a new life and home nearly five hundred miles away, in Berkeley, California.

CHAPTER NINE

Alone in the Spotlight

I know I'm supposed to say I do a lot of work on
these characters, but I don't. They kinda live in me.
It's a residence hotel. They say things and express
stuff that I would never express. It's exactly like
being schizophrenic. Whoopi disappears. I've learned
that I have some control over them, but once the
performance experience begins, there's not much I
can do. I'm just the one who takes care of all the
business. It will sound just as crazy as can be when
people read this, but that's the way it is.
—WHOOPI GOLDBERG, JUNE 1987

Certainly it was important to Whoopi Goldberg's professional
growth to have been a constantly working actor at the San Diego
Repertory Theater. However, of even greater vocational value were
her experiences in the art of improvisation. Working with the Spontaneous Combustion improv group was an excellent training ground. It
sharpened her insights and expanded her ability to think fast on her feet
in front of audiences. This gift of spontaneity was helped even further by
her performances with partner David Victor. In their joint skits they
extemporized on basic situations created by themselves or as a result of
suggestions from the audience. By playing out riffs on a given premise,
they were spontaneously creating characters.

As one-half of Victor and Goldberg, Whoopi stood out from her
white male partner in several respects. Goldberg was black, which was
unusual and at a time when integrated casts remained a strange, if not

upsetting, novelty to both white and black audiences. Moreover, she was female, and that made her quite distinctive, since most stand-up and improv performers during this period were male. In addition, Whoopi's overall visual image was different from the norms of the time. With her "odd" dreadlocks, casual garb (often loose trousers, a sweatshirt, and canvas sneakers) in an age when comedians dressed more formally, and her unique facial contours, Goldberg could not help but make an indelible impression on an audience. In addition, there was the surprise generated when this performer, oddly named Whoopi Goldberg, popped out onstage and proved not to be what her name suggested—a Jewish, white comic.

Additionally, Whoopi possessed yet another quality which made her a rare commodity in the world of show business during the late seventies. It had nothing to do with her race, outfits, or clever stage name but derived from her special gifts. She could skillfully observe the inequities and inanities of contemporary life and express herself in a pungent manner. Audience members—whether white or black, male or female—responded well to her piercing commentary, which made them think while simultaneously amusing them due to the structure of her verbal shtick and physically unique stage presence. Although her fabricated life stories and characterizations were tied into her partner's onstage responses, it was definitely Goldberg who was the heart of the duo act.

In many ways, Goldberg was a female version of Richard Pryor and Eddie Murphy. Those two comedians had pioneered mainstream audience acceptance of audacious, cocky African-American comics who employed crude language and gross comedic situations to underscore their shrewd observations, tied to their take on racial issues. Like Pryor and Murphy, Goldberg had learned to make audiences intellectually *and* emotionally respond to her acerbic patter, which always contained some real truths.

For Whoopi, these late-night gigs with David Victor in and about San Diego, at the Comedy Store and other venues, were not done primarily to get much-needed revenue. (Actually, in the beginning they would perform gratis just for the opportunity to exercise their craft in front of a live audience.) Of greater importance, these improv sets were a major outlet for Whoopi's uninhibited self-expression, something very central to her. In the real world, necessity frequently required that she bite her tongue to avoid engaging in caustic retorts when dealing with snotty welfare caseworkers, condescending employers, or male-biased club owners.

However, when Whoopi stood in front of an audience, she lost many of her inhibitions and allowed her heartfelt thoughts and feelings to rip. Because her hard-edged remarks were cloaked in comedy, her listeners paid attention to her sarcastic and ironic opinions. For Goldberg, it was spiritually very nourishing that others enjoyed her views on life's absurdities. Such audience respect did wonders for Goldberg's ego. It made all her life's sacrifices seem worthwhile.

In many respects, Whoopi was a professional sponge, always hungry to learn more about her craft. One such occasion occurred in late 1980. The Blake Street Hawkeyes, a Berkeley, California, performance troupe, visited San Diego. (The group had first appeared in Iowa—hence, its name Hawkeyes—and was an outgrowth of the Iowa Theatre Lab. In the mid-1970s, this avant-garde theater nucleus had moved to Berkeley. There they followed the performance tenets of Jerzy Grotowski, as described in his book *Towards a Poor Theatre,* 1968). As part of their show tour of Southern California, the Hawkeyes also offered workshops on their performance credo. At one of these discussion sessions in San Diego, Whoopi was one of only two audience members.

During this seminar, Whoopi invited the northern Californians to attend an upcoming Victor and Goldberg club performance. When the visitors saw the team perform, they were impressed by their artistry. Bob Ernst, a pivotal member of the Hawkeyes, would later recall being intrigued by Goldberg's unique stage presence: "She was different but shared a common aesthetic—of physically-based, collectively created theater." The Hawkeyes asked Victor and Goldberg to come north to perform in Berkeley. The offer was accepted, especially by an enthusiastic Whoopi.

Weeks passed. The night before Whoopi and David Victor were to fly to San Francisco for their Berkeley stage engagement, Victor suddenly announced that he was unable to leave San Diego. Some accounts of the episode insist that illness prevented him from going. In other renditions of this career-shaping event, it has been suggested that his mounting concern at leaving his safe home turf led him to drop out of the gig. Whatever caused him to change his mind, a determined Goldberg was left stranded at the last minute and had to honor the commitment on her own.

Whoopi recalls vividly that trip to the Golden Gate city, where she was met at the airport by David Schein, another founder of the Blake Street Hawkeyes: "I got off the plane saying, 'I'm really sorry, but it is just going to be me.' " According to her, Schein responded with "Just do what you do when you work with Don [Victor] and make the audience your partner." The practical advice was sound, but it made her visibly nervous. Her concern prompted the very supportive Schein to add, "What's the worst that can happen? You do twenty minutes, and if you're bad, you'll know it, and you'll get off the stage."

All too soon it was zero hour and a still-flustered Goldberg had to face her audience in Berkeley. By the time she walked onto the stage, she had convinced herself that she just might possibly get through the ordeal. She told herself: "Okay, I can do this. If it doesn't work, it doesn't work. So I did a lot of talking real fast so no one would see that I didn't know what the fuck I was doing but it would look good. And that was the birth of me as a solo character artist." She was on for an hour. At the end, she knew that she could do a solo performance.

By the time a triumphant, beaming Goldberg returned to San Diego, she was justifiably excited about expanding her career into the realm of solo appearances where it was *just* herself *and* the audience. Obviously, Victor's inability to accompany her on the pivotal San Francisco jaunt dampened the rapport between the longtime partners. It soon led them to dissolve their working relationship. Thereafter, when Whoopi was not performing at the San Diego Repertory Theater, she worked on her solo act, both developing routines and seeking outlets to test her new material.

In the process of perfecting her craft and seeking acting jobs, there was little quality time left for her to be with her daughter, who was often left in the care of accommodating friends or theater coworkers when the child was not in school. Whoopi's absence so often during Alexandrea's formative years was the start of a distancing between mother and daughter that would take years, in the future, to begin to mend.

Validated and buoyed by her rewarding fresh career direction, Goldberg became more audacious at the repertory theater. She now not only pleaded for bigger and better stage roles—which was nothing new for her—but often insisted that she should be considered for a given choice part. Had Whoopi not campaigned and then been cast in the showy lead role in *Mother Courage,* she might have left San Diego far sooner than she did. However, the demanding rehearsals leading up to the June 1981 opening of this major production were all consuming. And once the show opened to acclaim, Goldberg was committed to being on hand for a month of performances that ended on July 12, 1981.

With her obligations to the rep completed, ambitious Goldberg soon packed her belongings and, with seven-year-old Alexandrea in tow, left town. As would be true each time she moved up the rungs of her career ladder, she was caring and wise enough not to burn bridges behind her. She departed San Diego on very friendly terms with the repertory troupe and would remain supportive of their stage activities in the years to come.

For those who knew Goldberg, it was no surprise that she chose to relocate to Berkeley, California. This college town of thirty-thousand students of the University of California at Berkeley was still very much a center of the 1960s counterculture, where hippies, flower children, the drug culture, and anti–Vietnam War protests had thrived. While passé elsewhere in the country, this era and its style still hung on in Berkeley and parts of neighboring San Francisco. It was the free-spirited culture that appealed to the ex–New Yorker. For another thing, this very cultured community, located about eleven miles northeast of San Francisco, was visually appealing, with its beautiful tree-lined, hilly streets and impressive college campus. Geographically, it was also ideal. Via the BART subway system, it was a short hop into San Francisco, thus making it a convenient suburban-urban residence. Besides, Berkeley was the headquarters of the Blake Street Hawkeyes, and Goldberg felt an affinity for this performance group. She intended to work and grow with them artistically. And, most importantly, Whoopi had fallen in love again. Her new lover was David Schein, a pivotal force at the Hawkeyes who also happened to be white.

Goldberg set up a household with her daughter, Alex, and Schein. It was a novel experience for Whoopi to no longer be a single parent and to be able to share the responsibilities for her daughter's welfare. It also allowed her to be a bit "selfish" about her own creative needs.

However, there were complications abounding in this new relationship. For example, Whoopi once said of this extended love affair: "I met a new man who had, like, sperm of doom. Every time this sperm of doom got near me, we were having kids. I got pregnant with him using a diaphragm and an IUD at the same time. I was twenty-five—this was around 1980. While I was still twenty-five, I got pregnant with him again, this time using some fucking European bullshit sponge; I could have cut a sponge from the supermarket and put it in there and put some cream on it and had the same effect. . . . My choice, when I discovered that this could become something that would happen a lot, was to have my tubes done. I did that when I was twenty-six."

Several factors combined to prompt Whoopi's decision *not* to have more children. "I couldn't have those babies because it was not the time or the relationship. I was not prepared to take care of them, and it was not affordable at all. Those were tough times. I was on welfare for a while. . . . I was already raising one child, and my thought was: I don't want to be a single parent again."

She also remembers: "The man and I had great discussions before I went for those abortions. I felt it was important for him to say whatever he had to say. But he understood that I was not prepared and he was not prepared. One day, we hoped we would be, but unfortunately our rela-tionship didn't work out. But, yeah, we wept . . . We wept going for those abortions, we wept coming back . . . because both times this was something made from love."

According to Goldberg, whose first abortion, after all, had been undertaken at age thirteen: "I had all my abortions in the early weeks. I don't feel that there is life in the first four weeks. . . . People never know they're pregnant until after a month or two, so that the first four weeks is sort of like *stuff* coming together." She reasoned: "I have a problem with second-trimester abortions, because that's a person."

Over the years, Whoopi would become committed to pro-choice regarding the abortion issue. The actor has explained, "My commitment to choice comes from my belief that you have the right to decide whether you want to have children or not. The bottom line is that if someone does not want to have a child, they should not be forced into it. That's be-tween the woman, her man, if she chooses to make him aware, and God, whoever God is."

Her cumulative personal experiences with abortion over the years led Whoopi to become a pro-choice agitator in the early 1980s. By then, she, Alexandrea, and playwright-performer David Schein were living to-gether in Berkeley, across the street from the Herrick Hospital. Antiabor-tion supporters constantly picketed in front of the facility. "It got so awful that I went out with a man I used to live with—David Schein—and started handing out a hanger for every leaflet they handed out, because these people would harass women going in and say devastating stuff. It's just mean. It's certainly not the way to get people over to your side."

As with most performers—especially comedians—a great deal of Whoopi's onstage material came from her offstage life. For example, Whoopi's several abortion experiences over the years inspired and shaped, to a degree, one of the onstage characters in the growing repertoire for her one-woman show. She has said, "The character in my show, the thirteen-year-old [southern California] Valley Girl, a surfer chick who self-aborts, uses a hanger, too. The rest of her story has very little to do with me. I was not the kind of girl that I'm portraying. She's rejected by everybody. . . . One of the things she describes is the hooking of the top of the hanger, which I wish I had known about. Sometimes what they would do is straighten the hanger, like I did, and then hook and twist one end, so that when they put that end inside they didn't get the perforation. In the show, I do it very slow because I want the audience to understand what we're talking about. We're talking about a wire metal hanger with one end that is looped and twisted and then inserted in the vagina, up into the uterus, and moved around."

Goldberg points out: "I made the character white because nobody would have given a fuck about a poor woman of color—that's the bottom line. I wanted the people I knew were coming to my shows to see *their* children, to see and relate to their *daughter.*"

Another major character was a seven-year-old black girl who would give anything to be blue-eyed, white-skinned, and blond. If that were accomplished, she knows life would be so much better. She certainly would be asked to be a guest performer on her favorite TV show *The Love Boat.* This fictional creation is an amalgam of traits derived from Goldberg herself as a child and of those observed in her own daughter.

By the fall of 1982 life had settled down satisfactorily for Whoopi. She was gaining a reputation for her one-woman show, originally known as *More Than One Person* but later called *The Whoopi Goldberg Show.* By the time of her October 15–30, 1982, engagement at the Blake Street Hawkeyes Theatre (at 2019 Blake Street in Berkeley), the entertainment had been renamed *The Spook Show.* The program note explains the title: "This show is dedicated to all spooks living, dead, and yet to be born." (Later, the show's title would negatively resonate with some blacks who recoiled from the word "spook," which had long been understood as an

epithet for a stereotypical, not-so-bright black.) The program notes listed
The Spook Show as being written by Goldberg, with additional material by
David Schein and direction by Schein and Goldberg.

While these showcase appearances in *The Spook Show* were slowly
earning Whoopi a reputation in the Berkeley artistic community, they
were hardly paying the bills. Most all of Schein's energies and scant funds
were directed to the Hawkeyes' survival. As for Whoopi, when not performing on Blake Street with the Hawkeyes, she was busy networking
with both the Berkeley and San Francisco artistic community. Rather
than take part-time jobs, as she did in San Diego when funds ran low,
she was committing all her "spare" time to searching for new showcase
venues to present her act. She was also seeking out other opportunities to
participate in new artistic ventures before audiences. As a result, Whoopi
once again was forced to turn to welfare.

What had annoyed her before in San Diego about the bureaucratic
system and its too often patronizing caseworkers was not much different
in Berkeley. What made a difference now—to a degree—was that Goldberg was a veteran of the system and had learned to deflect her anger at
the disdainful treatment she received from the bureaucrats. But she was
not alone. She and David formed a joint household, and dealing with and
reacting to the frequently humiliating red tape of the welfare system
became a shared experience.

Thankfully, within the next year, Goldberg would be off welfare for
good and would never have to endure such a degrading ordeal again. But
it was not a phase of her life quickly or easily forgotten. Once she began
to gain further acclaim and fame, it would become part of the mantra of
interviewers to cite the adversities (drug addiction, poverty, welfare de-
pendence, abortions) that this young woman from the Chelsea projects
had overcome to succeed as dramatically as she did. Reference to those
experiences continued for years.

When the press dredged up her troubled past, Whoopi would become upset and actually admit that some of the problems were of her
own making. As she explained to Nancy Jo Sales in the February 17,
1997, issue of *New York* magazine, a good portion of the "legend" came
about by her own past exaggerations and the press's credulity. It was
Goldberg's contention that because she was black and came from the
New York City projects, the reporters bought into the stereotype far too
easily.

An opposing view, however, would construe such "about-face"

statements by Whoopi as a subconscious or even calculated desire to discourage the press from exploring her problematic existence in much of the 1970s, a period of her life which has yet to be fully documented. Also to be considered is Goldberg's apparently recurring habit to adjust— either innocently or deliberately—her recollection of certain happenings to whatever new lifestyle she has adopted.

Goldberg was more relieved than government budget watchers to finally get off the welfare treadmill. She proudly insists that "the greatest thing I ever was able to do was give a welfare check back. I brought it back to the welfare department and said, 'Here, I don't need this anymore.' " According to the actor, the day she returned her welfare money, she saw her old, vicious caseworker applying for public assistance: "It's sad I know to say this vindictive thing, but she had been hell, this woman, and now maybe she would get somebody who was just as nasty as she was so she could understand not everybody wants to be on welfare."

She also confesses that when life improved and she knew she was finally finished with the odious welfare process, she "kept the Medi-CAL card and had it framed just to remind me."

CHAPTER TEN

Love and No Marriage

I'm not a stand-up comedian. I'm not always funny
and can be quite biting; I want people to take
something with them, be it a feeling that's good or
uncomfortable. Of course, entertainment is
important, but in these trying times some sort of
education without a lot of preaching is called for.
—WHOOPI GOLDBERG, OCTOBER 1992

Whoopi's first residence in Berkeley was near Herrick Hospital.
Bolstered by a comfortable pair of shoes and a positive attitude, she found that almost everything of note in Berkeley was
within a "reasonable" walking distance from her new cottage. That included the headquarters of the Blake Street Hawkeyes. Located between
Milvia Street and Shattuck Avenue, the intimate theater lab and workshop was a small but vital facility for creative souls such as herself.

Several blocks away from the Hawkeyes' center was Telegraph Avenue. This crowded north-south thoroughfare was crammed with book
and record stores, used clothing shops, inexpensive restaurants and cafes,
and sidewalk vendors. It attracted a heavy sprinkling of ever-present
hippies, the meandering homeless, gawking tourists, and preoccupied
students. On Telegraph, near Haste Street, was the weekly farmers' market, where, from 11:00 A.M. to 3:00 P.M. each Sunday, Whoopi, her
daughter, and her live-in lover, David Schein, could shop for fresh, or-
ganic produce.

Farther northeast, Goldberg could hike through People's Park;
above it was located the University Art Museum. She could also visit the

74

sprawling campus of the University of California at Berkeley. Slightly farther north, where Bancroft Way intersects Telegraph, is Sproul Plaza. It was there that the so-called Free Speech Movement began in 1964, when students protested the arrest of a Berkeley student for having dared to distribute political flyers on the plaza. If the mood so struck her, Whoopi could next head westward toward the bay and then north over to Marcus Books on Martin Luther King Jr. Way, above Hearst Avenue. That landmark emporium had long specialized in books "by and about African Americans."

What made life so exciting in Berkeley was the buoyant intellectual and artistic atmosphere that permeated this college town. And if one craved more performance-art theaters, art-gallery showings, and museum exhibits, one only had to jump onto the BART subway system and head down to Oakland or over to San Francisco. This wonderful, civilized environment excited Whoopi, expanding her mind and soul. She was also making new friends, for she had discovered that there were many others like herself who were stimulated by the outpouring of talent show-cased at the city's avant-garde theaters. It would motivate Goldberg to experiment with all facets of creative expression—including performing, scriptwriting, and producing.

In other settings Whoopi, with her dreadlocks, ultracasual clothing, and an open, interracial love relationship, might have been considered a bizarre outsider to be avoided. But here everyone—no matter what their economic status, ethnic affiliation, religious belief, or sexual bent—seemed to be welcome, especially if they contributed to the dynamic artistic scene. In addition, there was no stigma attached to being periodi-cally on welfare. Many of the others whom Whoopi knew from the Hawkeyes and other area theater groups were scraping by financially, thanks to public assistance. By now, President Ronald Reagan's adminis-tration had begun deemphasizing government funding to the cultural arts. However, Whoopi and other artistic souls (especially those women who headed single-parent households) found creative ways around the cutting back of art subsidies. They had gone on welfare!

Very quickly Goldberg came to appreciate the broad-minded atmo-sphere of her new hometown. As she would enthuse later to the media, "You can say anything in Berkeley and at least someone will get it. Berke-ley people let you try out new material. They don't hassle me. When I played in San Diego and L.A., I was picketed by the KKK and the Nazis. I do a thing about abortion, about a fifteen-year-old surfer girl, a valley girl who gets pregnant. The right-to-life people spent two thousand dollars on a mailing to get people to picket my show."

Thus, it was little wonder that, in relatively short order, the distinctive-looking Goldberg—with those big, inquisitive eyes and that broad, warm smile—became a familiar and popular sight in Berkeley's artistic community. Soon she would expand her recognition factor into San Francisco's theater district.

For Whoopi, the week was never long enough to accomplish everything she wanted to do. There was the matter of tending to daughter Alexandrea when she was not in grade school. If Whoopi still refused to be a housekeeper and could scarcely cook, there were certain household chores she had to accomplish as well as take-out food that had to be purchased. Then, too, there were the demands of performing onstage, refining her own stage act, and doing creative chores for the Hawkeyes. Last but not least, there was the need to find time to maintain her romantic relationship with David Schein.

Sometimes Goldberg's busy schedule was interrupted by a domestic crisis. For example, there were those increasingly difficult periods when she found it hard to communicate with her preteen daughter. Alexandrea badly wanted more of her mother's affection and attention and must have resented having to turn to her substitute father, David Schein, or to neighborhood friends and their parents for counsel and interaction.

Also interrupting Goldberg's work schedule were unexpected disastrous situations. For example, there was the time in Berkeley—before Goldberg ensured that she would not become impregnated again—that she discovered she was pregnant again. As Whoopi recalls, she went to Oakland's Feminist Health Clinic for an abortion. The treatment she received there shocked her sensibilities: "They segregated me from my partner—it's his baby, too—and made me listen to this rap about how men did this to you, so we've got to stick together. I ask[ed] the woman there for a towel to scream into. She says, 'Oh, come now, you can handle this. You're a woman.' The doctor starts, and I wail. She tells me, 'Shut up. You're scaring everybody.' Is this how feminists treat each other? I don't want to be one—not if they don't give you a towel to scream in or let you hold your partner's hand."

As Goldberg settled into her Berkeley life, she frequently performed in improvisational skits with David Schein and other members of the Blake Street Hawkeyes. In addition, she often collaborated with Schein, Bob Ernst, and the others (Freddie Long, James Cave, John LeFan) on performances of short plays, such as *Dick Jones*. As time went on, Schein, Goldberg, and others were also busy preparing more ambitious productions. One of them was *Reverence for the Dead,* a musical spoof in which Lee Harvey Ozball, the accused assassin of U.S. president Hennessy, returns from hiding to stand trial and live as normal a life as possible on death row. His mother arranges a defense based on "excess salt in his diet" and gets him released, whereupon he forms a rock band. For this project, Goldberg and Schein coauthored the book.

Yet another Hawkeyes undertaking—long in development—was the very ambitious *Token,* which dealt with the great London Plague. Written by David Schein and directed by Bob Ernst, it eventually would be produced at the Theater Artaud, a huge space on Florida Street (between Seventeenth and Mariposa) in San Francisco. Meanwhile, for the Actualist Festival (in the 1982–83 period), Whoopi and Schein were seen in a sketch in which she was a telephone-sex operator.

While Goldberg was participating in projects with the Hawkeyes and absorbing as much of the area's cultural offerings as possible, she continued to revamp her one-woman show. Because her particular style required that she interact *with* the audience and not perform *at* them (as did many stand-up comics), she constantly put herself on the line with patrons in her club appearances. Her aim was to gain, through experience, sufficient confidence and smoothness of delivery to make her organized but still spontaneous offering as seamless and fresh as possible each time she performed.

According to Peter McCarron, today a San Francisco computer consultant but then a student of performance art in the Bay Area, the Whoopi of the early 1980s was a very eager entertainer who was always "pushing the envelope." She appeared to thrive on walking a tightrope. As part of this risk taking, she would invite hecklers in the audience to match wits with her. When they shot forth a barb, she would retort, but always in character. Sometimes an audience member would do an abrupt turnaround, suddenly simpatico with Goldberg's presentation, and laugh appreciatively. On such occasions, a mock-surprised Whoopi might just turn to the former heckler and ask, "Hey! Are you feeling all right?"

By mid-October 1982 when Whoopi's *Spook Show* was showcased at the Hawkeyes Theatre, she had already performed selections from her one-woman show at several performance-art sites in Berkeley and San Francisco, including 544 Natoma, Studio Eremos, Mariposa Studio, and Hospitality House. The promotion for Goldberg's appearance promised that "*The Spook Show* will offer a glimpse of Ms. Goldberg's variety of characters, including a young Southern California girl [newly popularized as 'Valley Girls'] faced with abortion at age fifteen, a junkie's inspiring interpretation of 'Blee T' [a spoof of Steven Spielberg's movie, *E.T. the Extra-Terrestrial,* 1982] . . . and many more."

The same publicity circular read: "Whoopi Goldberg's rare and exciting form of theatre/stand-up comedy utilizes a humorously caustic view of the world. It is a combination of joy and sadness that has moved audiences from coast to coast with an insight not often found in standard comedy or theatre." Once again explaining to audiences and reviewers alike the meaning of the show's title, the program notes stated, "Ms. Goldberg identifies the 'spook' as a universal thread within us all and offers her audiences an awareness of themselves and what's going on." In the playbill for *The Spook Show,* Whoopi gave special thanks to several members of her inner circle. These included her mother and daughter, her lover, David Schein, and several collaborators associated with the Hawkeyes.

Carolyn Wendt was on hand to review *The Spook Show* for the October 1982 issue of the (Bay) *City Area Monthly.* She reported, "On stage, Whoopi Goldberg doesn't bumble her way through a no respect routine or joke about what happened to her on the way to the office; five-minute Comedy Store gigs just aren't her style. It's this theatrical background that affords her the ability to present her comedy as an art form built on characterizations, as comedy beyond the T & A [tits and ass] jokes." Regarding Goldberg's parade of onstage figures—which then included a seventy-seven-year-old Jewish woman who had just learned she had gonorrhea—Wendt observed, "All are long-standing Goldberg characters, created in such a way that they are separate people with histories of their own, a myriad of aces and situations that reach a wide-ranging audience."

Bernard Weiner (*San Francisco Chronicle*) complimented her by saying, "Goldberg displays a talent for sharp caricature and a sterling sense of comic timing." He added: "She has an astounding ability to capture the gestures, inflections and speech pattern of a wide variety of types: a heroin junkie, a vapid surfer chick, an Italian confessing to a priest, a West Indian angry at a film critic, a scam Swami Spooktanananda, a streetwise burglar. Her comedy is often trenchant and funny." Regarding Whoopi's series of character sketches, Weiner concluded: "I look forward to seeing Goldberg develop a full-length piece."

That the above San Francisco reviewers approved so heartily of Goldberg's ever-evolving show substantiated what critics had already noted and would observe in months to come as Whoopi presented her one-person offering along the California coast and elsewhere. For example, the *San Diego Union* said, "With no apparent script she evolves each character vocally and visually before your eyes, and the results are fascinating." The *Los Angeles Times* wrote, "Goldberg is superb, providing in her performance an accessible and eloquent example of that essential human component which will always attract audiences and without which theatre is pointless." And the *Calgary* (Canada) *Times* declared, "A veteran stand-up comic, she is often outrageously funny, but without ever sacrificing the humanity of her characters."

Starting on March 4, 1983, for three weekends Whoopi undertook to present her one-person show—a condensed version entitled *Goldberg Variations*—on a double bill with David Schein, who was offering his own performance piece, *Out Come Butch*. Their venue was the Valencia Rose at 766 Valencia Street in San Francisco.

Bernard Weiner (*San Francisco Chronicle*) recorded in his March 8, 1983, column: "Schein and Goldberg are members of the innovative Blake Street Hawkeyes. Traditionally, audiences at their tiny Berkeley studio treat the space as a theater laboratory and the performers as artists, worthy of respect and admiration. . . . At San Francisco's Valencia Rose, there is a drinking/smoking/nightclub atmosphere. This is not a theater lab; audiences have popped in for a good time."

This reviewer reported that during Whoopi's opening set she chose to combat the noisy crowd by venturing out into the audience to confront the most vociferous face-to-face, which, according to the *Chronicle* reviewer, "defused any hostility."

Commenting on Goldberg's depiction of her two characters (the elderly woman discussing her gynecologic exam and a young black teenager mortified by her nappy hair), Weiner observed, "Each had its wonderful moments—Goldberg is a moving performer, with a superb command of body language and a wonderfully expressive face—but at times she seemed unsure how much she wanted to be an actor, working within the sketch, and how much a stand-up nightclub comic, working the crowd."

With her ever-increasing momentum as a "new" performer of note in the Golden Gate city, Whoopi, who had added a Siamese feline named Eartha Catt to her household, was now often profiled in Bay Area publications. Such opportunities gave her a forum to vent her feelings about her craft in particular and life in general. She informed Carolyn Wendt (*City Area Monthly*): "I like to show all types because I want to open things up for everybody. I'm a natural person, so ordinary people can identify with me and see me not just as a black or a woman but as a human who can be many people. Most theatre today is black or white or radical feminist or something that's unnaturally separatist. I want to expand that market."

To Alice Kahn of the alternative newspaper the *San Francisco Express,* Goldberg said: "I try to do as many ethnic groups as possible [in my act]. I don't slur people, but I do whatever is in character."

As to why she was not participating in more feminist activities, Whoopi responded,

> You can look at me and tell I'm a woman. Every day I make some progress. I'm a credit to my race, my sex, etc. I feel no kinship to any one group, and it pisses me off when people tell me I should be doing this or that. Why don't they go out there and do it? . . . I'm working on a piece now where this woman goes into a gay men's dining place, and it's all beautiful—mauve walls, plants, space, real silverware, painting. . . . Then she goes to a lesbian place, and it's all brick. Its got deer heads, ya know, plastic forks and spoons. And she's trying to figure out: What's the difference? What does it mean? . . . I want people not to take themselves so fuckin' seriously. Why are there all these factions? Gay men, Lesbians for Gay Men, Pseudo-Lesbians for Pseudo-Gay Men. It's as bad as going from colored to Negro to black to Afro-American. You want to call me something—call me by my name.

Whoopi also declared to the press, "I guess I just see humor in what happens to me in daily life. Like I went to this gynecologist and he gets

out a rubber glove and blows it up. He shows it to me and says, '*Moo.*'
. . . Or here in Berkeley I meet these people who used to be hippies. I
met this guy, he shows me a picture of him[self] five years ago . . . hair
down to his ankles, round glasses, eighteen women every minute. Now
he's a fundamentalist. Why? 'I was smoking this joint and the smoke
blew into a cross and I saw Jesus Christ.' "

Then, too, according to Goldberg, there was the occasion when "I
was down in lower Sproul [a thoroughfare in Berkeley] and I saw this
street lady and this street man dancing to the drummers. She was shaking
all over, twirling and posing, and all of a sudden her underwear fell
down to her feet. They were these *huge* white pants—boxer shorts. And
you know, everything froze—traffic stopped, birds froze, and I started to
laugh. I have no class. I laugh at this stuff. I see people slip, I laugh.
Everybody turned around. It was politically incorrect not to be cool when
underwear falls down."

On another tack, the ethnically conscious Whoopi told the media:
"What I've noticed about the comedy clubs in San Francisco is that you
don't see many blacks doing comedy. There are a whole lot of black
comics, and it bothers me that I have to put it in this kind of perspective.
Why aren't there more Chicano comics, Chinese comics? It pisses me off
that I have to think in these terms."

Summarizing her creative goals, Whoopi would admit, "With my
humor, I want to give a lot to people. I want to piss 'em off but I want to
give 'em a lot of love and teach them about people who may be a little
different from them, people they may be scared of."

CHAPTER ELEVEN

Steps Up the Ladder

Before [David Schein], there was just me and Alex,
and anything I got to do was always just a little bit,
because I always had to be Mommy. Now I'm a
woman with a great man. He said, "Go for it." And
here I am.

—WHOOPI GOLDBERG, JULY 1984

By 1982, Whoopi was settled into a relatively comfortable lifestyle in Berkeley, California. She, David Schein, and Alexandrea may not have been enjoying fancy living quarters, but it was still home. The funky cottage provided Goldberg and her daughter with their first real stability in several years. Whoopi might still be financially dependent on welfare, but creatively and intellectually, it was proving to be an extremely challenging artistic period for her.

As part of the Blake Street Hawkeyes, the perpetually busy Whoopi was absorbed in the world of performance art. When not writing skits and plays herself or in collaboration with others, Goldberg visited the many other theater groups clustered in the Bay Area. A cultural sponge, she enthusiastically watched them perform, met with their members professionally and socially, and fervently exchanged ideas with them about craft. (She joined the board of the Theatre Artaud, the former San Francisco cannery that had been converted into a three-hundred-seat performance space for experimental productions, and was able to participate in creative decision making there.) Her stimulating friends in these artistic circles included—above and beyond David Schein and Bob Ernst—actors-writers-producers Ellen Sebastian, Mary Alice Fry, Mark Gordon,

Nina Wise, choreographer John LeFan and his wife, Freddie Long, music director Candice Natzig, and many others, all of whom were reaching out into uncharted waters to express themselves through their craft.

More so than most of her female peers, Whoopi had overcome a number of obstacles and prejudices to reach the already impressive position she occupied. In an interview for the *San Francisco Express*, Alice Kahn cited a shopping list of the many personal, ethnic, religious, social, and cultural roadblocks that the actor had to confront in her life. It was a lot to cope with for a single mother struggling for professional recognition. These impediments included, according to Kahn, the fact that "Whoopi Goldberg . . . is black, Jewish, a welfare mother, and an ex-junkie whose father is gay." (This out-of-the-blue reference to the alleged sexual orientation of Goldberg's dad would not, to this author's knowledge, crop up in later Whoopi interviews and profiles. Whatever the full truth of the matter, it should be noted that Whoopi's dad would die of an AIDS-related disease in the 1990s.)

Above all, it was nurturing and wonderful for Whoopi—who had always been the looked-down-upon outsider—to be now increasingly validated and respected by her peers. Adding to her growing satisfaction was that word of mouth about her talent was spreading beyond the confines of northern California, where she was beginning to win Bay Area theater awards. Her performance art had already brought her to the attention of Bill Lee and John Moffitt, the creators and executive producers of the ABC-TV network comedy show *Fridays*. Cast in the mold of NBC-TV's *Saturday Night Live, Fridays* was 70 (later, 100) minutes of live late-night comedy entertainment devoted to satirical skits. At one point, Goldberg was contacted about joining the clamorous troupe. No agreement was ever reached, and the boisterous *Fridays* continued on without Whoopi's participation. The program was eventually canceled.

One of the reasons that Goldberg turned down the *Fridays* appearance was her fear that a sudden influx of money would lead her astray. She outlined to Leah Garchik (*San Francisco Chronicle*, February 6, 1983) why she had not joined that TV program: "There'd be a couple of pairs of shoes for the kid [Alexandrea] and a couple of packs of cocaine—and it would be gone." Since the time of that TV offer, she insisted that her life had become more grounded and that she had again abandoned drugs. She further told Garchik that she was now prepared "to deal with making decisions" and that she could handle success and money. "I'm more prepared. I wouldn't put it all up my nose." (This apparent candid openness about her vices and missteps would be a trademark characteristic of the performer throughout the years. However, there have been critics who have insisted that this blunt response was an ongoing subconscious or conscious ploy on her part to appear daring and hip as well as using her past misfortunes as a way of suggesting how many obstacles she had so valiantly overcome.)

Although reaching out to find a real talent agent on the West Coast and to further promote her career, Whoopi was nevertheless concerned about the artistic corruption that fame could bring to her doorstep. For example, she hypothesized to the *San Francisco Chronicle,* "You get used to making $40,000 a week on a sitcom. Where do you say no? No one's offered me $40,000 yet. But I hope if they offered it to me to play some stereotype, I'd turn it down. It's a struggle. Popularity brings on a whole lot of stuff. You want to please everybody."

Yet another explanation for Goldberg's not pushing harder for *Fridays* or other show-business opportunities was that she felt safe and satisfied in her Berkeley–San Francisco environment. It was the age-old dilemma of whether to be a big fish in a little pond or a little fish in a big pond.

The opportunity to overcome her provincialism occurred as *The Whoopi Goldberg Show* continued to gain word-of-mouth fame and, in turn, made Goldberg a more desirable commodity. Her growing fame led to her appearing on San Francisco's KQED-TV's *Comedy Tonight* program on January 13, 1983. (Four years later, Goldberg, by then nationally famous, would return to KQED-TV's *Comedy Tonight* for four starring TV appearances.) There were also additional performances of her one-woman show along the California coast and in Canada and a chance in mid-1983 to go abroad. Schein convinced her to accept the mind-broadening opportunity to see Europe, and she agreed to make the trip.

The culturally expanding trek overseas—where she performed *Whoopi Goldberg Abroad*—led Goldberg and Schein first to Holland and later to Germany. In the latter country, especially in the smaller towns, she was considered an intriguing oddity by the citizenry, who had never before seen a black performer. The Germans called her *die schwarze Schauspielerin,* which means "the black actor." It was an amazing, positive experience for Goldberg, although it required sacrificing time with her daughter, who was left behind in Berkeley under the care of Whoopi's mother and friends.

When the couple returned to Berkeley, Whoopi was ablaze with energy from her stay on the Continent, which inspired exciting new material for her ever-changing stage act. In particular, she devised new dialogue for that section of her program devoted to the hip Manhattan character she called Fontaine. He was a college graduate who had dropped out, become a druggie, and was now a burglar to boot. One night, in a fervor of creativity, Goldberg dashed off the routine that became Fontaine's European monologue in *The Spook Show/The Whoopi Goldberg Show.*

As she recalls the aesthetic process, her inspiration occurred when she and Schein were touring in Amsterdam. There they visited the historic Anne Frank house, where the young Jewish girl and her family had spent two frightening, claustrophobic years during World War II hiding from the Nazis. She was compelled to visit the shrine because "I saw the movie and I thought I'd go and check it out. I got there and went up into that room. Well, I just fell apart. I wanted to tell somebody about this, and I figured, Why not Fontaine? Why not this junkie? Here's the last guy that anybody thinks would have any feelings about it. But he goes into this empty room, and the history moves him. And it completely changes his attitude towards people."

With her expanded repertoire, Goldberg brought her solo turn to the Old Globe Theater in San Diego in the fall of 1983. Her pals from the San Diego Repertory Theater days turned out in record numbers to see their alumna perform. Lynn Schuette, founder of a performance space called the Sushi Gallery, would recall how impressed she was by the advances Goldberg had made in her craft: "She had honed her acting skills with the Hawkeyes, and she could twist the audience around her little finger. You could hear a pin drop. At that point, we thought, She's going to make it."

Fontaine and the other inhabitants of her special world were not Whoopi's only focus. In particular, she had long been intrigued with a unique, one-of-a-kind comic called Moms Mabley. The latter was a pioneering black comedian who became a legend in comedy circles for breaking down barriers against women and blacks in the field of stand-up. Goldberg first became aware of her when she was a child back in

New York and had seen Mabley's performances on TV. Mabley left a strong impression on Goldberg because she "was the only black woman in her field for over fifty years."

The future Moms Mabley was born Loretta Mary Aiken on March 19, 1894, in Bravard, North Carolina. She first came to New York in 1923 and was soon appearing at Harlem's famed Cotton Club and, later, at the Apollo Theatre. She toured frequently on the black club-theater circuit with Jimmie Lunceford's band, occasionally coming to Broadway (*Swinging the Dream, Blackbirds*) and, along the way, making a few films in the 1930s (*The Emperor Jones; Boarding House Blues*). By the 1940s, the salty, down-to-earth comedian had fully developed her Moms Mabley character ("a good woman with an eye for shady dealings"). This onstage persona appeared in a baggy dress, floppy hat, and as the years progressed, minus her false teeth. Her folksy routine revolved around her character as the commonsensical, advice-giving mother who recited her spicy anecdotal tales to the audience.

As the decades passed the gravel-voiced entertainer, with her bawdy jokes and anecdotes, grew increasingly more raucous. Finally, after decades of struggling professionally (especially due to racial discrimination), she gained national prominence in the mid-1960s. This newfound stature led to a new batch of ribald Moms Mabley record albums and eventually to a starring role in a mainstream movie, *Amazing Grace*, in 1974. In May 1975, she died of heart complications. Her well-attended funeral was held at the Abyssinian Baptist Church in Harlem of which she had long been a member.

By the early 1980s, the idea of creating and presenting a solo act onstage as Moms Mabley became an incessant passion for Goldberg. She envisioned the self-crafted project as both a homage to Mabley and an opportunity to make a major mark in the one-person-show arena. She'd be following in the distinguished wake of such theatrical performers as James Whitmore (as Harry Truman), Julie Harris (as Emily Dickinson), Hal Holbrook (as Mark Twain), Eileen Heckart (as Eleanor Roosevelt), etc.

While further developing her alter ego as Moms, Whoopi became convinced that someone might beat her by impersonating the fabulous Mabley onstage. She was also aware that because Mabley was black and not Establishment mainstream, she might not find a way to present her to the world. Her concerns led her to worry aloud. "I know it's my thing;

how many good black female comics are there with a knowledge of Moms? It's a real-life project now because I know I can do it, do it well."

By mid-October 1983, Whoopi had refined her Moms Mabley routine into a fully developed act and not just a curtain-raiser, as she initially planned. She felt It was now ready for that crucial audience reaction. One of her first forums for *Moms Mabley* was in Berkeley at the Hawkeyes' theater on October 7 and 8, 1983. The nearly hour-long production was directed by Ellen Sebastian.

Bernard Weiner reported in the *San Francisco Chronicle* of this theater piece: "Goldberg, a talented actor and comedian in her own right, impersonates Moms well, even down to the inability to pronounce certain words properly because of lack of teeth. . . . Though Goldberg occasionally ad libs with the audience and tech crew, there is no intent in this re-creation . . . to update the materials. . . . And though some jokes don't work as well as they might, much of Moms' stuff is truly funny, captured with a wonderful sense of comic timing by Goldberg." Weiner suggested that the show "needs some tightening and revision" but concluded, "Even in its current shape, it's an entertaining revisit with a black artist we shouldn't forget."

After *Moms Mabley* completed its weekend presentation at the Hawkeyes' theater, Whoopi moved her showcase in November to Eli's Mile Hi Club on Grove Street in Oakland. Thereafter, there were other Bay Area venues which presented her interpretation of the late comedian. Midway through this Mabley tour, Goldberg took *The Spook Show* to New York. It was not until mid-1984 that she returned to the Golden Gate city to continue her run as the beloved Mabley.

This time around, the production was featured at San Francisco's Victoria Theatre, and tickets for the event sold at a relatively steep fifteen dollars, with valet parking, no less, offered to patrons. The revamped show now included musical interludes by a pianist as well as special taped onstage segments of Mabley, fellow comedian Slappy White, and civil rights leader Martin Luther King Jr. These clips had been added to enrich the program's historical context. Bernard Weiner in the *San Francisco Chronicle* said of the return engagement: "*Moms* is like stepping into a time warp. Goldberg re-creates her with such care and precision, in everything from costume (flowered print dress, ratty sweater, floppy hat, mismatched socks, bathroom slippers) to timing and inflection." The critic applauded Goldberg's "wonderfully salacious way."

Weiner observed: "She submerges herself so well into that old lady's persona that little of the more original Whoopi we've come to know and love is visible." He also suggested: "The show—and the performer—could benefit by taking an intermission and coming back to present Whoopi Goldberg as Whoopi Goldberg, in sketches from *The Spook Show, Goldberg Variations,* new bits or whatever."

Steven Winn, also writing in the *Chronicle,* agreed with Weiner: "Goldberg has to bring her angular, manic inclinations down so far to get Mabley's dated, half-logy musings about sex and the good ole days right that it is like Picasso trying scrimshaw. There's something technically impressive in this feat of radical scale reduction but you wonder where Whoopi went in the process." Winn concluded: "For the most part, *Moms* doesn't come alive as a piece of theater because the performer vanishes inside the role instead of vitalizing it. The past here is all too present."

Edward Guthmann in the weekend *San Francisco Sunday Examiner & Chronicle* declared, "Goldberg offers her fullest, most deeply felt character."

Moms Mabley remained at the Victoria Theatre for five weeks, ending its run in late June 1984.

In the midst of Goldberg's *Moms Mabley* schedule (1983–84), she received an offer she "just couldn't refuse." Jack Davis of San Francisco's Intersection for the Arts Theatre had written to an associate involved with the Dance Theatre Workshop on West Nineteenth Street in New York, mentioning that Whoopi was a talented find who deserved a Manhattan showcase. Eventually, this New York performance group made Goldberg an offer to come east to perform *The Spook Show.* Her lover, David Schein, encouraged her to take the opportunity to reach a far bigger and more important audience.

Although most of the time ambitious, Goldberg still remained fearful of taking the next substantial leap in her career. She was concerned about how she would fare once under the microscope of knowledgeable New York critics and experienced theatergoers. It would be devastating, so she fantasized in her less secure moments, to fail big time and have to live with the ignominy the rest of her life. On the other hand, the New York offer had several potential pluses. Besides the hoped-for career break, it would provide an opportunity to see her mother. Moreover, it was also a chance to satisfy another childhood ambition—to serve retribution on all those who had treated her as such an outcast in her formative years. Goldberg said, "I wanted to go back to the neighborhood. I figured, I'm going to show these guys. They had laughed at me. Treated me like shit."

So, in early 1984, Whoopi flew to the East Coast. Daughter Alexandrea remained behind in Berkeley with David Schein. He was involved in trying to launch a production of the ambitious, expensive-to-mount *Tokens*, for which he and Whoopi had coauthored the book.

As the excited, nervous Goldberg jetted to Manhattan, she was only partially aware that what lay ahead was the start of what she had always dreamed of—to become a truly important show-business celebrity.

PART III

The Newborn Star

CHAPTER TWELVE

Mike Nichols
Enters Laughing

I found that a lot of the people who'd made it tough
for me [in New York City] hadn't moved an inch.
They were still in the [old] neighborhood. They were
still in their parents' houses. They hadn't seen
anything outside the neighborhood. . . . [T]hat
killed, for probably the rest of my life, that infantile
desire to just have a little bit of revenge, to twist the
knife a little bit. It was a revelation. Now I feel joy
that I was the odd man. It gave me an out that I
didn't recognize at the time. I've spent a lot of time
recovering from the feeling of being inadequate. I'm
building from that now. But then I did all kinds of
weird shit to try to get people to like me.
—WHOOPI GOLDBERG, JUNE 1987

Even before Whoopi Goldberg arrived back in Manhattan in January
1984, the Dance Theatre Workshop was issuing press releases
about the forthcoming *Spook Show*. The publicity bulletins enthused: "Charismatic black theater artist WHOOPI GOLDBERG blends social
observation and political satire with a searing brand of stand up comedy. . . . In *The Spook Show* she brings to life an array of poignant,
electrifying characters, both black and white, women and men. They are
the 'living dead and the actual deceased' people fighting to be heard from

the margins of society, and Ms. Goldberg gives them passionate and eloquent voice laced with high humor."

The Spook Show was presented by the Dance Theater Workshop's Economy Tires Theater series. Produced by David R. White and Caron Atlans, Whoopi's stage event was part of the 1983–84 season, which had as its theme "Character and Confession: New Experiences in Narrative Theater." It was to be staged at the Bessie Schonberg Theater, located in the workshop's complex, a converted garage at 219 West Nineteenth Street. Goldberg's New York debut was taking place just a few blocks from where she had grown up in the Chelsea projects. She couldn't have been more excited to be making good in her old neighborhood. Now, for a rare change, her mother, Emma, could be really proud of her daughter in front of all her friends in the projects.

Opening night for *The Spook Show* occurred on Friday, January 27, 1984, at 11:00 P.M. with late-evening performances thereafter every Friday through Sunday until February 19, 1984. As before, her show consisted of several offbeat characters who each took their turn, front and center. She insisted she never knew what might pop out of the mouths of her people, for they were in control and she was merely the vehicle through which they spoke.

Her cast of unusual personalities included the sassy Fontaine, an educated junkie who was a burglar by profession. ("My name is Fontaine, and love is my game. And when I kiss the girls, hey, they're all aflame. Hey, come on, let me kiss your hand. No, the one with the diamonds on it.") The audience soon learns that this glib dude is far more than he seems, as when he reveals he has a Ph.D. in literature. ("I don't like to brag about it 'cause I can't do jack with it.") In the midst of the Fontaine sketch, she would suddenly switch into a snide stewardess maneuvering a rattling beverage cart down the plane's narrow aisle. Later, the monologue would veer into a touching description of Fontaine's visit to Anne Frank's shrine in Amsterdam, Holland. At this point, the hipster allows an amazing self-revelation: "I discovered what I didn't think I had—a heart."

Then there was the adolescent Valley Girl, a pregnant airhead. ("One time, like, you know, like, I was on the beach and, like, these people came up to me and they said, like, 'Are you a Valley Girl?' And I said, 'No, I'm a surfer, because before there was the mall there was the ocean, okay.") This "surfer chick," abandoned by family, friends, and church, attempts an abortion by drinking a mixture of Comet bathroom cleaner and Johnnie Walker Red. She then follows the instructions she heard somewhere: "You know, like jump up and down fifty-six times." When the brew fails to do the job, she uses a wire clothes hanger to rid herself of the fetus. She reasons aloud: "Like you can't go surfing with a baby on your back."

Yet another of Goldberg's *Spook Show* characters—and perhaps the most endearing—was the nine-year-old black girl with pigtails that "don't do nuffin', don't blow in the wind." The youngster dreams only of being blond and white. To aid in her desired transformation, she has even soaked in a bath of Clorox bleach. The young miss wants nothing more than to be accepted by the white majority so that her cherished dream will finally be realized—to be a guest star on TV's *Love Boat*.

Sometimes Whoopi would present Inez Beaverman, an elderly woman dwelling on thoughts of death. At other times, her gallery of characterizations onstage would include a Jamaican, a self-sufficient soul involved with a much older man who at least has money. Not to be overlooked in Whoopi's repertoire of unforgettable characters was her touching interpretation of a crippled young woman who insists, "This is not a disco body." By the skit's end, this physically challenged female is set to marry a nice young man, although she is still convinced his under-lying motive is a need to be "kind to crips." As this feisty woman com-pletes her monologue and the stage darkens save for a spotlight on the actor's face, she invites the theater audience to her pending nuptials. She urges, "Please come. We're going to have a disco pool party." While the audience is still laughing at the irony of her final comment, Goldberg's damaged woman hobbles and boogies into the wings.

There were many unique aspects to this quite singular production. For one thing, Whoopi relied on only a few props in her performance. Her audacious Fontaine wears a trench coat and dark shades. Thanks to a naturally husky voice, androgynous clothing, and flip patter, Goldberg was convincing as this hip *male* crook. Her sad nine-year-old's blond tresses that constantly shake and flip from her array of head gestures was nothing more than a light-colored shirt tucked over the top of Goldberg's head and allowed to run down her back. Her crippled person used crutches, and the adolescent surfer chick was animated by attitude and body language.

During the course of her raucous onstage monologues—geared to awaken the audience's collective mind—Goldberg's alter egos would chat about a range of engaging topics. These sharp observations ran the gamut from Abe Lincoln to TV's Mr. T. ("A guy with a Mohawk I'm supposed to relate to. This motherfucker is a throwback, man.") Her language was salty, her perceptions shrewd, as when she dismisses the movie *The Big Chill* as being about "a lot of motherfuckers sitting around crying about the sixties." She was also fearless in interacting with the theatergoers. Fontaine, her crotch-scratching doper, walks into the audience, jibing and jesting with the theatergoers.

No two shows were ever the same, for Goldberg depended largely on inspiration and energy from the audience. And she brazenly demanded that theatergoers take an active role in the high-energy outing. She reasoned, "They can't just come in and sit. How can you change people if they just sit there? If you're right in their faces and you're fondling them and talking to them, they go out of the theater saying more than just 'Oh, we went to a show.' Sometimes I'll have an audience that just sits there staring, and it's hard; it becomes work. I say, 'Hey, you people should be twirling in the aisles. Wake up! Sometimes I have entertainment executives come to the show, and they can be the worst audiences. They sit there half-dead, and I think, You know how hard this stuff is, you know what I'm trying to do—lighten the fuck up! And believe me, I have no qualms about saying that to people."

Sometimes her harsh intrusion on a seemingly complacent audience backfired. During one performance back in San Francisco, Goldberg was unaware that one overly sedate aisle sitter was actually a theater critic. "He had a coat in his lap and he was sitting there doing nothing. I said, 'What are you doing under that coat, man? You have this big smile on your face. Is it for the reason I'm thinking of?' I found out the next day who it was when I read the review. He called Fontaine . . . a 'jive-talking, black, foul-mouthed version of George Carlin.' People must come in with open minds and decide during the course of the show if they'll allow themselves to be swept away."

On another occasion, she performed *The Spook Show* at Manhattan Community College on Chambers Street: "They gave me the business, and I gave it right back to them. One of my characters is a handicapped woman, and one guy started laughing at her, because many times that's our impression of handicapped people, we think they're amusing. She looked at him and said, 'Do I scare you?' he said, 'No,' and she said, 'I always wanted to be like you, but one of us got the shitty end of the stick. I guess it was you.' "

Sometimes her aggressive, in-your-face presentation would get overly strong reactions from obviously shaken theatergoers. "I've been slapped, pushed down, shoved, and spit on. That's okay. I say, 'You want to be like that, I'll just go back up and deal with you from the stage. I'll get ya.'" There were even times when audience members unleashed their reactions to her showcase after the show. For example, after one performance, she was slapped hard backstage by a right-to-lifer who was extremely offended by her Valley-girl abortion skit. How did Goldberg react? As she recalls, "Well, I'm not in jail, so I didn't kill them. But . . . no one has done it since, and I would not advise anyone to try and do it now."

Whoopi was not an overnight success with *The Spook Show*. She remembers: "The first night in New York we had thirty people in the audience. The first weekend it was like fifty, and they were ready to go away. They were ready to have me go away. Then we got this review that if I had done—I don't know—something sexual to this reviewer, I couldn't have gotten a better review. And suddenly it packed the house."

The pivotal critique came from Mel Gussow of the highly regarded *New York Times*. In its Friday, February 3, 1984, edition—a week after *The Spook Show* had opened—Gussow wrote a valentine to the comedic "newcomer." "Whoopi Goldberg is revealed as a fresh and very funny character comedian with a distinctive point of view and rich comic potential. . . . Quickly we realize that Miss Goldberg is not simply a stand-up comedian but a satirist with a cutting edge and an actor with a wry attitude toward life and public performance. Despite the outrageous quality of much of her commentary, she averts bad taste and retains her winning personality."

He closed his enthusiastic review with: "It would not be inaccurate to suggest that her comedy is a cross between Lily Tomlin and Richard Pryor, but, given the wide audience she deserves—and with more material—it may not be long before people will try to compare future comics to the inimitable Whoopi Goldberg."

Thanks to Gussow's rave assessment, word spread that it was worth a trip off the beaten path to see this curious and daring theater newcomer. One of these aisle sitters who attended a late-night performance was comedian-actor Mike Nichols. After performing successfully for years with partner Elaine May, he had turned to directing plays and films. In early 1984 he was preparing a New York stage production of *Hurlyburly*, featuring William Hurt and Sigourney Weaver. Another member of the acting ensemble was Judith Ivey. During the rehearsal period, Ivey and Nichols developed a little game in which they would each take turns coming up with the most unique, offbeat theater experience possible and then take the other to see it. It was through her masseur that Ivey first learned of Whoopi's showcase. In turn, she invited Nichols and his wife, Annabel, to join her and her own escort for a late-evening show at the Dance Theater Workshop.

Goldberg has two versions of what transpired that particular evening. She told the *Aquarian Weekly* (November 14, 1984): "Now, you know who Mike Nichols is, right? But you don't necessarily know what he looks like. I always pick some people to play to, and that night I saw these four beaming faces, really into it, so I played the show to them. It was a good night. I was on."

Years later, in the fall of 1988, Whoopi would tell Darrah Meeley (*Screen Actors* magazine) about Mike Nichols's surprise visit to the Dance Theatre Workshop that February evening in 1984: "I spotted him immediately. I think I've never been as good as I was that night, because I wanted to pay homage to someone who did what I wanted to do. Someone who became what I wanted to become—which is a consummate performer. Someone who understood and could make the leap between stage and film and do all these great things. I'm not interested in directing, but I like the idea of it. So there I was, sort of shining. And when you're hot, you know it."

Whichever version is more accurate, Goldberg's distinctive presentation moved Mike Nichols very much. He recalls that he "fell on my keister laughing, and then I went backstage to tell Whoopi and to meet her, and I burst into tears, made a complete fool of myself. She has a gigantic spirit, and you're sort of slowly exposed to what she's like. . . . She has a way of cutting through everything, both personally and professionally. She just gets right to it."

As Whoopi recalls the career-making event, Nichols came back to her tiny dressing room. He knocked, and when she opened the door, he stood there silently for what seemed like an endless amount of time. "He was crying and I was crying. He told me he'd be interested in producing me anywhere, anytime." Goldberg was definitely flattered by his obvious enthusiasm. However, at the same time she had too much street savvy to be overwhelmed by his impromptu offer. She couldn't quite believe that this notable was willing, on the spot, to commit to producing her show—

as she wanted it—on Broadway. It seemed far too good to be true. Besides, she had already made a commitment to return to San Francisco to do her *Moms Mabley* one-person show that June. Thus, after exchanging pleasantries, it was agreed that Nichols would be in touch with Goldberg in the near future and they would take matters from there.

Undaunted by Whoopi's failure to make a specific commitment to his on-the-spot offer, Nichols immediately became her biggest booster. He hyped her to the press as "one part Elaine May, one part Groucho [Marx], one part [famed monologist] Ruth Draper, one part Richard Pryor, and five parts never before seen." He proclaimed to all that he was dazzled by her "gigantic" spirit, above and beyond her talent. He bubbled to the *New York Daily News*: "Her compassion and her humanity are enormously moving and quite startling in somebody that funny."

Meanwhile, other influential sources were now spreading the word about Goldberg's captivating performance. The *Village Voice* reviewed her—twice!—and Liz Smith made note of her talent in her nationally syndicated gossip column. As a result, Whoopi was soon being interviewed on a local TV news show (*Live at Five*), chatting from behind sun shades with newscaster Jack Cafferty.

Adding to the newcomer's fast-growing reputation was an enthusiastic review by Cathleen McGuigan in the March 5, 1984, issue of *Newsweek*. She said, "Whoopi doesn't do one-liners or impressions, or self-deprecatory shtick. Like [Richard] Pryor, she treads that treacherous territory that falls somewhere between stand-up comedy and legitimate theater." McGuigan added: "Her acting control is especially evident during bits of improvisation with the audience; at a recent performance, she contended with a heckler without even going out of character as the crippled girl. Clearly, this isn't entertainment for anyone just out for yuks."

Another booster was journalist Bob Weiner, who, upon witnessing the one-woman production, made a point of coming back repeatedly to see Goldberg shine. He was often accompanied by show-biz big shots and club owners. Weiner later explained: "Everybody knows I hate everything and everybody. But I thought Whoopi Goldberg was the funniest, most moving performer I'd ever seen." Thanks to Weiner's enthusiastic promoting, club owner Greg Dawson offered Goldberg a home at the Ballroom on Twenty-eighth Street for an extended run of her show. Topping this promise, producer Joseph Cates suggested presenting her in a "classy off-Broadway venue," where she could properly "build as a theater artist." Now everyone seemed to want Whoopi for this or that personal appearance. For example, Larry Josephson, New York City's WBAI radio personality, asked her to write material for Radio Foundation, which produced *The Bob and Ray Show*.

With such ongoing hype, many other celebrities soon found their way to the Bessie Schonberg Theater. Backstage visitors included Bette Midler, Jerry Stiller and Anne Meara, Burt Bacharach and Carole Bayer Sager, not to mention superagent Sam Cohn and supermanager Sandy Gallin. When Goldberg moved her showcase to the Hudson Guild Theater in the Chelsea projects, notables followed her there, as they did when she was appearing at Manhattan Community College and elsewhere in New York City.

If such attention was a sweet balm to Goldberg, it was even more exciting to Whoopi's mother, Emma, who was on hand every evening to watch her daughter perform in front of the glitterati. Whoopi said: "Oh, she tried very hard to be calm. But then we'd go back home from the theater and just scream: '*Aaaaahhhh! We met Burt Bacharach! Aaaaahh-hhh!* He hugged me! Yes, he did, yes he did!' We'd be crazy, y'know, just nuts." In addition, there were happy reunions with other close members of her extended family and neighbors. However, for the most part Whoopi felt alien from many of the people with whom she had grown up or known as a young adult. That included her ex-husband Martin and many others whose lives had gone in such different directions from hers.

All too soon, Whoopi's successful Manhattan engagement came to an end. She returned to the West Coast—this time to southern California. Beginning on March 10, 1984, she fulfilled a commitment to perform *The Spook Show* at the Wallenboyd Center in Los Angeles. She was joined by David Schein, and they performed on a double bill. As had been the case in New York, celebrities found their way off the beaten path to see Goldberg's presentation.

One of those who saw Goldberg work onstage in Los Angeles was Warner Bros. vice president Diane Sokolow. She was among the growing number already considering the uncommon Goldberg for possible screen roles in upcoming major motion pictures. The clan of Los Angeles–based comedians (Robin Williams, Lily Tomlin, and others) took Whoopi under their collective wing, proclaiming her a major talent and now one of their own. It was a fast, heady, upward-bound trip for the amazed, newly arrived comedian.

Whoopi was hardly back in San Francisco to reconnect with her daughter and David Schein when she flew to Glasgow, Scotland, for a comedy festival. Then, once more unpacked in the Golden Gate city, she honored her commitment to appear in *Moms Mabley* in June 1984—for a several week run. (Years later, on a May 1993 NBC-TV special, *Bob Hope: The First Ninety Years,* Goldberg would reprise her Moms Mabley character.)

Much as she loved submerging herself into her role as the cantankerous, cackle-prone Mom, a lot was happening to Goldberg in rather short order. She was no longer "just" a local character but a person increasingly mentioned and praised in the national press. The increase in exposure was due in part to her having signed with the well-positioned talent-management firm Katz-Gallin-Morey & Addis, which represented such personalities as Dolly Parton, Mac Davis, Paul Rodriguez, and Debbie Allen. Gallin had been one of Whoopi's earliest champions in New York, having insisted that "Whoopi Goldberg is going to be a very big star." Thereafter, Gallin campaigned to sign Goldberg as a client, and she finally agreed. It would be Goldberg's live-in lover, David Schein, who would give Gallin some sage advice regarding Whoopi: "Just let her do what she wants. She's very surprising when she does what she wants."

Whoopi's burgeoning career left her breathless and somewhat ambivalent. As she explained to Edward Guthmann in the *San Francisco Sunday Examiner & Chronicle* in late May 1984, "The biggest deal for me is being able to dialogue with people I respect, like Jack Nicholson and Robin Williams, and meeting people like Michael Jackson and Alice Walker [author of *The Color Purple*]. But there's the other side, too, which is not so [much] fun—which is phone calls and talkin' money [with her agent] and learning to say 'No,' and finding yourself looking in the mirror at this egotistical bastard you've turned into in a matter of moments."

On the other hand, Goldberg assured Guthmann that she was remaining levelheaded: "Luckily, I've got people around to say, 'Hey, bitch, put some deodorant on it.' That kinda stuff'll keep me steady—that and my kid and my old man [David Schein] and my funky little house."

This led Guthmann to observe: "Looking at Whoopi, it's hard to imagine a less corruptible, more unaffected woman. Dressed in oversized painters' pants and a thermal undershirt, she wears her hair Buckwheat style, in a fury of small braids. Like Moms Mabley, the lady she plays so brilliantly in *Moms,* she has a warm, wide-as-a-frying-pan smile."

During this period of mounting hoopla over one-of-a-kind Whoopi Goldberg, Mike Nichols kept in touch with his "find." Goldberg said: "I get this package in the mail with a Ruth Draper record in it and a letter from Mike repeating the offer, saying if I want to come back to New York, he'll produce me, just pick a theater, a time, whatever. . . . It was a very hea-vy letter."

After further discussion with Nichols, Whoopi finally accepted the director's offer to produce her one-person show in New York. By now, all the available off-Broadway houses had been booked for the fall season. However, due to a play dropout, the Lyceum Theatre at 149 West Forty-fifth Street suddenly became available, and Goldberg committed herself to a run-of-play agreement. According to Goldberg, Nichols's attitude was that "the worse that could happen was it would fail dismally, but it won't hurt you."

Even with this qualification, it was now a reality. Whoopi Goldberg would be making her Broadway debut.

CHAPTER THIRTEEN

Broadway Bound

I kinda feel like I'm on the brink of something, in
the eye of a hurricane. It's real nice, and it's real
awful, too.
—WHOOPI GOLDBERG, MAY 1984

With Whoopi's career momentum now shifting into higher gear, she sensed that her life—both professionally and personally— would probably never be the same again. And she knew that this transition would deeply affect those closest to her. It had already made several of her peers in the Bay Area theater world regard her differently—either with newfound deference or with thinly veiled jealousy.

By this point, Goldberg must have understood that her relationships with her daughter, Alexandrea, and her lover, David Schein, would suffer the most from her latest career decision to go to New York. She had to appreciate—at least subconsciously—that her life on Broadway, for however long, and theirs in Berkeley, California, would cause much more than a geographic distancing. She would admit later, "I was tempted to say no 'cause I didn't know what it was going to do to my family. I knew they didn't want to come. If they had said, 'Don't go,' I would've been unhappy for a while, but I wouldn't have come."

To ease into this emotional and geographic separation from her family, it was decided that before Whoopi settled into her New York rehearsals, she, David, and Alexandrea would pile into their Volkswagen van and drive across the United States. Their immediate destination was the woods of Winooski, Vermont. "We had a little money," Whoopi explained. "I had never been on a real vacation, and David comes from

103

there. And I'd never seen Vermont. We walked and swam and made a leaf hut where you could go and think if you wanted to."

The few weeks of vacation came to an end, and the trio drove down to New York City. Then Schein and Alexandrea returned to northern California—Schein to the Blake Street Hawkeyes and Whoopi's daughter to grade school.

Goldberg's run-of-the-play contract was not a lucrative one. Because it was a one-person show, there was no Actors Equity requirement that her show be considered a standard production with the prescribed salary scale provided for a Broadway star. (Goldberg would insist that it was she who refused to rejoin Actors Equity. When she was working in San Diego, Equity started a witch-hunt of Equity actors performing under other names in regional, nonunion houses. She had angrily quit the union.)

Because of her non-Equity status, Whoopi's salary was only a little over $300 a week. It was not a lot of cash, but it was certainly an improvement over her struggling years as a welfare mother. She also received several perks, including a provision for free living quarters and food expenses during the run, a secretarial assistant, if needed, and appropriate transportation nightly to and from the theater. Wanting to be near her mother and her "roots," Whoopi selected a spacious two-floor apartment in her old Chelsea neighborhood.

Long recognized for his golden touch with most every creative project he undertook, Mike Nichols had assembled a high-caliber team to showcase Goldberg. Produced in association with Emanuel Azenberg and the Shubert Organization, the show boasted such experienced hands as Tony Walton (once married to Julie Andrews) as visual consultant, Jennifer Tipton in charge of lighting, and Otis Munderloh doing the sound.

The Lyceum Theatre, with 928 seats, was far smaller than many of the Broadway barns that housed musicals. However, it was still a far bigger cavern than Goldberg had experienced either off-Broadway, at the Economy Tires Theatre, or back in California. Above all, it presented a problem of sorts to adapt Goldberg's characters to the far bigger theater while maintaining the intimacy between actor and playgoer that Whoopi's production required.

An easy assumption might have been that given his experience and success, Nichols would have exerted strong control over the reshaping of Whoopi's show for Broadway theatergoers. However, since the project was written by and starring Goldberg and he was "merely" a coproducer and production supervisor and not the director, he walked a delicate tightrope, albeit one he had created. Moreover, being himself an alumni of the improvisational school of comedy, he respected the medium's need for unbridled spontaneity and self-inspired creativity. Having "discovered" this special talent and being one of her early mainstream champions, he was extremely respectful of, or at least enchanted by, Whoopi and her irrepressible personality.

For her part, Whoopi was in awe of the mighty Nichols, an Establishment success in so many creative areas. She reasoned: "He's one of the few directors you can name who has been a performer as well. He knows exactly what's going on. Working with him is going to make me a much better actor. . . . He's right in step with you all the way. If you're improvising, he knows. Most directors don't have an actor's perspective. Mike Nichols does." On another occasion, she said, "Nichols. It's like God came and said, 'Come with me.' "

When the preparation period began, Nichols and Goldberg worked their way through her characterizations, dissecting and reassembling each skit. He became a watchdog, voicing the need for changes whenever the star's monologues veered dangerously far from the particular playlet's major thematic thrust. As Whoopi went through her intricate paces, he would stop her if she began to meander. If she found this artistic vigilance demanding and sometimes annoying, she acceded to many of his suggestions.

However, Whoopi's aesthetic sensitivity could only handle so much advice or faultfinding. She was already feeling nervous and vulnerable about facing cynical Broadway critics and jaded theatergoers. As a defense mechanism, her innate iron will and self-containment took control, which led her to either contest several of Nichols's suggestions openly or ignore them. During the course of the exhaustive rehearsal process, she stubbornly refused to refine or reslant aspects of her character sketches as the far more experienced Nichols advised. (Much later, Goldberg would admit that she wished she had been more amenable to her mentor's wise recommendations.)

During the weeks leading up to the opening, the publicity firm of Bill Evans Associates, in conjunction with Salters, Roskin, and Friedman, worked hard to drum up appropriate interest in this unusual Broadway vehicle and its equally untraditional solo performer. Part of the process was to make the actor less accessible than she had been to the media, to create a demand for information about her.

There were many background angles that would be employed to promote Goldberg, even if some of the slants carried potential negative associations and considerations. In the course of press releases and/or publicity profiles and media interviews regarding Goldberg, it was touted that the newcomer was a native New Yorker, a high school dropout, a former drug addict and street person, a onetime welfare mother, a founding member of the San Diego Repertory Theater, and a participant in the still-innovative Berkeley–San Francisco counterculture. In addition, there was the added benefit of Whoopi's peculiar and surprising stage name, made even more mysterious by her refusal, at this time, to supply her "real" name, her actual age, or any concrete information about her ex-spouse. In addition, there was an overlapping of misinformation already circulating about her, fueled by the elaborations and fabrications she had previously created to enhance her stage background.

Finally, there was the "gimmick" of Whoopi's unusual look—ranging from her outré dreadlocks to her distinctive facial features and her bohemian way of dressing. (Ironically, years later, her choice of casual garb would be considered "cool.") That she considered herself an underdog due to her untypical appearance was reflected in her statements. For example, she told friend Janet Coleman in a July 1984 *Vanity Fair* interview that her one-woman program "grew out of desperation. Of people saying, 'Well, no, we can't cast you in this, because well, heh-heh, you know, you don't quite . . . uh . . . look, like, uh, you know . . . .' And I'd go, 'What? What don't I look like?' And they'd say, 'Well, frankly, you're not Barbie [doll].' Or, 'This is a movie for Meryl Streep to make or Goldie Hawn to make.' And I'd go, 'But what's the difference? I'm good.' "

Goldberg also said, "I've been an actor almost twenty years and I couldn't get enough work, so I developed a blend of straight theater, stand-up comedy, Greek comedy—political satire and world assessment through characters." She admitted that for the past decade she had been trying to find talent agents who believed enough in her—as she was—to represent her and help her career progress. These themes of being unacceptable because of her differences would be voiced over and over again by the actor throughout the years.

In considering the task of promoting the Whoopi Goldberg of 1984, her unorthodox lifestyle had to be handled carefully. While it was fine for sophisticated, progressive San Franciscans to accept the fact that Goldberg was a single parent living with a lover of a different race and for Manhattanites to tolerate her persona, it was unlikely that Whoopi's lifestyle would appeal to inhabitants of America's heartland. While the comedian's relationship with David Schein was never hidden, it was a touchy item that often got lost in the barrage of verbiage that Whoopi unleashed about herself and life in general whenever the media interviewed her.

Then there was the topic of Goldberg's race. In 1984, being a member of an ethnic minority did not carry the degree of "stigma" that it had for decades past in the United States. Liberal whites—especially in the creative arts—thought it proper and hip to accept talented blacks into their fold. However, this process led to the more famous and visible Goldberg being regarded as a spokesperson for her race—a role she was neither automatically qualified for nor would have consciously chosen to accept. It sometimes caused her to make inopportune statements, such as when talking to the *Amsterdam News,* a black-oriented publication: "We haven't made leaps and bounds in our progress, but we move slowly—that's good." Such pronouncements—meant to be diplomatic but truthful—coming from one who was rising in the esteem of mainstream white circles, were not likely to endear her to the African-American community.

As for mainstream white America, even in the mid-1980s, most of its populace typically lumped all black performers together into one category. Thus, Goldberg was automatically compared with two black male stand-up comics: the older Richard Pryor and the younger Eddie Murphy. In a way, it was a valuable association for her, since they were currently very successful. However, it also created for critics and audiences alike false expectations of an act filled with fast-paced, raunchy one-liners that Whoopi could not and did not want to fulfill.

Rather, this raspy-voiced comedian (a Marlboro chain-smoker), who had a rare take on life, wanted to be accepted and embraced on her own terms. However, as her professional day of judgment came nearer, she wondered how success might drastically alter her life. She confided: "I read all those biographies about what drove [successful] folks nuts. People change toward you. I want to do good work. I don't think I can compromise that and live. 'Cause if I have to shake my tits or play somebody's fuckin' maid for the rest of my life, it isn't worth it. My stuff—that's the one thing I know no amount of money can stop me from doin'. 'Cause that's the reason why I'm here on earth. I like to think that Moms [Mabley] and Lenny [Bruce, one of her stand-up comedy idols] are leading me. Moms and Lenny are saying, 'Do it. It's going to piss a lot of people off.' "

The backers (Mike Nichols, Emanuel Azenberg, and the Shubert Organization) of Whoopi's one-person show most likely believed its street-smart, urban tone would prove too controversial for out-of-town tryouts. Consider the extended pro-choice nature of the "surfer chick" skit, the drug-infused slant to the Fontaine monologue, and the theme of racial discrimination evoked by the nine-year-old black child wanting to be white.

As Whoopi prepared for her Broadway debut, Mike Nichols and the other backers decided not to call it *The Spook Show*. At first, the producers titled it *Whoopi Goldberg Variations*, then simply *Whoopi Goldberg*, thus avoiding the problem of reviewers and potential patrons dealing with the multilayered meaning of the word "spook," which might refer to ghosts, as Goldberg insisted, or to a demeaning slang term referring to African Americans, as others contended. As time would prove, calling the show *Whoopi Goldberg* would produce a surprise in many less informed playgoers who thought the show was headlining a white, Jewish comedian in stand-up routines revolving around extremely serious issues. (Ironically, many potential black patrons were still unaware that this strangely named woman was actually a "sister" and only belatedly became members of her audience.)

Thanks to her talent representatives, Whoopi was beginning to receive film offers. In the early fall of 1984 she made a business trip to Los Angeles, having already flown there earlier in the year to test for a movie role. While there, she found time to perform at the Comedy Store. Among those who caught her performance at the popular forum were Barbra Streisand, Michael Jackson, and Jack Nicholson. Such famous fans helped build Goldberg's reputation with the press and, in turn, with the public.

Once again, back in New York City, she turned to her New York legitimate theater debut. After eighteen preview performances at the Lyceum Theatre, *Whoopi Goldberg* opened on Broadway on Wednesday, October 24, 1984. Tickets for the ninety-minute presentation (with one intermission) ranged from a high of $27 on weekdays to $30 on weekends. (At Goldberg's insistence, management set up a policy of half-price student tickets.) As patrons entered the venerable theater, a notice posted in the lobby read: "Please be aware that *Whoopi Goldberg* contains strong language."

On most nights, her repertory included six characterizations from her gallery of nineteen personalities. As she would explain to Harry Haun in a November 1984 *Playbill* article, she doesn't "write characters. I just do them on the stage. Some lines I know work, so I remember to use them, but I don't write them down. These characters are very much people living in my head. They are all distinct, different individuals, and it's the job of the actor to keep them that way. Actors are schizophrenics essentially, which is how we can produce these vastly different people. In a sense, I see myself as a medium, something from which these people spring. If I had not lucked out and gotten into theater, I could be in Bellevue."

Her basic selection of character sketches for the audience included Fontaine the druggie; the Valley Girl; the crippled bride-to-be; the Jamaican woman who becomes the companion to a fossilized but still lecherous American millionaire; a humorous, aged street beggar who once did tap steps with the legendary dancing Nicholas Brothers; and the nine-year-old child who craves blond hair, blue eyes, and white skin. As always, the showcasing of these figures involved audience participation. During the Fontaine routine, her persona would trade quips with unsuspecting laid-back playgoers. Her over-the-hill male dancer might unexpectedly scrounge quarters from patrons in the front rows. Or, often at the conclusion of her little-black-girl sketch, she would persuade rows of the orchestra section to create a chain of handclasps.

At the end of each performance, Goldberg would always step to the front of the stage and, talking directly the audience, term her success "a big kick in the backside for avant-garde artists across the country. The fact that you came here to see me negates the myth that artists should not come to Broadway. If I can do it, anybody can." She always stressed that she was still "a little kid from downtown livin' a dream eight times a week." And she promised and warned, "Now that I've made it through that door, I'm gonna bring as many people as I can with me before it closes."

To use one of Goldberg's own favorite words, many reviews for her Broadway debut were "amazing!"

Clive Barnes in the *New York Post* wrote: "She seems to have every-

thing going for her—including a quite sizable talent and a more than
sizable nerve." While he noted that in her role as social commentator she
had a "friendly habit of dangerously provoking a white audience's guilt,"
he emphasized: "She is clearly an actor before anything. And on her own
terms an extraordinarily good actor." He predicted: She "will become a
cult hero. She is possibly a cult hero already."

Douglas Watt in the *New York Daily News* headlined his review
"Whoopi Goldberg: Long May She Whoop." As to her repertory of social
conscience–provoking characterizations, he judged, "The voice changes
and mannerisms are astonishing[ly] expressive throughout. There is a
tendency at times to sentimentalize, but that is almost always subject to a
cutting edge, and there is probably an overindulgence of raunchy humor
dotted with ripe puns. But these are minor matters." He concluded:
"You'll laugh with her, love her and be wounded, too."

Far less enthusiastic was *Weekly Variety*'s reviewer, who insisted:
"The black actor-comedian is an ingratiating and clearly talented performer, but her thin and unchallenging material seems too carefully calculated to soothe conventional audience sensibilities." He pointed out:
"Although Goldberg has a background as a street entertainer and comes
with overblown management comparison to Richard Pryor, there's nothing dangerous or threatening about the handful of characters she essays,
all of who are designed to engender maximum audience sympathy." He
acknowledged, "In only one of the monodramas, however, does the writing combine with the acting to create a satisfying dramatic experience.
That's the wistful nine-year-old black girl. . . . In this poignant sketch
Goldberg creates a memorable image of human longing."

Joel Siegel, appearing on WABC-TV, was downright negative: "Mike
Nichols . . . should know from his performing days [that] this kind of
show needs some kind of thread to stitch the sketches into something
more than nightclub routine. A word or two from Whoopi out of character might have helped. Nichols should also have recognized her writing is
just not up to her talents as a performer. . . . This act—and that's what
it is—doesn't belong on Broadway. She does have tremendous potential
as a performer. Maybe another season there'll be a reason to take in
Whoopi."

And then there was the notoriously surly John Simon (*New York*
magazine). He rated her a "fraud" and no better than a "three-legged
horse."

Goldberg's published retort to Simon: "His head is up his butt. He couldn't do to me [because of the then current trend to be politically correct to a black performer] what he does to everyone else, which is talk about how ugly they are and their thighs and noses, so instead he attacked my integrity and said the only kind of people who would enjoy this show are pregnant teenagers, any kind of black person, and bleeding-heart white liberals lookin' for guilt. He said I changed my name to Whoopi Goldberg for the show, to get white people to come."

Whoopi also found it difficult to deal with the barbs thrust at Mike Nichols because he had not sufficiently mainstreamed the product. A visibly wounded Goldberg offered, "People say it's not a show for Broadway because it doesn't have a point, that it's overly sentimental, that Mike Nichols should've made it harder, that it didn't reflect enough of the black experience. However, none of them could say I was not a good performer or actor, [not] even John Simon."

In the weeks that followed, the show and its star gained a kind of cult status. It became the "in thing" to see this offbeat performer. There were sufficient ticket buyers to keep the production alive. As Goldberg settled into her Broadway run, her boyfriend, David Schein, and her daughter, Alexandrea, came east to see her perform. They had stayed away, so it was said, for fear of making Whoopi nervous by being in the audience before she had become comfortable with the show. Goldberg acknowledged that her daughter "couldn't give a s——" about the Broadway hullabaloo, and besides "she's seen me do this stuff before." As for Schein, he found the New York scene too commercial and phony. The duo soon returned to their less complicated life in Berkeley.

How did the qualified Broadway success change Whoopi's lifestyle? Edward Guthmann of the *San Francisco Chronicle* had reviewed and interviewed Goldberg often. He was in New York in December 1984 and reported for his hometown newspaper: "The limo pulls up to the Lyceum Theatre stage door, where Whoopi Goldberg's dreams materialize eight times a week, and the newly minted 'Toast of Broadway' emerges, dressed in a stylish black cloak. Whoopi greets the theater staff—stage manager, curtain pullers, lighting technician, ushers—and leads the way up a circular staircase to her sliver-sized dressing room. She slips off her cloak, starts opening fan mail, and asks in her husky, nicotine-stained voice, 'So how's San Francisco? Are people surprised that I'm still hangin' on out here?' "

In reality, she was doing a lot more than just hanging on. She was the center of media attention, from big metropolitan daily newspapers to campus weeklies, across the country. Among those who had seen her Broadway performance were such notables as Diana Ross, Steven Spielberg, and Martin Luther King Jr.'s widow, Coretta, each of whom had paid homage to the actor-comedian backstage after the show. By now, Goldberg was such a recognizable face that the paparazzi spotted her wherever she went.

And she made good media copy, even if the facts were jumbled. One evening she went alone to see the Royal Shakespeare Company's *Much Ado About Nothing*. She happened to chat with singer Paul Simon, and he offered her a ride home. The press published their photo and said she was Simon's date. After Warren Beatty came backstage at the Lyceum to offer his congratulations to Whoopi, they left the theater together, and according to Goldberg, "the next day it's in print [with a photo] and I'm like 'Warren Beatty's new score.' " (Such incidents led the celebrity-circuit novice to observe: "I understand now why famous people stay off to themselves, 'cause it's f——in' dangerous.")

As for Goldberg's material needs, the only thing she professed to want for herself, now that she had the luxury of a rented limousine and driver, was new leather pants. (She still frequently wore her grandfather's black cashmere coat and usually wore a knitted Rasta tam covering her unusual hairdo.) As for her family, she admitted she would love to have the money to send her mother on a cruise, get her daughter assorted treats, and buy David Schein a word processor.

As for her next career move, she insisted that she still planned to return to Berkeley in the springtime and that she intended to remain an integral part of the Blake Street Hawkeyes.

Using the catch phrase "Her Time Has Arrived!" from Mel Gussow's *New York Times* essay on Goldberg's Broadway debut, many ads and follow-up stories touted Goldberg as a likely contender for a Tony Award in mid-1985, even though the production had closed on March 10, 1985, after 150 performances. Much to her disappointment, Whoopi, the Broadway sensation, was not even nominated for a Tony. However, she did receive a Theatre World Award as well as a Drama Desk citation for her outstanding talent.

Although she did not win a Tony nomination, Goldberg would soon receive artistic validation. HBO chose to tape an expanded performance of *Whoopi Goldberg* with some preshow commentary by the star, seen backstage, where she walks from dressing room to dressing room and encounters her assorted personas. Produced by Goldberg's Whoop Inc., in association with Broadway Video and D.I.R. Broadcasting, it was directed by Thomas Schlamme. The cable special was entitled *Whoopi Goldberg: Direct from Broadway* and debuted on Saturday, July 20, 1985, at 10:00 P.M. Reviewing the offering, John O'Connor of the *New York Times* wrote: "Whoopi Goldberg is reaching for something special in her act. She grasps it often enough to merit close attention." The *Washington Post* said, "She is an original, and the five monologues she presents . . . are flaky, funny, gritty, bizarre and quite unexpectedly touching." The *Village Voice* opined: "Caricature is her strongest suit. This charming entertainer could emerge as a great American comic."

Repeated airings of this cable program brought renewed praise and expanded popularity throughout the United States for Goldberg's one-woman showcase, as did the slightly abridged (75-minutes-long) home-video release of the special called *Whoopi Goldberg Live* (1986). The cast album of her Broadway show did even better. It brought her a coveted Grammy Award.

CHAPTER FOURTEEN

The Color Purple

I'm working on things that will change the face of
film. That sounds very bourgeois—I'll rephrase it.
The stuff I want to do is what *isn't* being done.
When you go to movies, you don't see many women
who look like "people next door." They look very
fashionable. Love stories and adventure stories should
involve people who look normal, like you and me.
There's no reason why I shouldn't be able to do a
love story with Robin Williams or William Hurt,
except that people say, "We can't do this. Our
distributors in the South won't be able to handle an
interracial relationship." That keeps the spirit of
stupidity alive. This pabulum they're sending people
out of fear is bullshit. The whole swing back to the
"white American dream" is wrong because there are a
lot of children who will never look like that.
                    —WHOOPI GOLDBERG, DECEMBER 1984

During the Broadway run (October 1984 to March 1985) of her
one-woman show, Whoopi Goldberg began to make her presence
felt in other entertainment mediums as well. She was especially
drawn to television, not only to showcase her versatility as a performer
but also as a means of reaching a far broader audience than stage work
would allow. In turn, television began to embrace Goldberg, as it had,
over the decades, many other newly touted celebrities. The rising star
appeared as a comedy-skit guest on NBC-TV's *Saturday Night Live* on
November 3, 1984, and did readings on PBS-TV's *Reading Rainbow*. The

114

latter was an educational series hosted by LeVar Burton, created to encourage children to read more. Goldberg was also among the famous to participate in the ABC-TV special, *Night of 100 Stars II* (March 10, 1985), which had been taped earlier on the stage of Radio City Music Hall. It featured brief appearances by a wide variety of name talent from many eras, including Ginger Rogers, Dinah Shore, James Stewart, Lana Turner, Sarah Vaughan, and a beaming Whoopi.

When not performing in one venue or another, the always-on-the-go Whoopi was basking in her newfound celebrity status. As a guest correspondent for *California* magazine, she wrote excitedly in its March 1985 issue: "And here I am. In the thick of it all, meeting and greeting anyone and everyone I've ever wanted. My face appears in newspapers, on billboards, on TV. I can go places that would turn me away before, dress as I please, and be fussed over, pampered. I am discussed in many different circles and by people from all walks of life—truck drivers, garbage men, street people."

While Goldberg found all this "sudden" attention flattering and exhilarating, she also admitted: "I get homesick. For the Bay and the Bay Bridge, the hills of Berkeley, Project Artaud, Top Dog in Berkeley. This was fun, exciting, great, but it's not home." And, of course, there were Whoopi's daughter and David Schein, who had remained in California to lead their lives as best they could without Goldberg's participation.

As Goldberg's Broadway stint came to a close in March 1985, there was a great deal of speculation as to what her next career move would actually be. There was talk that she and David Schein would go to London to present *Reverence for the Dead* on the West End stage. It was also rumored that she might team with British film star Jeremy Irons in a proposed New York stage production of *Antony and Cleopatra*, to be directed by Mike Nichols. However, a more exciting plum appeared—the lead in Steven Spielberg's forthcoming screen adaptation of *The Color Purple*, Alice Walker's acclaimed 1982 novel.

Alice Walker, born in 1944, had grown up in a segregated town in rural Georgia. A lonely child who wrote poetry in the fields where her sharecropper parents toiled, she shared a four-room home with seven siblings. At seventeen, with a suitcase and a typewriter given her by her mother, she left home for Spelman College in Atlanta. There she developed her craft as a writer and poet. She later studied poetry at Sarah Lawrence

College in Bronxville, New York. In the years following, she joined the civil-rights movement, was a social worker, and also taught literature and writing at several colleges. Her first poetry collection, *Once*, was published in 1968, followed by *Revolutionary Petunias* (1973) and *Good Night, Willie Lee, I'll See You in the Morning* (1979).

Meanwhile, Alice Walker's debut novel, *The Third Life of Grange Copeland*, appeared in 1970. It focused on the harsh destiny of Georgia tenant farmers. Next came *Meridian* (1976) which dealt with a woman's struggles in Mississippi's civil-rights movement of the 1960s. Her heartfelt saga *The Color Purple* was written as a series of touching letters over a period of many years between two uneducated sisters—one in the rural South and the other in Africa. The novel offered a sensitive portrayal of untutored black women who reached out to embrace life and individuality in the first decades of the twentieth century. *The Color Purple* was awarded the 1983 Pulitzer Prize for fiction.

Having struggled so hard to get *The Color Purple* published, the very retiring, frequently ill Alice Walker had forced herself to promote her novel (loosely based on the story of her great-grandmother) both before and after it won the Pulitzer Prize. Part of her publicity campaign involved a series of radio and TV question-and-answer sessions both around the country and especially in the San Francisco area where she lived.

Whoopi Goldberg recalls that one day in 1983, while she and her daughter were driving around Berkeley, she heard Walker reading a selection from her prize-winning fiction in which two of the characters discuss God. Goldberg remembers: "My kid made me pull over, because I talk about God a lot, and she thought it was funny that somebody else was saying the same kind of stuff. So I knew I had to read it." Whoopi promptly bought a copy of *The Color Purple*. Enthralled by its message and artistry, Whoopi sent the famed African-American author a letter (via the book editor of the *San Francisco Chronicle*). In that correspondence, the actor said, "You don't know me but my name is Whoopi, and here's all my reviews from the Bay Area and Europe and Canada, and I just read *The Color Purple*, and if there's a movie, I would very much like [to be in the project]. I'd be dirt on the floor. I'd do anything. And here's a list of references you can call just so you know I'm not a flake."

To her amazement, Whoopi received back a very flattering note from Alice Walker, who acknowledged that she had already seen Goldberg onstage in her San Francisco one-woman showcase and that she was indeed impressed by the actor's potential to play in *The Color Purple* onscreen. (Walker would later recollect, "I had seen her perform in a very small theater in San Francisco, and during the show she came out and shook hands with members of the audience. I was one of them, and I knew that night she was magical.") Walker also mentioned in her reply to Goldberg that she had "already sent your stuff to L.A." What was in Los Angeles was director-producer Steven Spielberg!

At first blush, white, Jewish Steven Spielberg, the son of an electronics-firm executive, might have seemed an extremely odd choice for directing the screen version of this richly ethnic literary property. However, for several reasons this director-producer-screenwriter was just the right person for the project. Having made his screen reputation and fortune with megahit thrillers (*Jaws*, 1975), elaborate science fiction escapades (*Close Encounters of the Third Kind*, 1977; *E.T. The Extra-Terrestrial*, 1982) and spectacular action adventures (*Raiders of the Lost Ark*, 1981; *Indiana Jones and the Temple of Doom*, 1984), he was anxious to prove to himself and to the film community that he could handle sensitive drama as well. He was also a very bankable commodity at the box office. As such he was looking for the right property to launch his career move.

Meanwhile, Oscar-winning film composer Quincy Jones had read *The Color Purple* and approached producers Jon Peters and Peter Guber, who held the screen rights to the novel. While Jones discussed the possibility of writing the film's score, he urged the filmmakers to allow him to become coproducer on the venture. To guarantee Jones's participation as film composer, they gave him a coproducer's credit, which he intended to exercise. It was Jones who then suggested Steven Spielberg as director.

In fixating on Spielberg to head the production, Jones reasoned, "I don't know how to punt. I have to go for the ultimate. I have never seen a black dramatic film made with total quality from top to bottom that could stand up against any major picture. I wanted a great director who had the sensibilities in every aspect to make this a great film." Jones also concluded that Spielberg—rather than such more obvious choices as African-American directors Gordon Parks or Spike Lee—could attract the big-budget financing needed to make the production "fly," since *The Color Purple* was a very ethnic story and therefore not deemed capable of huge box-office takes.

When Spielberg read *The Color Purple,* he became fascinated by its sensitive study of the heroic Celie, an impoverished young southern black woman in the early 1900s, and her heart-wrenching domestic experiences over a forty-year period. He soon indicated that he wanted to be part of this important screen venture. After executive producers Peters and Guber approved of Spielberg as director of choice, Jones and Spielberg flew to San Francisco to visit the reclusive Ms. Walker. When the visitors arrived at Walker's modest residence, their limousine was so huge it wouldn't fit in her driveway. It gave her pause to wonder about these Hollywood people.

During the course of Alice Walker's dinner with Spielberg and Jones, she came to trust this Establishment filmmaker. As she would later recall, "What impressed me about that meeting was Steven's absolute grasp of the essentials of the book, the feeling, the spirit. He loved Sofia; he loved her fighting spirit and her strength. Right away he saw everything visually." By the end of their meal, Walker had decided to accept him as the film's director. (She later wisecracked to a friend, "Well, maybe if he can do Martians, he can do us.") In giving her blessing to the project and to Spielberg, she agreed that she would write a screenplay of her book. She would also be allowed to make casting suggestions and be a consultant during the filming.

Months passed, and it was now the spring of 1984. Whoopi was in Manhattan doing her off-Broadway showcase when she received a phone call from Steven Spielberg, who said he was considering her for a new movie project he was planning. "He called me and said, 'I can't come to see you. Can you come to see me?' And I thought, Ah-ha, let me check my book to see . . . well, I guess I can squeeze you in. So there I go." (Goldberg also remembers: "My management initially said, 'You don't have to go audition for him.' I said, 'Are you crazy?' One of the great things about Steven is that when he hears about something new, he wants to see it in case he can work with it. . . . Apparently, enough people had said to him, 'Man, we're hearing about this girl.' ")

Whoopi flew to Los Angeles, where it was agreed that she would meet with Spielberg at his screening room and audition by performing her stage act for him and a "few friends." Goldberg recalls: "I'm told there's going to be ten people there. I arrive, and it's Michael Jackson, Quincy Jones, Ashford and Simpson—people I wasn't ready for. But I figured the worst I could do is stink. They've seen people stink before— they've stunk themselves, you know." After she completed *The Spook Show* act for a group of eighty people, she presented a special bonus piece for the famed filmmaker. It was a skit that her management team and friends had advised her not to do because they believed "it would be insulting."

The routine in question was a black-oriented spoof of Spielberg's blockbuster feature *E.T.* Goldberg's variation has the extraterrestrial landing in Oakland, California, where there are no working phones; the skit ends with the alien visitor on dope and in jail. According to Goldberg, Spielberg "loved it. And he said, 'I think I might be directing *The Color Purple,* and it's yours if you want it.' " Whoopi's reaction to this amazing statement was: "My teeth caught cold, 'cause all I could do was grin."

After the shock wore off, Goldberg told the moviemaker, "Yeah, I can do Sofia [a subordinate character in *The Color Purple*]." Her reasoning was: "I figured if I was not meant to be a movie actor, he could cut out whatever he needed and still have the whole movie to content himself with."

However, Spielberg stunned Whoopi by responding that she was too small in stature to play Sofia and that, instead, he envisioned her for the lead part of Celie. The heroine, Celie, is raped repeatedly at age fourteen by her brutal stepfather and gives birth to two children from whom she is almost immediately separated. Later, as excess baggage, she is shunted off to marry a tyrannical older man, Mister, who had wanted to wed her sister Nellie. Later, in revenge, the sadistic Mister tears Celie away from her beloved sibling and makes her life a living hell.

In retrospect, the craziness of what happened next in the discussion between Whoopi and Spielberg is permanently etched in Goldberg's mind: "I was arguing with him, saying, 'I don't want to play Celie. I don't want to mess you up if I'm not good.' The director kept saying, 'I don't know what you're talking about.' Then a little voice said, 'Goldberg, shut up. Take the gig, and if it sucks, he'll fire you.' That's what we did, and it was great."

What finally helped give Goldberg confidence in accepting Spielberg's astonishing offer was the approval of another attendee at her screen audition—Alice Walker. Goldberg recalls: "Apparently, she approved of Steven's casting me. She just looked at me and asked if I enjoyed canning. I said yes. So she said, 'Yeah, you'll do fine. But let's not talk about Celie. Let's just talk about canning.' So whenever we got together, we'd talk about canning."

Although Whoopi had the blessing of Spielberg, Jones, and Walker for the lead role in *The Color Purple,* their choice still required the approval of the film's backers and the movie's distributor, Warner Bros. She was told "they" would let her know in the next months. Filled with joyful anticipation as well as artistic concern over her abilities to handle such a demanding role in her debut motion picture, Goldberg returned to New York. There she continued to perform in *The Spook Show* and to await the final decision from the Hollywood powers-that-be.

As the weeks passed, there were times when Goldberg wondered if she would ever hear back from Steven Spielberg. Meanwhile, *The Whoopi Goldberg Show* opened on Broadway, and her professional fame began to grow, as did the rumors of whether she would finally be approved for the role of Celie. By early 1995 it was official. The part of Celie was hers; she was to be paid an extraordinary—by her standards—salary of $250,000!

Meanwhile, the rest of the mostly black cast for *The Color Purple* was assembled. Danny Glover, who had shone in *Places in the Heart* (1984) for which costar Sally Field had won an Oscar, was cast as Mister, the pivotal male role. He is a hard-hearted bastard, a farmer who marries the much-abused young Celie and continues to emotionally and physically mistreat her over the years, until she eventually rebels. Quincy Jones "discovered" Oprah Winfrey for the part of Sophia, the strong-willed black woman who marries Mister's son Harpo and later is cowed into humble submission to white folks. She was a recently arrived Chicago-based talk-show host whom he had accidentally caught on TV one day during a stopover in the Windy City.

For the crucial role of the beautiful Shug Avery, the sultry juke-joint singer who is Mister's adored mistress and ironically becomes the champion and lover of subservient Celie, the filmmakers had originally hoped to entice famed rock singer Tina Turner for the part. When she refused, Margaret Avery was eventually chosen over such possible candidates as Patti La Belle, Lola Falana, and Diana Ross. Others selected for the cast ranged from established personalities like Adolph Caesar (as Old Mister) to relative newcomers such as Rae Dawn Chong (Squeak) and Laurence Fishburne (Swain).

One of the great obstacles to bringing the project to the screen had been the preparation of an appropriate, that is, commercial, screenplay that would appeal to a broad spectrum of filmgoers. When it was decided that Alice Walker's own adaptation—her first such screenplay—did not satisfy Spielberg's vision of the film, the director had great difficulty in hiring a replacement screenwriter who was not only capable of doing the

Steven Spielberg directing Whoopi Goldberg on location in North Carolina for her first film, *The Color Purple* (1985). (Courtesy of Photofest)

Whoopi Goldberg, as Celie, finds love and understanding with blues singer Shug (Margaret Avery) in *The Color Purple*. (Courtesy of Photofest)

Whoopi as kookie Terry Doolittle in *Jumpin' Jack Flash* (1986). (Courtesy of Photofest)

Star Whoopi Goldberg and director Penny Marshall on the set of *Jumpin' Jack Flash* (1986). (Courtesy of Photofest)

Billy Crystal, Whoopi Goldberg, and Robin Williams go formal to host the fund-raiser Comic Relief (1986). (Courtesy of Photofest)

Whoopi as two of her most famous stage characters, Fontaine and the Little Blond Girl, from her one-woman show, distributed for home video (1986). (Courtesy of Photofest)

Undercover cop Whoopi Goldberg and her friend-in-need (Sam Elliott) work the mean streets in *Fatal Beauty* (1987). (Courtesy of Photofest)

As the would-be reformed cat burglar, Whoopi Goldberg finds misadventure with her San Francisco pal (Bob Goldthwait) in *Burglar* (1987). (Courtesy of Photofest)

As the ex-junkie recently released from the Betty Ford Clinic in her cable-TV special: *Whoopi Goldberg: Fontaine.... Why Am I Straight?* (1988). (Courtesy of Photofest)

Thanks to a growing friendship with her young charge (Neil Patrick Harris), a Jamaican-born domestic finds a meaningful new life in Baltimore, Maryland in *Clara's Heart* (1988). (Courtesy of Photofest)

Going dramatic as the distraught out-of-work actor in the surrealistic film *The Telephone* (1987). (Courtesy of Photofest)

Playing a young teen involved in the civil-rights movement in the South of the early 1960s— from the daytime TV special, *My Past Is My Own* (1989). (Courtesy of Photofest)

Whoopi as the sharp pool hustler in the made-for-TV movie *Kiss Shot* (1989). (Courtesy of Photofest)

Whoopi Goldberg as born-again medium Oda Mae Brown comforts Molly Jensen (Demi Moore) in *Ghost* (1990). (Courtesy of Photofest)

Whoopi as the determined housemaid protecting her employer's child (Lexi Faith Randall) in *The Long Walk Home* (1990). (Courtesy of Photofest)

Life is a constant battle for temperamental opposites (Whoopi Goldberg and Jean Stapleton) stuck at a desert truck stop in the short-lived TV sitcom *Bagdad Café* (1990-91). (Courtesy of Photofest)

job but who was interested in this very "specialized" project. Spielberg finally settled on Menno Meyjes, a Dutch-born writer who had attended college in the United States, where he had studied film. Later, one of his unproduced screenplays, *Lionheart* (about the Children's Crusade in the Middle Ages), had come to Spielberg's attention and led to his being signed to adapt *The Color Purple*. By anyone's standards it was a strange choice given the screenwriter's ethnicity, nationality, and gender. But then again, that was part of Spielberg's genius.

To achieve the desired "authenticity" for the production, it was decided initially to film *The Color Purple* in Alice Walker's hometown of Eatonton, Georgia. However, the town had become so modernized that the filmmakers had to search elsewhere. Finally, Marshville, North Carolina, a community of only a few thousand, was selected. (It was located a block off the main route between Charlotte, North Carolina, and Myrtle Beach, South Carolina.) There scenic designer Michael Riva, the grandson of Marlene Dietrich, made use of the town's existing structures, which could be dressed down to represent turn-of-the-century buildings. Other old edifices, including a sixty-year-old church scheduled for demolition, were moved to the location site on a Marshville side street. To add to the overall period atmosphere, additional building fronts were constructed on the shooting site. Meanwhile, on a former plantation in nearby Wadesboro, an authentic antebellum house was restored and reconstructed to serve as the home of Mister.

As part of Alice Walker's contract for permitting the making of *The Color Purple,* she designated that besides the mostly all black cast, at least half of the technical crew must be black, female, or of third-world origin. Complying with the demand, Spielberg chose his crew accordingly, bringing some one hundred behind-the-camera workers with him to North Carolina. Once on location, he hired over two hundred locals, who became laborers, security guards, and extras on the spread-out film site.

During the eight weeks of location work in North Carolina, the cast and crew sweltered in the over-100-degree humid climate. Most of the production team stayed at the Holiday Inn in nearby Monroe, where they could escape the extreme heat in their off-hours but could not find any public establishments serving liquor, since the town was "dry." Accompanying Whoopi on the shoot was daughter Alexandrea, who ended up with a bit role in *The Color Purple* as a walk-on crowd extra.

During the many weeks of filming, Whoopi, the fledgling film performer, took Oprah Winfrey, the fledgling actor, under her wing, and the two became fast friends, a kinship that has lasted through the years. Whoopi would remember the off-camera times during the weeks on location when she, Oprah, and Rae Dawn Chong would "sit and gab in the fucking Holiday Inn. We went to see Patti La Belle in concert. Also Springsteen. I took Oprah to buy cowboy boots. We'd talk about everything. Girl talk about guys, mostly. You know: 'Whoopi, what's the craziest thing that's ever happened to you?' And I said, 'My Rolodex.' So Oprah and I went through my Rolodex together, and she was going, 'Oooh, girl! Oh, shit! I want this number!' How we['d] just call each other 'ho.' That's for whore. . . . 'Hey ho!' "

Despite years of stage experience, Whoopi was very much the novice, and she felt a great responsibility toward the film's production. She has admitted, "I was in a panic . . . because, you know, you don't want to mess up a Steve Spielberg movie."

Fortunately, according to Goldberg, "Steven made it very easy for me to make the transition [to film from the stage]. He would say, 'There are eight million mute people in this [camera] box here. They're all in one room looking through a one-way mirror; you can't see them, but they see you. They're mute, so you can't hear them, but they hear you, and they enjoy what you're doing.' And that's how the camera became my friend."

Then, too, she adds, "Celie was in me, waiting to jump out. . . . The cat [Steven Spielberg] just gave me all kinds of faith. Plus, we had a lingo, because he's a movie fanatic like me. He would say something like 'Okay, Whoopi, do Boo Radley right after the door opens in *To Kill a Mockingbird* [1962].' Or he'd say, 'You know the scene where Indiana Jones finally finds the girl at the end? That kind of relief he has? That's what I want.' He'd give me directions like that, and I could do them because I knew what he wanted." (Spielberg would say of Whoopi's acting in *The Color Purple*: "That performance came out of her soul.")

Goldberg was also comforted by the fact that she considered Spielberg a kindred spirit, just as she had found director Mike Nichols compatible on *The Whoopi Goldberg Show* project. It all revolved around what Whoopi called presenting "the child-eye view of adult behavior." She explained the "view from a child in a grown-up's body" thusly: "I believe Spielberg is the same way, and I think that our biggest connection was that there are so many naïve ways that we have in common. That was a surprise. Because I like to think of myself as very cosmopolitan, very *in.*"

To bridge the change of acting venue from stage to screen, Whoopi kept telling herself how many parallels there were between the two mediums. "It's like doing seventy performances a day. You come in, do a piece, and somebody says, 'Cut!' The curtain comes down, and the performance is over. Then you start another one." Her courage and confidence level were also bolstered because she had rationalized thusly: "I love film. I watched movies; I knew I wanted to do that. For me the transition from the stage was not very big, because I started out with the best."

Her screen debut came down to exercising her best creative intuition and building a performance from there. She noted: "My attitude was that I drove Celie to work every day and let her off at the soundstage. But as soon as the scene was over, Celie would disappear and Whoopi would come back in full force. . . . That approach worked just fine with Steven."

However, she would later admit that she really had no standard of comparison to judge how she was doing during her first crucial filmmaking experience. Thus, when a reporter asked her, "Can you tell how you're doing when you're looking at a camera lens?," she responded, "Well, no, I can't, but I can't tell how I'm doing onstage, either, really. Even though an audience is there and will give you a response, you, as the performer, are going, 'Oh, God. Aw, man, I shouldn't a said that; that doesn't make any sense.' But it works for the audience."

Actually, Goldberg had no cause to worry about her creative output for the perfectionist Spielberg, who ruled the set with an iron hand. (The director's "dictatorial" nature was belied by his still-youthful looks, benign manner, and trademark baseball cap.) From the start he had great faith in Whoopi's screen-acting potential. This was substantiated when he shot the telling moment when beautiful Shug (Margaret Avery) sings plaintively to forlorn Celie and the two start their very special, life-affirming relationship which changes their lives forever. Goldberg handled the mimed moment wonderfully well.

Rolling Stone's Steve Erickson would later single out and praise this sequence: "In the picture's single best bit of acting Goldberg simply watches Shug, one emotion after another bubbling to the surface of that face, each bursting the emotion that came before and then waiting to be contradicted by the next." And the most amazing thing about this acting highlight was that, according to Goldberg, it was "the first scene we shot. It was also the first time I'd ever been on a soundstage."

Whoopi also vividly recalls one of the last scenes to be filmed dur-

ing the grueling schedule. It was set at the dinner table, where the
women square off against the men: "I'd spent two months not hardly
saying anything, and I was so ready to talk and [Spielberg] purposely—
which was great, you know—he built it up and boy, when he said, 'Roll
it,' it was like 'Yes! I'm ready to talk now, and I don't give a shit!' "

As the days and weeks of filming *The Color Purple* progressed, Goldberg developed confidence both in herself as an actor and in her ability to
"carry" the film. Her self-assurance allowed her to stand up to Spielberg
when she felt he was suddenly imparting the wrong nuance to her characterization. (Alice Walker would write in her personal journal, "I
cheered inwardly to see Whoopi stand toe to toe one day with Steven and
insist that Celie would not age the way he was envisioning her but would
look more like colored women do as they age. A matter of posture and
gait, not wrinkles and a white wig.")

Another who recalls Whoopi during the making of her debut feature film was casting director Reuben Cannon. He would say more than a
decade after the movie was completed, "She's the closest thing to genius
I've ever seen. [It] was the scene where Shug is introducing Celie to
herself. There's a very intimate, important part where Shug shows Celie
her face in a mirror. Spielberg yelled, 'Cut!' And Whoopi said, 'Not yet!
There's another moment.' And she was right, because Celie and Shug
needed to give each other a look. That was her first film, and she didn't
hesitate to tell Spielberg exactly what was on her mind. She had confidence in her own instincts."

During much of the first half of filming in North Carolina, Alice
Walker was on the set or nearby daily. She consulted with Spielberg and
his crew about last-minute dialogue changes, how a particular set should
be dressed to reflect reality. However, after a month or more of watching
her beloved book being translated to the screen—not as her vision but
that of Spielberg's—the physically worn out author departed to recuper-
ate back in northern California with family and friends. By then, she had
many second thoughts as to how she had sold out to Hollywood in order
to have her book and its message carried to a far wider audience than her
printed words had reached.

One of Alice Walker's gravest concerns was how Spielberg and
screenwriter Menno Meyjes had downplayed Celie's survival over the
decades and diminished the woman's ultimate victory of coming into her
own, starting a sewing business and making a home in which to welcome
her returning sister and Celie's own grown children. Instead, Spielberg

and writer Meyjes, being men, had opted to strengthen the part of Mister. Walker said, "It's just that Celie's industry is not made anything of." (Later, she would tell an interviewer that had she been directing this movie, she "would have been much more interested in showing the development of Celie under Shug's loving attention in Memphis." According to Walker, what added insult to creative injury, since Mister was based on Walker's own grandfather, was that the filmmakers had sanded away the complexities of Mister's character onscreen and made him very one-dimensional. Walker said, "To think of him reduced to one layer, and that of brutality, was a torture.")

Later, in Alice Walker's autobiographical *The Same River Twice: Honoring the Difficult* (1996), she would describe the process and her varied reactions to having *The Color Purple* brought to the screen. In the course of the detailed narrative, Walker confessed that two moments would always stand out from her filmmaking experience. One was the cultural shock of discovering that Steven Spielberg's favorite film was *Gone With the Wind* and that his favorite character in that epic was Prissy, the besieged black maid. Walker's reaction to this revelation was: "The only appropriate response would be to faint." The other defining moment for Walker was to learn that Whoopi Goldberg had never read the full *The Color Purple* script beyond her scenes.

CHAPTER FIFTEEN

And the Winner Is . . .

I don't think it'll ever be like that again. It will never
be that new or that glorious. . . . Because it was my
very, very, very first time [in a movie]—the very first
time, you know? And there will never be on-screen
again: 'And introducing . . . Whoopi Goldberg.' It
was an amazing moment of my life, to work with
Steven Spielberg and to be part of that film. So,
yeah, it can be different and exciting, but it'll never
be that moving for me again.
—WHOOPI GOLDBERG, JUNE 1987

Once the location work for *The Color Purple* was completed, the
cast and crew returned to the Hollywood soundstages where they
finished the shooting of the film. After that, Whoopi returned to
her family in San Francisco.

Meanwhile, *The Color Purple* went through weeks of editing and
other postproduction work. During this period, a growing national controversy erupted over the forthcoming release of the film. The first protest
occurred when the movie project was announced. Attorney Legrand H.
Clegg II, the leader of a Los Angeles–based group called the Coalition
Against Black Exploitation, insisted, "The elevation of Alice Walker's
book to the status of a movie will be devastating to the black community.
The book's degradation of the black male and its subtle promotion of
lesbianism as an alternative to failed heterosexual relationships convey a
negative message that is potentially destructive to the black family."

During and after the filming of the picture, Clegg and his group would hammer home their points of criticism. By the time the movie was nearly ready for its release, the very vocal Clegg and his followers were demanding a special screening of *The Color Purple* so they could judge for themselves just what was wrong with the picture. When the request was refused, several members of the coalition picketed producer Quincy Jones's production office in Los Angeles. Earl Walter Jr. declared, "We've asked some specific questions about . . . [the movie's portrayal] of incest, lesbianism and black male abuse of black women. And we aren't getting any answers."

As the arguments over *The Color Purple* grew more heated, Whoopi had her own thoughts. Her sentiments were reserved for airing publicly months after the movie's distribution. Goldberg said: "A lot of people [other factions besides the Coalition Against Black Exploitation] complain, the movie doesn't have enough lesbianism, it doesn't have enough this or enough that. And it is very cute in places. But it's necessary, because in Idaho and in Nebraska it makes it easier to ingest. It takes it out of the realm of a black movie into a people's movie."

She also "thought this furor over the treatment of black men in *The Color Purple* was a pile of shit. . . . But here you have this movie *Purple Rain* [1984—starring Prince] where women constantly get smacked around, thrown in trash cans, told to go topless in a lake, I mean, dumb, dumb shit. Nobody said a word. I don't understand it." Then, too, according to Goldberg, "it's not like . . . [*The Color Purple*] is a [concocted] lie where Steven Spielberg said, 'Oh yeah, I'm going to ruin it for black men and write this [false] stuff that happened [to the female characters due to their relationships with brutal black men].' And I resent people who use this movie as a way to get publicity for a bogus issue."

On a more positive note—which Goldberg voiced at the time *The Color Purple* was to be released—she insisted the movie was infused with universal themes: "It's not about blacks. It's not even about sexism. It's about a search of self. Celie has no idea that to be kissed you don't also have to be hit. Just look into my eyes. I know what I'm talking about. I've been around the block a few times." She also said, "It is a movie about someone discovering they have more power than they thought."

In defense of director Steven Spielberg, Goldberg said, "This film really isn't such a departure for Steven, not if you look at his work beyond the obvious special effects. *Close Encounters of the Third Kind* is really about man's search for something more than his everyday life offers him. That's what raised the film above all the other movies that were similar to it. And I feel like Celie is a lot like [the alien visitor] E.T. [in Spielberg's classic movie of the same name]. It's a whole new world of discovery for Celie, just as it was for E.T."

Whoopi further declared, "Steven [Spielberg] is able to see things because he loves movies, and this movie was a labor of love. No one else could have made it. I gave my faith and trust to him, and he gave his to me." (In retrospect, years after the movie was released, Goldberg would say, "We were lucky to come out of the running in the hands of Steve Spielberg. You know, we ate a lot of garbage about that film, but I think we all just did the best we knew, and he nurtured us. We were all like little plants. Man, he turned us into roses.")

———————

By early December 1985, *The Color Purple* was ready for release. By then the 155-minute feature had been given a PG-13 rating. Spielberg and the studio (Warner Bros.) worked hard to avoid the film's being placed in the R-rated category, which would have severely limited its box-office potential. They greatly downplayed any element of overt lesbianism in the final footage. In the movie version the telltale kiss between Celie and Shug is presented so ambiguously that it could be regarded by viewers as an act of friendship rather than a demonstration of budding sexual love.

Ironically, the physical and emotional abuse of the women characters by the menfolk in *The Color Purple* was graphically heightened without concern that more violence would contribute to a R rating. The Motion Picture Association of America, Hollywood's self-censoring review board, seldom considered onscreen violence a sufficient cause for restricting viewership to adult filmgoers only.

Increasingly curious to see how she had fared in her movie debut, Whoopi attended one of the prerelease screenings of Spielberg's newest picture. She still recalls vividly, "When I saw *The Color Purple,* I had my eyes closed. There I was with my zits five hundred feet tall."

Finally, on December 17, 1985, *The Color Purple* made its official debut in the United States. The highly imaginative, if not terribly accurate, advertising tag for the elaborate movie was: "It's about life. It's about love. It's about us. . . . Share the joy."

In reviewing this new picture, Kathleen Carroll wrote in the *New York Daily News,* "Spielberg turns . . . [the film] into a four-hankie tearjerker that reaffirms the importance of love in such a tender, inoffensive way that it could have been directed by the late Walt Disney."

David Denby in *New York* magazine declared, "The picture never stops to just observe something: it never allows a little bit of life simply to pass by. For over two hours, we look at these tumultuous doings and cardboard characters—vicious, ignorant men and saintly life-affirming women—and we have only the vaguest idea as to how they actually make a living or what their relationships with their neighbors or their community are supposed to be."

Janet Maslin in the *New York Times* reasoned, "What's more crucial is the film's peculiar unevenness and its way of combining such wild extremes. Some parts of it are rapturous and stirring, others hugely improbable, and the film moves unpredictably from one mode to another." Richard Corliss (*Time* magazine) concluded, "Everyone seems reluctant to let loose here, taking a cue from their too reverent boss." Julie Salamon (*Wall Street Journal*) argued, "From the moment this movie opens, with the pretty picture of young black women frolicking in a sunlit field of purple flowers, you get the sense that we are in for *The Sound of Music* approach of making it through hard times. Suffer a little, sing a little."

On the other hand, Gene Shalit of NBC-TV's *Today Show,* Gene Siskel of the *Chicago Tribune,* and Roger Ebert of the *Chicago Sun-Times* all praised the movie. Ebert wrote, "It is a great, warm, hard, unforgiving, triumphant movie and there is not a scene that does not shine with the love of the people who made it."

If the reviews as a whole for *The Color Purple* were mixed when comparing the film's artistic merits with the focus and strengths of Alice Walker's original novel, there was at least general consensus in other areas: The rich cinematography by Allen Daviau was excellent, Quincy Jones's lush score was more Hollywood than representative of the story's ethnic origins and the cast was mostly excellent. Whoopi herself was singled out for praise.

The entertainment trade paper *Daily Variety* reported, "As Celie, Whoopi Goldberg uses her expressive face and joyous smile to register the character's growth." Arthur Knight, in the *Hollywood Reporter,* complimented the performances, and in particular the star, "whose emergence from slavery to radiant womanhood is a joy to behold."

Sheila Benson wrote in the *Los Angeles Times:* "Like the book, the film's fondest indulgences are its female characters, the most compelling of which is Whoopi Goldberg's Celie, of the slow, incandescent smile. Her growth comes with the sweet inevitability of stop-motion flower photography, from a clenched bud to a full-blown, heavy-laden flower. It is a most touching debut."

Vincent Canby in the *New York Times* also praised the new ingenue. "The film has a star who functions much like an anchorwoman on a news show. In the early part of the film, Miss Goldberg's Celie is required simply to react to the other performers, but with her large, shrewd eyes and her big, expressive mouth, she can, by reacting, out-act everybody else on the screen. And when, near the end, Celie takes control of her life, mincing no words, the audience hoots with pleasure."

As *The Color Purple* went into North American general release, special interest groups, including the National Association for the Advancement of Colored People (NAACP), continued to speak against and picket the movie. Goldberg's acid response expressed her disgust: "If a black director had made the film, the NAACP wouldn't have said shit. The branch here [in Los Angeles] complains there's no work for black actors. So Spielberg goes mostly with unknown black actors and the NAACP says black men are depicted in a bad light, the movie's fucked up, and you shouldn't go see it."

The Color Purple went on to become a major financial hit. It would gross $80.26 million at the box office and would earn an additional $49.8 million in home-video rentals. The film's success is even more impressive when one considers the feature cost $15 million to make. (Originally budgeted at $12 million, Spielberg kept the cost down on *The Color Purple* by accepting an up-front $40,000 for his directorial assignment, which is the minimum acceptable by the directors' union. During shooting, whenever the picture went over budget, the director would tell the line producers to deduct any cost overage from his own pay.)

When the nominations for the March 1986 Academy Awards were announced, *The Color Purple* garnered eleven nominations: Best Picture, Best Screenplay Based on Material from Another Medium, Best Cinematography, Best Art Direction/Set Direction, Best Score, Best Song ("Miss Celie's Blues [Sister]"), Best Costume Design, Best Makeup, Best Actress (Whoopi Goldberg), and Best Supporting Actress (Margaret Avery, Oprah Winfrey). Ironically, Steven Spielberg was not nominated. The very obvious snub of this talented filmmaker further fueled the furor over the film. A perplexed but resigned Spielberg said, "When I'm sixty, Hollywood will forgive me. I don't know for what, but they'll forgive."

Film producer Dan Melnick observed of the academy's deliberate rebuff of Spielberg's direction of *The Color Purple*: "It's as if the nominators expressed their awe for the Sistine Chapel while snubbing Michelangelo." (Spielberg would finally win a Best Director's Oscar for his brilliant handling of 1993's *Schindler's List*.)

Despite her anger that Spielberg had been left out of the Oscar nominations, Whoopi was jubilant about being nominated for an Academy Award. It was a culmination of a long-cherished dream. "I have written and made acceptance speeches at my house since I was a little kid. It drove my mother and brother so crazy that the Oscars would come around and they would leave. They'd go into the other room and watch it on another set, because I would stand up and give this speech. So to get nominated, get the certificate, and go to the nominees' lunch was great. I know in my lifetime—I like to think—I will get one. It might not be for a while. I loved the idea of getting nominated. It's like a title— Oscar Nominee, Whoopi Goldberg."

Much as she might fantasize about winning an Academy Award as Best Actress, she had learned not to anticipate rewards before they were given. Recently, she had been highly touted as a strong contender for a Tony Award for her one-woman Broadway show and then had not even been nominated for the prestigious stage prize. Besides, Goldberg realistically understood that she was up against strong competition for the lead actor Oscar: Anne Bancroft (*Agnes of God*), Jessica Lange (*Sweet Dreams*), Geraldine Page (*The Trip to Bountiful*) and Meryl Streep (*Out of Africa*).

After weeks of anxiety, Whoopi attended the 58th Annual Academy Awards on the night of March 24, 1986, at the Dorothy Chandler Pavilion where Alan Alda, Jane Fonda, and Robin Williams were the hosts. One of the highlights of the 195-minute telecast was a segment entitled "Once a Star, Always a Star," in which onetime leading man Howard Keel serenaded such other M-G-M contract stars as June Allyson, Leslie Caron, Cyd Charisse, Kathryn Grayson, Ann Miller, Jane Powell, Debbie Reynolds, and Esther Williams. Another special moment occurred when internationally famous film directors John Huston, Akira Kurosawa, and Billy Wilder presented the Best Picture of the Year award to *Out of Africa*.

During the evening's program, in what proved to be an extremely surprising result, *The Color Purple* did *not* win a single Oscar prize. In the Best Actress category, it was veteran film and stage star Geraldine Page who was victorious for *A Trip to Bountiful*. (It was Page's eighth nomination for such a prize.) Goldberg later claimed it was no surprise that she had lost or that Page had won.

As Goldberg later explained as a guest on the *Oprah Winfrey* TV show, "[From] day one they started in with, you know, she's [Geraldine Page] been nominated eleven [actually eight] times and hadn't won and I thought, Well, this—please, God, give it to her now because I don't want all these people mad at me, you know. So I could just go and sort of have a great party [at the Oscars], you know, and be excited and stuff." (Despite the failure to receive an Oscar, Goldberg did win some trophies for her film debut. She was awarded a Golden Globe Award as well as the Image Award from the NAACP, which had a change of heart about the movie. For Whoopi, who had endured the wrath and repercussions of the NAACP's initial negative reaction to her movie, the Image Award was a bittersweet honor.)

If Whoopi did not have an opportunity to accept a Best Actress Award, she did appear before millions of TV viewers to present the Academy Award for Best Editing. The winner in that category was Thom Noble for his work on *Witness*. He was not there that night, so Goldberg got to accept the prize on his behalf. With an impish look on her face, Goldberg told millions of TV viewers, "Thom isn't here tonight. However, if he *was*, I'm sure he would have wanted to thank his mother . . . and some of us might have thanked *ours*." Everyone within hearing immediately understood it was Whoopi's creative way of thanking her parent in front of her peers.

Goldberg would later recall this impromptu Oscar episode. "My mother was sitting there, and I wanted to acknowledge her. I wanted her to know that I wanted to thank her, and so that was the best, most humorous way I could do it." Whoopi also points out that much to her chagrin, she did not "get to handle the Oscar at all. I didn't get to touch it because if they're [i.e., the winner—Thom Noble] not there, they don't give you the statue. This 'person' holds it. I wanted to say, 'Bitch! Gimme that, let me hold it for a second!' but I couldn't." On a more serious note, Goldberg has acknowledged that her on-camera words of thanks to her mother that Oscar night were not just on her behalf. "I was speaking for Steven [Spielberg] and Oprah [Winfrey] and Margaret [Avery] and Danny [Glover] and all the people who didn't get to go up on the stage at all."

After the ceremonies, she disappeared, not showing up at any of the postshow parties. It was not because she was angry. "People assumed that," she would later confide. "I was ready to go party. Are you crazy? I had [actor] Michael J. Fox with me, and we were going to boogie all night. Instead, while I was presenting the editing award, I got very sick. I have ovarian cysts, and one burst while I was standing there. On tape, you can see me lean on the podium. I was in pain! Poor Michael ended up taking me to the hospital."

Looking back at her Oscar defeat, Goldberg would reason later, "I was probably lucky not to win. If I had, there'd have been nowhere for me to go. People would have wondered if I was just a flash in the pan. Now they'll wait for me to get better."

However, in retrospect, Whoopi remained extremely angry at the NAACP's picketing of the film and even the Oscar Awards ceremony and the effect it had on her career. "I gave the Hollywood chapter of the NAACP the big old finger during *The Color Purple* thing . . . which cost us, I believe, an Academy Award for that film. All the fervor that the NAACP created, saying the film misrepresented blacks and how could this white guy do this movie. . . . It just was insane to me."

Goldberg learned and realized years later that the storm of protest surrounding *The Color Purple* reaffirmed to white establishment Hollywood that despite the potential profits of a mainstream black-oriented film, such projects were fraught with political repercussions. Part of the film industry backlash was to brand *The Color Purple*'s leading players— especially Goldberg and Oprah Winfrey—as personalities too closely associated with troublesome moviemaking. Goldberg said, "To this day, I feel that there is a sour taste in the mouths of Academy members as far as black projects are concerned because of the NAACP's stance." She further explained, "I realized that we had shot ourselves in the foot for five years because nobody wanted to make movies with us for fear that there was going to be this terrible backlash. So when the NAACP cut us off at the knees, they in fact cut film out from under us for five years."

As a coda, Whoopi is the first to point out: "By the way, after the Oscars, the same branch of the NAACP bitched because *The Color Purple* didn't win anything. That says there's some bullshit floating around here."

Later, in December 1990, Goldberg was designated the NAACP's Entertainer of the Year. It was an irony not lost on Whoopi, who accepted the award from the group who had made her life miserable during and after the filming of *The Color Purple* because she felt she deserved it. Goldberg told the assembled NAACP membership that while she appreciated their tribute, "I really could have used your help several years ago when you kicked my butt about stuff that was untrue. So thanks for this, maybe this means we've both grown up."

CHAPTER SIXTEEN

Flavor of the Month

I'm living out a whole lot of people's dreams and fantasies, and it's up to me to have the best time I possibly can.

—WHOOPI GOLDBERG, DECEMBER 1984

In late 1985, *People* named Whoopi one of the twenty-five most intriguing people of the year. The magazine profiled her—the new national craze—in her modest home in an unpretentious neighborhood of Berkeley. The magazine's interviewer noted that when off-camera, Whoopi wore a dental retainer. ("When I got my wisdom teeth out, my teeth started moving.") The reporter also observed that the rising star kept a huge crock of Turkish taffy on the fireplace mantel and that she was an incessant chain-smoker. Her household boasted two adopted kittens who were named Bud and Lou, after the comedy team of Abbott and Costello. Among Goldberg's other possessions were a stack of books in her bedroom, which included novels by Alexander Solzhenitsyn and Anaïs Nin, a biography of writer Yukio Mishima, and a history of the Polish Solidarity movement.

According to *People*'s chronicler, strewn about Whoopi's house were heaps of videocassettes and an alarm clock bearing on its face the photo of New York City's Guardian Angels. On the coffee table in her living room she had a Mickey Mouse telephone, and in another downstairs room there was a framed original of Abe Hirschfeld's caricature-style cartoon depicting her dressed as six characters from her one-woman stage show. The same room also boasted a framed honorary degree from the University of Charleston in West Virginia, which read: "To experience

134

Whoopi Goldberg is to expand your mind, awaken your conscience and view the world through new eyes. . . ."

Whoopi told *People*'s readership that she intended to remain level-headed despite her current career success. She was proud that she had been able to assist financially her actor-playwright friends at the Blake Street Hawkeyes with their production of the musical *Tokens*. She reasoned aloud, "I've been taken care of by people, so I'm continuing the tradition. That's why I live here. This is where I know people will say, 'Hey, don't get Hollywood with me: I remember when I had to drive you to the welfare office.' I depend on my friends for that, to keep my ego in check, 'cause it's real easy to go the other way."

According to Goldberg—at least publicly—she desired nothing more than to attend PTA meetings as a responsible single parent, take and give acting classes, and shop in neighborhood stores without being the center of attraction. She professed that she wanted to remember "how to be a real person, not turn into this parody of myself, which is very easy to do. . . . I don't want to wake up one morning and find myself having slipped into darkness."

Despite Goldberg's wish to remain rooted in reality, it was tough to do. She was already fast becoming a household name across America as a quirky, interesting entertainer—someone imbued with today's sensibilities. Then, too, she had been "adopted" by a wide variety of Hollywood's screen luminaries during her visits to the movie capital, where she often stayed at the Hotel Chateau Marmont. Her pals in Southern California included Robin Williams, William Hurt, and Timothy Hutton, who treated her like a peer. She explained: "These are people I'd like to work with because I know they're gonna challenge me, and I can't wait. *I can't wait!* I hope I'm not sounding like a goody two shoes, but I used to dream about acting. I wanted this, and they handed it to me on a silver platter."

Goldberg also admitted she was no longer a practicing Catholic: "I still believe in God. I don't agree with everything the Catholics are into, but I also don't agree with everything the Jews are into or the Buddhists and all the other religions I encompass and embrace. I'm kinda formulating my own." Regarding downplaying her sensuality, she insisted that it was intentional: "I myself am rather asexual. I prefer that, in work and dress and things, because it's easier for people to see you talking about doing different roles if they're not looking at this particularly sensual thing."

Asked about her current goals, she replied: "What I really want is someday to walk by some people and hear them talking about me. Maybe they'll be saying that they don't like me personally but they'll say this girl is not just a flash in the pan. She's doing work she's always wanted to, and I'm glad."

Interestingly enough, in talking to the press about a wide variety of topics, Whoopi had little to say about her daughter, Alexandrea, now a teenager. Perhaps she was intentionally protecting her youngster from the glare of the public spotlight. As for her longtime lover, David Schein, who was drifting out of her life, she now referred to him as "my semiboyfriend." She reflected: "I came to New York and did my show, and it was tough on him, so he went away." David, who still writes plays, eventually relocated to Chicago.

In mid-1984, Whoopi insisted, "I feel like I'm blazing a trail for normal-looking people. Yeah, I mean, I'm blazing a trail for the art of acting, I hope." Once she returned to Berkeley after the closing of her one-woman Broadway show, there was no way she could lead an average—let alone normal—existence. While the glitterati of New York City had courted Goldberg during her successful stage run, the Hollywood set outdid itself to make her part of its lavish social scene.

For some in the film colony, Goldberg offered the dramatic allure of being an ex-junkie and a former welfare mother, a person who had risen from adversity to stardom. For others, this outspoken, oddly garbed, and strangely coiffed female provided the opportunity to demonstrate political correctness. There were, of course, other entertainment figures, like Robin Williams, Elizabeth Taylor, Dustin Hoffman, and Billy Crystal, honestly drawn to this unique, multitalented woman who was insistently different and multidimensional compared to the average Tinseltown newcomer.

Who can blame Caryn Johnson, the former street person from the projects, for being overwhelmed by her welcome in the most fashionable and hippest circles that Hollywood had to offer. The outspoken, one-of-a-kind Whoopi now found herself invited to nearly every major happening on the Los Angeles social scene. And since she obviously stuck out in any crowd, she became a favorite subject of the paparazzi. During the height of the media blitz, they sold a slew of candid photos to the press depicting Goldberg going to, participating in, and leaving an array of Southern California A-list parties.

Whoopi might turn up at a Los Angeles art-gallery opening, or she might be found attending an antidrug fund-raiser hosted by first lady Nancy Davis Reagan. As the media would duly report, Whoopi flocked to these outings, obviously as enthralled at being the center of attention as her hosts were in having snared her for their latest entertainment function. Typically, Goldberg could be observed at such diversions engrossed in serious conversation with other celebrity attendees. It was a wild, heady period for Whoopi and one on which she thrived.

When asked what she, the newcomer, talked about with these notables, who generally had a far different background, Whoopi said, "I'm pretty up-front about whatever's going on in whatever company I'm in. It's easier for people to judge where I go and forget what I do. If I show up somewhere, it takes on a new connotation. People aren't sure where I'm at with my politics. It's true that I hang out with people who make lots and lots of money. But I'm talking my politics to their politics, and we get into a good discussion. Which they might never hear otherwise, because the people they hang out with wouldn't have my politics. Maybe you can even alter their politics, but you have to be open to them. You can't just say, *Oh, you believe that? Well, I think you're f——ed!* But from the outside, all people see is where I'm hanging out, and they go, Oh, of course! She's selling out!"

Without a doubt, Whoopi was thrilled to rub elbows with such esteemed company. She could be as starstruck as the next person. "[T]he scary thing is you get there and they know you, "she said. "They know who you are! So you'll be coming out of the bathroom or something, and someone'll stumble back onto your feet, and you're just about to say, 'Hey, look.' And they turn around and it's, like, Gene Kelly. And he goes, 'Oh, Whoopi, I'm sorry,' and it's like— And you have this conversation with them, and you want to say, 'I can't believe I'm standing here talking to you; I'm dying.' "

Another time, she would remember: "I had appeared at an AIDS benefit that Elizabeth had organized. Afterwards, Elizabeth came up to me and handed me a slip of paper. 'Whoopi, this is my private home telephone number. Call me sometime and let's get together.' " Elizabeth Taylor said that to ME! But what do I do about it now? Do I dial that number and say, 'Hey, Liz, this is Whoopi. Whatcha doin' tonight? . . . Wanna go get a burger?' "

It never occurred to Whoopi that her being invited to an array of choice social functions was perhaps motivated by any number of ulterior purposes. Caught up in the flattering rush of attention, it did not seem to enter into Goldberg's head that she might be overexposing herself on the social front. It was not part of her thought pattern at the time that her celebrity status would reach the point where, in the more jaded Hollywood enclaves, she would become passé as the next crop of offbeat personalities arrived.

Eventually, this realization came crashing down on Whoopi in a most cruel manner. Having gobbled up Goldberg's novelty value in their ongoing saturation of overreportage, the media began to cast sly innuendos that perhaps this Oscar-nominated actor was overdoing a good thing far too often. Soon the buzz around town was that Whoopi was so compulsively and egotistically drawn to celebrity social events that "she'd go to the opening of an envelope."

When Goldberg finally understood that for many she had become a "joke," she was emotionally devastated and embarrassed. "That hurt very deeply," she later told a *Los Angeles Times* interviewer. "I guess no one realized how new all of this was to me." It left her tremendously vulnerable, which she covered up as best she could with an air of bravado and indifference. In the end, though, it was a bitter lesson about being a celebrity that she learned the hard way. It made her increasingly cynical and far more discriminating, to the point where she became relatively reclusive when it came to any socializing with film-industry luminaries. This huge slap in the face from the media forever spoiled her naive enthusiasm about being part of the mainstream social set in the entertainment business. Even years later, in 1990, she could not forget how cruelly the press had treated her infatuation and enthusiasm with celebrity nightlife. At that point, she told the *Los Angeles Times*'s Pat H. Broeske: "Now every time I go anywhere or do anything, it is always in the back of my mind whether or not I want to read about myself in the morning. I guess all that I am interested in reading about, so far as I am concerned, is how I affected you in a film."

Before she starred in *The Color Purple,* Whoopi had entertained a few film offers, most of which sought to exploit her singular personality in a potentially career damaging way. After she played Celie, she found herself in a similar situation for different reasons.

Back in mid-1984, Whoopi had said, "I want to be a character actor. A working character actor. The ZaSu Pitts of the eighties." However, her having enjoyed a key role in *The Color Purple* and the ensuing Oscar nomination made that goal a noncareer option for the ambitious Goldberg. She was now on the Hollywood fast track. She reasoned that she should follow up her on-camera role as Celie with something of equal or even greater importance. She told her agents and others, as she had with her stage work, that she did not want her film career to be limited by her race, gender, or looks. It was Goldberg's optimistic belief that if she dreamed big—without narrowing down her options by virtue of "accepted" screen-casting conventions, prejudices, and dictates—she could somehow convince the studio top executives to give her a wide variety of important, career-building movie parts. She was very wrong.

Throughout Hollywood's history, blacks—like other minority groups—have been treated poorly by filmmakers. In the early years, silent movies depicted African Americans as household domestics working for whites or, at the other end of the spectrum, as jungle savages. During the fledgling years of American moviemaking, as on the Broadway stage, such roles were frequently played by whites in blackface.

By the 1930s black actors, such as Louise Beavers, Willie Best, and Stepin Fetchit were hired to play African Americans on-camera, even if the only parts they could obtain were as servants or African natives. When an occasional black stage star such as Paul Robeson arrived on the entertainment scene, he had to go abroad to find screen roles that barely matched his massive talents. In a rare exception in highly segregated Hollywood, a black performer actually could win an Academy Award, as did Hattie McDaniel in 1939, when she received the Best Supporting Actress Oscar for her spunky portrayal of Mammy in *Gone With the Wind*.

There were also blacks like Bill "Bojangles" Robinson, a talented tap dancer and vaudeville personality who made a limited mark in American movies of the thirties. His celluloid success was largely relegated to dancing and singing on-camera with child star Shirley Temple. Trumpeter-bandleader Louis "Satchmo" Armstrong suffered a similar fate, playing musical specialty numbers to support major white movie stars. Meanwhile, a separatist black cinema had arisen in the United States. It was filled with very low budget, often crudely fashioned films (compared to

Hollywood's standards) geared to play in separate black cinema houses located mostly in urban centers.

In the World War II era of the 1940s a cadre of Hollywood black talent emerged—Lena Horne, the Nicholas Brothers, Dooley Wilson—who were relegated to specialty acts in mainstream American films. Typically, they appeared in self-contained musical sequences which could be deleted when the pictures were distributed in the still-segregated South.

In the next decade, the fifties, such black personalities as Dorothy Dandridge, Sammy Davis Jr., Harry Belafonte, Sidney Poitier, Diahann Carroll, and Eartha Kitt tried to become major Hollywood stars fashioned in the "conventional" white mold. However, they found their career options severely limited by filmmakers fearful of breaking down the color barriers on-screen. Of the newcomers, Poitier proved to be the most resilient of the black contingent. By the 1960s he was allowed to demonstrate his acting versatility in mainstream pictures—many of which established precedents for those black performers who would follow—and he even won a Best Actor Academy Award for *Lilies of the Field* (1963).

In the 1970s a surprising—given the bigoted climate of the day—trend hit Hollywood. It was the age of black-exploitation cinema, which began essentially with Melvin Van Peebles's *Sweet Sweetback's Baadasssss Song* (1971), a low-budget film about an urban black rebel, and gained momentum with *Shaft* (1971), an M-G-M feature. In it Richard Roundtree played a hip, upscale black private eye who roamed the streets of Manhattan, rousting his clients' enemies by day and bedding a bevy of curvaceous women by night. Before the black film cycle wore itself out in the late 1970s, a number of black action movies were churned out by mainstream Hollywood. These entries exploited the black idiom and lifestyle in colorful, often violent films that ranged from *Slaughter* (1972) and *Superfly* (1972) to *The Soul of Nigger Charley* (1973) to *Blacula* (1972) and on to *Coffy* (1973), *Three the Hard Way* (1974), and *Foxy Brown* (1974). Before the era of black-exploitation films expired, the genre made stars—of sorts—of ex–football players Fred Williamson and Jim Brown, as well as shapely Pam Grier, wily Ron O'Neal, and karate-chopping Jim Kelly, among others. By the end of the decade, genre overexposure had created such a backlash in white Hollywood that black-exploitation films and its several stars were relegated mostly to screen history.

One of the few African Americans in Hollywood to professionally survive the 1970s black action movie craze was outrageous, in-your-face comedian Richard Pryor. He rode to fame costarring with white funnyman Gene Wilder (*Silver Streak*, 1976; *Stir Crazy*, 1980; etc.) and through such stand-up, solo-comedy concert films as *Richard Pryor Live on the Sunset Strip* (1982). (Unfortunately, Pryor's near-death experience from freebasing drugs in 1980 stalled his screen career, just as being stricken with multiple sclerosis would later effectively halt his show-business life.) Meanwhile, another black comedian, Eddie Murphy, an alumnus of TV's *Saturday Night Live*, arrived on the mainstream American film scene with such major big-studio hits as *48 HRS.* (1982), *Trading Places* (1983), and *Beverly Hills Cop* (1984). With such credentials, Murphy soon became one of the highest-priced film talents of the 1980s. However, like Pryor, Murphy was the great exception within the still-white-controlled Hollywood environment.

Thus, as Whoopi and her management descended on Hollywood to select her follow-up vehicles, she had to cope with the ingrained way the studios dealt with and controlled blacks in films. It also didn't help that mainstream movie executives thought of her as a too vocal personality who boasted of her own agenda—circumventing discriminatory casting at the movie studios.

Goldberg declared, "I can make myself *into* anything. I am going to *fight* to do roles that people would never send to me, that they would never consider me for, because their state of thinking is not advanced. The *country's* thinking is advanced. The country can take anything." She also said, "My job as an actor is to be a chameleon—to be able to do anything that's put before me. That's the art."

She also acknowledged: "I have credibility as an actor, as a good actor, and as a funny person. So people are saying, 'Oh, wow! We could use Whoopi on this. She could bring something different to it.' Still, I found some scripts that I really liked, but I'm getting resistance to having me do them, for old Hollywood reasons: 'Well, you know, we want somebody more beautiful who can make people believe this man could fall in love.' And I'm saying, 'Where's the magic in Hollywood, then? If you can't make me beautiful, then there *is* no magic here.' And they say, 'Well, it was an easy choice for [Steven] Spielberg to put you in *The Color Purple*.' And I say, 'That's a pile. That's garbage. Because the job of an actor is to take a given role and make it work.'"

Part of her campaign to buck the Hollywood system was to be confrontational with studio executives. As she outlined her modus operandi, she would say to the industry's decision makers: " 'Why are you making these movies like this?' 'I want to make this movie.' 'I would like to work with this person. You interested?' 'Why won't you let me read for this?' 'I heard you won't let me read for this. Is that true?' And they go, 'Well, no, it's not that it's not true, but you know.' And I go, 'Well, why? Don't you think I'm good?' And it's not done in a mean way; it's just that I'm trying to understand why everything takes so long. Why there's so much bullshit in the process of making a good movie. Why people settle on half-baked, half-assed stuff when it's so much easier to do it right."

Or another occasion, she would describe her goal as "I don't want them to say, 'Oh, she's a black actor, we can't use her.' I want them to say, 'Oh, here's a great role. Call Meryl Streep. Call Diane Keaton. Call Whoopi Goldberg.' "

But Hollywood power brokers were not listening to Whoopi's wishful thinking. It was bad enough for her ego and career momentum that her brazenness was not producing the desired results with studio executives. To make matters worse, they, in turn, kept advising her that she should alter, that is, dilute, her unique self to fit more into the acceptable Hollywood mold—as if that were even possible for her to do. Despite years of overcoming prejudice and insistence on stereotypical conformity, idealistic Goldberg was shocked at the Hollywood system and what it wanted to do to her. "I was too naive. I couldn't believe anybody would bring you somewhere and then want you to change. These guys would say very delicately, 'Whoopi, maybe you should do something with that—you know.' . . . And I would go, 'What?' They would go, 'You know.' I would have to say, 'You mean, my hair. You want me to change my hair? No, I'm not going to change my hair.' "

Sticking firmly to her beliefs, Whoopi kept attacking the movie industry. Meanwhile, she made use of her novelty presence by appearing in a wide range of television assignments. They ranged from costarring with Carol Burnett, Carl Reiner, and Robin Williams in a 1986 ABC-TV comedy special to playing a street-savvy con artist named Camille on a May 1986 segment of the TV series *Moonlighting*. For the latter guest-starring role she was nominated for an Emmy.

Eventually, a new screen role did come her way, but only thanks to Shelley Long, the blond ex-star of the enormously popular TV sitcom *Cheers*.

CHAPTER SEVENTEEN

Hurdling Jumpin' Jack Flash

I had to make those "shoot 'em up" movies. *Jack Flash* was just a full, blown-out, silly, fluffy movie. *Burglar* was the same thing. I loved them. I know it's politically incorrect, but I do love them. I love blowing up buildings and shooting the bad guy. What I really wanted to be was the gangster, but I knew they would never let me be that. Fun movies. They were never meant to cure cancer, only to take away the mind.

—WHOOPI GOLDBERG, NOVEMBER 1992

Shelley Long had a professional background in improvisational theater and local-TV-news, magazine-style telecasting. In 1977, at the age of twenty-eight, she moved from Fort Wayne, Indiana, to Los Angeles, where she appeared in failed television-series pilots, took guest roles in television series, and won semileads in low-budget films such as *A Small Circle of Friends,* (1980). All of which led to her participating in better-quality movies: *Night Shift* (1982) with Michael Keaton, and *Losin' It* (1983), with a fast-rising Tom Cruise. She debuted in the TV sitcom *Cheers* as Diane Chambers, the high-minded, prissy bar waitress who suffers a love-hate relationship with the pub's womanizing owner-bartender, played by Ted Danson. *Cheers* became a bigger hit with each succeeding year. Shelley agreed to make a quirky romantic comedy entitled *Sweet Dreams* (a.k.a. *Knock Knock*) during her 1985 summer hiatus from *Cheers*. However, she and the film studio, Twentieth Century–Fox, had artistic differences over the shape of this quasi-romance, quasi-spy outing. As a result, she dropped out of the screen project.

All this occurred while Whoopi Goldberg was making her assault on Hollywood. Somewhere along the way, Barry Diller, then head of Twentieth Century–Fox, and the movie's producers, Lawrence Gordon and Joel Silvers, thought that Goldberg would be a good substitute for Shelley Long in their stalled screen comedy. They planned to revamp the project so that it would be more like a *Beverly Hills Cop* (1984). The studio reasoned that if black stand-up comedians like Richard Pryor and, especially, Eddie Murphy could succeed in movies—particularly action hits—then why not Goldberg. That Pryor and Murphy were males and better suited to on-camera action than Whoopi did not seem to enter into the equation. Nor was it considered relevant that Whoopi, a far better actor than Pryor or Murphy, could have adapted to romantic comedy— the original intention of this project.

Whoopi eventually accepted the Twentieth Century–Fox film offer for several reasons. It was a chance to work in a mainstream action comedy. She would be the lead actor. Her negotiated fee was close to $1 million, and she needed something creative to do. In discussing the projected film with the press—which many of them considered quite a surprising "comedown" after her dramatic role in *The Color Purple*— Goldberg insisted that she relished the idea of doing something different. She said facetiously: "My life's dream, of course, is to play a swashbuckling pirate-detective, you know. And this film gives me a little leeway to do that."

Whoopi's statements to the media were, of course, rationalizations for the reality that a job was a job. However, she also displayed such a wonderful knack of convincing herself of her "real" reasons for doing the project that she actually came to believe her own hype. She was forthright and accurate when she mentioned her concern that the movie was being rewritten "to 'fit' it to me, which is a terrible mistake, because you don't want to fit it to me, you want it to be full enough to where you don't have to get crazy but blank enough where you can add stuff and build it."

In the course of adapting the screenplay to "suit" Whoopi's talents, seventeen writers were involved in the revisions of the movie, now retitled *Jumpin' Jack Flash,* named after a popular song by the Rolling Stones. The transformation reflected the studio's decision to change the film's leading role from a kooky, romantic heroine, as Shelley Long would have played it, to a bizarre asexual individual, dressed in absurd, oversized, unfeminine clothing. As such, Whoopi's character can love, but only from afar, the heroic British spy whom she rescues in the course of the movie. This all fit in with Hollywood's conception at the time that a performer such as Goldberg—who was black, offbeat, and unconventional in looks—could *never* attract the physical love of a handsome leading man on-screen. This was especially true because Twentieth Century–Fox intended to keep the cast roster basically white—to appeal to middle America—despite the presence of African-American Whoopi. (It would be a recurring theme of Goldberg's Hollywood features that she would rarely be cast with other African-American players, thus making her screen characters seem quite removed from the black community. As a result, many black filmgoers had difficulty in relating to Whoopi's film characters.)

To its credit, *Jumpin' Jack Flash* boasted an extraordinarily talented cast, many of whom were burgeoning comedians: Carol Kane, Annie Potts, Jon Lovitz, Phil Hartman, Jim Belushi. However, neither they nor the more "serious" members of the acting team were allowed much chance to give their potentially interesting characterizations any dimension in the final hodgepodge that was the script.

Only later would Whoopi reveal some of the behind-the-scenes misadventures in making what became a problem-plagued film: "It's a mistake to try to rewrite things for me. Only I can take the material that's already there and have some fun with it. They'd said I could—which is why I said yes to the script. Eventually, I sat in a room with an executive, who said, 'Well, I know we promised you all this, but frankly we've got you. You have signed on the dotted line. You have to make this movie, and you're going to do it *this* way.'"

Whoopi continued to protest the watering down of her once-engaging screen character, who had now become a foul-mouthed generic weirdo. She recalled: "They were trying to be so careful not to point her up as being black that what they did was they made her so bland that she was boring. And I said, 'What's the difference between Shelley Long and me or Meryl Streep and me or Robert De Niro? Well—no, there isn't. Scriptwise, I mean. I could fall in love just as quick as Shelley Long could."

Weeks dragged on as the revisions piled up. Finally, the movie was set to begin production on October 21, 1985, in New York and Los

Angeles, even though the script was going through yet additional re-writes. After a few days of actual shooting, Howard Zieff, the film's direc-tor, found himself released from the project. Goldberg said, "What happened? . . . I don't know what happened. I had nothing to do with it, though they made it seem that I did. The producer just called me one day and said, 'We're changing directors.' I don't know what happened. I just know it was awful. I don't think they should do such things."

Years later, Penny Marshall, comedian turned movie director, would reveal another piece of the *Jumpin' Jack Flash* production puzzle—how she came to make her film directing debut with this feature. As she told TV late-night talk-show host Greg Kinnear, she was having lunch with Whoopi Goldberg shortly after Howard Zieff had left the project. Whoopi told her, "Penny, why don't you do it? You'd be great as a director." Penny reportedly replied that she had never directed anything and had never thought about directing. (Actually, Marshall had replaced Jonathan Demme as director of the 1986 screen comedy *Peggy Sue Got Married* but then had been replaced herself by Francis Ford Coppola.) In any event, Goldberg and Marshall supposedly approached coproducer Joel Silver about their idea. He liked the concept, and the rest is history.

If the above story is true, Whoopi came to regret her casting inspi-ration, because neither she nor Penny saw eye to eye during the course of filming, which finally finished in early March 1986. Goldberg would admit to Pat H. Broeske in an April 1990 *Los Angeles Times Calendar* section piece: "We disagreed over a lot of things—including the tone of the comedy. Penny wanted it big and broad. I like subtlety."

At another time, Whoopi fumed, "No. Donald Duck could have directed that film and the producers would have gotten what they got. Penny Marshall [of TV slapstick sitcom *Laverne & Shirley* fame] should have been the actor in the movie. We clashed, because I had been on the movie for a while before they brought her in and had been going in a specific direction. The producers had given me some leeway to play with things, and she had her own very definite idea of how it was going to go. There were times when she'd be standing behind the camera giving me nuances as I was working, as the camera was rolling, showing me what she wanted to see." (This was all in sharp contrast to Whoopi's excellent working relationship with Mike Nichols onstage and Steven Spielberg on *The Color Purple*.)

By the time *Jumpin' Jack Flash* was released, in October 1986, Whoopi's starring assignment had gone through a myriad of alterations, turning her character into a nearly unisex, quirky, swearing action "hero." Regarding her on-screen role in the completed project, Goldberg was quoted in the film's press kit as saying: "She is an offbeat kind of girl. She reads spy novels and watches old movies and has a good time by herself. She is a normal person in an abnormal situation. It's not so much what happens to her but how she reacts to what happens to her that makes her fun."

Actually, Whoopi's Terry Doolittle is a screwball character who wears funky clothes, keeps an assortment of strange toy animals on her office desk, and jive-talks to anyone in sight. She is a whiz data-entry operator in the foreign-exchange department of a major New York City bank. Bored by her repetitive job, she rebels at authority and is equally eccentric and messy in her bachelor-girl home life. One day, her computer terminal is accessed by a mystery hacker, Jonathan Pryce, with the handle "Jumpin' Jack Flash." As it develops, the interloper is a British spy trapped in unfriendly territory, Communist Eastern Europe. He implores her to help him find his way back to safety. She agrees to do so, which leads her into overactive physical contact with an assortment of madcap killers, spies, and traitors. Undaunted, she dons disguises and uses her wits and survival techniques to obtain the needed data to assist Jumpin' Jack Flash. In the process, she falls in love with him just on the strength of his e-mailed notes to her. Eventually, her efforts lead to his rescue, and she now dreams of finally meeting him. When he breaks a dinner date to thank her, she is heartbroken. However, he eventually appears, and in a Cinderella-type finale, her Prince Charming asks her to lunch. End of movie.

As expected, the critics were not enthusiastic about the mishmash known as *Jumpin' Jack Flash*. In the *Village Voice*, Jan Hoffman likened Whoopi's screen character to a "black take" on Marlo Thomas's old sitcom *That Girl* and to Mary Richards (of TV's *The Mary Tyler Moore Show*), "the screwball single working girl." Hoffman wrote: "The film wallows in the predictable. Whoopi's shtick is always played against targets big as elephants: wealthy people, British aristocrats, police, bank managers." Vincent Canby complained in the *New York Times*, "She's a volatile natural resource that can't easily be contained by means as frail and soft-headed as those offered by *Jumpin' Jack Flash,* her first and—let's hope—her worst motion-picture comedy."

Jeffrey Ressner (*Hollywood Reporter*) said: "Goldberg has the chance to camp it up royally in a couple of scenes, but otherwise her brand of humor leans heavily on four-letter street jive. In fact, she swears so often you get the feeling the movie might make even Eddie Murphy blush." He added, "Most of the yuks are below-the-belt jabs, including a questionable climax where she escapes a tough jam by biting a villain's crotch."

On a positive level, Michael Wilmington wrote in the *Los Angeles Times* that if this would-be comedy "proves anything, it's that its star, Whoopi Goldberg, is an absolute movie natural: She can shine in the most ragged circumstances. . . . She makes *Jumpin' Jack Flash* seem a lot hipper than it really is, revving it up past its meager potential."

David Ansen in *Newsweek* advised: "Forget the silly story; the fun is in the hip one-liners, the interplay between Whoopi and her coworkers at the bank, the spectacle of a bewigged Goldberg sneaking into a British Consulate ball masquerading as a Supreme." He concluded, "Two things are clear: the movie provides a generous helping of laughs, and Whoopi proves herself a screen comedian with a long and bright future ahead of her."

Made at a cost of $15 million, the picture grossed only $11 million in domestic film rentals in the United States and Canada. However, it did fairly well overseas and became, when released to home video, an extremely popular rental item. As a result, the movie turned a profit.

Whoopi would later declare, "Making that movie was awful. It was a fucking terrible experience that made me an ugly person, and I didn't like that. The fact that the film has done well is no consolation. None. The producers wanted me to be the female answer to Eddie Murphy. But I'm not the black female answer to anybody. At the outset they said, 'We want something original. You put it together with the writers.' They went through a lot of fucking writers. But very little of what you see on the screen was on paper. It's me."

She also complained, "I got the 'artistic-control' *handshake* in the beginning, but I've learned never to assume anything again. From now on, every minute detail will be spelled out in my contract so that I know where I stand at all times. It was quite an education—like graduate school. . . . I'm not even positive that the producers wanted to make this movie work. It's a piece of shit that flew for some reason. It flies because I'm cute in it. It doesn't have any redeeming quality, and it's not a great performance."

———————————

By the time Whoopi had completed shooting *Jumpin' Jack Flash,* in March 1986, life in the fast lane had accelerated even more for her. In mid-January, she had been named Female Star of the Year at the ShoWest industry trade convention in Las Vegas. She was the first black woman to receive such an award, which she happily accepted at the conference in mid-February in the gaming capital.

Of even more importance to Goldberg was her participation in the founding of *Comic Relief.* The concept was the brainchild of established producer-screenwriter Bob Zmuda, who had previously organized an American Cancer Society benefit for the late comedian Andy Kaufman. It was Zmuda's idea to gather together a group of prominent Los Angeles–based stand-up comedians and have them appear at a fund-raiser on behalf of the homeless. Among the first to volunteer were Robin Williams, Billy Crystal, and their pal Whoopi.

From the start, it became a crucial cause for Goldberg. "I was a welfare mother. I could be a welfare mother again. . . . I have lived on skid row. . . . And I could again. That's why I'm doing *Comic Relief.*" Furthermore, she said, "I don't understand how people are living in dumpsters . . . how we can cut budgets [for the poor]. There's more than enough opportunity here [in the United States]." To prepare for the event, she and her copartners did on-site research. "We went to shelters, and we read articles about the homeless. A guy said to Billy [Crystal], 'Just tell them we're NOT all bums.' . . . It was a great response. Kids called up wanting to know if they could send in a dollar. Everybody wanted to help, because it was *us,* all of us, taking care of us."

To promote the *Comic Relief* event, Goldberg, Williams, and Crystal flew to Washington, D.C. in March 1986 for a press conference that included Sen. Edward M. Kennedy. Next, the trio flew to New York City to meet with the press and hype the event. They stayed at the plush Hotel Pierre in a $1,000-a-night suite, which led one Manhattan reporter to ponder the bizarre thought of talking with these celebrities about the 2 million homeless while they were in such a swank setting. He noted that a nearby buffet table offered lobster and caviar.

A few days later, on Saturday, March 29, the highly touted, sold-out fund-raiser was held at the expansive Universal Amphitheater in Los Angeles. Among those performing were Steve Allen, George Carlin, Sid Caesar, Dick Gregory, Michael J. Fox, Bob Hope, Michael Keaton, Jerry Lewis, Weird Al Yankovic, and Henny Youngman. Goldberg, Williams, and Crystal were the masters of ceremonies at the star-studded happening. They made their opening appearance dressed in tuxedos. The formal outfit made Goldberg look both cute and unisexual. As both a master of ceremonies and a performer, it was the first time that Whoopi, used to doing comedy skits, did real stand-up in which she had to deliver a barrage of funny one-liners. It proved to be a nerve-racking experience for her. It is very noticeable that she defers throughout the lengthy program to spotlight-grabbing and quite manic Williams and Crystal, who were used to working together in impromptu skits.

Comic Relief was packaged in conjunction with HBO, which aired the event as a cable network special. Excerpts of the lengthy live show were later released as a home video, which proved very successful. All proceeds from the multimedia charity show went to projects in the National Health Care for the Homeless program.

Initially, Comic Relief was intended to be a onetime thing. However, it was so successful, raising over $2 million, that the founders and its guiding figures, Whoopi, Robin, and Billy, were asked to repeat the event year after year. It became an American institution and one forever after closely associated with Goldberg, Williams, and Crystal. Another offshoot of this high-profile charity affair was that, over the years, it gave added credence to Goldberg as humane. Increasingly, as her career prospered, Whoopi would become involved in a myriad of charities as spokesperson, fund-raiser, or advocate. Another offshoot of Comic Relief was that it bolstered her professional career. In a similar fashion with Jerry Lewis and his Multiple Dystrophy Telethon, Comic Relief became such a well-regarded and highly promoted event that Whoopi gained many new fans and reinforced the support of loyal followers by her unstinting efforts on behalf of this almost yearly event.

CHAPTER EIGHTEEN

Viva Las Vegas

Of course, nobody has asked me about my first
husband [who is black] because nobody wants to
know about that.
—WHOOPI GOLDBERG, MARCH 1991

After her initial experiences in Hollywood moviemaking—especially *Jumpin' Jack Flash*—it was clear to Whoopi that because she was black, female, and unconventional in looks, few screen projects would easily come her way. This led her, increasingly, to the realization that she had to reach out to make overtures to the studios and independent producers for work. Quite a state of affairs for an Academy Award and Emmy nominee but a reality Hollywood in 1980.

Thus, Goldberg soon became adept at learning through the Hollywood grapevine what movie projects were in the works and what roles she might then ask to be considered for as casting got under way. One such property was the screen adaptation of William Goldman's whimsical novel *The Princess Bride* (1987). Rob Reiner, the former husband of Penny Marshall, who had directed *Jumpin' Jack Flash,* was signed to direct this feature film for Twentieth Century–Fox. Goldberg's friends Billy Crystal and Carol Kane were soon signed for extended cameos in this fairy tale-adventure-spoof. Subsequently, Cary Elwes was cast as the swashbuckling hero, Mandy Patinkin as his helpful pal, and Chris Sarandon as the evil Prince Humperdinck. Idealistic and still very naive about the politics of moviemaking, Goldberg had the notion that she wanted to audition for Buttercup, the Princess Bride. It did not seem to matter to Whoopi, or so she allowed, that she, the actor, was black and the screen role she coveted was conceived as a blond, fair-complexioned, beautiful maiden. According to Goldberg's way of thinking, if she wished and tried hard enough, she could convince studio executives to cast her against type in such a part.

With this tunnel-vision optimism, Goldberg, posing as a casting agent, called director Rob Reiner.

Agent: You still haven't got a Buttercup?
Reiner: Have you got one?
Agent: It's amazing casting.
Reiner: [growing impatient] I'm waiting. I'm waiting.
Agent: Whoopi Goldberg!

Reiner ended the phone call thinking it was a bad joke. Whoopi said, "They thought it was the stupidest thing they'd ever heard. It hurt so bad." Eventually, Reiner hired a white actor, Robin Wright, the future Mrs. Sean Penn, for the heroine's part in *The Princess Bride*. It was a rebuff that Goldberg has never forgotten. Years later, Whoopi, still determined to break the rules, would seek to audition for *Single White Female,* the part eventually given to Bridget Fonda. Said Goldberg at the time, "What a great twist, if they had decided to put me in that part. I'm not gonna stop doing it, stop trying to get the gigs. I also want to do Eleanor of Aquitaine, you know."

Another screen project of this period that never reached fruition for Whoopi involved heartthrob John Travolta. He was then suffering through a career slump after the failure of *Perfect* (1985) and other recent vehicles (including *Two of a Kind,* 1983). Goldberg and Travolta spent about a year developing a projected joint comedy for Cannon Films, but the concept never gelled, and it was eventually abandoned. Unlike *The Princess Bride* fiasco, this time around it was Travolta who regretted the missed opportunity.

Travolta would later say of this down phase in his life: "I was feeling sort of out of it. Then two wonderful things happened. Whoopi Goldberg wanted to make a movie with me—and she was the hottest thing going. And Princess Di wanted to dance with me [at a White House function they both attended]. And I thought, Even when things are bad for me, they're pretty damn good."

Finally, another picture deal came Whoopi's way. If *Jumpin' Jack Flash* had been rebuilt on the concept that Goldberg was "another Eddie

Murphy"—albeit female—Whoopi's next screen venture took this conceit a giant step further. Based on characters in a series of comedy-crime novels by Lawrence Block, *Burglar* was set to go into preproduction at Warner Bros. under the direction of Hugh Wilson. (Wilson had directed, among others, the first *Police Academy* movie in 1984.) The probability of this project receiving a green light to start shooting depended on whether Eddie Murphy or Bruce Willis would accept the title role of the reckless cat burglar. Meanwhile, Goldberg, at loose ends for screen work, agreed to the subordinate part of a bizarre poodle groomer who was the main character's sidekick.

In late May 1986, Bruce Willis, who had never officially signed for *Burglar,* dropped out of the film, and the worried studio, at a loss as to how to proceed without its bankable star, closed down the project. Frustrated at suddenly being jobless, Goldberg switched into her aggressive, assertive mode: "I called [Warner Bros. executives] a week after they'd shut it down and said, 'I can do this.' And they said, 'Of course!' " Thanks to her initiative, she now had the lead role in this reactivated film.

According to Goldberg, her reassignment in the on-again *Burglar* was a fast deal. "They just said, 'Here's some money,' and we started making the movie." In actuality, the script had to be altered to enable Whoopi—albeit in her now standard unisex mode—to handle the lead. As the revised screenplay developed, it was announced that Goldberg would be playing a lesbian burglar named Bernice Rhodenbarr, a variation on the actual characters of Bernie and his Sapphic pal in *The Burglar in the Closet* (1978), one of the Lawrence Block novels on which the *Burglar* screenplay was being based. As further script redrafts occurred, it eventually developed that Goldberg's part would be heterosexual and that her sidekick, a character named Carl Hefler, would be a gay poodle groomer.

By the time the "final" script for *Burglar* was frozen for production, it was decreed that Whoopi's character should essentially be of no particular gender, as had been the case with her creation of Fontaine the druggie in her stage presentation. Goldberg claimed to be unmindful of this decision, that is, because she was black and "unpretty," her screen character should not be given a sexual life of any sort, let alone having a stated gender. Whoopi said, "My attitude is that I can play anything. I meet with resistance, but people forget that playing different genders is nothing new. . . . I'd like to play Bob Marley [the reggae musician]. I'm not saying actors should be *allowed* to play anything, but they *should* be able to play anything. That is the art form."

Having adjusted to her latest film assignment, there were several positive reasons why Goldberg wanted to do *Burglar.* The child within her relished the idea of being in another shoot-'em-up movie. For another, she could help in the casting. It was Whoopi who dragged director Hugh Wilson to a comedy club to see Bob "Bobcat" Goldthwait perform. Goldberg had worked with the manic comedian on a bill with Robin Williams in San Francisco a few years earlier. With her prodding, Wilson approved signing Goldthwait—he of the strangled, jarring voice—to play the effeminate pet groomer and pal. Another friend of Goldberg's who won a small role in the film was Mike Nesmith of The Monkees, who had a few moments on-camera as a cabbie.

In addition, *Burglar,* which began production on July 22, 1986, was to be largely filmed on location in San Francisco, thus taking advantage of the city's hilly turf for cops-and-crooks car chases à la Steve Mc-Queen's classic action hit *Bullitt,* made eighteen years earlier. It gave Goldberg a great sense of satisfaction to return to her home area, now as the star of a sizably budgeted feature for a major studio. When scenes for *Burglar* were shot on the streets of the Bay City, Whoopi frequently encountered or entertained pals from her Blake Street Hawkeyes days as well as neighborhood friends who knew her from her home in Berkeley, which she still maintained.

Those "dropping by" to see Whoopi in her on-location dressing room would be greeted by the actor who would be chain-smoking, nibbling M & M candies, and frequently playing with her key chains, which sported brown and blue glass eyes. These eyes underscored Goldberg's penchant for wearing blue contact lenses when performing—or sometimes, if the mood hit her, only one lens, giving observant fans the occasion to note that she was performing with one blue and one brown eye. Her wearing blue lenses on-camera had been the starting point of the highly publicized friction between Whoopi and Spike Lee. The black filmmaker had made sharp comments publicly suggesting that Goldberg was trying to disguise her African-American heritage.

Goldberg took umbrage at Lee's snide comments and insisted that, like any white performer, she was entitled to alter her appearance for her roles or to suit her moods and that, she was not African American but very much an American. Or, as she phrased it during a November 1986 seminar on comedy held at the UCLA film school: "I would caution Spike

Lee to think about his own feelings about being black. If I can have green eyes today and blue eyes tomorrow, so be it. People do this whole trip about black; I'm not interested in that. My answer to Spike is, I hope everything goes well. But stay off my eye color, because if I want to change it, I will."

On another occasion, she would further argue the point brought up by Spike Lee: "If I wanted to be white, I suspect I wouldn't look the way I look. I don't care if you don't like me, that's okay. You're entitled. But don't like me because my politics are weird to you or because you don't like my choice of phraseology or the work that I do. Don't make contact lenses a priority. Get to the me. You don't like me, fine. But be up front about it." With such hard feelings on each side, it would be years before Goldberg and Lee mended their fences.

Meanwhile, making *Burglar* proved physically exhausting for Goldberg. The script's several on-camera chases required the cast to jump around hilly San Francisco both on foot and in careening vehicles. One day, while driving to the set, Goldberg's vintage Porsche, a recent gift to herself, went out of control. She veered into a tree to avoid hitting a neighbor's home. In the process, she suffered a torn ligament in her left leg. Filming had to stop for a few days while she recovered.

In describing her new screen project, Whoopi called it an "entertainment," while Warner Bros. termed *Burglar* a "comedy/adventure." A confused misfire might be a more appropriate description for this R-rated, 102-minute feature. Its "plot" revolves around Goldberg's Bernice, the owner of a Haight Street, San Francisco, bookstore by day and a hope-to-be-retiring cat burglar by night. Having already served prison time, Bernice has good cause for alarm when a corrupt ex-cop, played by G. W. Bailey, blackmails her about a past caper and threatens to send her to jail again if she doesn't give him $20,000 in cash and a mink stole for his nagging wife. Meanwhile, a dumb but wealthy dentist (Lesley Ann Warren) hires Bernice to break into the living quarters of her ex-husband (Steve Shellen). Bernice's mission is to steal the jewelry the former spouse had purchased with money skimmed from the doctor's dental practice. Bernice reluctantly agrees to this final caper and finds herself on the scene when the ex-hubby is murdered. Now she must solve the homicide to prove her innocence. Bernice's partner-in-sleuthing is hyperkinetic Carl Hefner, played by Bobcat Goldthwait.

When the film was released in March 1987, reviewers did not take kindly to this pieced-together turkey. Mike McGrady wrote in *Newsday:*

"It's Whoopi, the performer, who attracts our sympathy. One would feel for any gifted actor who keeps appearing in lemons."

Katherine Dieckmann said in the *Village Voice*: "It makes one uneasy to chastise a black woman performer for appealing to the lowest common denominator and achieving spectacular wealth in the process, just like so many white movie stars do. But Goldberg built her reputation on critiquing caricature, and now she's made herself into one, a cartoon in braids and shades." Dieckmann added a sidebar to her review: "One subversive moment occurs when Whoopi Goldberg confronts a pompous psychotic lawyer who's been murdering innocents to conceal his gay love affair. She bitches him out; he tries to drown her, she rises from near-dead and they duke it out in a sylvan glade. . . . I mean, here's a black woman beating on a middle-aged white urban male professional in this moody, foggy forest. It's weirdly great."

And Vincent Canby in the *New York Times* wrote: "Because of her talent, plus the fact she has no serious competition, Miss Goldberg is the premier black actor in American films today, but you wouldn't know it from her appearances since *The Color Purple*. . . . What's happening to Miss Goldberg (with, I assume, her cooperation) is the kind of exploitation less often associated with people than with corporate takeovers. It's as if Miss Goldberg had been 'acquired' by Hollywood, which set about to liquidate her assets as quickly and heedlessly as possible." Michael Buckley in *Films in Review* summed up a universal sentiment: "Several times during *Burglar*, Whoopi Goldberg exclaims: 'I gotta stop doin' this sh———.' She should listen to herself."

Made at a cost of $17 million, *Burglar* grossed only $8.1 million in domestic film rentals in the United States and Canada. Like *Jumpin' Jack Flash* it recouped some of its production costs from foreign distribution, TV and cable screening rights, and especially from home-video profits. It was becoming a ritual with a certain cadre of VCR owners that whenever a new Whoopi Goldberg picture was released on home video—no matter its subject or quality—they would rent the offering, which helped keep Whoopi's screen career going.

————————

Having completed three major motion pictures in a year's time, Whoopi Goldberg was considered a financial, if not an artistic, success in Hollywood. She was the first to admit that she was in a peculiar movie-industry position: "This star business. It's kind of, like, no one's quite sure what to say about me and where to put me, so they made me a star and figured that'll cover whatever comes down. It's just a real blessing to be a *working actor. A real* blessing."

When asked who her movie role models were, she confided, "Mostly men: Spencer Tracy, John Garfield, Jack Lemmon. . . . Those are the guys I watched, those are the guys I wanted to be [as a child]. They did stuff I always wanted to do. I never saw any damsels that looked like me, but I could always imagine that I could be swinging through Sherwood Forest."

If Whoopi was having a hard time positioning herself in the film business, she was having an equally difficult existence as an ethnic role model. When she had first risen to popularity on stage in *The Spook Show,* she was considered an inspiration to her race for having overcome so many obstacles. Later, when she costarred in *The Color Purple,* Whoopi, along with other participants, took a great deal of flack from African-American organizations, which considered the film a giant disservice to blacks everywhere.

Thereafter, when Goldberg went from *The Color Purple*—a relatively artistic film—to such duds as *Jumpin' Jack Flash* and *Burglar,* many in the black community accused her of having sold out to "white Hollywood." As a guest on TV talk shows, she even had to defend herself against irate callers who insisted that the typically breezy wardrobes she now fancied wearing in public did not reflect well on the black race. In short, it was very hard for Goldberg, the reluctant role model, to win major support within the black community. As far as the white establishment of the film industry was concerned, Whoopi was generally perceived as an eccentric outsider who had yet to really prove her box-office worth.

Whoopi, no longer involved in a romantic relationship, found ways to be good to herself by redecorating portions of her Berkeley home. One of her purchases was a large white, old-style porcelain bathtub. She said, "This is the one bourgeois thing I got when everything started to happen, because I always wanted a bathtub like this."

She also created a spacious loft bedroom for herself. And then she bought a new bed. "When everything started to happen," she explained, "I decided the one thing I wanted was a really *nice* bed—the kind of bed that needs someone to be in it."

Despite her run of unisex screen roles and her seemingly nonerotic persona off-camera, Whoopi Goldberg was actually a very sensual woman with healthy sexual appetites. Now that playwright-performer David Schein was no longer the special man in her life, she felt a great void.

Then twenty-seven-year-old David Edward Claessen entered Whoopi's world. He was a Dutch-born, documentary filmmaker-cinematographer who had begun his career in Holland and France. He had been previously married and divorced. Claessen and Whoopi first met around the time of her participation in the initial *Comic Relief* in late March 1986. According to several people who knew Goldberg at this time, there was an immediate attraction between the handsome, curly-haired white filmmaker and the black performer. Goldberg would describe the "instant" romance: "We set off our own atom bomb, and we've been enjoying the mushroom cloud ever since." They soon became inseparable, and in Goldberg's home he became almost immediately a surrogate dad to Alexandrea, who had formerly relied on Goldberg's then-boyfriend, David Schein, as a father figure.

As their romance blossomed, Whoopi and Claessen discussed the possibility of their doing a documentary together on the homeless once she had completed *Burglar*. In the meantime, while she was in San Francisco filming *Burglar,* he would be a frequent on-the-set visitor. Then, on Labor Day weekend, 1986, during a holiday break in the shoot, the in-love duo impulsively departed for Nevada.

There, in Las Vegas, on Monday, September 1, 1986, Whoopi and Claessen were married by Dr. John Peter Levendis at the Candlelight Wedding Chapel, on the Las Vegas Strip, at 2855 Las Vegas Boulevard South. (This was the same chapel—"The Number One Choice of Recording, Stage and Movie Personalities"—where Bette Midler had tied the matrimonial knot with Martin von Haselberg on December 15, 1984.) Goldberg used her given name, Caryn Johnson, for the brief ceremony.

According to the presiding pastor, who knew something about celebrities—he had married TV's Lone Ranger, Clayton Moore, the month before—the minute Whoopi walked into the wedding chapel, she looked familiar to him. He immediately remarked to her, "You remind me of an actor." Her response was a wide grin. He would later describe her smile as "a combination of an angel and a bit of impishness." Later, when the media asked his impression of the famous bride, he responded, "I always considered her something of a rascal, but she was very dignified, a radiant lady." As for the groom, Dr. Levendis described him as "a very gallant sort of man."

It was not long before the press learned of the interracial nuptials and printed their own take on the unusual union. In their September 22, 1986 issue, *People* magazine would list the event in its "Wedding" column and subtitle the blurb on *the* matrimony of the moment with "A Hollywood Do for Whoopi G. and Mr. Who." (Facetious as this magazine caption may have been, it was a correct prognosis of what would soon prove to be an ill-matched—at least professionally—union.) Other onlookers had their own special take on this mixed marriage. For example, as far as many in the black community were concerned, Goldberg had once again let down her people by wedding outside her race. Few seemed to recall or care that Goldberg's first husband, Alvin Martin, was black. It didn't fit into their mode of wanting to chastise the too-successful Whoopi.

From Las Vegas the newlyweds went to Los Angeles, where the *Burglar* cast and crew were now scheduled to complete the shoot at the Burbank studio. To acknowledge and celebrate the marriage and gain a great deal of "free" publicity, Goldberg's manager, Sandy Gallin, and her agent, Ron Meyer, hosted a dinner for the couple at Gallin's Beverly Hills home. On Sunday, September 7, an intimate crowd of three hundred well-wishers flocked to Gallin's house to toast the couple, who were scheduled to exchange rings in the presence of their friends as well as Alexandrea.

Among the eclectic celebrity attendees were Jane Fonda, Cher, Lesley Ann Warren, Bobcat Goldthwait, Robin Williams, Barry Manilow, Kenny Rogers, Quincy Jones, Barry Diller, Dolly Parton, Howard Zieff, Mel Gibson, Carol Burnett, Tony Danza, George Segal, and Elliott Gould. Goldthwait, who had been recently married himself, told the partygoers that Whoopi had caught the wedding bug from him. When asked what he thought of the guests of honor, Robin Williams said, "Blessed." Actor James Woods concluded, "I've got a vibe they've got something great going." *Playboy* magazine founder Hugh Hefner insisted, "They've got a serious case of the cutes." When asked for his comments, Carroll O'Connor mumbled, "Love her, don't know him." *Comic Relief* producer Bob Zmuda told one reporter on the scene that he recalled meeting Claessen at a Comic Relief press conference: "He's very handsome, very hip. I believe it was him I met." On the other hand, Elliott Gould was more positive. He insisted that the groom was "a real sweet, sensitive guy." In the course of the evening's festivities, host Sandy Gallin toasted the couple, wishing them "a long, loving life together—filled with health, happiness, success, and peace of mind."

Following the completion of *Burglar*, Whoopi, who now had the flu, and Claessen flew to Europe for a belated six-week honeymoon. They decided they would live in Los Angeles in a Hollywood Hills home, which they would share with one of her managers when Goldberg was in town. Mr. and Mrs. Claessen were now set to live happily ever after.

CHAPTER NINETEEN

Call Me "Eddie Murphy"

> I really liked the idea of running around and
> jumping over cars and kind of being macho. I
> wanted to do that kind of role, and this script [for
> *Fatal Beauty*] let me. I also liked the idea that there
> hasn't been anyone quite like me in a role like this.
> So I also felt this was an opportunity to bust down
> some doors in Hollywood and to open up some
> chances for different kinds of people. That's very
> important to me.
> —WHOOPI GOLDBERG, OCTOBER 1987

Still unable to solidify the reputation she earned in *The Color Purple*,
Whoopi Goldberg and her management team worked strenuously
to find a viable screen property. Their ideal goal was to move
Whoopi away from her current action-moviemaking syndrome (*Jumpin'
Jack Flash, Burglar*). Asked about her career plans in the fall of 1986,
Goldberg insisted, "I'm choosing things I want to do and going to the
studios and saying, 'Hey, what about this?' Because if I wait, I'll be doing
hookers and mammies and abused women for the rest of my life." When
asked what three screen roles she would most have liked to have played
in movie history, Goldberg listed: Captain Queeg in *The Caine Mutiny*,
Billie Dawn in *Born Yesterday*, and anything in the Japanese film
Rashomon.

Actually, she almost had one of her moviemaking dreams come
true. In 1986 she was slated to star in a Hollywood remake *of Born
Yesterday*, which had earned actor Judy Holliday an Academy Award years

161

before. As part of Whoopi's announced two-picture deal with Cannon Films, she was to costar in a new edition of *Born Yesterday* with Walter Matthau. So serious was the Cannon company about this project, with its very offbeat casting, that it even announced the project with large display ads in film-industry trade papers. Next it was revealed that Garson Kanin, who had written *Born Yesterday* for the Broadway stage and then adapted it for the screen in 1950, would update it for this new edition.

Months passed, and the *Born Yesterday* project faded from industry preproduction charts. According to Goldberg, it all was caused by her refusal to costar in *Public Enemy,* the movie that would have teamed her with John Travolta. Not that Whoopi had anything against working with Travolta on-camera. Rather, she regarded the intended script as just awful. She recalls: "The stipulation was I had to do another film for them [Cannon Films]. Unfortunately, on my way to the mailbox, I could *smell* the script that they wanted me to do. And I said no, because nobody starts off to make a bad movie. So they said, 'Well, then, you're not going to do *Born Yesterday*.' People were saying it was better not to do it, anyway, that it should be geared to someone like Bernadette Peters or Madonna. But the idea was not to imitate Judy Holliday but to be as different as I could be from Judy Holliday. I suppose when I grow up, I'll get to it." (So far, Goldberg has never gotten to do *Born Yesterday*. However, it was finally remade—with dismal creative and financial results—in 1993, featuring Melanie Griffith, Don Johnson, and John Goodman.)

For a time before Whoopi and Cannon Films agreed to disagree and go their separate ways, it was mentioned that Goldberg and Walter Matthau might be paired in *Autumn in the Air,* based on an original screenplay by Garson Kanin. That project never came to be, nor did a suggested remake of Budd Schulberg's *Face in the Crowd,* which had been a hit for Andy Griffith and Patricia Neal three decades earlier. In fact, Schulberg was already at work on the updated screenplay for producer Gene Kirkwood. An enthusiastic Goldberg was hoping to snare Don Johnson as her on-camera partner. He was then riding high on the crest of his popular TV series *Miami Vice,* (1984–89). She even sent Johnson a cassette of the original film, hoping he would agree to take over the Andy Griffith role in the remake, but nothing came of all these efforts. However, Goldberg did get the opportunity to work with her chum Johnson on his hip TV police drama. For "Streetwise," the December 5, 1986, episode of *Miami Vice,* Whoopi sang backup vocal on the original song performed during the segment's opening scene.

Another potential Goldberg screen vehicle of 1986 was *State of Emergency*. It was based on a true story about an American newspaper reporter, to be played by Whoopi, her white husband, and their child, who are stationed in apartheid South Africa. An eager Whoopi said, "People have been asking me when I was going to do something serious again—well, this is it." Unfortunately, this high-concept idea was never realized.

While Whoopi was sifting through good, bad, and off-the-cuff film offers, she participated in a three-day campaign through nine California cities, starting in Los Angeles, along with actor Shari Belafonte-Harper and thirty-eight other celebrities. Their mission was to promote the state's latest clean-water initiative. At the same time, Goldberg and her new husband, David Claessen, "settled" into their Hollywood Hills digs. Her Berkeley, California, period had now effectively ended.

Partial these days to cranberry juice and puffing on Vantage cigarettes, Whoopi filled her Los Angeles house to the rafters with memorabilia, such as *Jumpin' Jack Flash* watches, neon sculptures, vintage movie posters, and even a Groucho Marx doll. Sometimes Alexandrea stayed with her mom and stepdad. At other times, daughter and mother, who frequently did not see eye to eye about any important things, such as schooling, dating, and discipline, lived apart. Because Alexandrea still had close ties to friends and school in Berkeley, the teenager remained up north, generally supervised by her maternal grandmother, Emma Johnson, who had moved to the West Coast to help her family.

By now, some Hollywood observers wondered if, artistically, Whoopi Goldberg was merely a flash in the pan. Although it was acknowledged that it was not easy for someone of Goldberg's special looks, ethnicity, and gender in a male-dominated industry, everyone harped on the fact that she should be striving for "another" *Color Purple*. But, Whoopi countered, "They [the critics] want me to do Othello. I want to do all different roles." Such assignments included doing action movies which appealed to the little child in her; at least, that's what she told herself and others in those days. She admitted they were bits of fluff, but she insisted that in making them she "had the best time: motorcycles and leather jackets and blue contact lenses!" These movies also helped pay the bills and kept her in the public's eye until something worthwhile came along.

On January 17, 1987, Whoopi appeared on the televised 19th Annual NAACP Image Awards. She had forgiven the NAACP for the unpleasantness they generated a year earlier regarding *The Color Purple*. Five days later, Goldberg and Bruce Willis were guests on the NBC-TV musical variety special *The Pointer Sisters: Up All Night*. A month later, on February 24, 1987, Whoopi was a presenter at the 28th Annual Grammy Awards, aired on CBS-TV.

Meanwhile, thanks to Cher, Goldberg inherited another screen assignment. Actually, she had first seen the script two years earlier, in 1985. Then she had been interested in starring in this antidrug story about a beautiful undercover cop who sets out to find the source of a deadly drug called Fatal Beauty that had recently become available through illegal street sales. However, singer–film star Cher became attached to the screen project. Later, Cher dropped out, preferring such screen parts as *Moonstruck* released in 1987, for which she won an Oscar; *Suspect*, also a 1987 film; and the following year's *The Witches of Eastwick*, with Jack Nicholson.

When Cher abandoned the cop action movie, Whoopi again contacted M-G-M, which was set to release the film. She asked to be considered seriously for the lead part. "I told them I could do this. But they said that the movie would be more interesting with Tina Turner because there had to be a reason for the man to fall in love with her." Such blunt reasoning was deeply hurtful to Goldberg no matter how tough, aggressive, and hip an exterior she presented to the public. Months later, she would say about this latest professional rejection, "Too many times Hollywood seems to be saying that if you don't have tons of makeup on and change your clothes every five minutes, the woman can't ever find happiness. That perpetuates the myth."

Then, in a turnaround, Tom Holland, who was now scheduled to direct this M-G-M entry, retitled *Fatal Beauty*, contacted Goldberg. He asked her to take the lead part. Later, Holland explained his reasoning. "I had a lot of white-bread actors who could cut it but none that could bring the conviction to it, the street smarts that Whoopi could. She brought truth and conviction to the role."

Before signing on for the picture, Whoopi learned that the producers intended to revamp her screen role to "fit" her "special" qualities. For example, the part originally had the heroine named Rita Rizzoli. The producers now decided that it didn't suit Whoopi and planned to rename the character "something like Clovis or Cleotia. I said, 'Oh, no, you don't.'" The filmmakers were convinced that they needed Goldberg to make the delayed project happen, so they acceded to her wishes. They also had to meet Whoopi's demand for a salary of nearly $2.5 million. (This was quite a jump from the $250,000 she had received for *The Color Purple*.) She said, "the movie was written with a beautiful woman in mind, and they resisted me. When they finally did come to me, they had to pay an ugly woman's price."

The making of *Fatal Beauty* was a perfect example of all that can go wrong in a film made by committee. By February 23, 1987, when the movie went into production, Eddie Murphy's *Beverly Hills Cop 2* was in prerelease screenings around Hollywood and seemed to be a certified hit. The *Fatal Beauty* filmmakers decided to mimic that new film's comedic formula, which included the lead playing an outrageous law enforcement agent who is a constant joker. To accommodate these copycat goals, *Fatal Beauty*'s original hard edge and *film noir* ambience were discarded. In the process, Goldberg's character, less unisex than her film roles in *Jumpin' Jack Flash* and *Burglar,* was converted into a carbon copy of the wise-ass, foul-mouthed Axel Foley of Eddie Murphy's *Beverly Hills Cop* series. As shooting progressed, most of the creative aspects that had piqued Goldberg's original interest disappeared.

One item that director Tom Holland fought about and won was the choice of the movie's leading man. Once Goldberg had been contracted for *Fatal Beauty,* the film's producers suggested that black actor Billy Dee Williams be made Whoopi's leading man. Holland refused, insisting that the main male role had to be played by a white man, as originally intended in the script. He felt this interracial mix of Goldberg's character and her screen co-lead would make for far more interesting interaction.

However, casting a white actor to play with or against Whoopi soon proved to be a minor victory at best. Now the film's decision makers were apprehensive about having a final product in which an interracial romance was even suggested. And even worse, in their minds, was to allow black Goldberg and white actor Sam Elliott, eventually chosen to play the male lead, to engage in an on-screen romance. Nobody even dared to suggest that the mixed couple be allowed to indulge in bedroom sex play. With all this in mind, the script was whittled down further, leaving these two key characters with merely a suggestion of a romance. (Goldberg and Elliott's sizzling bedroom scene—between the sheets—was deleted after West Coast preview audiences objected strongly to the interracial comingling.)

Later, Whoopi joked about the lack of on-screen romance in *Fatal Beauty*. She claimed that there was *never* any real scorching sex scene

intended for the picture. She insisted that the amorous relationship between the two characters was *always* geared to be only intimated, thus
diverting attention from the real issues, an unacceptable interracial romance and Whoopi's lack of film-industry clout to demand that such a
mixed relationship be treated normally.

Even as late as postproduction, the executives involved with *Fatal
Beauty* worried that it was still too daring for the mid-1980s to permit
Sam Elliott's character to survive a gun skirmish in the story's climax.
They lobbied to have him die in the film's finale. An annoyed Goldberg
said: "In every movie about a white man and a black woman, one of them
has got to die. In every picture but *Guess Who's Coming to Dinner* [re-
leased in 1967 with Sidney Poitier] you've got to step into the street and
get run over by a truck if the [romantic] chemistry works."

As a result of the controversy over whether Elliott's character should
live or die, *Fatal Beauty* went through more expensive rewrites. Goldberg
had to fight to keep her "love" interest physically alive at the movie's end.
Nevertheless, despite all of Whoopi's campaigning to have it otherwise,
all that remained to suggest the on-screen sexual relationship between
Goldberg and Elliott was, to quote entertainment reporter Kristal Brent
Zook in the *Los Angeles Weekly,* "a hug, a rumpled sheet, one final
[chaste] kiss and an implied promise of future nookie." The studio's
official rationale for excising footage depicting intimacy was that at test
screenings it slowed down the narrative. As one executive told Stephen
M. Silverman of the *New York Post*: "The scene was not quite as we
wanted. It wasn't as strong a statement as we wanted."

On a later occasion, Goldberg would hark back to *Fatal Beauty* and
the way filmmakers then treated her on-screen characters' interracial "romances." She said that if her character in that picture had been a prostitute and Sam Elliott's character had left fifty dollars on the dresser
drawer, the bedroom scene would have stayed in. She was also upset on
another level: "For them [i.e., studio power brokers] it was such an
amazing, incredible thing that a man as attractive as Sam could be interested in a woman who looked as unconventional as they thought I did.
And that's what bothered me."

During the filming of *Fatal Beauty,* Goldberg had to contend with
other major story-line distortions. As the story's synopsis became more
botched and confusing, Whoopi herself rewrote a key scene to bolster the
faltering plot. Ironically, because of the sequence's high quality, it would
leave filmgoers thinking it had been lifted from some other movie. Later,

in reviewing this segment and her growing disillusionment with the movie, Goldberg recalled: "Well, it is pretty close [to what I wrote], you know. I did a lot of drugs in my life and thought the best way to get the information out in the scene was to draw from what I knew. It's very sad what they did to *Fatal Beauty,* because it started as a nice and gritty little shoot-'em up about a cop who hates drugs and drug dealers. Originally, my character had scars on her back from when some drug dealer kidnapped her as a teenager and beat her. Because of that, she went around shooting drug dealers. That didn't gel correctly for me as an explanation of what a radical police officer she was. So they said, 'Well, come up with something better.' So Sam [Elliott] and I talked about it and I told him, 'I'll probably make this weird end run,' and he said, 'Run on.' So I did, but then they cut our love scene out."

If Goldberg didn't have her say concerning many aspects of the film, she did interject her personality and life experiences into other facets of the production. Some of her prized possessions found their way on-screen as set dressing. Her Aunt Jemima cookie jar, people-shaped banks, several posters, and other items from her own "Negrobilia" (her collection of campy caricatures of her race) wound up in the film. Whoopi said of these politically incorrect items: "For years, these things were horrible representations, and it wasn't cool to display them until collectors let everyone know how much they were worth." In contrast to others who saw the new popularity of such black collectibles as symptomatic of rising racism, Goldberg countered: "I like it. It's part of Americana."

By late May, *Fatal Beauty,* released finished shooting. Goldberg and director Tom Holland, who had experienced tense times during the production, left on amiable terms. Both were on hand at the Hollywood Roosevelt Hotel to join Sam Elliott and the rest of the film's company for a wrap party.

During the course of *Fatal Beauty* in October 1987, reckless Los Angeles undercover cop Rita Rizzolli (Goldberg) learns that a San Fernando Valley businessman (Harris Yulin) is manufacturing and selling a new killer drug. However, Rita's harried precinct boss (John P. Ryan) won't permit her to follow up on the case. Nevertheless, she stubbornly does so on her own, and soon everyone is chasing everyone else, with bodies dropping everywhere. Among those involved are a pair of two-bit drug dealers (Brad Dourif and Mike Jolly) as well as self-contained Mike Marshak (Sam Elliott), the high-powered drug dealer's chief of security. It is he who ends up joining forces with the law enforcer (Goldberg) he's been hired to obstruct.

There are bits and pieces of this R-rated (originally X-rated for its violence), 104-minute feature that do come alive. There is the amusing sequence in which Goldberg's character is strutting undercover as a whore, dressed in a very tacky outfit and crowned with a frilly blond wig. There is also a bit where Whoopi's on-camera character, a tough cookie who frequently impugns the virility of some of her male adversaries and threatens to castrate others, has a verbal tussle with a snotty society lady (Jennifer Warren). The interlude ends with Whoopi punching the society snob in a brawl, during which they shatter a plate-glass door.

There are also the subtler personal touches that Goldberg sneaked into the film, such as graffiti on her precinct-office wall, where she lists all those people she encountered who fell victims to drugs. One of the names scrawled on the wall is Caryn Johnson, Whoopi's own real-life name. Among the many *Fatal Beauty* scenes structured to rip off *Beverly Hills Cop 2*, Goldberg's cop arrives at a messy murder scene where a white cop snickers and says, "This place is a real mess. You know where we could find a good maid?" Whoopi's character zings back, "People like you are the reason abortion is legal."

Janet Maslin noted in her *New York Times* review: "*Fatal Beauty* asks whether a woman can be just as loudly, obnoxiously macho as a man, and answers with a resounding yes." Kevin Thomas, in the *Los Angeles Times*, described the result as "a rickety, ultra-bloody star vehicle that allows Goldberg to strut all her outrageous stuff and also to try to sock over a strong anti-drug message. Whoopi is fun, but the picture self-destructs on several counts and succumbs to hypocrisy in trying to preach against drugs while exploiting violence to the hilt."

Roger Ebert said in the *Chicago Sun Times* that he liked "the way Goldberg handled the same basic situation that Eddie Murphy flunked in *Beverly Hills Cop 2*. What you have in both movies is a black street cop who ostensibly doesn't fit in with the chic folks of Beverly Hills. While Murphy handled the confrontations with a smug and even shrill self-confidence, Goldberg allows uncertainty to creep in. Even in a scene where she is bashing a society woman in the chops, she allows herself to seem apologetic."

Made at a cost of $18 million, *Fatal Beauty* grossed only a meager $4.7 million in domestic film rentals in the United States and Canada. Its poor showing was evidence of the further diminution of Goldberg's box-office value. In judging the final product, Goldberg herself admitted, "It should have been a grittier, ugly movie." Furthermore, "when things went weak in the script, people said, 'Well, now, let's have Whoopi go into her Eddie [Murphy] parody.' There's quite a bit of Eddie in the movie. It was not written that way." But, looking for some virtues to the nonsensical outing, she did say, "I'm glad it's pretty. It looks fantastic. It is entertaining. It does move. And you'll never see a sexier couple than Sam [Elliott] and me."

Back in March 1986, Whoopi had lost the Best Actress Oscar to Geraldine Page. On June 13, 1987, Page died at the age of sixty-two. By that point, in one of those "small-world" quirks of Hollywood moviemaking, Goldberg had already made a feature film with Page's actor-husband. The latter was making his screen directorial debut with *The Telephone,* a low budget feature. Like Goldberg's own screen name, his "Rip Torn" was intended as a funny word combination.

In retrospect, it is difficult to discern what potential commercial prospects intrigued either Rip Torn or Whoopi Goldberg. However, at the time, it was a near spontaneous happening that almost turned into spontaneous combustion. Torn was looking for a simple project to show off his nascent abilities as a film director. Once the concept of having Goldberg star in the venture as the box-office attraction was suggested, everything fell into place quickly. Now committed to the movie, Whoopi worked with screenwriters Terry Southern, an Academy Award–winning coscreenwriter of *Dr. Strangelove,* and Harry Nilsson, better known as a songwriter. What the trio eventually did—or at least so it seems in retrospect—was essentially to string together a half dozen on-camera routines for Goldberg to perform, all of them revolving around a schizophrenic young actor holed up in her apartment.

This New World release was shot on location in San Francisco—which appealed to Goldberg—and was filmed over the course of a brief two-week period. (Actually the shoot went two days over its intended ten-day filming timetable.) Although it was designed for Whoopi to be the whole show, there were also cameo performances by such name performers as Elliott Gould, John Heard, and Amy Wright. Herve Villechaize, who had played Tattoo on TV's *Fantasy Island,* was hired as one of the film's several off-camera voices.

Torn displayed a dash of nepotism by hiring one of his children,

Danae, as an off-camera voice. Then Goldberg had the notion that her then-available husband, David Claessen, should be hired as the film's cinematographer. This suggestion upset Torn, who had already selected someone for the project. (Eventually, Claessen would be listed as the picture's cinematographer, while David Myers would be billed as visual consultant.) According to a key source on the picture, "Torn raised hell about bringing David in. The battles started with that and never seemed to cease." As one cast member told gossip columnist Marilyn Beck about life on *The Telephone*: "When Rip would stalk off [the set], it would be producers Robert Katz and Moctesuma Esparaza who would cajole him back—they were the real heroes."

In this essentially improvisational, one-character movie, which owes a great deal to Jean Cocteau's 1930 one-woman drama *Le Voix Humaine* (*The Human Voice*), Goldberg's character shuts herself up in her cluttered apartment at a time of extreme professional and personal despair. Her crises revolve around being out of work and having just been deserted by her lover. Her sole companions at home are a goldfish and an adored owl. Her only lifeline to the world is her zebra-striped phone. During the course of this "art" film, she calls her girlfriend, then the local video store, and later the police to register a complaint. She also has a one-sided conversation with her grocer, the phone company, her agent, and an Irish priest whom she has selected to be her confessor. Throughout the 82 minutes on-camera, Goldberg's alter ego exhibits a variety of ethnic screen impressions: East Indian, Korean, French, Japanese, and Latino, among others.

When *The Telephone* was released in early January 1988, the film's press kit quoted Whoopi as saying that there only was one thing she worried about during the filming: "Is what I'm doing going to interest and please the audience?" In actuality, though, she was far more focused on the battles she had with Torn, which did not end with the film's wrap-up.

On September 2, 1987, months after *The Telephone* was completed, Whoopi filed suit against New World Pictures and director Rip Torn because the film company planned to release the director's final cut of the picture instead of the one she had approved. She claimed in Los Angeles Superior Court that her picture contract gave her the right to attend all editing sessions and to share in the editing cuts to the picture. She also alleged that she was not permitted to attend such sessions or to partici-pate in the footage cuts. Instead, she insisted, she was given a video of a work print of *The Telephone* and allowed to make separate cuts. Whoopi's suit further claimed that both New World and the producers (Robert Katz and Moctesuma Esparza) of the movie stated that they preferred her cut to Torn's and that they had planned to release her version. However, said Goldberg's complaint, Torn and the Directors Guild of America (DGA) filed for arbitration after learning of the producer and studio's decision, and on August 11, 1987, the arbitrator ruled in Torn's favor.

The arbitrator's decision was based on his determination that Torn had not been aware of New World's special editing agreement with Whoopi and that Goldberg's husband, David Claessen, had apparently done the editing on her final version of *The Telephone*. It was ruled that a disclaimer be placed on all prints of the movie stating it was edited in violation of the DGA basic agreements and that trade-paper ads be taken out explaining the situation.

Upset by the arbitrator's ruling in Torn's favor, Goldberg further pursued her lawsuit, insisting that the version of the movie that New World planned to release was artistically inferior to the one she had suggested. As a result, she wanted $100,000 in damages, $5 million in punitive damages, and an injunction against the release of Torn's rendering of *The Telephone*.

On October 20, 1987, Los Angeles Superior Court judge Leon Savitch handed down his decision. He concluded that because of Goldberg's antipathy toward Torn, she had refused to participate in the editing process jointly with the director. As a result, the court found in favor of the defendant, reasoning: "I just don't believe this would have great impact on her [Whoopi]." Goldberg was not on hand in the courtroom; as she was in Baltimore making her next movie, *Clara's Heart*.

Two days later, on Thursday, October 22, 1987, Torn informed the media, "I'm breaking my rule about hanging out the family wash because Whoopi unfortunately has already dragged *The Telephone* through the mud and it needs at least a rinsing of the truth." Torn noted that his star was a good actor but she "had been badly advised about her attitude toward this production" and her suit only served "to disparage this film." Furthermore, Torn said, "I was always willing to meet with her in the editing process. The film was shot in twelve days, but that was fine because we were using a two-camera technique to capture and be able to 'match' Whoopi's wonderful spontaneous creativity. The problem was that for many key sequences we really only had the output of one camera to consider in the editing."

Torn emphasized that he had found himself engaged in "artistic disputes" over the fact that Claessen refused to shoot "substantial portions of other actor's heads. It forced Torn to go to filmed screen close-ups of the leading lady's goldfish and owl. Torn also insisted that "anyone who cares to look at the arbitration transcripts will see that they [i.e., the producers] stated emphatically that they preferred mine [final cut of the movie]."

The Telephone went into limited release in early 1988. It won no favor with the critics. Kevin Thomas concluded in the *Los Angeles Times*: "Very quickly you feel trapped with Goldberg's disintegrating actor in her funky San Francisco apartment, but instead of developing empathy for Goldberg's Vashti Blue, you just want to get away from her."

Kyle Counts, writing for the *Hollywood Reporter,* was even more dissatisfied with the film: "*The Telephone* isn't a movie, it's eighty-two minutes . . . of self-inflicted character assassination. Strained and monumentally unfunny. . . . Torn's direction is so insensitive . . . you'd swear a good portion of the film was made up of first takes: Goldberg's timing is off, as if she's medicated or low in energy, or in the presence of people she doesn't trust."

With such a poor critical response and a limited theatrical release, *The Telephone* soon disappeared from distribution, only to show up later in home-video format. But this was not to be the end of Whoopi's encounters with the family of Rip Torn and Geraldine Page. Two years later, she would find herself costarring in a feature with Torn's actor-cousin from Texas—Sissy Spacek. As for Rip Torn, he has never directed another motion picture.

PART IV

Scrambling on the Hollywood Treadmill

CHAPTER TWENTY

Treading Water—
Hollywood Style

[A]cting is all I ever knew I wanted to do. I know I
can do it. I know I'm good at it. This movie stuff
could all fall apart tomorrow. That's okay. I have the
four-letter word to fall back on: T-O-U-R. That is the
saving grace. I have my theater work to fall back
on. . . . As soon as people see what you're doing,
what the press says doesn't matter. It's all in the box
office.
—WHOOPI GOLDBERG, JUNE 1987

By the spring of 1987, even optimistic Whoopi Goldberg had to
admit that she was treading water as a screen actor. On the big
screen, the Oscar-nominated actor had been reduced to starring in
three unimaginative action films in which she was shoehorned into being
a second-string Eddie Murphy clone, and an asexual one at that. It also
had to be apparent to her that no matter what the strength of her will,
she could not overcome a trio of casting obstacles created by the Hollywood establishment: her lack of typical screen beauty, her being black,
and her being female.

In addition to not conforming to Hollywood's standards of what
constituted a movie star, she was also still having a difficult time being an
acceptable role model for her race; not that she had ever wanted to be.
Because she was such a dramatic success story, it was "expected" by
many in the black world that she would devote herself to being an

inspiration and role model for all African Americans. It was also assumed by many blacks that she would also want to crusade for any cause brought to her attention. Whoopi was not—by the standards and expectations of certain segments of the black community—doing enough for her race.

Besides Goldberg's contretemps with the outspoken Spike Lee, she had continuous vocal scuffles with the very sensitive NAACP. In addition, she was subject to ongoing friction with the Coalition Against Black Exploitation. A year earlier, they had included Whoopi in their criticism of those involved with *The Color Purple* who had allegedly created unflattering stereotypes of African Americans. Now, in March 1987, a dozen members of the coalition picketed for an hour in the rain outside Los Angeles's Hotel Ambassador, where Whoopi was the guest speaker at the Black Women's Forum. According to Hasani Webb, spokesperson for the coalition, Goldberg was their target for several reasons: "We object to the profanity and vulgarity she exhibits in her work which denigrates our race." Webb also noted that Whoopi was "not being socially responsible" and that she "has a negative influence on black youth." Adding to the community's overall disappointment was her marriage to someone outside of her race.

Despite these criticisms, Goldberg was doing something right for some people. That same month, March 1987, she received the Hans Christian Andersen Award for outstanding achievement by a dyslexic (a learning and reading disorder which strikes 15 percent of the population). Said Whoopi, "After years of being considered as retarded [in school], I think I am doing pretty good."

As if making back-to-back movies, participating in charity fundraisers, and representing an array of black causes were not enough, Goldberg kept herself active in television. Within a two-day period in mid-May 1987, she emceed the ABC-TV special *Happy Birthday, Hollywood.* On May 19, 1987, she was a cohost on the televised *1st Annual American Comedy Awards.* That same evening, she also hosted the syndicated antidrug special *Scared Straight: Ten Years Later.* With such a performance schedule, Whoopi was proving that quantity, if not always quality, could help boost a celebrity's popularity with the public.

Whoopi was understandably concerned about the potential effects of fame on her as an individual. In a June 1987 *Playboy* interview she told David Rensin: "I think I fared pretty well. I read movie-star biographies. Sid Caesar's autobiography prepared me for one big aspect of being popular that I hadn't anticipated. He wrote that the biggest down, the biggest crevice most people fall into, is 'Am I going to wake up and not be good at this anymore?' That's what scared Sid, Marilyn Monroe, John Belushi, Errol Flynn. Am I going to wake up suddenly and not be able to do this anymore? I don't have that fear."

She also acknowledged: "Sometimes it's tough to keep my ego in check, but I blame it on the people around me, because suddenly I can't do any wrong. They tell me shit that's not true. And if enough people tell you that your shit doesn't stink, you start thinking that maybe it doesn't. Sometimes it's hard for me to get my head through the fucking door. Meanwhile, I'm actually thinking that all this star stuff is a goof, because I'm really just a kid from the projects. But no one wants to hear it. People think I'm bragging. But, shit, I see Jack Nicholson, and I'm a puddle on the ground. It's hard to think of myself in those terms. This is all new for me."

She also said: "People, friends, suddenly treat you differently. They don't even wait for you to change and become an asshole. They just assume you're going to be one and treat you accordingly. This is very painful when all you're trying to do is figure out that you're still okay."

Regarding the filmmaking business, Goldberg acknowledged to *Playboy*: "I think this is a motherfucker of a business. I work sixteen hours a day. I sit around. Then I have to come every time someone says, 'Action.' I do eighty, ninety performances a day when I'm working on a movie. But people don't understand that movie people are still human beings. They say, 'Your name is in magazines, you're making movies, and you're complaining!' I'm not. I'm freaked because I'm in the middle of it and I can't tell what I'm doing. But I'm also lucky to have friends who can still say, 'Look, bitch! Don't get cute.' My kid's like that. She says if she has to make her bed, so do I."

One topic that was certain to surface when the media conversed with Whoopi was racial discrimination. Her mid-1987 response was: "When I grew up, it was never an issue. My mother would say, 'Look, you're black. You woke up black this morning, you'll go to bed black tonight. But it doesn't make any difference. It doesn't mean that you will be better or worse at school. It doesn't mean that you will get or not get jobs,' which was kind of—in this field—not exactly true. But I didn't know that until very recently. People kept saying, 'You know, there aren't a lot of black movies.' And I didn't get what they meant. In New York, actors are not black and white. They're actors. You have Diana Sands and

Alan Alda doing *The Owl and the Pussycat*. But you come here [to Holly-
wood], and people say, 'You're good, but shit, we can't have an interracial
couple.' Is there a law that says you can't? 'Well, no. It's just that our
audience wouldn't be ready for it.' "

Then there was the matter of her drug-filled past, a subject which
she had so candidly detailed for public consumption on many prior
occasions. These revelations of her "past" were now causing her problems, even though she was now a certified movie star. "I have to take
tests all the time for movies. Honey, now they want blood. I hate it. I
fight it. I say, 'Are you asking me if I do drugs? Why don't you ask me?
You think I'm not going to tell you? You think you won't be able to tell?
Why do I have to give you blood? How do you know I'm not clean for X
amount of time just to be clean for you?' I give urine. No blood. I don't
like needles. I wouldn't give blood to anybody. I don't like anybody
poking me. If you want to know if I'm into drugs, you'll just have to keep
your eyes on me."

When asked how she adjusted to discrimination in the film business, Goldberg answered, "I didn't get used to it at all. I just kind of
ignore it, and I tell other people to do the same. I'm always asked what
advice I have for black actors. Simple: Don't think about being black. It's
not like you can pretend to be a white person."

Whoopi expanded on this concept: "I don't deal with people and
their color, because it means I can't work. As soon as I put a limit of
being a black and a woman on myself, that narrows down the field of
work to nothing. To nothing. Actors have no color. That is the art form.
Actors are supposed to be able to do anything. Be anyone." To make her
point clear, she added. "You can see that I'm black. It's not something I
consciously think about. It just is. It's like having a dick. You don't think
about having a dick. You just have one."

Whoopi wants to be judged by her talents, *not* by her color or even
by her gender. However, her egocentric nature bristles at being lumped
into an ethnic category. In addition, there is her apparent antipathy to
shouldering the burden of being responsible in any way for the deeds of
the entire black community. Whoopi, a very intuitive person in all phases
of her life, prefers to be spontaneous rather than contemplative in dealing
with personal and social issues. Devoting time to studying ethnic issues is
not something that would seem to appeal to her nature.

As to her outspoken stances on key political issues: "I don't think
about solidifying my career first. I'm going to get out there. [T]oo many

things have happened in the past that people have to listen to. . . . You cannot deny that homelessness in America is fucked. There's no way to negate it. There's no conversation. You cannot deny that the government has done little or nothing to alleviate the problem. I don't understand why anyone would take offense or be pissed at me for saying that the issue with abortion is choice. . . . As an American citizen, I have a right to speak out. . . . I gotta keep people aware. And I will for as long as I can."

Goldberg also voiced her stance on political correctness: "I like the idea of being able to talk to people about certain issues that affect men and women. For example, abortion. Otherwise, I'd have to think about life as a woman, then as a black person, then as a black woman. Then what happens if I add Catholic? It's endless! I'm trying in my own way to maintain a humanistic view of everything. . . . I don't want to represent this or speak for that. That only leads to people fighting, and then someone says you're not fighting hard enough for women with behinds that sag closer to their knees."

When asked her thoughts on the infamous Hollywood casting-couch system, tell-it-like-it-is Whoopi said, "I've never fucked my way anywhere, if that's what you mean. Could never do that. . . . The only time I think about being a woman here is when I see how women treat one another. Basically, people don't fuck with me, because I don't intimidate anyone overtly, like by being glamorous. I'm sure that if someone has to spend two hours on her makeup and then she looks at me and knows I spend five seconds just wiping myself off, it may be a bit intimidating. In the same way, I look at some women and think, Goddamn, if I could just look like that for five minutes, I would be happy."

As to future career plans, Goldberg enthused: "I'm going back next year [1988]! Listen, I go on the road by myself, take the old man [her husband] if he wants to go. And I *work*. And once I get on the stage, it doesn't matter what's happened before. It's like heaven, man. It's like fucking heaven. I *come* when I work. I fucking come when I work. That's what matters, not being some star. Stars don't get to do anything. Stars only *are*. They're a state of mind. I'm not a star. I'm a working character actor."

Finally, when *Playboy* asked Whoopi what words of advice she had for her legion of fans, she said, "I got lucky. I know that. So I'd like to have people remember that all I've gotten is a little bit of recognition and not to be afraid of me. Please cool out."

In mid-April 1987 it was announced that Whoopi's next feature, now that *Fatal Beauty* and *The Telephone* were history, would be *Clara's Heart*, in which she would play a domestic. Some trade journals reported this casting as "Whoopi Goldberg as a black Mary Poppins." As expected, this did not sit well with many African Americans, who felt that Goldberg was again betraying her race. They contended that when Whoopi first started in movies, she had promised in interviews that she would never play a stereotypical servant on-camera. And now, less than two years later, they claimed she was apparently going back on her word. In fact, the role she would play was hardly stereotypical.

Actually, *Clara's Heart* was a project that had been in the works for Whoopi since 1985, when producer Martin Elfand approached her on the matter. "They asked me over the course of three years to do that film. Every year they'd ask me, and every year I'd say, 'Not yet. I still want to do some other things,'" which included trying screen genres other than drama. "There's only two I haven't done—the Western and the detective movie. *Jumpin' Jack Flash* was the screwball comedy, *Burglar* was a piece of fluff; *Fatal Beauty* was my cop movie. *The Telephone* should have been the weirdo scare movie, but it didn't work that way."

When queried whether her onetime stage character of the Jamaican (who weds the "old raisin" and inherits his money) had any bearing on her getting this new film, Whoopi responded, "I suspect that might be one of the reasons they offered me the part. 'Oh, she can do it, she's got the accent.' It's possible. I'm sure that there are strains of that lady in me." The movie which would feature Goldberg as a noble Jamaican who relocates to Maryland to work for a white family was based on Joseph Olshan's novel of the same title, as adapted to the screen by Mark Medoff, who won a Tony Award for *Children of a Lesser God*. Originally, David Anspach was to direct the feature. However, by the time filming was to get under way, Robert Mulligan, who had directed *To Kill a Mockingbird* and *Summer of '42*, was in charge.

The story of *Clara's Heart* focuses on a well-to-do, spoiled white youth progressing into manhood and, in the process, learning to let go of his troubled past. He is bolstered through these worrisome times (the death of an infant sibling, his parents' divorce, and the domestic tug-of-war over whom he will live with) by smart, sassy, compassionate, Jamaican-born Clara, who has recently become the new maid in the boy's

Baltimore home. The sensitive youngster's companionship with and growing esteem for Clara provides the silently grieving maid with the emotional support necessary to deal with her own unresolved tragedy: being raped by her own son, who later committed suicide. As the film progresses, emotionally healed, self-sufficient Clara at last permits herself to be vulnerable and finds new joy in her rather austere life.

Much of the location work for *Clara's Heart* took place in the Baltimore area, in such locales as the Pub Congress Hotel, St. Anne's Church, the historic Belvedere Hotel, and the city's "Harlem" area. Other filming took place in St. Michaels, Maryland, across the Chesapeake Bay from Annapolis, where a Civil War–era estate, restored in the 1930s, filled in as the home of the film's central characters, including the boy's parents.

In *Clara's Heart,* Mark Medoff not only played therapist Dr. Stevens; it was he who had discovered fourteen-year-old Neil Patrick Harris for the key role of the confused, angry youth. Medoff first met young Harris when the boy participated in a drama camp Medoff conducted in New Mexico a few years earlier. Others in the cast included Michael Ontkean and Kathleen Quinlan as the teenager's parents, actor-monologist Spalding Gray as the pompous bereavement counselor who becomes Quinlan's new love interest, and Beverly Todd as the feisty Jamaican who knows the shocking secrets of Clara's past.

For many reasons Whoopi enjoyed working on the prestigious, well-mounted *Clara's Heart*. After all the conflicts on her recent feature films, especially *The Telephone* and *Fatal Beauty,* it was a relief to be so in tune creatively with this movie's well-respected, mainstream director, Robert Mulligan. According to Goldberg, he "allowed me to do what I could do, just as Steve [Spielberg] did in *The Color Purple*." She also noted that Mulligan "reminded me that making movies is a collaborative process. Not all actors feel like that, but I do. I want to be part of the process when it goes up on the screen and my name is above the title. Because if it doesn't do the box office that Eddie Murphy's movies do or it isn't *The Color Purple* that critics want to see, if I have no say in it, I get a little mad that I have to eat it."

On the set of *Clara's Heart,* a special rapport developed between Whoopi and the wide-eyed acting novice Neil Patrick Harris. The two kindred souls not only became pals during this shoot, they have remained so over the years. For example, in 1992, by which time Harris had become the star of the hit TV sitcom *Doogie Howser, M.D.,* he was a guest on Goldberg's syndicated TV talk show. It was obvious from their interaction on-camera, and especially from what one could overhear of their whispered confidences between commercial breaks, that they still held one another in very high esteem.

The slickly prepared *Clara's Heart* boasted Freddie Francis's lush cinematography and Dave Grusin's emotionally stimulating score. Released in October 1988, the movie failed to please many of the nation's critics. Tom Matthews complained in *Boxoffice* magazine: "*Clara's Heart* practically oozes with warmth and heart-tugging tenderness. Clara is so noble, so good, so insightful that she nearly glows and Goldberg (who slips in and out of her Jamaican accent) fills the role with an Oscar-baiting earnestness." The trade journal prognosticated: "There is very little room in the marketplace for a soap opera this routine."

In her mixed review, Janet Maslin wrote in the *New York Times:* "*Clara's Heart* . . . has in Whoopi Goldberg virtually the only actor who could turn Clara from an affront into a likable heroine. Funny and sarcastic in delivering the screenplay's snappy rejoinders, Miss Goldberg is also comfortable with the character's sentimental side. Indeed, she appears at ease in every way, and for the first time seems genuinely to become the character she is playing." Nevertheless, Maslin added, "the film is exasperatingly slow in getting to the bottom of [its plot device], and the secret itself doesn't do anything to explain Clara's character."

A generally dissatisfied Roger Ebert reported in the *Chicago Sun Times:* "I kept waiting for *Clara's Heart* to turn itself around, to stop being an insufferably overwrought melodrama and start applying intelligence to the situation of its title character. It never happened. Here is a bad movie into which a great character seems to have dropped from another dimension." However, in a tribute to its star, Ebert added: "Goldberg is magnificent. The character belongs in a different movie, even a different universe, from the rest of the ludicrous plot."

The film prompted Ebert to note: "Looking at her choices of projects since *The Color Purple,* however, it is easy to imagine she has been ill-served by her agents and advisers. She has been denied true relationships, except with weirdos, strange neighbors, computer buddies, and nerdy little boys. (*Fatal Beauty* is again an exception, with her friendship with Sam Elliott.) She is always the being from another planet. How come? She is not a conventional beauty, but I've always thought that her face and eyes and smile contained a warmth and personality that shone like the sun."

Support for *Clara's Heart* and Goldberg's performance came from a surprising quarter, the *New York Amsterdam News,* a strong media outpost for the black community. Its reviewer, Mel Tapley, wrote in its October 22, 1988, issue: "If they [the naysayers] object to the role talented Whoopi is playing—that of a maid or housekeeper—they can't really hear the humanity ticking away in *Clara's Heart,* and they don't see the tears and joy and understanding and real sympathy that radiate from performances of Whoopi Goldberg."

Tapley put the matter in historical perspective: "They [African Americans] sneered and vilified Hattie McDaniels [sic] and Louise Beavers and Butterfly McQueen a couple of generations ago for their portrayals of [screen] domestics because they felt the shudders and shivers of slavery. It was the shame of a conquered people of the fat bourgeoisie, not the proud recognition of the strength of survival."

With such generally negative critical response and the public's resultant indifference, the underrated *Clara's Heart* was neither a critical nor financial hit. Made at a cost of $14 million, it only grossed a meager $2 million in domestic film rentals in the United States and Canada. Despite its box-office failure and the jibes she endured from the black community for playing an on-camera domestic, Goldberg would say years later on CNN's *Larry King Live,* "I've got a special place in my heart for *Clara's Heart.* You know, that's one of my favorites."

CHAPTER TWENTY-ONE

Marriage on the Rocks

So now phase two starts. I lived through the first
three years. . . . I didn't end up dead. But this year
[1987] was the toughest. Suddenly everybody wanted
me to make *The Color Purple* every movie I did.
—WHOOPI GOLDBERG, OCTOBER 1987

The end of 1987 was a time of transition for Whoopi in many subtle
ways. She had made six feature films and assorted television network appearances. At thirty-two, she was no longer the ingenue.
Once the antiestablishment heroine, she had become just another celebrity. For some African Americans she had failed as a role model for her
race.

Goldberg had tired of black action groups condemning her for one
alleged misstep or another. Long irritated at suppressing—at least by her
own outspoken standards—her thoughts on these often humiliating criticisms and challenges, she finally lashed back at the black community's
disparaging comments. She told Allan Carter of the *New York Daily News*:
"Many black men have complained about me because I don't think black
or white. If I thought of myself as just a black actor I would never work
again. And I'm a bad role model because I say the 'F' word. How about
my involvement with the homeless, *Comic Relief,* human rights. I also
help support five or six AIDS patients. . . . How about that?"

As for the claim that she did nothing to help blacks get jobs in her
films, she countered, "How many actors do you know that get casting
approval? They don't come to me and say, 'Whoopi, who do you want in

this movie with you?' But I know my crews have more blacks and Chinese working on them than any other."

In addition to her busy professional life, her home life became more complicated. Whoopi was a mainstream star frequently on location for her work. In contrast, her stay-at-home cinematographer husband, David Claessen, was relatively unknown both in the film industry and to the public. There were rumors of dissension in the Goldberg-Claessen household, which led the press to ask Whoopi about the status of her year-old marriage. By now she was experienced in using diverting quips and ambiguous remarks to redirect the media's attention when they interrogated her about sensitive topics. So when pushed to discuss her marriage, she said with pointed vagueness: "It's working so far. It might not work later, so stick around and you may get lucky."

Regarding her relationship with daughter Alexandrea, now fourteen, Goldberg said, "Once they hit their teens, they don't want to see you." When asked if her daughter saw her movies, Whoopi admitted offhandedly, "Sometimes she goes with her friends. I got a big teen following, which I didn't know. These kids voted me their favorite. Because of the kids I cleaned up my junkie [stage] character. He doesn't shoot up drugs anymore."

If Goldberg's film career and personal life seemed to be drifting, one area absorbed her attention and interest: charity work in general and the homeless in particular. Such volunteer efforts gave Whoopi's life focus and status. On November 14, 1987, along with pals Robin Williams and Billy Crystal, she cohosted *Comic Relief II.* The relatively new, live fundraiser had become an annual stand-up-comedy event and on HBO. *Comic Relief II* was not only more slickly handled than the prior year's fundraiser; the cable licensing rights, the home-video edition, and the CD-album excerpts grossed more revenue than its predecessor for organizations dealing with the homeless.

In another charitable arena, Goldberg was named Entertainment Buddy of the Year. This was a new award given by AIDS Project LA at its third annual Commitment to Life Celebration, held in early November 1987 at the Wiltern Theatre in Los Angeles.

As she had promised months before, Goldberg now chose to return to her professional roots—the stage. This time, she was no longer the unknown theater personality who had a surprise success on Broadway. Instead, having established a wide fan base throughout the country because of her films and TV work, she decided to tour with her one-woman show. Asked why she would do a "rehash" of her Broadway success rather than something fresh, such as a new play, she said, "I don't like stage scripts when I'm working on my own. So if the audience is sitting there going, 'What is she doing?' I'm responsible to go up and say, 'Hey, it's okay—I'm just having some fun, you know? You paid twenty bucks, lighten up. Why sit there and have a bad time when you can have some fun?' I don't expect people to agree with everything I say nor like it. But I do think people are entitled to have a good time, and I like doing it. I'm a big ham sandwich ready to be eaten, and I like it. I really do."

Her theater showcase was now entitled *Living on the Edge of Chaos*. It featured her repertoire of familiar characters. There was her Surfer Chick, who allowed Goldberg to deliver a strong message to audiences: "Your kid could end up in the women's bathroom with a hanger in her crotch. That is why abortion is legalized—so that women do not have to be on bathroom floors anymore."

Goldberg's act also included her previously debuted Crippled Lady and Fontaine. The latter, like Whoopi, had undergone startling changes. Fontaine, the junkie with a Ph.D., decides to go clean and undergoes substance-abuse treatment at the Betty Ford Clinic in Palm Springs, California. A prime reason Fontaine cleaned up his drug dependency was because Whoopi felt responsibility toward her young enthusiasts: "I didn't realize how many kids watched and liked my show [*Whoopi Goldberg: Direct from Broadway*]. I was surprised. When I'm in a movie, you see me smoke cigarettes, but you don't see me drink alcohol. And there are no drugs in my films—just because I think of my [own] kid. If other kids are saying, 'I really love your work! I can't wait till you do something else,' I have to take that into consideration. I don't want to promote drug use, because Fontaine makes drugs look very hip. For him they work. That's how he gets through. So somehow he's going to clean up."

A little girl who contracted AIDS from a blood transfusion joined Whoopi's repertoire of fictitious personalities in her stage act. Another of Goldberg's new characters was seventy-seven-year-old, sex-driven Inez Beaverman, a lounge singer who once worked with Frank Sinatra. Additionally, there was a mental-institution patient, a man whom the audience first meets as he eats rose petals and delivers a telling thank-you speech.

When asked which of her inventory of stage alter egos she preferred best, Goldberg admitted it was the crippled lady, "because she is very gentle. And very wry. And very understanding of people, because the first thing she does is ask, 'Are you okay talking to me, because some people are uncomfortable with handicapped people.' . . . Soon you forget that she is handicapped and start focusing on her story about falling in love with a guy who isn't fazed at all by her handicap. He invites her to go swimming, and she says, 'Look, no. Forget it.' And he goes, 'Well, why not?' She does these things and discovers he's right. She's human. All that's wrong is a physical inability. Oh, yeah! You got a mind in there. You're a human being. You're in love. Sex! Yes! Handicapped people have sex! Of course! It's a revelation."

Whoopi's stage return premiered on December 26–30, 1987, at the Theatre Ballroom of the Golden Nugget Hotel in Las Vegas. In reviewing her brief Nevada stint, Joe Delaney wrote in the *Las Vegas Sun*:

> This critic-columnist hasn't been this moved by a performing artist since the first time we saw Marcel Marceau in person at a refurbished theater on Second Avenue and Twelfth Street in Manhattan. . . . Once a welfare mother, streetwise, not afraid to take on the establishment, putting her talent where her mouth is, working for causes she believes in, causes some of us are not yet ready to face, like the homeless and AIDS: there is a message as well as much mirth in her performance. . . .
> If there was a fault in her first show Sunday, it was an imbalance between the two. . . . There was a tiny minority there to see an academy Award nominee. . . . Everyone got what they paid for but this small faction resented the message content, for whatever reasons. . . . Perhaps Ms. Goldberg or some announcer voice should make a prior statement like "This performance is for mature audiences only."

Back in Los Angeles on a temporary break, Whoopi received an award from the California Theatre Council. The twelfth annual ceremony was held at the Mark Taper Forum on January 18, 1988, which Los Angeles Mayor Tom Bradley had named Whoopi Goldberg Day in the City of Angels. The emcees were actor René Auberjonois and Goldberg's longtime friend Ellen Sebastian, now artistic director of San Francisco's Life on the Water Theatre. Other celebrity guests included Michael J. Fox, comedian Bob Goldthwait, and actor Judith Ivey. The event raised $40,000 for the council's program to foster nontraditional casting.

Ten days later, Whoopi did four performances of her solo showcase at her alma mater, the San Diego Repertory Theater. Proceeds from Goldberg's appearances went toward an $80,000 challenge grant given to the rep by the local Parker Foundation. *Variety* noted: "She's one of the most versatile actors extant, and her range of talent creates characters and moments that you don't forget." The reviewer said of the segment dealing with the AIDS-infected youngster: "Goldberg's depiction of the little girl, remaining innocently cheery as she becomes more and more outcast, is classic in its poignancy."

One of Whoopi's next theater stopovers was at the Mayfair Theatre in Santa Monica, California. Her performances there were taped and later edited together for the HBO special *Whoopi Goldberg's Fontaine: Why Am I Straight?* This one-woman show was also made into a record, which would be nominated for a Grammy Award. Goldberg paused long enough in Los Angeles to appear in the low-budget *Beverly Hills Brats,* which went almost directly to home video when released in 1989. Whoopi can be seen in the film briefly, driving her new red Porsche convertible.

By early May 1988, Whoopi had finally embarked on her twenty-city *Living on the Edge of Chaos* tour. She was well aware of the inherent problems she would face, for she was now a well-known movie star performing in the theater. As she told Rick Kogan of the *Chicago Tribune,* "I know that I will be judged a little more harshly because of that. But what can I do about it?" Besides, she was more concerned with the exciting potentials of teaching her audience something about life: "People do not leave a show like this thinking about toilet paper and McDonald's. . . . There is turmoil in the world now, and I think my characters have some interesting insights into that."

On occasion, Whoopi's offstage, not her onstage, performances produced a strong reaction. When she performed in Atlanta, Georgia, she chose to lunch one day at the swank restaurant in the Ritz-Carlton Hotel, where she was staying. Arriving at the plush eatery, she was refused service because she was wearing a very casual outfit—sports shirt, blue jeans, tennis shoes. The hotel's general manager informed her that she could only be served if she changed into more appropriate attire.

When Goldberg declined to do so, the snub was heard around the country. A hotel spokeswoman attempted to exert damage control. "The Ritz-Carlton," she said, "is not in the business of setting social mores or standards. We do have to respect the wishes of our other guests who do come in semiformal attire. We talked to Ms. Goldberg about it, and she understood."

Not quite so! Whoopi told her side of the story when interviewed on a local Atlanta radio station. She said that strict dress codes should *not* apply when "you have the money to spend and you're clean and presentable." And where did Whoopi eat that unpleasant day in Atlanta? She was finally served lunch in the Ritz-Carlton lobby, not in their showcase restaurant.

Whoopi had interrupted her scheduled tour for a movie assignment. *Homer & Eddie* had originally been written as a road-buddy movie for two guys. When Whoopi joined Jim Belushi in the new movie, "her" role was altered to a degree—but not by much. In fact, her on-screen character still retained a male name—Eddie. She described the part thusly: 'I play sort of a psychotic person. You're not sure if it's a guy or a girl. I think of him as a guy who's in the process of dying from a tumor that makes him very prone to violent behavior."

Even on paper *Homer & Eddie* must have seemed a chancy project at best: A mentally retarded dishwasher (Belushi), who is innocent and childlike, picks up an escapee from a mental asylum (Goldberg). The latter joins him on his odyssey home to Oregon to see his parents for the first time in twenty years. The weird duo make their way across America in Eddie's ramshackle car. They stop along the way, where they just happen to learn a variety of life lessons, including pairing Homer the virgin with Eddie's seedy prostitute cousin. Goldberg relied heavily on a variation of her unisex druggie character, Fontaine, for her role in this movie. It proved to be a wrong choice. Within the film, her alter ego has a pathetic encounter with her dying mother and also indulges in an antisocial penchant for robbing and murdering strangers. Rather than aiming for a sympathetic performance, Whoopi, with bad guidance from both the script and director, emphasized her character's bizarre behavior: talking aloud to herself and becoming frozen by a series of phobias.

The completed *Homer & Eddie* was such an obvious fiasco that it sat on the shelf for nearly two years before gaining scant release. When it did appear, *Daily Variety* called it "a downer from beginning to end. Unfavorable comparisons with *Rain Man* (1988) are bound to be made." This bungled entry prompted Janet Maslin to point out in the *New York Times*:

"Eddie, for her part, has a sufficiently confused sexual identity to use the men's room in one scene and have Homer refer to her as 'he.' " Reacting unfavorably to Whoopi's latest androgynous film role, Maslin wrote, "Whoopi Goldberg remains one of the great unclassifiable beings on the movie screen."

Homer & Eddie was so badly received that Skouras Pictures, which was to distribute the picture throughout the United States, dropped their release plans after a few disastrous test engagements, which led to a lawsuit between the producing company, Kings Road Entertainment, and Skouras. The legal action in Los Angeles Superior Court was dropped in late 1990 when Kings Road received payment from, and an audit of, the relatively minuscule receipts from Skouras's extremely limited showings of the failed Homer & Eddie. As for Whoopi's reaction to her latest box-office misfire, she said, "When I saw the first cut of this movie, I thought, I'm not going to talk about it—ever! I don't want to know from it. I mean, it sucks. I don't know why they ever released it."

If Whoopi was spinning in several directions and bouncing from media to media in an effort to revive her faltering career, she also was in a down spiral with her second marriage.

By late spring of 1988, the one-and-a-half year union between Whoopi and David Claessen, which had been deteriorating for a long time, was virtually over. The May 23, 1988, issue of People magazine quoted Whoopi as having told the London Daily Mirror: "He only married me to further his career as a filmmaker." When asked what this statement meant, Goldberg's publicist replied, "No comment." By August of that year, the Goldberg-Claessen marriage had ended, and she was already dating studio cameraman Eddie Gold, whom she had met while filming Clara's Heart. Gold, white, Jewish, and some ten years older than Whoopi, was a far cry from the twenty-year younger and much handsomer David Claessen. On October 4, 1988, Whoopi filed for divorce in Santa Monica, California. Publicist Lee Solters, Goldberg's spokesperson, stated that she and Claessen had been "separated for some time" and that Goldberg was currently sharing a residence with cameraman Eddie Gold.

When Goldberg divorced her first husband, Alvin Martin, the marital split was accomplished quietly and peacefully, in part because they had a child. However, over the years Whoopi would have no kind words for ex-husband number two. She would tell *Jet* magazine in November 1989 that this union had been "very costly to get out of." In March 1991 she confided to *Ebony* magazine interviewer Laura B. Randolph: "The man walked off with a car, a house, and all my cash. And he didn't come with nothing." Goldberg also claimed that Claessen came into her life "with air. Bad air at that." When *Ebony's* Randolph asked if she would consider marrying again, Whoopi answered, "The last one cost me too much money. It left a permanent scar."

Still later, for the January 1997 issue of *Playboy* magazine, Whoopi told David Sheff about the unusual background of her failed second marriage. A terse, inference-packed statement, it says a lot even in its brevity. "And then [after her first divorce] I didn't get married. I went out with a couple of people and then slipped back into a little drug haze and woke up married to somebody else. . . . Yeah, and it took me about a year and a half to get out of that."

When contacted by this author in the period between late 1996 and early 1997, David Claessen declined to be interviewed regarding his relationship with Goldberg. Claessen has spent recent years as director of cinematography on commercials, documentaries, and some feature films. He did reveal, "I remarried five years ago to 'the funniest wife I have ever had' and divide my time between Los Angeles and Marin County, California."

As for the now-single-again Whoopi, life was still not simple. There were always those invisible celebrity watchers who insisted on their own take involving notable people. In the period after David Claessen and before she began dating Eddie Gold, Goldberg began traveling in social circles with one or another women friends. According to Whoopi, this started a lot of false grapevine gossip: "People assumed that I was gay because of . . . the way I look and because of the way they assume gay women are. I would show up in places alone or with a friend who happened to be female, so this created a lot of fervor." Her participation in the 1987 march on Washington, D.C., to fight for gay rights and more federal funds for AIDS research added more fuel to the fire.

Angered by the accusations of being a lesbian, Whoopi commented about these self-proclaimed moralists: "I'll tell them if they ask me, 'No, I'm not gay.' But people don't want to know that. They want to insinuate and *push* you out."

On another occasion, when interviewed by Vito Russo for the gay publication *The Advocate,* the unpredictable Goldberg was again asked to respond to the rumor that she was gay. "It's possible," she said. "I'm not practicing at the moment, but I will not say it will never happen or hasn't happened in my past."

CHAPTER TWENTY-TWO

Beam Me Up,
Captain Picard

I go in and I'm really sage and I get to wear great
hats. I also get to hang out with some extraordinary
people, like Patrick Stewart, LeVar [Burton], and
Jonathan Frakes.

—WHOOPI GOLDBERG, AUGUST 1993

Whoopi Goldberg had been a major *Star Trek* fan since its original small-screen airing in 1966–69. As a child living in the
Chelsea housing projects in New York, she sat fixated in front
of the TV set watching the weekly program. Goldberg remembers: "I
would tune in on Thursday nights, and it was like heaven." Lieutenant
Uhura (Nichelle Nichols), the communications officer aboard the USS
Enterprise, especially appealed to the youngster. She was not only a
woman, but she was black. Goldberg recalls that she was enormously
impressed by this female role model who demonstrated episode after
episode that "a black person had survived into the future."

When *Star Trek: The Next Generation* began its TV run in the fall of
1987, Whoopi was a devout follower of the program. She also had a
friend in the cast, LeVar Burton, the African-American actor who had
starred in the miniseries *Roots* in 1977 and, among many other acting
chores, hosted PBS-TV's *Reading Rainbow.* Goldberg had been a repeated
guest on that series. Whoopi told LeVar that she would love to be a guest
on *Star Trek: The Next Generation.* According to Goldberg, "he [Burton]
got the message to the producers, and they said, 'Yeah, right. Whoopi

193

wants to do *Star Trek!*' " Since the producers did not think Whoopi meant it, no job offer was forthcoming.

Then, in the spring of 1988, Goldberg's agents approached executive producer Gene Roddenberry, suggesting that Whoopi indeed would like to appear on *Star Trek: The Next Generation,* ideally in a recurring role. When Roddenberry heard this offer, he was incredulous. "I knew she was a star, so I didn't quite understand why she would take a secondary role on a series."

Now in its second season, the TV series was already undergoing cast changes. Denise Crosby's character, Lt. Tasha Yar, had been killed by an alien. She would be replaced as head of security by the already present Lieutenant Worf, the ship's Klingon officer. Another short-lived cast change about to occur was having Diana Muldaur's Dr. Katherine "Kate" Pulaski replace Dr. Beverly Crusher for one season as the *Enterprise*'s medical officer. Thus, there was room aboard the *Enterprise* for another occasionally recurring female character, such as the one Whoopi offered to play. Having Goldberg join the crew would also make the mix aboard the starship even more politically correct.

Whoopi remembers the *Star Trek* situation: "One of the characters had been killed off, and I asked them if they'd be interested in having me as part of the cast. And they said it would be okay as long as the rest of the cast said, 'All right.' And so I went in and met the captain [Patrick Stewart, who played Capt. Jean-Luc Picard] and just said, 'Please! I want to be on the show so bad! Beat me! Anywhere! Sometime!' . . . So they did. And that's how I got the job." She would soon express her enthusiasm about being a part of *Star Trek: The Next Generation,* "It's such a hot cast and real good scripts. I need actors. I don't need to be the star."

Beyond her love for *Star Trek,* why would Oscar nominee Whoopi Goldberg want to accept such an infrequent, subordinate role on a television series? On the surface it seemed such a comedown for a movie star. It was not until the summer of 1993, by which time she had concluded her stint on *Star Trek: The Next Generation,* that Whoopi admitted publicly all the reasons for her strange career decision: "I did it because, frankly, I couldn't get any work then. I liked the show, so I asked if I could be in it. . . . I did it as a tribute to my love of the show. I liked the idea of being in space. . . . I know I'm never going up in anybody's rocket ship. I know this because I don't even like to fly. . . . I thought being on *Star Trek* was a great way to sort of expand on the universe and be a part of it. Gene Roddenberry's vision always included a multiethnic group of people. I thought that was pretty amazing."

From the start, Goldberg made it clear to the producers of the series that because of other career demands she could only appear in occasional episodes and that she could only be available for a day or so of filming each time she was to appear in a segment. Even with this in mind, executive producer Gene Roddenberry was so impressed by Whoopi's enthusiasm and sincerity that he created a special new character for her to play. The role was that of Guinan, a highly insightful humanoid host and bartender who holds court over the spaceship's recreational lounge. The character was named after Texas Guinan, the popular nightclub hostess of the twenties.

As conceived, it would soon be Whoopi's Guinan who would make dramatic entrances, garbed in an ever-changing wardrobe of colorful, uniquely designed outfits topped by an array of strangely shaped hats. As part of Roddenberry's support of Whoopi's joining the *Star Trek* team, he had an elaborate new set constructed for the series to represent 10-Forward, the lounge where she was to rule. Goldberg said, "Roddenberry wanted a place where you could see the characters not 'characterizing,' where you could see them relaxing, and he needed someone in there to be a catalyst."

Goldberg's role of Guinan would have parallels in characters of later *Star Trek* spin-off series: Quark, the Ferengi barkeeper in *Star Trek: Deep Space Nine* (1993–   ) and Neelix the alien cook and morale booster in *Star Trek: Voyager* (1995–   ). In *The Next Generation,* Guinan is described as a member of a very old race of beings whose individual time span covers centuries of life. She acts as a confidante and counselor to the show's main characters while tending to the recreational lounge aboard the *Enterprise.* There is a hint that she knew Captain Picard from some earlier time.

As the wise counselor who dispenses advice, pinpoints problems, and proposes solutions, Goldberg would describe her character as "kind of like Yoda [from *The Return of the Jedi,* 1983]. She's very old and wise."

In retrospect, one of the intriguing creative questions regarding Guinan's presence in *Star Trek: The Next Generation* is why Whoopi's TV character was never more fully developed. Perhaps it was because she was not sufficiently exotic or enough of a counterbalance to the recurring major and minor characters of the sci-fi series. It could have been that the one-dimensional part she was given had nowhere to develop or that she did not push hard enough to have her part expanded due to her busy work schedule.

Goldberg made her debut on *Star Trek: The Next Generation* in the second season's opener, "The Child," which aired the week of November 21, 1988. She would receive special guest-star billing at the beginning of each episode in which she appeared. As the new, mysterious 10-Forward hostess, she advises the young ensign Wesley Crusher on the wisdom of whether he should join his mother, who has left the *Enterprise* to be in charge of Starfleet Medical. During the year 1988–89, Whoopi appeared in seven of the show's twenty-two segments. One of her more prominent offerings was "Q Who?" In this installment her character is explained further in reference to Q, a being from some other dimension. She has met Q somewhere else and dislikes any contact with him. Q, in turn, calls her a mischievous imp who is up to no good. It is in this segment that Q introduces Picard and the *Enterprise* to the Borg; thus, Guinan's role in this chapter expands greatly, as her race had encountered the Borg before. She warns Picard to remove the *Enterprise* quickly from any contact with them.

As anticipated, Goldberg's presence worked to the advantage of everyone. For the series it provided an added boost of publicity and credibility in having a performer of Whoopi's stature and popularity as part of the mix. It also gave Goldberg lots of publicity opportunities because of the offbeat casting and bizarre wardrobe. It was also a useful way to expand her fan base through the increasingly wide viewing audience of this show. Of key importance to her career, it provided her with an ongoing part on a successful series, thus allowing her to refer to herself as an employed actor—even when she was not doing a new movie, TV special, or a fund-raiser.

As the series swung into its popular third season, Goldberg was already well accepted by both the show's cast and TV viewers as a welcome addition to the program. She met with approval from her fellow actors because she did not try to dominate rehearsals on the set or to "hog" scenes on-camera, as she might have easily done. As a matter of fact, Whoopi so downplayed her presence in many of the episodes that sometimes she came across as overly low-keyed and almost too deferential in her interaction with fellow cast members. Strangely, too, there was a tentativeness to her performance as Guinan, which, on occasion, gave her performance an undesired flatness. This static quality was emphasized, from time to time, by an apparent nervousness on Goldberg's part, as if she felt out of place in the world of the future and that futuristic costumes made her uncomfortable.

For followers of the series, Whoopi was an intriguing, enigmatic presence. Since she was not present in that many episodes each season and her appearance in each of those segments was relatively small, she never wore out her welcome.

In her first year, Whoopi's character was supplemental to the episodes' plots and to the interaction among the ensemble cast. Then, as time wore on, her character grew, and she was allowed to do more as an actor. As her tenure extended, an increasing amount of Goldberg's type of humor emerged. This worked well with that "confide in me and I'll see how I can help you" quality which was a natural part of the character.

Because she was preoccupied with other outside acting assignments, Goldberg only made three appearances in the 1989–90 season of *Star Trek: The Next Generation*. However, she made up for it in the series' fourth season; she was aboard for eight segments. One of her most engaging episodes that year—or any of the series for that matter—was in "Clues," which aired the week of February 11, 1991. In this segment, Guinan is invited by Captain Picard to partake in a holodeck real-life adventure. The holodeck is a virtual-reality machine that can be programmed to simulate real life with various adventures to give variety to the crew's existence aboard the *Enterprise*. The holodeck program Picard selects describes a murder mystery in a twentieth-century Earth city. Picard is playing a private eye, and Guinan is his tough moll. She is somewhat confused by all the conventions and dress of this "game," in particular when the mobster holding them up in the detective's office is suddenly gunned down through the window behind them. Needless to say, Goldberg plays this situation for all its potential humor.

The fifth season of *Star Trek: The Next Generation* contained mixed blessings. The year 1991 was part of a yearlong twenty-fifth anniversary celebration of *Star Trek*. However, on the downside, Gene Roddenberry, the show's creator and guiding force, died of a series of strokes on October 26, 1991. As had become customary, Goldberg's Guinan, who also happens to be an excellent markswoman, was now part of the season's opening episode, "Redemption II." That show resolved the cliffhanger, involving who would become the Klingon emperor, that had ended the previous year's season. Of her six appearances during 1991–92, her most engaging occurred in the season's finale, "Time's Arrow." Here Data finds himself trapped in 1890s San Francisco and encounters a time-warp version of Guinan, a saloon keeper and madam as well as a friend of Mark Twain's, who is also featured in this entry. The plot premise was completed in the opening show of the next season, "Time's Arrow, Part II."

When *Star Trek: The Next Generation* began its sixth season, it found itself competing against a third *Star Trek* series. *Star Trek: Deep Space Nine*—an even more elaborate TV outing with an entirely new cast— began in syndication in January 1993. By now there were already rumors that *Star Trek: The Next Generation* would end after this its sixth season despite the fact that most of the recurring cast had eight-year contracts. There was even talk of some of the characters from *Star Trek: The Next Generation,* including Goldberg's Guinan, making crossover appearances on *Star Trek: Deep Space Nine*. Eventually, only Chief O'Brien and his wife and, later, Klingon security chief Worf would become permanent fixtures in the new series. Whoopi was in three chapters of the 1993–94 run, including "Rascals." In this fanciful outing, Captain Picard, Guinan, and two others crew members of the *Enterprise* find themselves transformed into beings with bodies of twelve-year-olds but still having the minds of adults. During the week of May 10, 1993, Whoopi made her final appearance of the season in "Suspicions."

By the time *Star Trek: The Next Generation* began its seventh and final season, Goldberg had left the series, although she had earlier announced that she would be available for the new batch of episodes. However, she was now too busy elsewhere. As for *Star Trek: The Next Generation,* after 178 episodes, it ended its lengthy television run during the week of May 23, 1994, with the two-hour segment "All Good Things." At this point, the show was dealing not only with the competition of *Star Trek: Deep Space Nine* but with the potential of yet another follow-up weekly property, *Star Trek: Voyager,* which premiered on January 16, 1995 on the UPN-TV network.

However, this was not to be the finale for the *Star Trek: The Next Generation* cast. They were assembled to appear in the seventh big-screen *Star Trek* adventure: *Star Trek Generations* (1994), in which some members of the old crew from the first TV series meet and mingle with the crew from *Star Trek: The Next Generation*. In this new theatrical release, Captain Picard and Captain Kirk finally encounter each other, with the latter dying during the course of the story. Goldberg made an unbilled appearance as Guinan. One rumor that circulated regarding Whoopi's not being billed in the film revolved around the fact that Nichelle Nich-

SCRAMBLING ON THE HOLLYWOOD TREADMILL

ols, unlike the other available members of the original TV series, supposedly had not been asked to appear in this new film. Allegedly, Whoopi felt this was a slight against Nichols, her "hero," and thus refused to be promoted in the cast list.

When *Star Trek Generations* was released in the fall of 1994, it received its usual mixed reviews from the critics. For example, Janet Maslin wrote in the *New York Times*: *"Generations* is predictably flabby and impenetrable in places, but it has enough pomp, spectacle and high-tech small talk to keep the franchise afloat." As for Whoopi's brief appearance in this sci-fi tale, Maslin insisted, "It's time for Ms. Goldberg to duck roles that require her to be patient, kindly and wise." Made at a cost of over $25 million, *Star Trek Generations* grossed over $74 million in ticket sales at the domestic box office in the United States and Canada.

In early 1995, when Larry King asked Whoopi on his cable-TV talk show if she planned to do more *Star Trek* movies, she replied, "I love *Star Trek*. I plan to do them as long as, you know, they have a costume that will fit me." However, when *Star Trek: First Contact,* the next big screen installment, was unveiled in 1996, Goldberg was nowhere to be seen. By then, she had abandoned flights of outer-space fancy with Guinan for more lucrative acting work on terra firma.

CHAPTER TWENTY-THREE

Whoopi in Transit

There's a script I'm interested in that they would
never have thought of me for because it's about a
Midwestern girl. Excuse me, but are there no black
people in the Midwest? I also want to do a cowboy
movie, but I guess we weren't there, either. It's very
peculiar. It's sort of like we were here in the early
1800s and then we disappeared. We came back as
cops and *Superfly* [1972], then we disappeared again.
Now we're sort of back in toothpaste commercials
and stuff. So it's tough.

—WHOOPI GOLDBERG, FALL 1988

One of the most intriguing aspects of Whoopi's hectic existence is
that every three to four years she undergoes a metamorphosis in
her professional and personal life which often leads her in new,
surprising directions. Such was the case in late 1988.

During that year, Goldberg returned to the stage with her one-
woman show, appeared in an HBO special, and made her bow on the
syndicated TV series *Star Trek: The Next Generation*. However, all this was
not sufficient for Whoopi, a highly energetic performer. She couldn't
resist a wide variety of guest shots on other TV shows, among them the
satirical *D.C. Follies,* the special *Free to Be a Family,* and, with several
other celebrities, oddball comedian Paul Reubens's *Pee-Wee's Playhouse
Christmas Special.* According to Whoopi, these undemanding TV guest
appearances were financially lucrative, demanded little time or effort, and
gave her easy access to a wide range of TV viewers. It never seemed to

200

Newlyweds Whoopi Goldberg and her second husband, cinematographer David Claessen (1986). (Courtesy of Archives Photos)

Whoopi Goldberg attending the 63rd Annual Oscar ceremonies, March 25, 1991, at the Shrine Auditorium with her daughter, Alexandrea. (Courtesy of Archives Photos)

A triumphant Whoopi Goldberg displays her Oscar for Best Supporting Actress in *Ghost* at the March 1991 Academy Awards. (Courtesy of Archives Photos)

Whoopi Goldberg hits the campaign trail for presidential hopeful
Bill Clinton in 1992. (Courtesy of Archives Photos)

Ted Danson and Whoopi Goldberg meet the press before the start of the Friars Club roast for Whoopi on October 8, 1993, in New York City. A few hours later, Danson's controversial blackface routine at the tribute turns the love fest into a tense media circus. (Courtesy of Archives Photos)

Whoopi Goldberg—the first woman to solo host the Academy Awards on March 21, 1994. (Courtesy of Archives Photos)

Whoopi Goldberg and fiancé Lyle Trachtenberg at Washington, D.C.'s Planet Hollywood restaurant in June 1994. Four months later, Lyle became Goldberg's third husband. (Courtesy of Archives Photos)

Confirming her superstar status, Whoopi Goldberg places her handprints in cement in the forecourt of Mann's Chinese Theatre in Hollywood on February 2, 1995. (Courtesy of Archives Photos)

Whoopi Goldberg and Broadway star and boyfriend Frank Langella exchange confidences at the Bushnell Theater in Hartford, Connecticut, while waiting for the start of the presidential debates (October 6, 1996) between President Bill Clinton and Republican presidential nominee Bob Dole. (Courtesy of Archives Photos)

occur to Whoopi that she might be overextending herself or diluting her unique appeal through constant overexposure.

During 1988, Whoopi continued to build her relationship with cameraman Eddie Gold, which had begun on the set of *Clara's Heart*. She said, "People never ask me to do stuff because they think, Oh, that's Whoopi. She would never want to just go out. So I asked him [i.e., Eddie Gold] to go for some Chinese food. . . . I have a pretty funny time with the old bald guy." For the November 14, 1988, issue of *US* magazine, Whoopi told Rita Kempley: "Yeah, it's pretty serious. It's not a new relationship—it's about a year old—and it's sort of amazing that it took so long for anyone to figure out that something was different. I mean, we've made no pretext about running around together over this year, and nobody noticed. Well, we just assumed that there were other things going on in the world." Soon thereafter, the couple became engaged officially. Whoopi even flew to New York City with Gold to meet his mother, Gladys, and the disparate trio went out one evening in Manhattan to celebrate Mrs. Gold's birthday.

Once again, Whoopi was now subjected to criticism from segments of both the black and white communities, who disapproved of her interracial romantic ties to Eddie Gold. Her reaction to the tasteless sniping about her white boyfriend: "I don't even listen. Nobody's going to tell me who I can sleep with. Who I sleep with and how I sleep with them should not be a problem because . . . if I'm looking to make peace in the world, then why do you want to mess with me and tell me I've done the wrong thing? Because [you think] I've let go of my culture? I'm *here*. I don't change my skin every day. Every day I'm out there, every movie I make I'm black. Every diamond I wear is worn on a black hand."

Toward the end of 1988, Whoopi evaluated her movie career. "In four or five years, I've made seven films and developed a body of work. While critics have not liked the material I've done, never have they ever had anything bad to say about my acting ability, which is why I still have a career. Cicely Tyson *wishes* she could have seven films behind her right now, and she's been around for 190 years. It's a slow process."

She went on: "Making movies is a compromise. You give a little; they take it! Don't get the wrong impression. I like doing movies. It's just an education. There's a lot of stuff you never think of, like I didn't know how many people were involved. So it's been a . . . learning experience—both bittersweet and wonderful. I like working."

She also confided: "I go looking for scripts. They don't send me stuff, because nobody knows what to do with me. I begged to be in *Ironweed* [which eventually starred Meryl Streep and Jack Nicholson]—I begged—because I thought that was a part I could've done. When I say that to people, at first they look at me, then an hour later they say, 'You know, that makes perfect sense.' " She further explained, "I like the idea that I'm working. I just won't let anybody tell me what I'm supposed to do, because if I wait for them, I'll never work. If I wait for a script written for someone who looks like me, you know I'd be mending shoes or [being] a waitress somewhere."

As to her unique look, which not only made her stand out from the Hollywood crowd but also inhibited filmmakers from considering her for certain parts, Whoopi said, "I've taken so much heat about my hair and the way I look. Well, this is it. And I'm not going to try and change myself because other people are not comfortable with me. I'm comfortable with me. I'm comfortable with it. So why should I be uncomfortable to make other people feel better? That's not a good idea to me."

On January 24, 1989, Whoopi was featured on a CBS-TV *Schoolbreak* special entitled "My Past Is Showing." It dealt with a 1961 sit-in to integrate a southern lunch counter and the dramatic repercussions the sit-in produced. The key role of Mariah Johnston had materialized for Goldberg because she had been meeting with CBS network executives about possible projects. At a lunch conference, she overheard an outline of "My Past Is Showing." She was so impressed by Alan Gansberg's script, which told its story from a black, *not* a white, point of view, that she asked if there might be a part for her. The network said most definitely yes.

When Gansberg learned that Goldberg was to be in his drama, he was ecstatic. "Whoopi is really fantasy casting for us. Feature film stars don't often do *Schoolbreak* specials, and what she'll do will elevate the whole project to a level we hadn't thought possible." While Goldberg provided a well-modulated performance in this hour-long drama, geared to youth audiences, her appearance on the program also sent a message to the entertainment industry that she was not finding it easy to get good screen roles if she had time to work on daytime TV.

Although her screen career was now faltering, Goldberg still earned high marks for her many charitable endeavors. For example, in mid-March 1989, she, Robin Williams, and Billy Crystal hosted *Comic Relief III* which aired as a four-hour HBO special. The fund-raiser generated over $3.5 million in pledges. Meanwhile, a few days earlier, on March 11, 1989, at the Century Plaza Hotel in Century City, California, Goldberg was the guest of honor at the Starlight Foundation's Humanitarian of the Year Award. Fifteen hundred people attended the sold-out, $275-a-plate, black-tie event, which raised $750,000 for the charity. In attendance with her daughter, Whoopi told the celebrity-filled audience, "It's very strange to hear the truth about things that I do. My feeling has been that if I didn't do it and this celebrity stuff doesn't last, I could be in deep sh–t. . . . It's not any great shakes, it's just what you are supposed to do."

––––––––––––

For many stars, acting in made-for-television movies is a distinct come-down from lead roles in theatrical features. If Goldberg felt this, she refused to admit it publicly. Thus, she accepted the starring assignment in *Kiss Shot,* her first TV feature. This debut, in 1989, came about when Jerry London, a specialist at directing well-mounted TV miniseries, was developing new projects for the CBS network. They asked him to work on a TV movie that would be a variation of Martin Scorsese's big-screen movie *The Color of Money,* released three years earlier. In that film, which costarred Tom Cruise, Paul Newman had reprised his role of Fast Eddie Felson, the pool shark in Newman's earlier screen hit *The Hustler.* The gimmick to be used in CBS-TV's project would be that it would feature female, instead of male, pool players.

While London was preparing *Kiss Shot* to specifications, CBS executives and Goldberg's representatives were in discussion about possible coventures. This prompted CBS decision makers to have Jerry London rework his script to accommodate a black female lead—Whoopi Goldberg. As the featured actor, Whoopi received a bit more than the usual $250,000 star salary for such work in the late 1980s. Because the TV movie was budgeted to use primarily nonunion support crews, the project was shot in San Jose, California—including footage at the Fairmount Hotel—where plenty of nonunion talent was available from nearby San Francisco.

To help Goldberg sharpen her pool-playing skills for the picture, director London hired a pool-trick player from Minnesota; he worked extensively with Whoopi for a week. By the end of the training session, she could do her own basic shots on-camera. Dorian Harewood, Whoopi's costar in this romantic comedy, was a pool expert himself, having played since the age of seven. During the four-week period of shooting this TV movie, London found Goldberg very amusing to work with on the set. "She was very profane, but in a funny way." According to the director, she would frequently say, "Jerry, I can't do this fuckin' line," and they'd stop and fix it.

In *Kiss Shot*'s Whoopi plays Sarah Collins, a single mother with a thirteen-year-old daughter (Tasha Scott). Sarah loses her job with a computer company in the Silicon Valley just as a balloon payment is due on her home mortgage. Eventually, it dawns on her to draw on her talent as a pool player to earn some quick dollars, a situation soon exploited by her newfound promoter (Dennis Franz). In the process of playing pool for money, she encounters a handsome, wealthy playboy (Dorian Harewood). An amorous relationship develops but quickly sours. Later, the duo are paired in a championship playoff during which they resolve their differences.

Televised in early April 1989, *Kiss Shot* was promoted with the ad line "The game of love is a lot like the game of pool. If you want to win you have to give it your best shot." The amiable, if conventional and derivative, offering received a critical drubbing. *People* magazine rated it a "D+" and implored: "Please, Whoopi, not another lovable, warmhearted character. Why can't Hollywood manage to find a vehicle for your irreverent talent? Dispense rage, sarcasm, controversy—anything but hugs and dopey dialogue." Chris Willman argued in the *Los Angeles Times,* "Other than her hair, which is braided and unbowed, the wildly subdued Whoopster is allowed no flamboyance whatsoever in her thankless role." *Newsday*'s Terry Kelleher found that Goldberg "offers a bland leading character who rarely has anything clever to say." Kelleher wondered aloud, "What's next for Whoopi Goldberg—a family sitcom?"

———————————

After making *The Color Purple* back in 1985, Goldberg surprised many with her choices of follow-up films, which saw her taking on Eddie Murphy–type roles in mindless action flicks. At the time, she claimed she liked doing them and that they should be accepted for what they were intended to be: lighthearted fare. By 1989 she was not only *not* being offered many of these type of action screen roles, she was now distancing herself from her string of bad movies: "Yes, I'm disappointed, but I take no responsibility for them. The studios take this nice, gritty script and turn it into pabulum."

Fortunately, Goldberg's fine work in *The Color Purple* stuck in some people's minds, which led to the first of her career turnaround assignments. Producer David Bell was preparing to shoot *The Long Walk Home,* based on a script by John Cork, then a University of Southern California film student. In the arduous process of bringing the project to fruition, Bell contacted Oprah Winfrey about starring in the film. She wanted to appear in the movie, but her TV-talk-show chores and other acting commitments made it impossible for her to accept the offer for several years to come. At this point in 1989, someone in the production office of New Vision Pictures suggested Whoopi Goldberg for the key role of Odessa Cotter. Much as Whoopi was intrigued by the prospect, she refused to agree until she knew who would play her colead. Meanwhile, Sissy Spacek, who had won an Oscar for *Coal Miner's Daughter,* had been approached to play Miriam Thompson in the movie. She, in turn, would not accept until she knew who her costar would be. Through diplomatic shuffling, both actors were eventually contracted for the dramatic feature.

Since *The Long Walk Home* was set in 1955 in Montgomery, Alabama, where sixty thousand blacks triggered the civil-rights movement, producer David Bell and screenwriter John Cork, who was from Montgomery, convinced their backers that the movie should be shot in Alabama, using actual historical sites whenever possible for the film. Originally, cinematographer John Bailey was hired to make his directorial debut with *The Long Walk Home.* However, after some days of actual filming on location, he was replaced by a more seasoned director, Richard Pearce.

If this change of directors caused tension on the set, so did the fact that the movie crew was re-creating civil-rights events that still angered many residents of Montgomery. While Spacek, who brought her family on the trek, stayed mostly to herself when not filming, Goldberg, with her usual enthusiasm, was on the set every day, whether she was on call or not. She was there to keep morale up and to participate in the filmmaking process even from the sidelines. There were rumors during the making of this movie that the two lead actors did not get along. One source said, "Whoopi thought Sissy was on a star trip, and Sissy thought Whoopi wasn't being professional. Things came to a head when

Whoopi's brother [Clyde] was hired to work [as a driver] on the movie."
When asked if any of this were true, Goldberg's spokesperson denied any
such problems.

The plot of The Long Walk Home focuses on two women in mid-
1950s Montgomery, Alabama. Each of the duo—a black maid (Goldberg)
and her white employer (Spacek)—are the mainstays of their families.
The drama deals with how each comes to terms with the bus boycott
by local African Americans after a black woman, Rosa Parks, refuses to
ride in the back of a public bus. As the boycott takes its toll on both
women and their families, the two disparate women bond. The good-
hearted but unworldly white woman has a rude awakening about the
injustice of racial discrimination. Suddenly she realizes that as a well-
bred southerner she had taken too much for granted about racial segre-
gation.

To better understand her character, Whoopi researched this crucial
period in civil-rights history. She even turned Method actor. She decided
to replicate, at least once, the long walk that these blacks had endured
because they did not have their own cars and because they refused to ride
on the bus. Each day, they traveled from their modest homes in Montgomery to the other side of town, where they were employed as domestics in more well to do white people's homes. After a strenuous day of
domestic chores, they had to trudge back home in time to cook, clean,
and nurture their own families before dragging off to bed. Then they had
to get up early the next morning and begin all over again.

Goldberg recalls: "That walk is long. I—I did a four—I think it was
a four-mile one—in sneakers, you know, and my dogs were killing me.
You know, but I was thinking about those women who—who did that
walk every day—every day for almost what? A year and a half, two
years—a long time, you know. And thinking about the things they had to
listen to and take. See, because somebody would eventually say 'cut' [on
the set]. You know. I could walk away and thumb my nose at the whole
thing and—and not want to be bothered for, you know, a day or two or
whatever. . . . [T]hat was available to me as an alternative. There was
no alternative for these women in the fifties."

Whoopi also admits the acting job "was a trip, because I went down
there kind of with a little bit of an attitude, you know, kind of like, 'Well,
what took you all so long,' and when—these ladies [who had lived
through the events] said to me, 'Sit down, child. Let me explain to you.
You did not buck the system. Okay, you didn't buck the system. It took

us a long time to figure out how to do it in such a way that nobody could point their finger to us and say . . . how disgusting or dirty or whatever we were, because we continued to go to work. You know, we continued to take care of business. We showed them that in fact one person who finds another person who finds another person can make a difference. We did not write ourselves off,' and that for me was a big awakening."

Thanks to preparation for her role, Whoopi developed fresh insights about her race and what African Americans had to go through just a few decades earlier. She explained: "You have to understand that we're talking about 1955, and the bottom line was you didn't sass or talk back or they killed you. Very simple. You died, or you lost your job—even worse, you know. So that was very bizarre for me, you know, because it meant I couldn't even give her, like, a nineties look. I couldn't suck my teeth in. I couldn't do nothing, you know. I just—I had to just, you know, sit on it. I had to sit on it, and people keep saying, Oh, you know, there was, you know, this quiet strength. It's this rage. It's not a quiet strength. It's this silent rage that I— I understand now what these people had to deal with, because there was nothing they could do."

Part of the film's plot focuses on how the black citizens bear up under the increased racial discrimination as they battle to gain equality with the white majority. When Goldberg was later a guest on Oprah Winfrey's syndicated TV talk show, the host asked her visitor about the tension while filming and the effect, "even if it's acting," of being called "nigger" by other cast members. Goldberg responded with "Oh, no, wait a minute, not just nigger, but nigger, nigger, nigger, nigger. . . . One guy [on the set] made a mistake and said it while we weren't shooting. I said, 'I'm the nigger you work for, you know.' "

One of the things that Goldberg is most proud of is that during this movie project she increasingly took an active role as a creative leader, not just a follower. During filming and postproduction there was much talk of shortening the film's lengthy running time. To do so, the producers— Howard W. Koch Jr., Dave Bell, Taylor Hackford, and Stuart Benjamin— had to choose which sequences could be cut. Goldberg said, "That was one of the areas where I had to take Burt Lancaster's advice and fight. When they were talking about scenes they thought they might be able to lose and two were my family scenes, I lived up to my reputation and went ape crap. But they're in there."

Once *The Long Walk Home* was completed, the front office debated whether to release it so close to the debut of the big-budgeted, highly promoted *Driving Miss Daisy,* which appeared the previous year. Both films had similar story lines involving a white employer and black servant. (In the case of *Driving Miss Daisy* it was a chauffeur.) The other option was to wait before distributing the new movie so it would not be compared unfavorably with the multi-Oscar-winning earlier film starring Jessica Tandy and Morgan Freeman. The latter course was taken by Miramax Pictures, which had contracted to distribute *The Long Walk Home.*

After sitting on the shelf a long time, the PG-rated, ninety-seven-minute-long movie finally opened in New York and Los Angeles in late 1990 so as to be eligible for Academy Award consideration, which did not happen. It then had a spotty release in the rest of the country in midyear and never made much money at the box office or impressed the reviewers.

Louis Menand wrote in *Vogue* magazine: "It's hard to give dramatic resonance to a conflict in which history, justice, and high moral style are all on one side and the other side has nothing going for it but bigotry and ignorance. But *The Long Walk Home* has to try." Menand added, "Whoopi Goldberg is the movie's surprise, for she turns out to be ideal in the role of a woman whose character is the antithesis of everything implied by the name Whoopi. She underplays the anger that inspires her to walk ten miles to work, and she underplays the weariness too. The performance holds the movie together."

Janet Maslin, of the *New York Times,* noted, "Because Whoopi Goldberg is the most prominent black actor of the moment, she is offered roles like this regardless of whether they suit her." But, Maslin conceded, "Ms. Goldberg accomplishes this [i.e., her characterization] with dignity, reserve and a lot more credibility than might be expected."

Though well-intentioned, *The Long Walk Home* was not especially appreciated at the time of its first theatrical release, it has since gained a minor cult reputation as a well-acted, solid drama. However, this film once again put Goldberg in the unenviable position of having to defend herself to portions of the black community who found her screen work in it offensive—no matter the historical context—by her choosing to play yet another domestic on-screen. Nevertheless, at the NAACP Image Awards held in January 1991, Goldberg won for the third time for her performance in *The Long Walk Home.*

Whoopi has always been proud of participating in this unheralded movie drama. Whenever someone compliments her for her "restrained" performance in this picture, she has always been quick to counter with "It's restrained because that's what those women had to do. They were mad, but they had to work to support their families."

CHAPTER TWENTY-FOUR

Winning an Oscar

I didn't know my career was so far down the toilet
until I read the reviews for *Ghost* [1990].
— WHOOPI GOLDBERG, AUGUST 1990

By the summer of 1989 it was no secret, not even to Whoopi Goldberg, how far her career had fallen or how much she had dropped in perceived public esteem. For example, back in 1984, *Esquire* magazine had named Whoopi one of the six most influential people changing the face of the entertainment industry. However, in its August 1989 issue, as an adjunct to its feature article on "Women We Love," *Esquire* printed as a sidebar about Goldberg: "Get a movie. Get a haircut. Get serious."

Several months before Whoopi went on location to make *The Long Walk Home,* she campaigned hard for another screen role. It was the offbeat part of the eccentric, fake medium Oda Mae Brown in the upcoming Paramount feature *Ghost.* One of her former managers, Barry Josephson, had slipped her a copy of the script and told her she must read it. Once she learned that the vehicle was to be directed by Jerry Zucker (he and his brother David were responsible for the zany comedy *Airplane!* [1980] and other hits), Goldberg pursued the possible movie assignment aggressively.

Whoopi was among the very first to read for the part of the phony medium in *Ghost.* After doing that, she was told that the filmmakers were looking for an unknown. Director Zucker later explained that initially he thought that Goldberg's overly strong personality would throw the film out of kilter. "I didn't want the role to be a vehicle for anybody," he said.

There was another consideration, according to Zucker: "Based on her earlier movies, I definitely had a preconceived notion of her as this kind of funny, crazy person. But that wasn't the role we were casting."

Thus, even though she knew she had a terrific handle on the role and had done a good job of reading for it, Whoopi suffered the humiliation of having to sit by while most everyone else in town auditioned for "her" part. "They wanted just about everybody." Goldberg recalled, "They woke folks up from the dead to talk about that part." Among the other contenders considered to play Oda Mae Brown were TV-sitcom star Nell Carter and rock singer Tina Turner. Still, Zucker would not make a final decision as to who would play the phony medium.

Goldberg kept in touch with the *Ghost's* casting people, insisting that she was best possible choice for the role. However, says Whoopi, "they just would not give me this role. And they looked everywhere: under rocks, bathrooms, everywhere." Then, she continues, "six months later, I got a phone call saying, 'You know, we couldn't find anybody better for this than you. So, do you want to do it?' I said, 'Yeah.'" Zucker has admitted that once he was ready to reconsider Whoopi for the screen part and actually met her, he "was surprised, because she had a warmth I hadn't realized was there before." It also developed that Patrick Swayze, who had been cast in the title role of *Ghost,* was a big fan of Goldberg's and had insisted that the filmmakers reconsider her.

Accepting the part was not a case of Goldberg's swallowing her pride after having been kept dangling so long. Rather, from her perspective, it was a victory of bringing others around to her viewpoint. Besides, Whoopi was a self-admitted workaholic who wanted to "keep the machinery oiled. . . . Work is work. The idea is to make it as good as you can."

Filming of *Ghost* began in July 1989, a few weeks after Goldberg finished her work on *The Long Walk Home.* Scenarist Bruce Joel Rubin, who conceived *Ghost,* explained the film's unique perspective: "The story is told from the point of view of the ghost. I was intrigued by the idea of capturing the sensations and emotions of a person who suddenly realizes they have passed from life into an immaterial world—a new universe."

Ghost revolves around New York banker Sam Wheat (Patrick Swayze) and Molly (Demi Moore), his sculptor/lover, who move into their dream Manhattan loft. Although the couple are deeply in love, Sam fears a commitment to marriage. One night on the way home from the theater, they are attacked by a mugger, and Sam is murdered. He is flabbergasted to discover that despite being dead, his spirit still remains on earth. The bereft Molly can neither see nor hear him, so she is unaware of his warnings once he discovers that Lopez (the mugger—played by Rick Aviles) acted in collusion with the couple's supposed good friend and Sam's coworker, slimy Carl Bruner, played to the hilt by Tony Goldwyn.

Later in *Ghost,* through an accidental encounter with Oda Mae Brown, played by Whoopi Goldberg, Sam discovers that this spiritual adviser is not such a fake, after all. She can actually see and hear him! He convinces the bewildered woman to help him communicate with Molly. Moreover, Oda Mae becomes Sam's confederate in exposing Carl's crooked manipulations. Once Bruner is dispatched, Sam resignedly departs for the hereafter. Before leaving, he and Molly reaffirm their great love. He tells her, "It's amazing. . . . The love inside. You take it with you."

Throughout the summer 1989 shoot of *Ghost,* Goldberg relished her role as the zesty con artist who discovers that she is a legitimate spiritual reader. Her greatest problem was in interacting with the ghost figure, whom, in their first scenes together, she cannot see. She explains, "Have you ever tried to work with somebody who was there but not there? It isn't easy. Not looking at Patrick was very hard and sort of crazy-making. Every once in a while we would be doing a scene and everything would seem to be going okay when suddenly Jerry [Zucker, the director] would call cut. I would ask him what the problem was, and he would tell me I was looking at Patrick. I would tell him, 'No, I'm not.' So we would shoot the scene again, and I would be looking all around and trying not to look at Patrick."

There was also a dicey moment in *Ghost* when it came time to film the scenes where Swayze's Sam enters Oda Mae's body so he can physically caress Molly, his lost love. Originally, it was structured that filmgoers would see Oda Mae, with Sam's spirit, inside her, being affectionate with Molly. Then it was realized that movie audiences might misconstrue the scene and think there was a lesbian relationship going on between the medium and the sculptor. So the sequence was reconfigured to have Sam's spirit enter Oda Mae's being. Then she fades from view, and the audience sees the embodied Sam sharing tender moments with the teary, emotionally fragile Molly.

Goldberg was among those in the production who had pressed for the three-way love scene to be redeveloped, as was done finally for the release print. "There was no reason for me to do a love scene with Demi. Demi closing her eyes and seeing Patrick plays much better. It's very well done. But I know more than one person who was very nervous when they saw *my* hand creep in there [on-camera, before the scene fades into the romantic interaction between Swayze and Moore]." Then, too, Whoopi had good reason to be so cautious about moviegoers' sensibilities. She recalled all too well the problem of the lesbian rumor that clung to her because of the suggested relationship on-screen between her Celie and Shug in *The Color Purple* (1985).

As to her *Ghost* costars, Goldberg said, "Patrick and Demi are different types of actors than I am. They needed more space and quiet between scenes. But I liked a lot of noise and bad jokes. And there was a lot of that. Jerry was always in a funny place, and Rick Aviles is one of the craziest people I've ever met. I had some of those days when things got heavy and I wasn't in the best of moods, but then one of the crew members would come along and tell me a really awful dirty joke. I would bust up, and everything would be fine again." Whoopi observed, "I think Oda Mae is the best part in the movie. I think it's written solidly, and when you have two actors like Demi and Patrick who allow you to just bloom and blossom in it without any attitude, it's happening. It's happening."

Despite the slight aura of hokum and sticky sentiment as well as the movie's inconsistent ground rules created for ghosts still on earth, critics responded well to the new release. Sheila Benson wrote in the *Los Angeles Times:* "In our increasingly fragile and unpredictable world, *Ghost* . . . might well strike a seductive chord. . . . Director Jerry Zucker is packaging the distilled essence of romantic yearning and he's done a canny job of it." As for Goldberg's performance, Benson reported, "Oda Mae, stunned to discover that for the first time her gift is real, is Goldberg in her element, giving the film its kick and energy. In the three-way scenes with Sam and Molly, as Sam's mouthpiece on Earth, translating, transposing, deleting in outrage when his language offends her, Goldberg is gleefully, wickedly funny. Working out the villain's comeuppance she's even better."

The *New York Times*'s Janet Maslin said *Ghost* "is nothing if not earnest. It's also eccentric enough to remain interesting even when its ghost story isn't easy to believe. . . . *Ghost* veers repeatedly from the somber to the broadly comic with a number of strange but appealingly offbeat digressions along the way." As to its cast, Maslin added, "Fortunately, the third of the film's three stars is Whoopi Goldberg, the one performer here who seems to have a clear idea of what she's up to. Dressed in a long teased wig and flowing gold robes Ms. Goldberg plays a disreputable medium named Oda Mae Brown . . . and Ms. Goldberg plays the character's amazement, irritation and great gift for back talk to the hilt. This is one of those rare occasions on which the uncategorizable Ms. Goldberg has found a film role that really suits her, and she makes the most of it."

With an ad campaign slogan "You Will Believe" and a surprise hit song, the Righteous Brothers' recording of the old tune "Unchained Melody" on the soundtrack, *Ghost* became the surprise summer hit of 1990. Made at a cost of some $25 million, it grossed $218 million at the box office in forty-one weeks of domestic distribution in the United States and Canada. Its soundtrack album sold over 500,000 copies. Later, when the videocassette edition of *Ghost* was released in March 1991, Paramount Home Video had preorders for 595,000 copies from North American video retailers alone, making *Ghost* the then-biggest-shipping rental title of all time.

When the Academy Award nominations for 1990 were announced in February 1991, Goldberg was among those chosen for Best Supporting Actress. Her competition included Annette Bening (*The Grifters*), Lorraine Bracco (*GoodFellas*), Diane Ladd (*Wild at Heart*), and Mary McDonnell (*Dances With Wolves*). On the day of this key announcement, Whoopi was still asleep when she was called with the good news, for it was 5:30 A.M. where she was: "The phone rang and I thought, Somebody is dead, or I owed somebody some money, all right, and . . . they just tracked me down and I picked up the phone and somebody said, 'Aarh, aarh, aarh,' and I went, 'What? What?' They said, 'Aarh, aarh, aarh.' I said, 'Slow down. Slow down please,' and they said, 'You've just been nominated,' and I just went, 'Yes, I love it,' and then it just sort of got stranger and stranger as the day went on, because there was a good possibility that I could win, and the six weeks before it were somewhat traumatic because it was so positive and so encouraging that I would be in the bathroom, in the movies and . . . voices would come under the stall saying, 'You know you're going to win, don't you,' you know, and it's like, 'Oh, thank you.' "

One person not so overjoyed by Whoopi's Oscar nomination was movie critic Roger Ebert. In a *New York Daily News* article on Whoopi Goldberg, he pointed out: "Ironically, the [Oscar] nomination came for the kind of work she has done many times before in the movies—while the Academy overlooked her inspired and truly wonderful performance in *The Long Walk Home*." (Other awards that Goldberg would accumulate for *Ghost* included a Golden Globe, a NAACP Image Award, the British Academy Award, an American Comedy Award, and the Saturn Award, given by the Academy of Science Fiction, Fantasy and Horror Films.)

Finally, after weeks of nervous anticipation, Monday, March 25, 1991, the night of the 63rd Annual Academy Awards, arrived. Feeling optimistic because of the Hollywood Oscar buzz that she was the favorite to win, Whoopi went all out on her full-length gown to wear to the ceremony. She hired Nolan Miller, the veteran costume designer who did the wardrobe for TV's *Dynasty* and who had recently designed chic outfits for Whoopi's new movie, *Soapdish*. Miller created her stunning ensemble for this special evening, which included jewelry accessories. Goldberg described it as "a very simple sequin black dress with the slit . . . a very nice slit, a breezy kind of slit." She attended the ceremonies at the Shrine Auditorium in Los Angeles with Alexandrea and others. (It was her daughter who explained to syndicated gossip columnist Liz Smith what the small tattoo of a bird over Goldberg's left breast signified. The girl explained it was the bird "Woodstock" from the Peanuts comic strip.)

When it came time to announce the Best Supporting Actress Award, the TV cameras focused in on Goldberg and the other category nominees. As presenter Denzel Washington announced her name as winner, Whoopi remembers thinking, Please God, don't let me trip [going up onstage]. She also admits that she hesitated before going up the aisle because "I was still sure that Denzel was going to go, 'Oh, no, no, I— that's what I was thinking, but here's the real winner.' I mean, I just—I wasn't sure still." Even when she went onstage she double-checked the winner's name on the card inside "the envelope." She had indeed won an Oscar.

Regarding her acceptance speech, Goldberg explains, "I was afraid that if I prepared a speech, people would think I had gotten cocky be- cause there was so much . . . I mean, the oddsmakers and the people in the newspapers . . . You had to stop reading news—I did. I stopped watching television, I stopped reading newspapers, because you start to think, God I really do want it. I do, and I didn't want to be humiliated mentally, not outwardly, but in here, you know, because the heat was so intense. It was like, 'Yes, you're going to win. Yes, you're going to win,' and I thought, What am I going to do if I lose? . . . So, I just thought,

I'm not going to prepare anything, and if it happens, whatever comes out will be me, and it did. I tried to say something to my brother. I made a half statement like—you know, the whole statement for that, 'My brother will never have to listen to me prepare another stupid speech again, because since I was small, that's what I did every year. I read these bogus little speeches . . . and so—and I forgot to— And I started that and my mind went [blank] and I forgot to thank people. . . . I remembered to thank Paramount."

Her actual speech included such statements as "Ever since I was a little kid, I wanted this. You don't know. I'm so proud to be here. I'm proud to be an actor, and I'm going to keep on acting, and thank you so much." As she left the stage, the jubilant Goldberg flashed one of her wide-mouthed, radiant smiles and quipped, as she look closely at her Oscar, "I was kinda hoping there'd be a battery pack in this!"

Like the other Academy Award winners, Whoopi was swamped backstage at the ceremonies by the media. When asked how she felt, she replied, "It will keep me very warm in my bed tonight. Aside from that, I don't know that it will do anything except put me in the history books as the second black female to win an Oscar."

She also said, "I hope it opens more doors for other good actors, but if we start talking about ourselves as black . . . immediately there's no work . . . because everybody will tell you there's no work for . . . ethnic people in Hollywood. So I always sneak in and let them sort of come around to 'Oh, you're black.'" Another Oscar chronicler on hand asked Goldberg if she thought there was anything bad about winning an Oscar statuette. Her answer: "Are you f——g nuts!"

After the Oscar telecast, a jubilant Whoopi went on the VIP party circuit. After stopping by the Governors' Ball, hosted by the Academy of Motion Picture Arts and Sciences, she was driven in her limousine to agent Swifty Lazar's annual Oscar bash: "Kathy Bates [who won Best Actress for *Misery*] and I both carried our Oscars in. Jeremy Irons [who won Best Actor for *Reversal of Fortune*] left his in the car, and we, I think, were the most eclectic bunch of winners. I mean, from Joe Pesci [who won Best Supporting Actor for *GoodFellas*] to Kathy Bates to Jeremy Irons to myself, it was just a very lovely bunch of folks."

Goldberg partied until two in the morning, then went home, where she was greeted by her brother, Clyde, and her daughter, Alexandrea. Drained by the evening, Goldberg told them, "You know what happened;

good night." However, before going to sleep, she called her mom to share the excitement of the victory.

Goldberg recalls that when she awoke the next morning, she began to laugh "because I thought . . . of all the things that have happened in my life. . . . A great many wondrous and fabulous things have happened, but this is the one thing that will never, ever, wear off. Every time I look at that Oscar, I'm going to know what it is and where it came from."

After her Oscar triumph, Goldberg kept her prewin vow to treat the "losers" in her category to a fancy meal and a night on the town. She hosted a dinner for Diane Ladd, Annette Bening, and Mary McDonnell. (Lorraine Bracco was on location in Mexico for a film and was unable to attend.)

A few weeks later, when she was a guest on Oprah Winfrey's TV talk show, Goldberg had a lot to say about winning the Academy Award: "It meant for me that I was as good as I thought I was and I was as good as anybody out there. It meant that I would not have to listen to or be picked on anymore with stupid comments like that woman from the *Times* [who said in a review, "Did anyone really like *Jumpin' Jack Flash*], you know. It meant that whenever anybody talked to me, they would now give me my title, which was Academy Award winner."

Nearly a year later, in February 1992, when TV's Mark McEwen interviewed Whoopi on *CBS This Morning,* he asked anew what it had felt like to win the Oscar and to explain the genuine look of pleasure on her face that March 1991 evening: "Baby, I was so happy. It was—it's one of those moments that you can never, ever. . . . There's not enough time in the world to explain what happened. But I wanted that so badly, and for all my life. And I wanted it also because it had taken fifty years for one of us to get it. . . . I'm going back for another one."

Three years later, on February 7, 1995, Goldberg found herself again visiting *CBS This Morning.* Once more, Whoopi was asked how it felt—now that time had passed—to have won an Academy Award: "I like the idea that I open my eyes and the second thing I see is Oscar, you know. . . . I—I love that. And I let people play with him because he—he really does represent a goal for people who want to act. It is—you know, it is one of those things that everybody wants. And I'm part of a select few in the history of film, you know, that has one. So I'm very, very . . . I'm just big proud. Okay? I'm just big proud."

CHAPTER TWENTY-FIVE

Personal Problems— Whoopi Style

Well, I've had a very peculiar career. People keep
telling me this. I don't tend to look at it like in the
future. It will be what it will be. I've had a great
time. I've had two bad experiences, and seven or
eight or nine movies and a TV show and stage stuff.
As long as the work keeps coming, I'm happy. That's
my thing. . . . . I don't like not to work.
—WHOOPI GOLDBERG, MAY 1989

If achieving fame had been a long, arduous process for Whoopi Goldberg, adjusting to its complex demands was equally difficult. Along
the way, she sometimes faltered by taking an inappropriate career
step. On other occasions, she made what proved to be a faulty choice in
her personal life. And at each turn in her professional or personal life, the
media were always monitoring her and eagerly reporting the infraction of
the moment and its aftermath. As with other luminaries, the press
glossed over Whoopi's brighter moments in favor of harping on negative
or unfortunate situations in her event-filled life. In addition, members of
the black community kept a constant vigil over her activities. They were
quick to cry, "No! No!" whenever this unwilling role model for her race
did anything that bothered a particular segment of black America.

While Whoopi had business managers, agents, and industry friends
(Robin Williams, Billy Crystal) to provide career advice, she lacked the
continuity and support a life partner could have provided in helping her

make wiser choices in her private life. She certainly had not been lucky or successful in her choice of mates. Her first two marriages had ended in divorce, and her romantic liaisons in the years between marriages and thereafter, including the long-term, live-in situation with Berkeley-based playwright David Schein, had not endured. In the late 1980s, Whoopi spent more than a year being involved with camera operator Eddie Gold, to whom she became engaged. However, by 1990, that amorous relationship had dissolved, and Goldberg was soon appearing on the social scene with a variety of new male friends. Among them were fellow *Star Trek: The Next Generation* actor Brent Spiner, who played the android Lieutenant Commander Data, and stage and film actor Eric Bogosian.

Adding to the instability of Goldberg's domestic existence was her frequently dysfunctional home life. For a long time after she moved to California in 1974, Goldberg had been physically separated from her mother and brother. By the end of the 1980s, Whoopi's mother would be taking care of Alexandrea in Berkeley, and Goldberg's brother, Clyde, would become her personal driver on her movie projects. Whoopi's only relative close at hand during much of the 1980s was Alexandrea. As Goldberg became more successful in her career, professional and personal demands kept her from being the full-time mom that her daughter sought. Thus, when Goldberg left Berkeley and relocated to Los Angeles to make movies, Alexandrea chose to remain in northern California. Cared for by Goldberg's mother, the teen drifted further apart from her famous parent. Whoopi was certainly aware of the widening breach. However, she had neither the desire nor the time to mend her fences with the girl.

Years later, in retrospect, Goldberg would admit, "You make specific choices with children. I didn't make the mother's choice. I chose my career. I should have cared more. I was selfish, and I am selfish. But I just felt that when opportunities came up, I had to take the ball and run. I would have become very angry and bitter otherwise. I've learned since what being a mother means, what those responsibilities entail. I know that I have to care more." She also acknowledged that it was an error to treat her child like a roommate, "like we were pals, without realizing that somebody has to take the responsibility."

The mother-daughter situation came to a crisis in 1989 when Berkeley-based Alexandrea—all of fifteen years old—informed Whoopi that she was pregnant, did not want to marry the father of her child-to-be, and planned to have and keep the infant. Once the controversial news broke in the media, Goldberg became the subject of many published and on-the-air discussions dealing with whether she was to blame for Alexandrea's condition.

Because of Whoopi's status as a celebrity, what should have thereafter remained a private matter between Goldberg and her child instead became a media-circus event. Whoopi was dragged into discussing openly with the press this very personal, sensitive situation. She candidly admitted when she learned initially of her daughter's condition, "I believe my first reaction was 'Gee, I should break your legs.' That was my first reaction. And then she [Alexandrea] said, 'Well, it won't change anything if you break my legs.'" Goldberg said she next asked her daughter what she wanted to do. The teenager replied, "I want to have it. . . . I got pregnant because I want a baby. . . . This is my choice. I'm choosing to have this kid."

Once Whoopi recovered from the initial shock of learning of her daughter's pregnancy, she had to admit that she was pleased that at least Alexandrea was "confident enough in me to tell me." It became clear to Whoopi that her daughter, having missed close family ties in her own childhood, wanted to create an environment in which she could give and find love. It was also evident that part of Alexandrea's deliberate plan to have a child was to create a new world for herself in which she was no longer overshadowed by her famous mother. The teenager could now be the center of attention and decision making in her own household. Absorbing and dealing with Alexandrea's complex set of motives proved hard for Whoopi.

And to make matters more complicated, Goldberg was more than annoyed that the media had chosen to target her daughter, who was not in show business, for their public speculations on morality. "I was hot when they went after my family. If someone wants to find crap, let them look for it on me. I'm the public figure."

Eventually, Whoopi came to terms with her girl's decision despite her belief that having the baby was "the absolute wrong thing." From experience Goldberg knew that having a child at a young age would be extremely demanding and stressful, but these were matters that Whoopi—too often an absentee mother—did not feel justified in explaining to her daughter. Goldberg also appreciated that she could not tell Alexandrea to abort the fetus. Since she had long been pro-choice and had had several abortions herself, morally she could *not* be a hypocrite. She had to give her daughter the freedom to choose. She further reasoned: "Whether you are pro-abortion or not, that [having a child] is such a personal choice that you should not be berated or bullied or mentally abused for making the choice."

Years later, when Goldberg wrote her own chapter for *The Choices We Made,* the book about celebrities discussing their own abortions, she explained her rationale in dealing with this major domestic problem: "She chose to have a baby. It would not have been the choice I would have made for her; I think fifteen is young. But she had the choice, and she took it. I thought, 'It may be wonderful for her,' so you stand behind her. A lot of parents don't stand behind their kids, which is why the laws don't allow parents to make this decision for their kids. For me, the laws are inconvenient, because I would have chosen for her to wait."

As to Alexandrea's pregnancy, Goldberg would report, "She was ecstatic about this baby, and this baby kicked all the time, because it knew that there would be a lot of wonderful things waiting for it. . . . My daughter was phenomenal. She was one of those women who floated around." Finally, at 7:28 A.M. on November 13, 1989—Whoopi's thirty-fourth birthday—Alexandrea gave birth to her six-pound, fifteen-ounce baby girl at a Berkeley hospital. The infant was named Amarah Skye Martin.

Goldberg was present for the birth and reported: "I'm blessed with this really funny grandbaby who just grins. She grins and drools, and that's pretty neat. I give her back when she does that other stuff because I don't want to deal with it. But I'm lucky." As the months wore on, she would say publicly, "Now I'm Grandma Whoopi. I think that I should be able to do some things better with my daughter's child then I could do with her. This kid is not going to have to worry about our next meal, for a little while, anyway. Having some money takes a little pressure off, but I can't say it matters much on an emotional level. It's hard to be a mother, it's even harder when you're a kid."

To celebrate the new addition, Goldberg suggested that four generations of her family pose for an ad for the Gap clothing chain. The end result, featuring Whoopi's mother, Whoopi, daughter Alexandrea, and granddaughter Amarah proved to be a popular item with the public.

A few years later, in the early 1990s, Goldberg acknowledged that the public at large had not made it easy for her to handle her daughter's becoming a mother. "I got a lot of angry letters from people when my granddaughter was born, because Alexandrea was a young single mother. 'You go around telling kids about birth control and safe sex, and your own daughter does not follow the advice.' She didn't. I know now because she wanted a baby. . . . My daughter got pregnant because she did not feel that singularly she was enough. Is it other people's business? I don't know. What people were criticizing is that they thought money was going to prevent her from getting pregnant, or fame would do it. You can't wear fame to bed. She wanted to get pregnant, and I figured if she was old enough to make that decision, I had better damn well be there for her."

Before *The Long Walk Home* and, especially, *Ghost* reestablished Whoopi's screen career, she seriously had been considering turning to television—rather than hard-to-find feature-film projects—as her major career outlet. It did not mean that she intended to stop making movies altogether. With Goldberg's enormous energy level and her capacity for a prodigious amount of work—not to mention the fees she still commanded per motion picture—that would not be a viable option. Rather, she thought that TV might become her home-base medium. Her plan—and that of her business-management team—was that she should accept lucrative network offers to star in a TV series.

Whoopi had already tested the waters in the fall of 1988 when she joined the cast of *Star Trek: The Next Generation* as an occasional regular. That interplanetary excursion had proved to be fun and no more demanding than her recurring appearances as an hostess of television specials and a guest on TV talk shows. With this in mind, Whoopi agreed to CBS network's offer to join their ranks as the star of her own weekly program. However, she made it clear that she did not intend to curtail any of her other activities.

The vehicle chosen to launch Whoopi as a TV-series star was *Bagdad Café*. The show was to be based on the 1988 German-made film comedy directed by Percy Adlon. That very offbeat movie featured zaftig Marianne Sägebrecht as Jasmine, a woman stranded in the Mojave Desert, somewhere between Los Angeles and Las Vegas, when her spouse dumps her by the side of the highway and drives off. Jasmine soon stumbles upon a shabby truck-stop cafe–motel run by a free-spirited, not-so-neat black woman, Brenda—played by CCH Pounder—who has an adult son. The son is caring for his infant and a teenage daughter. Like Jasmine, Brenda is separated from her husband. Time passes. The two women bond as they cope with an assortment of amusing, if bizarre, situations.

The well-received movie won an Academy Award nomination for Best Song with the composition "Calling You."

Actually when Percy Adlon had been preparing *Bagdad Café* as a feature-film release, he had contacted Goldberg's management about asking her to play Brenda, but she never replied. Later, Goldberg claimed that she had never been told of the offer. Unable to sign Goldberg for his art film, Adlon had chosen CCH Pounder for the major role.

The official news that Goldberg would star in a CBS-TV series was announced in March 1989. Preproduction began in July that year for the show, to be known as *Bagdad Gas & Oil*. It was stated that the program would be used as a replacement entry should one or more of the network's series fail in the 1989-90 season. By the time taping got under way in November, the show not only had a new title, *Bagdad Café*, it boasted a prominent costar, Jean Stapleton, who would be teamed with Goldberg.

A veteran of the Broadway musical-comedy stage, Stapleton had made her mark as Edith "Dingbat" Bunker, the well-meaning, bumbling wife of bigot Archie Bunker on TV's *All in the Family*. During her nine years (1971–80) on that acclaimed sitcom, Stapleton had won three Emmy Awards, two Golden Globes, and a People's Choice Award. In 1984 she almost starred in another TV series but dropped out before the pilot was filmed. The show was *Murder, She Wrote* (1984–96), which proved to be a lucrative venture for Stapleton's replacement, Angela Lansbury.

As the costar of a major TV comedy series that cofeatured the well-esteemed Jean Stapleton, Whoopi had to defend herself against the inquiring media. Many suggested that Goldberg had taken on the weekly grind because her film career was fizzling and, as a result, she needed work. A very sensitive Goldberg countered that she did not consider *Bagdad Café* a comedown: "One thing I'm not is a flash in the pan. I have not done anything I'm ashamed of. Things haven't always turned out the way I wanted, but I did the best job I could. They [the critics] built Whoopi's image; I didn't. As a girl from the projects, I'm not at all disappointed in the way things are going. This is what I've always dreamed about. And I'm still here, which is the phenomenal thing."

As usual, Goldberg had a way of putting a positive spin on most any situation. That her optimistic take on her career standing was not accepted by the majority of her doubters was another matter.

Protesting a bit too much, Whoopi also noted that her new TV project "allows me to exercise. It's like doing a weekly play. And I needed a steady gig. I need to stay put in California for a while. Plus I'm working with Jean Stapleton. Plus I've been told that I can be involved in some of the writing if we get picked up next season."

Goldberg even managed to find redeeming social values in her upcoming television job. Speaking to Oprah Winfrey on her Chicago-based TV talk show via satellite from Los Angeles, Whoopi pointed out, "As you know, my daughter, who is going to be sixteen this month [May], has a five-and-a-half-month-old baby. It seems to me there's not a lot of encouragement for young women to talk to their parents. One of the things that I want to make sure that happens on this show is that in my relationship, whether I'm right or wrong, there's a dialogue that goes on between the daughter and myself. Monica Calhoun plays my daughter. She was in the film. And we decided that we really want to make these issues, which come up about teenagers, something that they know they can go to their parents about, and if they can't, give them access to somebody else."

As to her illustrious costar, Jean Stapleton, thirty-two years her senior, Whoopi said: "[Jean is] like so amazing, because she's wonderful. I was kind of panicked in the first week because I don't know— I mean, there's cameras, and then there's audience. If you don't know how it works, it seems very peculiar, and she said, 'Listen. Get over it. It's like doing a play every week. Don't worry about it.' She brought me through. She's a gem, an absolute gem."

On another occasion, Goldberg would use Stapleton's high regard in the industry as a rationale that her own career was not slipping: "I find it interesting that anybody would think I was stepping down by working with Jean Stapleton. I mean, come on!"

During the taping of the initial batch of *Bagdad Café* episodes, Whoopi was busy juggling her hectic work schedule, which included completing *Ghost* (1990) and her usual assortment of TV specials. She also made time to travel to Australia and New Zealand in early 1990 for a six-week, sold-out tour of her one-woman show. In February 1990 there was her HBO special, *Whoopi Goldberg and Billy Connolly*, the latter being the Scottish comedian whom Whoopi worked with "Down Under." Thereafter, in the spring of 1990, Goldberg performed a stand-up comedy act at Caesars Tahoe in Stateline, Nevada, preferring to try out new material there rather than in front of too many peers in Los Angeles's more logical sites, such as the Comedy Store or the Improv.

Finally, on Friday, March 30, 1990, at 9:00 P.M., *Bagdad Café* debuted on CBS-TV. The ad line for the new show read: "Come to the hottest spot in the desert. In the Mojave stands an oasis of laughter. The food's lousy—but the comedy's four star." The cast not only featured Monica Calhoun, from the feature-film original, as Brenda's (Goldberg's) sixteen-year-old, man-crazy daughter, but there was Scott Lawrence, as Brenda's twenty-two-year-old son raising his baby girl, and, in an occasional role, Cleavon Little as Sal, Brenda's philandering husband.

David Hiltbrand in *People* magazine rated *Bagdad Café* a "B–" and stated: "This gets my vote for oddest concept of the year. . . . [M]ost of the humor is generated by Goldberg's tart tongue, as she plays a sort of Maude of the Mojave. The show has good chemistry among the major players and an unusual setting, but the writing needs to develop consistency."

Andrew J. Edelstein, writing in *Newsday*, was less encouraging: "The pairing might have worked, if only they weren't saddled with trite dialogue. ('Am I disturbing you?' someone says to café owner Whoopi: 'Too late, I'm already disturbed.') And it might have worked if the show had more resembled a 'small' production of the kind that some pay-cable services specialize in instead of an assembly-line, go-for-the-cheap-shot sitcom. . . . And it might have worked if you felt something for these women and could muster the patience to wait through subsequent episodes to see the bond form between them. But after tonight's debut, you're unlikely to return." More damaging, Edelstein pointed out: "With Goldberg's string of movie failures, Whoopi-bashing has become too easy. *Badgad Café* isn't going to begin her rehabilitation. She's too shrill and abrasive, her angry eyes constantly bugging out."

With unremarkable ratings, *Bagdad Café* bravely plowed onward until the end of the season on May 30, 1990. In audience-appeal ratings it remained far below the top twenty-five shows that season, which included such sitcoms as *The Cosby Show*, *Roseanne*, *Cheers*, *The Golden Girls*, *Empty Nest*, *Who's the Boss?*, *Dear John*, and *Coach*.

During the summer break from *Bagdad Café* both Goldberg and Stapleton did their best to reassure the media and TV viewers that their series would be back in the fall, that rumors of a rift between the two stars was promotional nonsense, and that they each admired one another's talent and each felt the series in which a black and white woman bond had plenty of admirable social value. Meanwhile, Whoopi found time to join Billy Crystal and Robin Williams to cohost *Comic Relief IV* at

Radio City Music Hall in New York. By that point, the first three *Comic Relief* benefits had earned over $8 million.

Meanwhile, CBS-TV, then third among the major networks in overall program popularity, took a long, hard look at the Goldberg-Stapleton sitcom. The network's entertainment chief, Jeff Sagansky, decided to take action. He installed Tom Patchett, cocreator and executive producer of such TV shows as *Alf, The Bob Newhart Show,* and *Buffalo Bill,* as the new guiding force on *Bagdad Café.* Analyzing the situation, Patchett declared, "The [original *Bagdad Café*] movie said there was reason for these two women to be together. I didn't see that in the series."

Not only did Patchett revamp the show's story line and character motivation (e.g., explaining why Stapleton's Jasmine decides to stay at the cafe when her husband comes to take her back to Wisconsin), but he added a new character, Dewey Kunkle, the nephew of one of the diner's regulars, who takes over the job as cook now that Brenda's son has left to find his real future. With her son gone, Brenda now must take care of her infant granddaughter, Amarah, named after Whoopi's own grandchild. To carry out the planned alterations, Patchett hired a new staff of writers.

Moved to Friday at an 8:30 P.M. time frame, the revamped *Bagdad Café* redebuted on September 28, 1990. *Variety* allowed that the sitcom "has improved but still lacks the spark to make it a first-rate comedy." The trade publication also said: "During the more dramatic moments, Goldberg and Stapleton shine brightest. Unfortunately, the program was conceived as a comedy, and there are few funny moments." It added: "The phony desert scenery also tends to detract from the show, which already appears to be walking a thin line."

The prognosis for the second season of *Bagdad Café* was not good. There were already reports that a very unhappy Whoopi Goldberg was making the situation on the show's set tense; she and management fought, often at cross-purposes, to resolve the program's weaknesses. It didn't help matters that Stapleton, a much more experienced veteran of the TV situation-comedy format than Goldberg, was getting all the praise and that her characterization was far more grounded than Whoopi's Brenda.

By the middle of November 1990, everything had gone from bad to worse on *Bagdad Café,* and a deeply dissatisfied Goldberg no longer showed up on the soundstage. There were grapevine rumors that CBS might sue Whoopi for breach of contract, but the suggested legal action never became a reality. Meanwhile, Whoopi was not part of the series' last few weeks on the air before the program was canceled as of November 23, 1990. (CBS-TV would bring back *Bagdad Café* in July 1991 to utilize two completed episodes that had not aired in the show's aborted second season.)

Goldberg's final words on the subject of the trouble-plagued *Bagdad Café* were spoken to Laura B. Randolph in the March 1991 issue of *Ebony* magazine. Discussing her TV flop, the star insisted, "It needed to end, but I did not end it, and I am taking the heat for a corporate decision that they were not strong or confident enough to stand behind without a scapegoat."

CHAPTER TWENTY-SIX

Love and Friendships

I try to find ways to make things happen. I'm
pleased I'm still around. I've made eleven films in
four years. I live at the beach. I drive a Sterling. I'm
a happy woman. . . . If it interests me, I go for it.
—WHOOPI GOLDBERG, FEBRUARY 1990

Whoopi Goldberg was in a strange career position in the late fall
of 1990. *Bagdad Café* had been canceled. However, she was
still a recurring player on *Star Trek: The Next Generation,* a
syndicated show that had gained strong approval among viewers. Then,
too, in all the hype to promote and salvage *Bagdad Café* for its second-
season bow late in September 1990, many commentators lost sight of the
fact that peripatetic Goldberg was the costar of yet another new TV series.
This was Ted Turner's TBS-TV animated series *Captain Planet and the
Planeteers.*

Captain Planet was a syndicated half-hour children's program with a
twist. It was a disarming cartoon show aimed at instructing youthful
viewers on the value of environmental correctness. Providing the voices
for the series' adult regulars were such personalities as David Coburn
(Captain Planet), LeVar Burton (Kwame), and Whoopi (Gaia). Gaia is the
spirit of Earth who awakens from a century-long sleep, only to discover
that mankind is pillaging the resources of the planet through its unthink-
ing behavior. Each week's episode would find Whoopi, the captain, and
his five young Planeteers combating a rogues' gallery of bigger-than-life
ecology villains. These evil ones—such as Verminous Skumm, Sly
Sludge, Zarm, Duke Nuken, and Dr. Blight—were given voices by an

228

impressive array of talent, including Jeff Goldblum, Meg Ryan, Dean Stockwell, Tim Curry, and David Rappaport. This politically correct but entertaining series drew quite a following, and Goldberg would remain with the program for the first three of its five seasons on the air. On some episodes Whoopi was also heard as the character TBD. (When Goldberg did leave the show, Margot Kidder replaced her as the voice of Gaia.)

As if that weren't enough activity on the small screen, in late 1990, Whoopi could also be seen as a guest on TV's *Sesame Street,* a coringmaster on the *15th Annual Circus of the Stars,* and as host of the Fox-TV special *A Laugh, a Tear.* It seemed amazing, despite such overexposure, that she had not worn out her welcome with the TV viewing audience. Such a feat—considering the output of her television work—attested to her enduring popularity with a wide range of television viewers.

Goldberg's status and ranking in the field of motion pictures was, however, confusing to say the least. After a string of unsuccessful movies and turning down such unlikely material as *Cold Dog Soup* in 1989, in which she would have played a cabbie frustrated by numerous attempts to buy a dog, Whoopi had a change of luck. There was her artistic success the following year in *The Long Walk Home* and her great commercial popularity with *Ghost.* So positive was industry and public reaction to her comedic Oda Mae Brown, the fake spiritual of *Ghost,* that Paramount, which had released that movie, quickly signed Goldberg to a multi-million-dollar moviemaking agreement in the fall of 1990, which included having her own office on the studio's Hollywood lot. This arrangement occurred a few months before Whoopi won a Best Supporting Actress Academy Award for her performance in that smash hit.

Ironically, once Paramount contracted with Whoopi, they were uncertain how to proceed with this very unusual screen personality. There was talk then, and in the months to come, of developing a follow-up movie to trace the further misadventures of New York's own Oda Mae Brown, but that *Ghost* sequel never materialized. Instead, for the production team of Herbert Ross and Aaron Spelling, Goldberg joined the cast of the screen comedy *Soapdish.* The production literally had an all-star cast, including Sally Field, Kevin Kline, Robert Downey Jr., Cathy Moriarity, Elisabeth Shue, and Carrie Fisher. It was a satirical—and sometimes slapstick—account of the goings-on behind the scenes of a major TV network's daytime soap opera. Whoopi was assigned to be Rose Schwartz, the soap's veteran scriptwriter who is also the confidante and best friend of Sally Field's character. On-camera, Field played with dizzying intensity the longtime, beloved star of the daytime drama.

Whoopi's only problem with the *Soapdish* assignment was that she had been handed a relatively small and thankless role that hardly used her talents. When asked why she had taken the supporting part, she admitted to Katie Couric on NBC-TV's *Today*: "It is a hard one—it is a hard one because I'm not in it that much. It's—the opportunity really to—to play with Sally Field and to be able to work with Kevin Kline and, you know, a couple of other people. And I liked the director a lot. Michael Hoffman was a really great kind of guy. . . . It—it gave me the opportunity to add the word 'and' in front of my name on the poster. It says—you see, it says, yeah, yeah, Sally Field, Kevin Kline, Robert Downey Jr., and Whoopi Goldberg. That's sort of like, yes, I won the Oscar, but I'm doing this, anyway. That's what that 'and' means."

Whoopi did find one reward in her small role in *Soapdish*. It gave her a rare opportunity to dress in a chic manner, which was the handiwork of veteran costumer Nolan Miller, whom producer Aaron Spelling had been using on the TV drama *Dynasty* to dress his leading ladies in haute couture. Miller had dressed many of Hollywood's sleekest actresses over the decades. When he heard that one of his *Soapdish* tasks was to provide Goldberg with a stylish wardrobe, he said to himself, God, what did I do in another life to deserve this? However, when Miller and Whoopi met, she immediately put things on the right track by telling him: "I know nothing about clothes. Can you please dress me?"

And dress her he did. He would later reflect: "I think Miss Goldberg has been dressed in films in the past, or dressed up for films, but it was always to make everyone laugh, to be funny. And this time she was dressed seriously as a woman. And I think it was a wonderful feeling for her, and she liked it." She did. She not only thought Miller was "very, very cool," but he taught her "That I could actually look any way I chose and be elegant. You know, all of those women [on the screen] who had great style and class—I could be part of that if I chose to be."

After the *Soapdish* shooting, a Goldberg-converted Miller proclaimed of Whoopi: "This film, I think, has changed her life. Her hairdresser told me, 'She's putting her hair up now. . . . Honey, she's crazy for you.'" In retrospect, Nolan Miller considers his biggest *Soapdish* achievement "getting Whoopi Goldberg in high heels and a bra."

Soapdish, which neither helped nor hurt Whoopi's acting career, grossed $15.7 million in distributors' domestic rentals. Goldberg followed this movie with a brief guest appearance in 1991's *House Party II*, a raucous and often uncouth ethnic comedy that earned a respectable $9.5 million in distributors' rentals at the United States–Canadian box office. Vincent Canby, writing in the *New York Times* about the film, said, "Whoopi Goldberg turns up several times in an unbilled cameo performance, playing the sort of joyfully ghoulish professor who haunts the imagination of every lazy student."

At this point, the upwardly mobile and affluent Whoopi Goldberg owned a ranch complete with main house, barn, and stables for her horses in West Cornwall, Connecticut. She also had an expansive beachfront home in Malibu that sat on a bluff a hundred feet above beach level and boasted 180-degree views of the Pacific Ocean. She had purchased the California home in 1987 for over $2 million. This ranch-style Malibu structure consisted of a compact main house, a separate apartment complete with kitchen and bath, as well as a guest house. In 1992, ever-acquiring Goldberg would add forty acres of land on the West Boulder River in Montana to her property portfolio, which now included a beachside retreat at Port Antonio on the northeastern coast of Jamaica.

Despite her choice of homes, Whoopi frequently stayed at the chic St. James Club and Hotel in West Hollywood. She chose to do so because she was so often on the Hollywood and Burbank soundstages, which made the proximity of the St. James and its refined room service a viable alternative for the increasingly upscale Goldberg. With her hard-earned wealth, she was, by now, becoming known as a collector of objets d'art, which ranged from fine paintings to antique furniture and on to such esoteric items as pricey genuine Lalique cocktail swizzle sticks made in the 1920s.

Even with the change in her lifestyle, the upwardly mobile Goldberg refused to change her down-to-earth public image to accompany her newfound existence among the rich and famous. In particular, she clung to her trademark dreadlocks. When she appeared on Phil Donahue's talk show in mid-1990 she explained how she engineered this hairstyling feat. According to Whoopi, the undertaking required her and longtime hairstylist Julia Walker to set aside a large chunk of time: "We divvy up the sides of my head. She takes this side, and I take this side. And we get a good movie or a good book, and for four hours we do this." That said, Goldberg observed about her coiffure: "I've been around, now, five years maybe. Five years ago, this was a weird, freak thing to people. Now there's Milli Vanilli and Tracy Chapman and all these people. And it's very chic and hip except when it's on my head. I like this."

Another thing that had not changed—and this went back to her childhood days in the New York City housing projects—was her enthusiasm as a film fan. She confided to movie reviewer Roger Ebert when they chatted at the Toronto Film Festival in September 1990, that her love of film was primarily why she did all those Happy Birthday salutes that peppered her television schedule. "I bring my autograph book, and I corner people and I talk to them." She said that talking to veteran stars had taught her a lot about the business: "Jessica Tandy told me, 'Take the work. People will tell you you're overexposed, but you only get better when you take the work.' Jimmy Stewart told me you have to be the big actor in little movies, and the little actor in big movies, that's how you get better. Burt Lancaster said, 'Listen, kid, this is a bitch of a business. You're gonna be okay. Tell the truth, hit your marks, do your job, and if it's you on the screen, then fight for it.'"

If Goldberg's fluctuating professional life was bewildering to friends and observers alike, her social activity was equally varied. Following the end of her romance with Eddie Gold, Whoopi found a new "best friend." Her selection was one that not even the most imaginative Hollywood matchmakers would ever have considered possible. She began to be seen everywhere in late 1990 and early 1991 with the screen's latest James Bond, British actor Timothy Dalton.

Born in England in 1944, the six-foot-two Dalton had gained his acting reputation playing Shakespearean roles in the provinces before he made his film debut in *The Lion in Winter* as King Philip II of France. It was while making *Mary, Queen of Scots* in 1971 with Vanessa Redgrave that the handsome, sardonic actor and Redgrave began a long-lasting professional and personal relationship. Alternating between stage, film, and TV work, Dalton made his American movie debut playing the sixth spouse of octogenarian Mae West in *Sextette* in 1978. Later, Dalton took over from Roger Moore the mantle of the screen's most famous spy, James Bond, in *The Living Daylights* and *License to Kill*.

Apparently, as green-eyed, cleft-chinned Dalton told pals, he had long been intrigued by Whoopi and was delighted when mutual friends introduced them in Los Angeles. After that, the unlikely couple became an item on the Hollywood scene. However, they always insisted—modestly and blushingly—that they were just good pals. They stuck to this story even when they arrived as a couple at the March 1991 Oscars, held at the Shrine Auditorium in Los Angeles, or thereafter appeared together on Arsenio Hall's late-night TV talk show. Arsenio tried his smiling best to break down their reticence about the true scope of their relationship. What the odd couple refused to confirm in words to Hall was fairly evident to viewers by their flirtatious, blushing interaction with one another on-camera.

Deeply involved with her new "beau," Whoopi maneuvered to extend their social rapport into a working professional relationship. Back in the spring of 1990 she told interviewer Pat H. Broeske of the *Los Angeles Times* that she would love to do a remake of the over-fifty-year-old classic screwball comedy *It Happened One Night* with Dalton: "But I'll do the Clark Gable role. He'll be a member of the royal family." That suggested venture never came to be, but another equally intriguing work situation did arise. They costarred onstage in *Love Letters*.

A. R. Gurney's *Love Letters* had debuted off-Broadway in 1989 and then had a brief Broadway run. Its structural gimmick was that it required only two actors, who sat at a handsome table with a couple of glasses of water and their scripts. For the show's two acts they read a lifetime of letters between Andrew and Melissa, two well-bred soul mates who live out most of their relationship by mail. After its New York run, the play—which was easy to mount—became a profitable phenomenon on tour, in summer stock, and in extended runs in different cities in the United States and England.

In Los Angeles alone, *Love Letters* had been running for sixteen months during 1990 and 1991. Over that period of time, 128 different actors played 65 different couples. Other statistics included the fact that Meredith Baxter held the show record for being paired with four different actors and that Charlton Heston had done the production with two different costars. When Goldberg and Dalton signed on to do the show, they were the first interracial couple to perform the play.

Whoopi and Timothy were scheduled to appear the weekend of August 3 and 4 at the Canon Theatre, on North Canon Drive in Beverly Hills, which would be the final performances of the extended Los Angeles run. Like their predecessors, neither of the stars received more than $1,500 a week. By tradition, rehearsal time was limited to four hours before curtain time plus as many additional private meetings as the actors themselves wanted to arrange. To deal with the contrasting ethnic status of Goldberg and Dalton, the couple used a variation of the adjusted script that playwright Gurney had created for such black actors as Alfre Woodard and Blair Underwood when they did *Love Letters*. Tickets for the Goldberg-Dalton performances sold out within two-and-a-half days of the announcement of the pairing.

Although their unconfirmed romantic association would fade by late 1991, the couple has remained good friends. This is a magical quality that Goldberg has had with many of her male friends—being able to perpetuate a platonic rapport after the romantic sparks extinguished themselves. In fact, Goldberg and Dalton finally did make a film together when they appeared in the generation-X comedy-fantasy *Naked in New York*, shot in the fall of 1992 but not released until 1994.

PART V

Life at the Top

CHAPTER TWENTY-SEVEN

At the Top
of the Hollywood Heap

Getting the paycheck. That's the biggest thrill.
Actually, I'm just thrilled that people come to see the
films that I make even if they are not critically
acclaimed. . . . My films will never gross Eddie
Murphy money. I'm not that kind of star. I have said
that from the start. But all I read is 'She's not as
good as she was in *The Color Purple.*' The old movie
stars did forty movies a year. They did big stuff, little
stuff, good stuff, bad stuff. That's what I want.
Unfortunately, now we have to deal with words like
'overexposure' and 'box-office receipts' and fucking
words like that.
                              —WHOOPI GOLDBERG, AUGUST 1990

In 1991, Whoopi had a very good year. She now had her family close at hand, since her mother, brother, daughter, and grandchild all lived in Los Angeles much of the time. Goldberg starred or appeared in five full-length motion pictures—one of which required her to go on location to South Africa—and, in addition, made an impressive showing on television. In February 1991 she could be seen in *Blackbird Fly*, a twenty-eight-minute drama about adolescent sexual abuse which aired over the Learning Channel. Others in the cast, besides Whoopi, included Esther Rolle and Rain Pryor. All of the cast worked without pay for this project.

As part of Whoopi's pact with the Nickelodeon cable network, she starred as Angela and was also executive producer for the daytime special *Tales from the Whoop: Hot Rod Brown, Class Clown,* for which she was nominated for a daytime Emmy Award. Nine days later, she was a guest star on the sitcom *A Different World* in the episode "If I Should Die Before I Wake." She was cast as the professor in whom a student with AIDS confides about her life-threatening condition. Whoopi received an Emmy nomination for her compassionate performance in this episode. Later in the year, as part of her three-project pact with HBO, Goldberg starred in, and was the executive producer for, the HBO special *Whoopi Goldberg: Chez Whoopi* (August 24, 1991). In this major entry in the *HBO Comedy Hour* series she played host to stand-up comics Jedda Jones and Chris Thomas and the singing group Rockapella.

In addition, Goldberg agreed to be a member of the Cannes Film Festival jury, which began its activities in the French resort city on May 9, 1991. Others on the ten-member panel included Polish-born director Roman Polanski and French director Jean-Paul Rappeneau. Among the pictures in contention for Festival prizes that year was Spike Lee's *Jungle Fever.* When the jury—and Goldberg in particular—chose Joel and Ethan Coen's *Barton Fink* as Best Picture, Lee was furious. He suggested that racial discrimination had motivated *Jungle Fever's* loss and that Whoopi, in particular, had once again let down the black community. The accusation reignited the antipathy between Lee and Goldberg and led to biting remarks from each party about the other.

Whoopi said of the *Jungle Fever* brouhaha, "Yeah. I didn't think the movie was very good. I'm *entitled* not to like it. I thought *Barton Fink* was a lot more fun, a lot more interesting. It's not enough to support *Jungle Fever* just because it's black. That wasn't his [Spike Lee's] best work, and he knows it. I don't owe allegiance to you because we're the same race." Later, Goldberg would add, "Spike hurt my feelings when he got on Arsenio [Hall's TV talk show] and put it in the words he did, saying he didn't get any support from me. I busted my butt to make sure Samuel Jackson [who played Gator in *Jungle Fever*] got an acting award, and Spike didn't talk about all the flak I took, being called nationalistic, for that. But then Spike's the master at getting attention. But sometimes when he's in the attack mode he doesn't realize he's attacking those who are also forging through the tundra."

Rising to her own defense, Whoopi insisted she was not prejudiced against Spike Lee's movies per se. She said, "I love *School Daze* [1988] because it was an insight into how we, as people, view ourselves: If you're light-skinned, you're cool; if you're dark-skinned, you're ugly. I loved the movie because I thought it would help people understand, it would help them get it."

It would be months before the latest Goldberg-Lee skirmish—played up in the African-American media—would die down and the two very different, high-profile black talents could resume being restrained antagonists.

After *The Color Purple,* Whoopi made a lot of foolish movies that, at the time, she defended as being fun action-movie projects. When discussing her arty film releases (*The Telephone, Homer & Eddie*), she would insist that they were well-intentioned projects that had gone bad along the way. Now, having won an Academy Award, Whoopi adopted a revisionist point of view in summing up her string of mostly unsatisfying movies of the late 1980s: "I did the pictures I was offered. Do you think I would sit around and say, 'Here's great scripts, here's crappy scripts; I'll do the crappy ones'?"

Now, however, in 1991, she was doing interesting roles in intriguing major film productions. Nonetheless, sometimes she still had to ask for parts. For example, when director Robert Altman (*M*A*S*H, Nashville*) began casting for *The Player*—which was to be filled with many big-name personalities in cameo assignments—Whoopi wanted to be part of this sharp, behind-the-scenes look at the Hollywood film industry. At first, Altman resisted her blandishments to be given the role of Det. Susan Avery: "A black Whoopi Goldberg did not fit the image I had of this thing," he later recalled.

Eventually, Altman gave in to Whoopi's pestering, and she signed on to join a star-studded cast in this jaded insider's study of the cutthroat movie business. In a brief but crucial role of a homicide officer, Goldberg tracks the murderer of a movie scriptwriter and soon becomes convinced that a certain hotshot film producer is the killer. According to Altman, Goldberg transformed what he had envisioned as a "functionary" character into a "side-slapping, tough-talking cop who casually twirls a tampon." The director remembers well this famous sequence in which Whoopi interrogates suspected killer Tim Robbins. In the process, she seemingly absentmindedly pulls out a tampon and starts to swing it around by its string: "That was a particularly dull scene, and I was at a loss as to how to do it. We sat down and she said, 'Why don't we do this?'

She wrote it herself. And that's when I realized that she's so far above any tag that's hung on her that it borders on the supernatural."

Whoopi recalls her inspired interplay on the set as she questions the suspect: "Whenever women are together for more than two days, they talk about their periods, and that's what I thought Detective Avery and Detective Broom [Susan Emshwiller] would surely be talking about in the police station." As to working with the esteemed Robert Altman, she opined: "By far the most emotional experience I've had on a film was with him. Every time we worked, I knew he was rooting for me, and when people believe in you, you can fly. I have a very [feisty] reputation in the business. I have no qualms about saying I disagree. You're not supposed to suck your teeth or have an opinion. There are all these don'ts. But they don't exist with Altman. You have the room to say, 'I really don't feel good about this.' And he'll say, 'If you feel that strongly, what do you want to do instead?' "

When *The Player* opened in April 1992, most critics endorsed the movie. The *New York Times* raved: "So entertaining, so flip and so genially irreverent." Julie Salamon, writing in the *Wall Street Journal,* concurred. "This is, above all, a wonderful movie—one that is both piercing and playful. It sparkles with gleeful wit, originality and complex characterizations." The high-profile movie went on to gross $8.42 million in distributors' domestic rentals.

In this sly story of how to literally get away with murder in Hollywood, Altman used a very sturdy main cast (Tim Robbins, Greta Scacchi, Fred Ward, Peter Gallagher). In addition, Altman persuaded a variety of familiar movie faces to make brief guest appearances in this arty production. They included a wide range of talent: Steve Allen, Harry Belafonte, Cher, Peter Falk, Elliott Gould, Jack Lemmon, Nick Nolte, Julia Roberts, Susan Sarandon, Lily Tomlin, Bruce Willis, and so forth. That Goldberg, in her brief on-camera interludes, could make such a lasting impression with filmgoers in the midst of this unending parade of on-screen celebrities is a testament to her scene-stealing abilities as a performer.

The irony of *Sister Act,* which became Whoopi's breakthrough starring vehicle, is that the smash hit comedy was originally slated for brash, funny Bette Midler. The project had been in development at Disney Studios for several years. Just as the picture was given the green light to start production in September 1991, Midler—so the story goes—had a change of heart about playing a brassy lounge singer forced to hide in a convent to protect herself from killer gangsters. Once there, she becomes involved in turning the lackluster nuns' choir into a hip world-famous singing group, and with the money their recordings earn, they are able to save their church from closing and help their needy parishioners. Midler reasoned that her audience might not accept her, a Jewish woman, playing a Catholic nun.

After Midler rejected the role, the studio went on a crash program to find a suitable replacement. Meanwhile, several script writers-doctors, including Carrie Fisher, were hired to revamp the project for a new leading lady. In the film's credits, Joseph Howard is the fictitious name used for the scenarist of *Sister Act*. In reality, a team of at least seven writers worked on shaping the film's plot line.

In retrospect, it now seems that the only actor in Hollywood who could have properly played Deloris Van Cartier, a.k.a. Sister Mary Clarence, was indeed Whoopi Goldberg. She had pulled off a rascally sort of character in *Ghost* and won an Oscar in the process. Then, too, the idea of portraying a woman of God on-screen was not a new concept for Whoopi. One of her aborted film projects in 1989 had been to star as Sister Thea Bowman, a pioneer in the movement that encouraged black Catholics to express their cultural roots within the church. If this property had materialized, Whoopi would have been seen on-camera as the Roman Catholic nun who was a lecturer, poet, evangelist, singer, and the only black member of the Franciscan Sisters of Perpetual Adoration.

As usual, it took some time before Goldberg was considered for the role. When finally asked to replace Bette Midler in *Sister Act,* she said yes. She reasoned, "I really wanted to do this because as I thought about the part I knew it would be another dimension to add to the odd and bizarre career that I've made for myself. And in the process perhaps I would learn some new things."

Part of the challenge of her *Sister Act* role was that she had to sing on-screen. To prepare for the daunting task, Goldberg spent a month before the start of filming to train with vocal coach Seth Riggs. She also worked with Marc Shaiman, who provided new music for the film plus adaptations of existing musical numbers, in selecting the proper array of songs to be featured in the comedy. As a result of all the preparation, Goldberg was able to carry off creditably her singing chores in the picture.

The star later gushed to TV interviewer Steve Kmetko on *CBS This*

Morning: "That's my voice. . . . That's me. That is, you are not going to hear anybody, no two tons of fun coming up and saying, you know, 'I sang for her.' That's me. That is my voice, you know, and that's—that's an achievement. Now, I'm not a singer. I mean, Patti La Belle sings, you know. But I warbled. . . ."

As for her primary *Sister Act* wardrobe—a nun's habit—Whoopi was flabbergasted the first time she caught sight of herself in the distinctive garb: "Oy. Oy. Yeah, it was wild. It was wild. It was a strange experience. You know, I went to a Catholic school so I saw a lot of those women, you know, rustling around in those things. I really have a lot of empathy for them now." As to wearing the nun's outfit for a long period of time on the sound stage: "They're heavy. They're ugly, you know . . . and they're tight around the neck. All you have is face, cheek, and chin. That's all there is. I didn't know I had a double chin till I put this damn thing on."

When the filming of *Sister Act* got under way in late September 1991, the final shooting scenario for the comedy had yet to be completed. This made it extremely difficult for director Emile Ardolino (*Dirty Dancing*) to work from day to day with his cast, since he did not have in hand the final vision and plot line of the movie. Location work for the film included using Hollywood's United Methodist Church for the convent interiors, St. Paul's Church in Noe Valley of San Francisco to double for St. Katherine's, and Fitzgeralds' Casino on North Virginia Street in Reno as the site of Deloris's lounge act.

Goldberg admits that during production "I was crabby because things weren't right." She further explains: "It wasn't easy. . . . We—you generally want to start out on a little bit more solid ground that we did, but . . . the bottom line is you get to work and you work with what you have, and—and just ignore everything else. Which is pretty much what we did. We had a lot of producers . . . and you couldn't make a move without calling L.A."

Whoopi also says, "One of the things that we fought for was to extend the relationship between myself and these nuns so you would get an idea that these were actual people. Of course, there were things we couldn't talk about that I would have liked to have talked about, but you know, that's—that's another movie, I think." When asked what she would have put into the plot line that was not part of the resultant movie, Goldberg suggests, "There are thinking nuns out there who have ideas and attitudes about what goes on and how women are treated in the—in the church; so I thought we'd . . . throw in one of those or two, and they said, 'No, no, no. Look, no. Forget it.' "

Before long it was common knowledge throughout Hollywood and even publicly that Goldberg was fighting a battle royal with Disney management over the shape and progress of *Sister Act*. Gossips insisted that an angry Whoopi was referring to her making this film as "picking cotton" for Disney. In a moment of pique, so the word went, she had T-shirts made with a picture of Mickey Mouse in blackface and a caption which read: "Nigga-teer." No one could predict whether Whoopi or studio chieftain Jeffrey Katzenberg would emerge victorious in their struggle over "control" of the film and, more importantly, whether the movie would ever be completed.

By December 20, however, *Sister Act* did wrap up production. Thereafter, Goldberg spent a long time reexplaining what really did or did not go on during the much-troubled production. She insisted, "I didn't make T-shirts. I've tried to clear this up for months. When there's trouble on the set, people don't write what's really going on because it's deadly boring. So other stuff comes up. . . . But you can't figure everything, so you just have to laugh." She confirmed: "Yeah, I sent him [Jeffrey Katzenberg] a hatchet and said, 'Let's bury this; we've got a job to do.' He sent me a pair of brass balls and said, 'Always keep these with you in case you lose one.' It was us trying to get to a place so we could make the movie."

Later, Goldberg discussed what happened during the filming of *Sister Act*: "They [i.e., Disney executives] weren't really as open as I hoped they would be. I just wanted to make things better. I don't know what their experience has been with other actors, but we had an antagonistic relationship."

She further elucidated: "We had too many producers, and the guy who was the producer got thrown away. One producer took his name off the picture. [Thereafter, when it was released], he put it back on. Our director was getting trashed. Fortunately, we had these wonderful women [actors] and some good times. You see that on the screen. . . . Anyway, Disney and I have come a long way since we began that movie.

"There's too many people, in my opinion, at Disney who (a) don't have enough experience and (b) don't understand really how to deal with people. Not just actors but people in general—crew, cast. My problems with Disney had to do with a lot of the lower-echelon people who, in their zeal and zest to make themselves noticed, started s——ing on me, and I didn't like it. And I made everybody very aware of it, very aware of it."

With filmmaking problems resolved or put aside, *Sister Act* was prepared for a late May 1992 release. As part of the promotional campaign, the studio had a special screening on May 28 at Cinema 2, across from Bloomingdale's in midtown New York City. Some three hundred real sisters from twenty-five religious orders in the surrounding boroughs attended. The biggest laugh from the nuns occurred at film's end when Whoopi's character tells her onetime former boyfriend, a hoodlum: "I've got two words for you, Vince—bless you." The biggest cheer from the nuns came when the pope gives the church choir a standing ovation. There was also appreciative chuckles from the special audience when the trio of nuns in *Sister Act* leave a biker bar, and one tough says to another, 'If this turns into a nuns' bar, I'm outta here.' "

Considering its prefabricated structure, it is not surprising that *Sister Act* did not especially appeal to the mainstream critics, even with a cast that included Goldberg; Oscar-winner Maggie Smith as the Mother Superior; plump Kathy Najimy, skittish Wendy Makkena, and acerbic Mary Wickes as a trio of nuns; and Harvey Keitel as a revengeful thug and Goldberg's ex-boyfriend. Janet Maslin insisted in the *New York Times*: "*Sister Act* has been retooled in a way that only partly suits Ms. Goldberg's broadly demonstrative comic style. . . . Scenes that might have played as mere snobbery with Ms. Midler now have a hint of racism, which might have been dispelled if the film had addressed it head-on."

"It stinks of calculations . . . but the suits [i.e., studio executives] will be happy." *Time* magazine chastised. "It will prove to them that films needn't be written; they can be assembled like Lego blocks."

The *New Yorker* was scornful: "The plot and the characters are almost insultingly perfunctory . . . and when there isn't any rock on the soundtrack the moviemaking is listless."

Despite the reviews, *Sister Act* proved to be a hugely popular picture. Most filmgoers found it hard to resist Goldberg's impish alter ego as she wildly leads her nuns' choir to new musical heights or to ignore the humor of her triumvirate of irresistible church helpers. Thanks to positive word of mouth, by the end of 1992, *Sister Act* had grossed $139.4 million at the domestic box office in the United States and Canada. Once her movie was a registered hit, its star quipped, "People wanted something hopeful. They were relieved to see a black face on-screen that wasn't running off with a beanbag chair." On a more serious note, Goldberg declared, "The financial success of *Sister Act* means I can open a picture. In the past, my biggest obstacle was Eddie Murphy. I was supposed to be this female Eddie Murphy and make money for all of these studios. I didn't live up to that."

In retrospect, Goldberg would say proudly, "My first $100 million movie. . . . I knew it was a good comedy movie. But it's always hard to know how films will take off. I don't think anyone thought it would do as well as it has. I think it's great, because it's the sort of success you need to really make your mark in Hollywood."

Not only was *Sister Act* a huge moneymaker, but Goldberg won a Golden Globe nomination in the Best Actor category, and she won a People's Choice Award as Favorite Movie Actress. More importantly, on a personal level, she and the Disney regime settled their differences. She gleefully noted that the studio "said they were wrong, and that was nice. And they said it before the movie started making money, which I appreciated a lot." She also acknowledged: "Disney's been really great in giving me some credit for it [i.e., the success]. I give most of the credit to [director] Emile [Ardolino] and his editor, but there must have been something there to work with."

Finally, above all, Whoopi has long given special thanks to Ms. Bette Midler for having turned down the screen role that did so much for Goldberg's career.

Scarcely had Goldberg completed her scenes in *Sister Act* in the late fall of 1991 than she was packing her bags to fly to South Africa for her next movie, *Sarafina!* This project began in 1985 as a concept in the township of Soweto, South Africa—then an oppressive, militaristic hot spot. Mbongeni Ngema, the famous African playwright, director, composer, and musician, was visiting his friend Winnie Mandela, then the wife of incarcerated Nelson Mandela, leader of the African National Congress (ANC). "We were talking about what was happening with the South African struggle at the time. With all the political leaders in jail, in detention, or in exile outside of South Africa, the children were left in the forefront of the struggle." Their discussion soon focused on the youngsters, who, even with the horrors of their existence, danced in the streets of their townships—segregated residential settlements. In fact, it would be these youths who played a key role in creating the social pressure which led eventually to Nelson Mandela's release and the subsequent dismantling of South Africa's apartheid system.

Following his discussion with Winnie, Ngema decided to combine two musical idioms: that of the *mbaganga,* the pounding hypnotic blend of indigenous African sounds, with elements resembling blues and gospel. It took Ngema two years to create *Sarafina!,* the story of a youthful South African girl who aspires to be a Hollywood star and ends up having a life-transforming experience through the terrors of apartheid. In the winter of 1986, the playwright met with musical composer Hugh Masekela in London, and together, on a piano, they worked through the play's structure and musical interludes. In June 1987 the musical premiered at the Market Theatre in Johannesburg, where it ran for ten weeks. Soon thereafter, Gregory Mosher, artistic director of Lincoln Center in New York City, invited the *Sarafina!* company to appear in the United States for a limited engagement at the 299-seat Mitzi E. Newhouse Theatre in the center's complex. It opened there on January 3, 1988, and was so successful that it moved to the Cort Theatre on Broadway later in the month. It went on to win five Tony Award nominations, including Best Musical. Meanwhile, a second *Sarafina!* company toured Europe, Japan, and Australia.

In the subsequent month, Mbongeni Ngema, in collaboration with William Nicholson, wrote a screenplay of *Sarafina!* Thereafter, Anant Singh, a third-generation South African Indian and one of the producers of the projected film version, suggested to Ngema that Whoopi Goldberg would be a good choice to costar in the movie. He envisioned her being cast as the steadfast teacher of Sarafina who dies for her beliefs. The part was based on Phumzile Miambo, a real-life schoolteacher in Durban, South Africa. She was the courageous individual who refused to teach her students the lies that the school and government authorities tried to pass off as historical truth and, for her beliefs, was murdered.

At the May 1991 Cannes Film Festival, Anant Singh met with Goldberg, who that year was a judge at this international film competition. Whoopi recalls: "We started talking. Who knew they had a film industry in South Africa? Anant said he was getting ready to do *Sarafina!* and I said I'd love to read the script. I liked it so much that I asked, 'Is there anywhere I can slip in here without it being too distracting?' " When Singh told Goldberg of the role he had in mind for her, she was thrilled. "I was hesitant at first because the last thing I wanted to do was come in and take a role from a South African. But the people on that end said I should come. I've always wanted to be in the eye of the storm, anyway, so I was both thrilled and nervous."

When Goldberg arrived in South Africa, she quickly found out that Soweto was quite like the United States in weird ways. "In both places there's a struggle to overcome what people on both sides have been raised to believe is true. The chains of apartheid have fallen, but the emotional and mental bonds are still in existence." (Goldberg was in Africa at the same time as her old nemesis Spike Lee. He was there to film scenes for his movie *Malcolm X*. On-hand observers who compared how each of these two Hollywood celebrities comported themselves on the foreign location sites gave Goldberg far higher marks than Lee for thoughtfulness and consideration of local people and customs.)

Cast in the lead role was twenty-one-year-old Leleti Khumalo, who was recreating her part from the original South African and, later, Broadway productions. To direct the venture, the South African and British filmmakers insisted they use a South African, and they chose Darrell James Roodt, who had been born and raised in Johannesburg. Internationally acclaimed Miriam Makeba, known as "the Empress of African Song" and "Mama Africa," was chosen to play the role of Sarafina's mother.

Feeling a responsibility to be a goodwill ambassador and not a typical Hollywood star, Goldberg refused to have her name placed on the film's credit above that of the real star, Leleti Khumalo. Whoopi also turned down the use of a luxury mobile home on the set in favor of utilizing the same caravan as everyone else. During breaks in shooting at the Soweto matchbox house—which was her on-camera home—Goldberg would stay and chat with real neighbors who had gathered to watch the filming. She was surprised to learn that so many in South Africa had seen her movies. *Ghost* was a big hit in that country, and *The Long Walk Home* opened during her last weekend in Soweto. At that time, *The Color Purple* still had not been shown in South Africa. Alice Walker refused to let it be screened there. As with all cultural visitors, Goldberg held her obligatory workshop at a community arts center in Soweto. There she answered questions with what was described as "willingness, conviction, and passion." She talked to the locals of the "small root" she had grown in the South African soil and of having now become part of the history of the country.

If Whoopi could adapt to the filming conditions in South Africa and the sweltering heat of the local climate, she could not abide a seemingly thoughtless act on the part of the recently freed Nelson Mandela, the African National Congress's president. Mandela decided to host a cocktail party for Whoopi and chose to have the event at the palatial home of a controversial insurance millionaire. On the appointed day, she was whisked from Soweto, a town of 2 million blacks, noted for its squatters' shacks, chickens, and dust, to a $10 million "palace" just twenty minutes away. There, at "this humongous house," a disbelieving Goldberg was feted by the famous President Mandela amid plush environs. The house boasted eight bedrooms, nine bathrooms, two swimming pools, a tennis court, a squash court, seven whirlpool baths, eight garages, and a dozen rooms for servants. According to a fellow *Sarafina!* cast member, "Whoopi was miserable. After days in Soweto, it was too much for her. She couldn't believe that Mandela—a man of the people—would choose a place like that to welcome her."

But the Mandela incident proved to be the least, relatively speaking, of Goldberg's problems on the South African set. It seemed that even before she arrived in Soweto she had become the target of a "declaration of war" by a local black group opposed to a project which would feature an American in a major role that could have been played by a South African. By the time she began filming the musical, she had received several death threats. Refusing to be cowed by this real danger, she not only continued making the movie; she sought out representatives of the warring faction: "We talked it over, and the problem was more or less fixed. But, yeah, you feel fear. They had issued a license to any nut who wanted to take me out."

During the extended process of "fixing the problem," Goldberg endured an eerie sense of unreality on location: "They have a shadow government down there and a secret police, and whew, those are rough guys. My passport disappeared from my hotel room while I was there. And—not the day that it disappeared but another day—a friend of mine was in my room while I was at work, and the doorbell rang, and the door opened, and outside stood two guys in leisure suits with suitcases and a maid, with her key. These were not men who worked in the hotel. Nobody knew where they came from, and nobody could ever tell us who they were. And then, just as suddenly, several weeks later, when I was packing to leave the country, in a book that I was reading about Alexander the Great . . . and that I'd been reading every day, I found my passport. . . . And the clicks on the phone and the voices that you hear! The big concern that everyone had for me was that they thought somebody was going to blow me away down there. And what everybody came to realize is it wouldn't have served anybody's purpose. It would be bad for the whites and bad for the blacks if it happened. So I was okay."

Despite the chaos her presence inadvertently caused, Goldberg came away with rich cultural and political experiences. It helped her to develop new perspectives on her ethnic heritage; for example, "watching a multicultural crew shoot this movie, you know, and realizing what an American I am. I used to call myself an African American. I'm not an African American. I've met African folks. I've been in Africa, and I am . . . as American as Planet Hollywood and Mickie D's." (This point of being an American and not an African American is a distinction Goldberg would make repeatedly and loudly over subsequent years whenever she felt an interviewer misclassified her.)

Hardly was Whoopi back in the United States when the Los Angeles racial riot broke out over the seemingly biased jury decision in the Rodney King case. The ironic juxtaposition of events in the two countries was not lost on her. Goldberg called the devastating and shocking L.A. riot a "huge scream of despair. Our situation has been coming for a very long time. I personally thought it would happen when that young woman was shot in a grocery store. Given the vileness of the racist and homophobic statements politicians have been making for years, we shouldn't be surprised that this is happening. You can't step on people that much before they rise up."

Sarafina!, set in trouble-plagued 1976 South Africa, had its first official showing at the May 1992 Cannes Film Festival. Four months later, it opened in the United States. Jack Mathews, in *Newsday,* pointed out, "The casting of Goldberg seems a wise move. She is a distraction at first, with a clipped South African accent and a role heavily underplayed, but her star power will ensure a larger audience for the film than it would have had otherwise." Mathews also noted: "The violent confrontations, shot like newsreel footage, and the tension between the children and the South African officials become almost unbearable at times."

In contrast, Donald Suggs wrote in the *Village Voice* that Goldberg "looks so out of place that you almost expect her to stare into the camera, break out in that Grinch-like smile, and say, 'Look! It's me, Whoopi! In Africa!'" He went on: "Fortunately, the strength of this movie—and of Whoopi's performance—is that it acknowledges how commercial, and yes, even campy, our vision of modern black nationalism can be. . . . Whoopi always seems very much the black American in this movie, but at crucial moments her wide-eyed idealism bridges the gap between the fantasy and the reality of the struggle better than a Malcolm X T-shirt. And her warm relationship to Sarafina is always believable. When the South African police finally come for her, she exits the classroom—and the movie—with a clenched fist. It's still Whoopi, but it's a sister act of an entirely different nature."

Janet Maslin of the New York Times wrote: "It's also clear that a tough, more realistic Sarafina! [compared to the stage musical] means a film at war with itself, as it tries to reconcile Fame-style high spirits with the misery of its characters' lives. It's no small accomplishment on the part of Darrell J. Roodt, the director of this vibrant film adaptation, that Sarafina! remains a forceful mixture of celebration and fury much of the way through." As to its Hollywood costar, Maslin declared: "Although Ms. Goldberg serves an inspirational purpose in the film and does this movingly (despite a laboriously achieved South African accent), the film never wavers from its focus on Sarafina."

Made at a cost of over $8 million, the PG-13-rated Sarafina! grossed only $2.9 million in distributors' domestic film rentals in the United States and Canada. Unfortunately, it was considered too arty, too ethnic, too political, and much too violent for most middle-American audiences. Nevertheless, Sarafina! remains one of Whoopi's most heartfelt performances. One of the film's really special moments occurs when Goldberg's character joins the young cast in native song and dance as they affirm their political passion to be free.

Rounding out her nonstop filmmaking in 1991, Whoopi found time to participate in the Canadian-made documentary Wisecracks, which had limited U.S. distribution in the summer of 1992. Created by Canadian filmmaker Gail Singer, the documentary interviews twenty-four female comics from the United States, Canada, Great Britain, and Australia. Among those heard and seen in this production were such disparate comedians as Phyllis Diller, Ellen DeGeneres, Pam Stone, Jenny Jones, Robin Tyler, and Whoopi. In reviewing this very specialized entry, Jami Bernard wrote in the New York Post: "All the comics in this well-made documentary have weathered the storm of sexism, hecklers, and people who stubbornly believe women can't be funny. But not all of them wear their femaleness as a badge; in fact, some go to great lengths to distance themselves from the old stigma." Bernard cites as a case in point "Whoopi

Goldberg's alarming assertion: 'Every twenty-eight days I remember I'm a woman.' "

Goldberg's fifth and final feature-length movie for 1992 release (Warner Bros.) was *The Magical World of Chuck Jones,* a documentary directed by George Daugherty which paid tribute to the great animator on his eightieth birthday. The rather hodgepodge 100-minute film contains a medley of clips from Jones's wildest cartoons as well as interviews with actors and directors whose personal lives and careers were strongly influenced by him.

During all this intense activity of Whoopi's 1991 moviemaking for the following year's release, only a few of the more astute Hollywood insiders noted that, by year's end, Goldberg and Paramount had ended their once widely touted multipicture deal. The studio, with all its changes of regimes, simply was not equipped to find proper screen vehicles to showcase the very talented but "special" Ms. Goldberg. Meanwhile, the Oscar-winning star had said yes to another venture. Her own TV talk show.

CHAPTER TWENTY-EIGHT

The New Talk-Show Diva

> I haven't changed from being me. A little older, a
> little quieter. But I haven't shut up. . . . I've learned
> there's a lot of stuff I don't want to be bothered with.
> I don't want to come to work and fight. And I've
> gotten a little harder, just in my view of reality.
> There are some things that you can't get
> around. . . . That in the eyes of the majority of the
> people hiring, I'm still first and foremost black.
> —WHOOPI GOLDBERG, OCTOBER 1992

A perfect illustration of Whoopi's ease in front of the TV cameras was her network debut as an awards-show hostess. The event was the 34th Annual Grammy Awards. Goldberg had several qualifications for the demanding job. It had become customary over the years to utilize the talents of well-known comics to emcee such major national TV events. The rationale of award-show decision makers was that comedians, with their ability to amuse audiences, were best qualified to host the typically overlong award programs. Show planners counted on the hosts to provide impromptu comic relief to keep TV audiences watching.

That Goldberg was both black and female gave the announcement special resonance when the National Academy of Recording Arts and Sciences selected her to host the February 1992 Grammys, to be held at Radio City Music Hall. However, it was left unsaid that having Whoopi aboard provided a display of political correctness on the part of the academy. Instead, when it was announced that Whoopi would emcee the Grammys, Mike Greene, then president of the organization, chose to focus on other aspects of their decision-making process. In discussing Goldberg's selection as Grammy host, Greene offered: "Not only is she a creative performer, but she represents the better side of our industry as a humanitarian who works on behalf of homeless children, human rights, substance abuse, and the battle against AIDS."

When Whoopi was asked what she most looked forward to in hosting the Grammys, she said it was the opportunity to mingle with the greats of the music world, even if she herself had "no talent musically." When questioned as to how she had gotten ready for the daunting task ahead, she responded, "I'd love to give you . . . a really long list of intelligent things to do. I just went out and had a good time last night; that's how I prepared."

Natalie Cole, Michael Bolton, Bonnie Raitt, Wynonna and Naomi Judd, Garth Brooks, Mary-Chapin Carpenter, and Luther Vandross were among the winners at the 34th Grammy Awards. However, Goldberg certainly made her presence known during the course of the evening. She delivered jokes with a deadpan look and good comic timing. Maintaining a very straight face, she told the audience, "In the category of New Faces of the Year, the winner is Michael Jackson." At one point in the proceedings, Whoopi was asked to ad-lib to cover over a sudden dead spot in the program. She promptly walked back onstage at the mammoth Radio City Music Hall carrying instead of wearing her shoes. Once back in view, she sniffed her footwear and told the audience, "I was afraid it was my [arm]pits. It was my feet." Then she embarked on an extemporaneous, stream-of-consciousness riff. She continued until one young man, part of her writing staff, trotted onstage front and center to put her shoes on for her. The nonplused Whoopi quipped, "Don't you love the way these white people can be trained?"

Whoopi was back on the West Coast by the end of February 1992. Then she joined a group of celebrities to help Elizabeth Taylor celebrate her sixtieth birthday. That Goldberg herself was a major celebrity was reinforced when Nor' East Miniature Roses, Inc. named its newest variety—a red and white hybrid—the Whoopi rose.

In early April 1992, *Publishers Weekly* reviewed the two-cassette audio book *There Are No Children Here* by Alex Kotlowitz. Judging

Whoopi's reading of the text, the publication decided, 'This story, largely unsentimental, is read with all seriousness by Goldberg, whose familiar husky baritone lends it empathy." Within a few months, Whoopi would turn author herself. While she had contributed introductions and chapters to other writers' projects, this was her debut as a full-fledged author of her own book, *Alice,* published by Bantam Books in the fall of 1992.

She chose as her format a children's story. On the surface, this tale—geared for children ages three to five—was an updating of Lewis Carroll's *Alice in Wonderland.* The narrative dealt with a young girl named Alice who thinks she has won the lottery. On the way to claim her big prize in New York, she is joined by her pal Robin and by Salvador De Rabbit, an invisible, top-hatted, card-playing eccentric. Later, when she discovers that her prize-to-be is another one of those sleazy Florida swampland schemes, it is Salvador who helps Alice pick up the pieces of her shattered hopes. The narrative was illustrated by John Rocco.

Why did Whoopi write the book that *Newsday* praised for its "breezy storytelling"? "Well, I just thought it was time to have a fairy tale with a little girl that kind of looked something like me. I always wanted to have black people in fairy tales. You know, we don't turn up that often." At another time, she said, "*Alice* comes from my mind. *Alice* is a gift, kind of, to my daughter. Because when she was a kid, there were no Alices. . . . And I like it because it's multicultural. . . . It has humans and animals and some animals who act as humans, some humans who act as animals. And it's a story of knowing what's in your own backyard. It's *The [Wonderful] Wizard of Oz,* it's all those stories that say, 'Oh, I actually have what I'm looking for, and that makes me a better person.' "

A few months after the publication of *Alice,* Goldberg found herself embroiled in a lawsuit—a copyright-infringement case concerning *Alice.* Screenwriter Christopher Jackson filed a complaint in the U.S. District Court alleging that he had written a semiautobiographical screenplay, *The Lover,* in 1988 about an African American who attempts to escape the ghetto and gain material success. The hero is assisted by his pal, an invisible rabbit. In his court filing, Jackson claimed that he had shown his script to Whoopi in 1991, hoping to persuade her to do the voice for the rabbit in the projected film. She had agreed. He alleged that *Alice* bore striking similarities to his screenplay. In the course of time, the suit was dismissed. Judge Consuelo B. Marshall ruled that any alleged similar scenes mentioned by the plaintiff in his papers were "common stock" and thus were "not protectable."

In early May 1992, Whoopi returned to the Cannes Film Festival, where she opened the American Pavilion by cutting the ceremonial ribbon. Two of her films (*The Player; Sarafina!*) were to be screened at the festival. Vivacious and accessible, Goldberg was always a favorite interviewee with the media at Cannes. Asked what she liked best about the festival, she said, 'You get to go to strange, odd parties, and you see the most amazing bodies, bodies you could never have in your life. Well, maybe once for six minutes you had a body like that.' She also acknowledged that she was very proud of her new movies being screened at Cannes. "I can hold my head up. I don't have to explain why and how. My [moviemaking] choices have not always been popular with the critics, but I notice that nobody gets pissed off at Meryl Streep when she experiments. And I don't remember the last time one of her movies made $70 million."

In May 1992, Alexandrea, a single parent, turned eighteen. Alexandrea's child, Amarah, was three-and-a-half years old. Now, finally, there was a growing rapport between Goldberg and her only child. Said Whoopi of her offspring: "We are close now only after a series of battles. . . . We had rows [in the past], and she'd say, 'You left,' and I'd say, 'I had my career.' " As to how Alexandrea regarded her parent's enormous success, Whoopi said, "I was handed fame on a plate. But I'm no celebrity to her. She just says I have a job a lot of people want to know about."

At this time, Alexandrea and Amarah were living in the San Francisco area where she was completing a college course. Alexandrea was no longer involved with Amarah's dad, although he still saw their child. By the fall of 1992, Alexandrea and Amarah had relocated to Los Angeles and for a time lived with Whoopi before finding their own place.

It was no surprise that producers and distributors were searching for that right, special personality who could create a lucrative talk-show franchise. Taking its cue from daytime's Oprah Winfrey and Montel Williams and late night's Arsenio Hall—each of whom attracted large numbers of both African-American and white viewers—Genesis Entertainment contacted Whoopi in the fall of 1991 about hosting her own talk show. By that point, she had been discussing the concept with such other notewor-

thy syndicators as King World and Buena Vista Television. It was Genesis's belief that because Goldberg then enjoyed the highest Q [audience
recognition] rating of all females in the entertainment industry, she
would be a hit with her new program.

Part of the attraction of Genesis's generous offer was that it provided
Goldberg with a five-year contract, some $4 million in up-front payment,
and most important, a large degree of artistic freedom and input to tailor
the show to her personality and concepts. Reportedly, Whoopi was anxious to cement the deal because it would provide the ready cash needed
to pay off debts accumulated during her former marriage to David Claessen. It would also satisfy another need. As she phrased it, "I'm thrilled to
have this opportunity to pursue yet another lifelong dream, which is to
talk to the most important and interesting people in the world today."

Goldberg also described the particular structure of her late-evening
program, which would air five nights a week, with a special one-hour
highlight edition on weekends. There would be no on-camera sidekick,
no grunting groupies, and no "posse," the inevitable house band with its
overly chatty, hip lead musician. Whoopi also insisted she would not use
the host-desk setup but rather a comfy living room with two overstuffed
chairs—one for her, one for the guest. She promised that she would not
be pushy, nor would there be any surprise personal questions thrust at
unsuspecting guests. She claimed that her visitors could do what they
wanted on air: "I'm not Barbara Walters. We can talk about whatever they
want to talk about, 'cause it's for them. There's no pressure on these
people, and it's not a show about me. It will be initiated by what they
want to discuss. I'm not going after people."

Whoopi also decreed that the program should be a half hour rather
than the usual one-hour, late-night formula. Moreover, she would be
taping three segments a day way in advance of the particular episode's
airing. "We don't have the pressure of talking about someone's current,
latest, hippest [thing]. We can talk to anybody, so we are kind of like an
asset to the other shows." Genesis Entertainment acceded to all of the
star's wishes.

Regarding the inspiration for her particular chat show, Goldberg
would tell Larry King on his TV talk show *Larry King Live:* "I've taken my
cue, really, Larry, from you and from a show in England called *Face to
Face,* and from Dick Cavett, because those are the shows I was interested
in. It gave you a chance to sit down and talk to somebody for a length of

time and get some ideas about who they are and move on. I think there's a space for it in our late-night situation."

Goldberg also insisted that her forthcoming venture was not a career move: "I don't make career moves. I do things because they interest me and it might be fun." Yet, at another time, she acknowledged that the cyclical nature of a show-business career—sometimes busy, sometimes not—had a part in her decision making: " 'Cause you never know when those slow periods are going to show up. Slow periods are funny, you know. They come in their own time. And this is . . . a unique opportunity for me to—to be able to talk to what I feel are the most interesting people of my time. . . . I'm not Mark Twain in terms of being able to chronicle the—the things that are happening around me, but I figured this would be the next best thing."

As far as being considered competition for the already existing talk shows, Whoopi concluded: "I sort of see myself as this sort of queen in an open car, passing and waving at the battlefield, you know."

As to the type of guest she hoped to attract, Goldberg said she hoped to talk to people "who I think are amazing politically, socially, and in entertainment. And talk about *them,* not just their newest project. . . . We'll probably have lots of people I don't agree with and wouldn't want to go to dinner with. I want the show to be what the U.S. is supposed to be—a melting pot with different ideals and beliefs."

By midsummer of 1992, everything was in place for the forthcoming *Whoopi Goldberg Show.* Whenever her schedule allowed, she taped nine shows a week over a three-day period, commuting from her Connecticut home to Hollywood. It was planned that by the time she took a break in November 1992, she would have 120 of the 180 contracted episodes completed. Enthused by the project, Goldberg helped design the set, even adding paintings from her own collection. Her daughter, Alexandrea, was employed on the program as the film-clip coordinator.

As Goldberg's debut approached, prognosticators tried to gauge the potential success of her new talk show. In their August 16,1992, edition, the *New York Times* published an article entitled "Handicapping the Late-Night Talk Show Hosts." Their forecaster predicted: "Industry buzz: Potential winner. She's hot at the box office, her guest bookings are great. . . . Weaknesses: Shows will be taped far in advance, so forget topical edge. The host is inexperienced, and the audience may tune in for Whoopi-the-comedian, not Whoopi-the-interviewer."

Time magazine sassed: "Quick, what does the world need one more

of? Right, a television talk show. Whoopi's starts this week on 180 syndicated stations—making it potentially available to 93% of the national
audience. The idea, she says, is conversation: one guest and half an hour
of talk. . . . The negatives, as they say in politics, are encouraging: no
monologue, no band to tootle when inspiration flags, no giggling studio
audience to which the camera can pan, and no Dan Quayle jokes unless
Quayle himself makes them." Since no pilot shows had been taped, there
were no samples to send out to the industry. Thus, for everyone, including the distributor and the star, it remained very much a guess as to the
outcome of Goldberg's foray into the chatfest arena.

Promoted with the tag line "It's Whoopi Time!" the TV show
debuted on Monday, September 14, 1992. At the beginning, as well as
the end, of each program a funkily dressed Goldberg, with eyeglasses
sliding down her nose, was seen strutting and jiving to her theme music.
For each show the camera would pan in from a distance, revealing a
black pianist performing cocktail-type music on stage right of the set,
while Whoopi and her guest would be seated in the plush but dimly lit
living-room environment, already chatting away. When the camera lens
came in for a close-up, Goldberg would beam and say quietly, "Hi,
there."

Her debut guest, which guaranteed and earned strong audience
interest, was Elizabeth Taylor. The most revealing statement Taylor made
was "I know it's hard to believe, but I am really shy. A lot of performers
are, and doing our thing on film or whatever is our way of releasing!" The
most bold remark the ex–Mrs. Richard Burton offered was "Without
homosexuals, there wouldn't be Hollywood." Goldberg's response was
"Go for it, girl."

Other celebrities that crucial first week of shows were Ted Danson,
Tom Metzger (the white supremacist), Elton John, and Robin Williams.
One might have thought Goldberg would have asked harder questions of
Metzger than she did, but she stuck to her policy of being polite and
nonconfrontational. The highlight of their interchange occurred when
Metzger promulgated his theory of the separation of races, and Goldberg
responded with "Where are you people going, because I sure as hell ain't
leaving." When she said to him, "Gee, Tom, if you move away, how am I
going to get to talk to you, man?" he said, "I'll call you."

It soon became clear that either for lack of adequate research preparation on any given guest or because of her be-the-good-host rule,
Whoopi was definitely not asking her celebrity visitors challenging or

stimulating questions. For example, she asked Liz Taylor: "Has your sense of self come a very long way from that little girl in *National Velvet* to the woman you are now?" Taylor said, "Yes." When Elizabeth began discussing the Betty Ford Clinic, where she had been a patient and met her most recent spouse, Goldberg ignored the open door and let the intriguing topic die.

To Ted Danson, she asked, "I've read that Ted Danson and Sam Malone [of his long-running TV sitcom *Cheers*] are very different." Reverting to one of his intellectual postures, Danson gave a rather inane response, and they traveled on to other matters. She asked Robin Williams: "What were you like as a child?" He said, "Shy." She countered, "Really." The lack of conversational interplay became too readily apparent.

Entertainment Weekly rated *The Whoopi Goldberg Show* only a "C+," describing it as "the warmest, most buttery new talk show on television." They decided that she "is doing her share to bring civility to the talk-show wars." However, the publication said, "The atmosphere on her set is so humid with respect and reassurance that this normally hard-headed performer seems to have gone all soft and squishy."

Rick Sherwood, writing in the *Hollywood Reporter,* was even less encouraging: "Given the gregarious nature of its star, *The Whoopi Goldberg Show* is a surprisingly staid affair. The result is a show that displays little personality and only marginally more style."

Variety's Jeff Silverman reported: "Fawning. Treacly. Reverent. Safe. Four adjectives you'd never think—or want—to associate with Goldberg are the very ones that infused the opening week of her entry into the chat arena."

After an initial decent rating for her debut show, Goldberg's talk forum slipped greatly in the viewership charts, not helped by the fact that in many cities the program kept changing its late-evening time slot. Soon it was rumored that executives at Genesis Entertainment wanted to "liven up" the show. One source said the aim was to "get her to be more confrontational with her guests, maybe even do a little stand-up comedy at the beginning of each show." Other insiders insisted that the problem was that "Whoopi refuses to change anything." Officially, Genesis Entertainment would only state that the star and her producers are having discussions about possible format changes. Another suggested change would be to have two guests per shows, with some thematic tie between the two interviewees.

The talk show plowed on through September, October, and November, with such guests as Christopher Walken, Neil Patrick Harris (Goldberg's *Clara's Heart* costar), Bernie Taupin, Burt Reynolds, Jack Lemmon, Tim Robbins, John Travolta, Quincy Jones, and so on. Many of the guests were drawn from the impressive client roster of Creative Artists Agency, the powerful talent firm that represented Goldberg.

Even when the half-hour show boasted a uniquely different personality, like singer Eartha Kitt—who did a two-part session—rarely did the ambience shift from low-key to interesting. Even with such zesty luminaries as Ms. Kitt, Goldberg remained overly deferential and unfortunately diffused the guest's energy level with such bland responses as "fantastic" or "amazing." Occasionally, a seemingly "square" celebrity would do something surprising, but such actions were never sparked by Whoopi. Charlton Heston was the star of one segment, and after chatting a bit, he kissed his host to see, he said, what people would think of an interracial kiss.

Frequently, the most lively moments on-camera would be just before or just after the commercial break, when the home audience could catch a brief glimpse of Whoopi and her latest guest talking animatedly. However, once the interview began anew, stodginess set in.

By Thanksgiving 1992, the judgment in the TV industry was that Whoopi's talk show was, to quote the *New York Times*'s Isabel Wilkerson, "an anti-talk show in much the same way that Ms. Goldberg is an anti-celebrity." By December of that year, *Daily Variety* was reporting that the talk show had guaranteed advertisers a rating of at least 4.0 and that Goldberg had slid from a 2.5 national Nielsen rating for a syndicated program to a 1.7. In its category, the show went from a thirty-ninth ranking to seventy-third place within a few months.

A very nervous Genesis Entertainment predicted through its president, Wayne Lepoff: "You will see an improvement in the interviews. What you are going to see primarily is Whoopi getting more involved in the show and more into the interviews." However, he reassured TV stations carrying the program, and home viewers as well, "You have to give a show time to grow, and we are committed to this year to see if it works out."

By early 1993 it seemed clear to everyone that Goldberg's program would soon be history. Nevertheless, Genesis Entertainment kept insisting it would not only last the full 1992–93 season but would return for a second season. They insisted that forty stations had already renewed for the new batch of shows. Then, in mid-March 1993, at an industry convention held in Las Vegas, Goldberg was quoted as saying, "My show is probably going to die. It's going to go elegantly, as it came in." A Genesis Entertainment executive responded that Whoopi's candid comments were "unfortunate" and that, in reality, no decision about the show's fate would be made until the May rating sweeps.

Before April Fool's Day, 1993, *The Whoopi Goldberg Show* stopped airing, but its final fate was still not official. By now, its star was throwing soft-pedaled blame shots for its failure on lack of advertiser enthusiasm, low-keyed support from her syndicator, and "crappy time slots around the country." By May 1993, the expected cancellation occurred when Genesis Entertainment announced that Whoopi's show would *not* return for a second season.

Despite the show's demise, Goldberg insisted she was glad to have done the high-visibility project: "I loved it. I got to meet many wild and strange people. It was great." On a more forthright note, she added that because she ran the show her way, "that's why they yanked my black ass off!" She added: "Hey! I just wanted to sit down and talk to people. I wanted [to interview] people whose work I like. I wanted to hang out and ask them: 'What made you do this?' Ya know, fan questions. . . . I have a reputation for being difficult, but that was my vision, and I didn't want to change it. We could still be on the air if I did a monologue and had an audience and 'whoo! whoo! whoo!' [imitating the signature Arsenio Hall gesture] and stuff. Maybe if I asked questions like 'How come your wife fooled around with your dog, huh?' I didn't want to do that. The critics said I was too nice to the people I was seeing. Fuck. I was really grateful they came."

All of these excuses still did not explain the fact that Whoopi had not really tried hard enough or did not have the skill to pull out of her guests those qualities that would make them fascinating to her TV viewers. The ultimate blame for the show's failure had to be laid on Goldberg's shoulders.

CHAPTER TWENTY-NINE

From Cartoons
to Comedies

My first screen kiss was with a woman [in Steven
Spielberg's *The Color Purple*, 1985], and I haven't
been kissed since [on-camera].
> —WHOOPI GOLDBERG, JUNE 1993

One of the most amazing aspects of Whoopi Goldberg's highly productive show-business career has been her instinctual knack for professional survival. Thanks to a great love of her craft and the rewards it brings—both tangible and intangible—she has been a nonstop worker, always exploring new avenues to expand her acting range and opportunities. As such, she has had many show-business irons in the fire. This has been her salvation on more than one occasion. Thus, when one area of her occupation fails to provide the quality or quantity of work she needs, she always has another work card to draw upon. Frequently, this new type of gig has helped reestablish her with the public.

That is what happened when her nationally syndicated TV talk show was canceled. Shrugging her shoulders at this major failure, Goldberg simply fell back on other types of television work: an interview subject on *60 Minutes*, an appearance at the televised *7th Annual Comedy Awards*, and a presenter at the *65th Annual Academy Awards*. She even turned up on *Aretha Franklin: Duets*.

With her television career stalled, Whoopi turned back to her movie career for solace. Thanks to whopping financial returns on *Sister Act*

(1992) and a good critical response to her contrasting performances in *The Player* and *Sarafina!*, Goldberg found herself still much in demand. She also tried a new area for her in the medium—performing as an off-camera voice in feature-length cartoon features.

In 1992, Goldberg drew upon her voice-over talents to participate in two full-length animated films: *The Lion King* and *The Pagemaster*. Both technically complex features would be in production for well over a year and would not be released until 1994. Disney's *The Lion King* was the studio's thirty-second feature-length cartoon production and took advantage of state-of-the-art, computer-generated animation to enhance the visuals of the overall production. Goldberg said she joined this Disney fare because "I was really trying to impress my granddaughter. . . . I wanted to have something she could go and see. . . . I love animation. I love the idea of being a voice."

The Lion King is the G-rated tale of a young African lion, Simba (voice of Jonathan Taylor Thomas as a cub and the voice of Matthew Broderick as an adult), who discovers the circle of life as he is trained by and then replaces his father, Mufasa (voice of James Earl Jones), as king of the jungle. Goldberg had the fun role of Shenzi, a hyena who revels at being at the bottom of the food chain. Along with two other hyenas (the voice of Jim Cummings as Ed and of Cheech Marin as Banzi), she allies herself with the evil Scar (voice of Jeremy Irons), who plots the demise of his brother, Mufasa. During the course of this eighty-seven-minute feature with songs, Whoopi joins in the musical number "Be Prepared," a rousing call to arms led by Jeremy Irons's Scar.

Janet Maslin of the *New York Times* was among the mainstream critics who reviewed *The Lion King* upon its June 1994 release. She rated the result "as visually enchanting as its pedigree suggests" but pointed out that "it also departs from the spontaneity of its predecessors and reveals more calculation. "She added: "*The Lion King* counts on the wittiest group of voices Disney has yet assembled." The feature went on to gross over $765 million worldwide. The soundtrack album was the biggest-selling CD album of the year. *The Lion King* won Academy Awards for Best Song ("Can You Feel the Love Tonight" by Elton John and Tim Rice) and for Best Original Score (Hans Zimmer).

Participating in the hugely popular film was a boon to Goldberg's career, associating her with another massive hit, as *Sister Act* had done previously. However, Twentieth Century–Fox's *The Pagemaster* was quite another story. It was an uneasy blend of live action and animated footage which told the meandering story of a timid youngster, played by Macauley Culkin, who gains self-confidence through several misadventures. These escapades are the results of a fantasy trip that springs from his taking refuge in the local library during a storm. Goldberg appears as Fantasy, one of three guides whom the overly intellectualized boy meets in the world of books.

When *The Pagemaster* debuted in November 1994, Caryn James warned in the *New York Times*: "*The Pagemaster* is the kind of well-meaning film some parents think their children ought to like, but it ignores a child's sense of fun." As to the effectiveness of Whoopi's gravelly, distinctive voice, the *Times* argued: "Fantasy (Ms. Goldberg) is a mauve-colored book who wears glass slippers and waves a magic wand, but her lines sound like castoffs from other Goldberg movies. When someone points to a bird in the distance and says: 'Look! Mother Goose!' She shouts, 'Hey, girl!' " Technically and creatively uninspired, *The Pagemaster* grossed only $12 million domestically.

After a cameo in the fitfully funny spoof *National Lampoon's Loaded Weapon I,* the film *Made in America,* also in 1993, returned Whoopi to a comedic vehicle along the lines of *Sister Act.* Originally, it had been planned as a starring role for Jessica Lange. When she dropped out, coproducer Michael Douglas and director Richard Benjamin were stymied in recasting the key part. At this juncture, Goldberg happened to see the script and told the filmmakers that she thought it was a sweet story and "it's a shame that I can't do it." Goldberg says, "That got everybody sort of thinkin' and saying, Well, maybe this [having a black actor play the part] adds dimension, because it gives us a lot more places to go comedically than it does if the woman's white." Before long, Goldberg was signed for the lead and the script was being adjusted to suit her talents and her ethnicity. Ted Danson, most famous for playing woman-chasing bartender Sam Malone on TV's long-running *Cheers,* was cast as Whoopi's leading man in what was now to be an interracial romantic comedy. Much of the production, which began filming in April 1992, was shot on location in the Oakland and Berkeley areas of northern California. It was like going home for Goldberg.

Made in America gave Whoopi a full-bodied showcase role as Sarah Mathews, a capable single mother who owns an African-culture bookstore in Oakland, California. Her brilliant daughter, Zora, is about to start college and now decides to track down her father. All the teenager knows is that her fiercely independent mother had gone to a sperm bank after

As a perplexed daytime-soap-opera writer, chic Whoopi Goldberg comforts the show's highly emotional star (Sally Field) in *Soapdish* (1991). (Courtesy of Photofest)

No-nonsense police detective Susan Avery (Whoopi Goldberg) quizzes a prime suspect (Tim Robbins) in *The Player* (1992), a satirical study of Hollywood. (Courtesy of Photofest)

As the enthusiastic star of her own TV talk program,
The Whoopi Goldberg Show (1992-93). (Courtesy of Photofest)

The passionate antiapartheid teacher (Whoopi Goldberg) inspires her prize pupil (Leleti Khumalo) in the musical drama *Sarafina!* (1992) set in South Africa. (Courtesy of Photofest)

Sister Mary Clarence (Whoopi Goldberg) hits a new high note with the nuns' choir in *Sister Act* (1992). (Courtesy of Photofest)

Flying high as Sister Mary Clarence, Whoopi Goldberg is joined by Wendy Makkena and Kathy Najimy in *Sister Act 2: Back in the Habit* (1993). (Courtesy of Photofest)

Finding romance on the set of *Made in America* (1993) with costar Ted Danson. (Courtesy of Photofest)

Romance blossoms between a widowed father (Ray Liotta) and his maid (Whoopi Goldberg) while the man's young daughter (Tina Majorino) looks on in *Corrina, Corrina* (1994). (Courtesy of Photofest)

Ever-wise Guinan (Whoopi Goldberg) counsels Capt. Jean-Luc Picard (Patrick Stewart) in the science-fiction entry *Star Trek Generations* (1994). (Courtesy of Photofest)

Caught in the middle between young love, Whoopi Goldberg's lounge singer Jane DeLuca wonders at the romantic future of her on-the-lam pal (Drew Barrymore) with an idealistic cop (Matthew McConaughey) from *Boys on the Side* (1995). (Courtesy of Photofest)

Bonding with a friend's mother (Kathleen Turner) in the women's drama, *Moonlight and Valentino* (1995). (Courtesy of Photofest)

Portraying real-life civil-rights activist Myrlie Evers in *Ghosts of Mississippi* (1996), costarring Alex Baldwin as the Mississippi district attorney who helps to prosecute her husband's murderer. (Courtesy of Photofest)

The jubilant new coach of the New York Knicks tries a tricky hoop shot in *Eddie* (1996). (Courtesy of Photofest)

A hardworking guardian angel (Gérard Depardieu) hopes to convince hard-hearted Whoopi Goldberg to warm up to young Haley Joel Osment in *Bogus* (1996). (Courtesy of Photofest)

There's no love lost between this bright Wall Street broker (Whoopi Goldberg) and her smarmy, lazy coworker (Tim Daly) in *The Associate* (1996). (Courtesy of Photofest)

her husband had died so that she could have a child by artificial insemination. With the help of her nerdy pal, Zora discovers that her biological dad is not black, as Sarah had always thought; he is a chauvinistic white boor—none other than the disreputable local used-car dealer Hal Jackson, famous as the king of asinine TV commercials. For much of the 111 minutes of this PG-13-rated slapstick comedy, Sarah and Hal are battling antagonists. Only belatedly do they discover that they have two major things in common: their love for their pretty, smart daughter and a growing affection for one another.

One of the more unusual aspects of *Made in America* was that it provided Goldberg with her first real on-screen love scene that survived. This was in contrast to the butchered footage of her on-camera interracial romance with costar Sam Elliott in *Fatal Beauty* or her lesbian embrace on-screen with another black character in *The Color Purple*.

When asked about her *Made in America* romantic sequences, Whoopi explained, "It was very uncomfortable. It's a wonderfully warm scene. But you know, having to kiss somebody in front of tons of people standing there, you know, judging, 'Well, that kiss wasn't s——, it was good'—it was like suddenly something you *think* you do really well at home is up for discussion in the movie house." Goldberg did acknowledge that the comedy's amorous moments made her feel young and kittenish: "I turned into a six-year-old, you know, because we'd rehearse and I'd come close and I'd drop my head because I just thought, Ohhhh."

When *Made in America* was released in May 1993, Kevin Thomas wrote in the *Los Angeles Times,* "Whoopi Goldberg and Ted Danson go together like Clark Gable and Carole Lombard—or Lucy and Desi. On the surface, of course, they seem like polar opposites, but they're well-matched in their ability to move deftly from slapstick to seriousness, rage to tenderness, indomitability to vulnerability."

Richard Schickel (*Time* magazine), who rated the picture "a nice little entertainment," observed: "It appears to be Goldberg's mission in life to redeem improbable situations. It's what she did so profitably last summer in *Sister Act,* and she's awfully good at it. There's something about her—a gritty, down-to-earth straightforwardness—that tends to promise some realization of our wan hopes that potentially explosive circumstances [the interracial romance] can be defused—at least for the running time of a movie."

Made in America was released with the advertising catchline "At the sperm bank, she asked for a tall, intelligent, black man. One out of three ain't bad." The movie grossed a very satisfying $44.9 million in distributors' domestic film rentals in the United States and Canada. Part of the reason for the comedy's stellar success was its familiar, TV sitcom–like premise and the succession of slapstick episodes: a runaway elephant, Goldberg's character charging through crowded streets on her wobbly bicycle. Another major factor was Whoopi's box-office clout, which had remained strong after the release of *Sister Act*.

Of equal or more importance as a key ingredient of the picture's financial success was that Goldberg in her new picture had caught America and filmgoers by surprise. She not only demonstrated that she could be sexy and romantic on-camera; she could be equally so off-camera. For as the media discovered and exploited, during the making of *Made in America,* Whoopi had fallen in love with her leading man, Ted Danson, a married white man with two young daughters.

CHAPTER THIRTY

The Ted Danson Affair

When Ted Danson said that I was a sexy lady, as
well as funny, on Arsenio Hall, it was the first time
that anyone had ever voiced publicly in the eight
years that I've been making films that I was actually
feminine, pretty, and womanlike. It's rare in my
career that I'm offered a romantic lead. . . .
—WHOOPI GOLDBERG, JUNE 1993

Ted Danson had been the star of *Cheers* since it premiered on NBC-TV on September 30, 1982. When not taping the long-running hit sitcom season after season, he spent his summer hiatus making TV movies—often in dramatic parts—such as *Something About Amelia* and *When the Bough Breaks*. His films in this period included such comedies as *A Fine Mess* (1986), *Three Men and a Baby* (1987), *Cousins* (1989), and *Three Men and a Little Lady* (1990) as well as the drama *Dad* (1989) with Jack Lemmon and Olympia Dukakis.

Edward Bridge Danson III was born on December 29, 1947, in Flagstaff, Arizona, the son of an archaeologist. His mother, a fervent reader, refused to have a TV set in their home. Ted grew up reading a great deal and playing cowboys and Indians with real Native Americans from the nearby Hopi and Navajo Indian reservations. In 1960 he was sent east to attend Kent, a rather strict boarding school in western Connecticut. Later, when he entered Stanford University in Palo Alto, California, he was already six feet two. Once on campus, he discovered acting and participated in school plays, which led to his transferring to Carnegie-Mellon University in Pittsburgh, noted for its drama program. By the time he graduated in 1972, he had married and divorced.

Danson has never talked much about his first marriage. All he has revealed in interviews is that "I don't really want to bring her into this. That wouldn't be fair. She's a nice lady. It just didn't work out."

Free of college and marriage, Danson moved to New York, where he appeared in off-Broadway productions and TV commercials, including one in which he was a walking lemon-chiffon pie mix. He made his Broadway debut in *Status Quo Vadis* on February 18, 1973. An avant-garde play costarring Bruce Boxleitner and Gail Strickland, it opened and closed the same night. Danson had much better luck in the world of daytime TV drama. From September 1974 until December 31, 1976, he was Tom Conway, a sleazy lawyer on NBC-TV's *Another World*.

During a self-help EST motivational workshop he took in 1977, he met environmental designer Cassandra "Casey" Coates. Nine months later, they married. He was twenty-nine; she was thirty-nine. The next year, the couple relocated to Los Angeles, where they both found work teaching at the Actors Institute. His movie debut came in the fine screen adaptation of Joseph Wambaugh's *The Onion Field*. Ted was cast as the Scottish-American L.A. policeman who plays bagpipes and is murdered early in the film. Thereafter, he gained parts in such made-for-television movies as *The Women's Room, Once Upon a Spy,* and *Our Family Business*.

On December 24, 1979, Ted's wife, Casey, gave birth to their first child, Katherine. During delivery Mrs. Danson suffered a massive stroke. Although the infant was fine, Casey was completely paralyzed on the left side of her body. The prognosis was that she might walk again one day but that she would not ever be able to use her left arm. During the next two-and-a-half years, Casey, with Danson's encouragement, worked hard to prove that prediction wrong. Thanks to extensive physical therapy and a strong will, she had a miraculous recovery. By this point, the Dansons had bought a two-story home in Santa Monica, which was restructured based on Casey's designs.

In 1982, Ted traded a lucrative contract—doing sophisticated TV commercials for Aramis scents for men—for his leading role on *Cheers*. In 1984, Ted and Casey became the parents of a second daughter, Alexis; she was born without complications. Throughout the 1980s, Danson was nominated for an Emmy for his *Cheers* role several times, but did not win one for his rambunctious Sam Malone until 1990.

Back in 1987, the Dansons founded the American Oceans Campaign (AOC), an environmental group devoted to preserving the cleanliness of the seas. Ted, in particular, became an impassioned speaker at ecological fund-raisers. One of his offshoot charity ventures was participating in the 1990 videotape *Help Save Planet Earth*. It featured Danson's commentary and boasted appearances by Jamie Lee Curtis, Whoopi Goldberg, John Ritter, and others. While Ted was at work making *Three Men and a Little Lady* in 1990, the tabloids, with information supplied by the Dansons' former nanny, suggested that Ted and Casey would most likely separate or divorce in the near future. Neither happened at the time. Despite rumors to the contrary, Danson insisted, "We are committed to each other, totally. The idea of my having more relationships boggles my mind."

It was in this period—the early 1990s—that Danson was a guest on Arsenio Hall's TV talk program with Whoopi Goldberg. Ted recalls: "Arsenio was talking about how most comedians aren't knockouts. Whoopi was coming on next, and I nailed him. I told Arsenio, 'You're wrong there.' " The actor remembers saying to the TV host: "Here comes a very sexy, very funny lady," which, says Danson, "got, I think, Whoopi's attention a little bit."

Goldberg recalled of this fateful TV meeting: "I've done stuff for Ted's organization, AOC, and we'd sort of say hello. We'd be loud in the street: 'Hey, Ted, it's me, Whoopi!' and then move on." She also would remember back to how she had felt when she first met Danson on the Hollywood scene—he was already famous for his *Cheers* work: "You think, I'm gonna be really cool, I'm not gonna be overanxious, I'm not gonna get nervous. And then suddenly it's like, 'Aaahhhh. Hi, hi, hi. . . . Wow, I love your show; I think you're great. . . .' I was just like one of those wind-up toys that go Bang! Bang! Bang!" She also says that when Danson stated on national TV, he wanted to work with her: "I sort of felt that maybe there was a little something to be investigated here. . . ."

In subsequent months, the pieces, with an assist from fate, fell into place. Jessica Lange dropped out of the projected *Made in America*. Goldberg was contracted to replace Lange, and the movie was then tailored as a vehicle for Whoopi. Then Danson signed on to be the film's leading man. Filming was to begin in northern California on April 13, 1992. A few days before, Danson left his family in their five-bedroom Santa Monica home and headed up the coast to Oakland.

Once the shoot began on *Made in America*, it became obvious very quickly to everyone that something was fast developing between Gold-berg and Danson that was not in their script. One on-the-set source reported, "Even hardened crew members, used to seeing stars flirt with each other, were shocked at the level of schmoozing between Whoopi and Ted. The kissing scene was outrageous." Other observers insisted, "The [key Goldberg-Danson romantic] scene [in *Made in America*] was simple, but it required ten takes. If anything, the chemistry between the two of them was too electric." A waiter at the hotel where Whoopi and Ted stayed during the filming was quoted as saying, "They might seem like an oddball pairing, but they looked like sweethearts to me. . . . On several occasions, they had dinner together, away from the rest of the cast and crew. . . . And they always sat at the same table, in an intimate candlelit corner overlooking the bay. . . . She'd gaze lovingly into Ted's eyes. He'd lean over and whisper in her ear."

During the weeks of filming, rumors filtered back to Los Angeles about the goings-on between Goldberg and Danson. A crisis developed when Casey Danson paid a surprise visit to the *Made in America* set to attend the party celebrating the end of filming Whoopi's scenes. Mrs. Danson arrived at the festivities only to discover that Whoopi and Ted had bypassed the celebration to take a private stroll in the nearby woods. That evening, when Danson returned to his hotel, coproducer Michael Douglas alerted him that Casey was on hand and that fireworks were under way. However, the warning did not prevent Danson from getting an "earful" from his angered wife.

Thereafter, when Whoopi left for Los Angeles while Danson and the crew remained in the Bay City area to finish scenes that did not involve Goldberg, she and Ted engaged in a long good-bye kiss that was noted by all on the set. The next day, when Danson returned to his trailer for a noon break, a three-piece orchestra in tuxedos was there playing classical music. The setup had been paid for by Whoopi.

The romantic interaction which transpired on the *Made in America* set remained, for a time, a quiet rumor, unconfirmed in the media. How-ever, matters changed by early September 1992. At the 9th Annual Amer-ican Cinema Awards on September 12, Ted Danson was one of the guests on the dais who spoke of the remarkable, unique Whoopi Goldberg. His praise and adoration left little doubt about his true feelings for his recent costar. A few days later, during the first week of Whoopi's new TV talk show, a very playful Danson was one of her on-camera guests. Soon thereafter, Liz Smith reported pointedly in her syndicated gossip column:

"When *le tout* Hollywood discovers who Whoopi Goldberg's newest crush is, that'll be when the wit hits the fan! He's funny, famous and attractive. Cheers, everybody." It didn't take even the uninitiated long to figure out that Ted Danson was the new man in Goldberg's life.

As the gossip persisted, there were the usual denials by both stars' publicists: "This is absolutely untrue," said one representative; another spokesperson claimed that the couple "are friends and that's all. There is no romance." As the "Inside New York" column of the October 13, 1992, issue of *Newsday* explained, "Everybody's denying it left and right, but this story keeps making the Hollywood rounds."

Fueling the speculation were the rumors that in late September 1992, Whoopi and Ted had enjoyed a not-so-secret weekend trek to Tijuana, Mexico. The *National Enquirer* would detail, "They sat and sipped margaritas at a cozy little café and at one point Ted took Whoopi's [hand] and kissed each finger. Later he presented her with a rose like a love-struck teen."

By mid-October 1992 the supermarket tabloids were having a field day with the romance that supposedly was not happening. It was reported that Casey Danson had left her husband at the end of September over the Whoopi affair and had moved with their two daughters to the Dansons' Malibu home, with Ted remaining in their Santa Monica house. It was further reported that a distraught Casey had checked into Los Angeles's Bellwood Health Center because she supposedly feared killing herself. According to a November 13 feature spread in the *National Enquirer* by Julia Coates, Casey was quoted as telling a friend from her residence at the Health Center, "My husband is a liar and a cheat who clearly doesn't love me. . . . He'd have a little fling, then come running back to me when he'd get scared or be in trouble. . . . Well, I won't be his mommy anymore. From now on, Mr. Ted Danson's on his own! I want out of our marriage."

By late October 1992, Casey was discharged from the Bellwood Health Center and supposedly rushed home to inform her spouse, who was caring for their daughters, that she wanted him out of their household for good. At this point, Danson was worth an estimated $80–$100 million, having earned well over $600,000 per *Cheers* episode in the series' later years on the air. It was speculated that if the couple should divorce, Casey could get half of their assets, including their $3.5 million Malibu beach home and their million-dollar-plus New York City condo.

Ousted from their homes, a nonplussed Ted Danson checked into a

$900-a-night suite at the Hotel Bel-Air. Within a few days, Whoopi had joined him in his suite (no. 164). According to a detailed account published in the *Star,* a staff insider revealed: "At first, Whoopi and Ted were really secretive. They stayed in the room almost all the time, and whenever Ted ordered room service, Whoopi would hide in the back bedroom of the suite until the waiter was gone. . . . In the mornings they act like little kids, sneaking out of the room separately. She'd get real embarrassed when people would see her sneaking out at 6 A.M., ducking down behind the steering wheel of her Ford Bronco and burning rubber as she drove out of the parking lot.

But lately, they've been growing bolder: The staff sees a lot of celebrities, but even they were taken aback when they saw them wandering in an enclosed private garden. . . . It was getting dark, and they were walking hand in hand. He wasn't wearing his toupee, and she was being very affectionate, cuddling close with a big smile and rubbing his bald spot."

As the Danson-Goldberg liaison at the Hotel Bel-Air progressed, it was not unusual, according to published reports, for Danson to shower his new love with expensive flowers and wine when she went back to the hotel in the evenings. When Whoopi would arrive back at the Bel-Air each night, she would frequently find stacks of other gifts as well as cheese, cookies, and candy, and on one occasion when she wasn't feeling well, a bottle of cold medicine to soothe her sore throat. At least once during his exile at the Bel-Air, Danson had his two daughters over to visit, and according to hotel-staff observers, Goldberg did her very best to become friendly with them.

By mid-November 1992, Whoopi had moved several batches of her own clothes and other personal items to Danson's hotel suite. It seemed that they had now established a permanent residence at the Bel-Air. There were even rumors that Ted was negotiating to have Whoopi join the cast of TV's *Cheers* for its last season (1992–93). The suggested premise, so some claimed, would be that Goldberg would play a wealthy businessperson who needs a money-losing investment for tax purposes. As such, she buys the Boston bar and then maneuvers to put it out of business. There was also scuttlebutt that Danson was attempting to get the producers of *Cheers* and the NBC-TV network to pay his more than $40 million divorce settlement to Casey when and if they divorced.

Then came Thanksgiving, 1992. A guilt-ridden Ted returned home for the holiday meal with his wife and children. Apparently, the tense domestic scene turned dramatic when a fight erupted between the Dansons. A few days later, so the *National Enquirer* reported, Danson met with his parents, who insisted that he end his much-hyped interracial, illicit romance with Whoopi. Bowing to the pressure, Ted reportedly broke off with Goldberg, leaving her to mourn their lost romance over the Christmas holidays. The *Star* jibed, "Cutting the dead wood of romance may be a bigger challenge to Whoopi Goldberg than rethinking her television career. Whoopi could be called as a witness in a divorce action unless lawyers work out a costly settlement."

This was far from the end of the seesaw relationship between Goldberg and Danson. Throughout much of 1992, Goldberg had been campaigning on behalf of Bill Clinton. Like Barbra Streisand, Danny DeVito, Warren Beatty, Robert De Niro, and other entertainment celebrities, Whoopi was one of the film-colony contingent who avidly supported Clinton's presidential race against George Bush. To promote Clinton's cause, Goldberg often entertained at political fund-raisers, quipping, "Hollywood is one place where you can come from nowhere and become somebody. In Washington, it's just the opposite." In the process of endorsing Clinton, Goldberg had become friendly with the candidate and his wife, Hillary. When Clinton won the presidency, Goldberg was among those invited to attend the inauguration in Washington, D.C., in January 1993.

At this juncture, Whoopi and Ted were supposedly a dead item, and he was purportedly making amends to Casey and the children. Also an eager endorser of Clinton, Danson reportedly told his family he was flying to Washington alone for the Clinton celebration bash. Instead, so the *National Enquirer*'s Julia Coates revealed, Danson headed to Goldberg's Connecticut home. Thereafter, the two of them went to Washington for the festivities. One source was quoted as saying, "At the Lincoln Memorial 'American Reunion' concert, Ted and Whoopi were together the whole time except when they were on-stage. In the tent behind the memorial they made sure their curtained little cubicles, which served as dressing rooms, were across from each other. . . . And Ted spent most of his time backstage in Whoop's cubicle." When news of all this reached California, Casey Danson, understandably, was livid, canceling any plans she had made to take back her errant spouse.

While the tabloids and other media had been turning the Whoopi-Ted situation into a feeding frenzy, the couple refused to comment. When Goldberg was interviewed on *60 Minutes*, she told a very curious

Ed Bradley: "You know I'm not going to confirm it; I'm not going to deny it. It's nobody's business. I'm not running for public office, you know?" At this juncture, some reporters found that the only way they could gain access to the couple was to promise not to discuss certain forbidden topics.

Then came the national press junket in Los Angeles sponsored by Warner Bros., which was releasing *Made in America.* In the crowded forum where Whoopi and Ted met the press, a few audacious souls broke their promise and inquired as to the status of the Goldberg-Danson tandem. This led Ted to hold up a sign, "That's Personal." In turn, Whoopi revealed her poster, "Next Question."

At a later press gathering at a Beverly Hills hotel, Whoopi angrily snapped when asked about the so-called affair. "That question is too personal. Our job is to tell you the things you want to know about this movie and what it was like working together." In a more subdued moment, Goldberg said of Danson to reporter Jim Brown on NBC-TV's *Today Show*: "We are good friends. But anything more than that, it's only to be shared with our friends and family. I—I take a very strong point of that because I value my privacy. I like that, you know. I like not having to explain why and how. I'll just say this. He is one of the best people I know and one of the best people I've ever worked with, and that should sustain anybody's curiosity."

Danson's response to such media needling was "I understand the curiosity. I understand it, but I can't be part of the conversation. I need to have privacy in my life. This is a big conversation. It involves a lot of people. . . . I need to have this conversation with those people who are part of my private life, not with people I don't know. . . . My life is incredible right now. Huge amount of stuff in my life. I'd love to share it with you on a personal level, but not to pick up and read in the paper—not for people in my life to pick and read it in the paper. It's personal."

One item Danson would discuss with the press was their recurrent query of what it was like to have an interracial relationship—on-screen. "My experience with all the black-white questions has been what a damn burden it is. I cannot imagine how Whoopi feels. 'Wow, you get to have a kiss. That's amazing that you get to have a sexual relationship.'" Goldberg said, "People say, 'Gee, you're black and you get to kiss this white guy.' Yeah, I'm kissing a man! This stuff never occurs to me. I go out with anybody who will go out with me."

Part of the *Made in America* publicity tour took Whoopi and Ted to

Europe. They flew together to Paris for promotional assignments and then hopped over to London, where they stayed at a $650-a-night suite in the swank Savoy Hotel. This transatlantic trip reignited the rumors about the seriousness of the duo's lasting love for one another.

By mid-1993, Whoopi had rented a $11,000-a-month house in a fancy section of Pacific Palisades, California. She had sold her Malibu home in January 1993 for approximately $2.2 million, about $1.05 million less than her initial asking price. Her newest abode—a Mediterranean-style walled estate—boasted a prized view of the Pacific Ocean, five bedrooms, five bathrooms, in addition to two guest cottages, servants' quarters, a library, a steam room, and a pool. Now even more driven to privacy, Whoopi said of her new seven-thousand-square-foot retreat: "In public, I have to act like everything's fine, everything's copacetic. But when I get home and I turn into a real person who has to deal with bills and family crises and whatever, there's no room for Whoopi Goldberg."

However, privacy was not something that fate would allow the Oscar-winning actor. In the late spring of 1993, while Danson was supposedly vacillating between life with Casey and the girls or with Whoopi, Casey Danson came across a box of love letters from Goldberg to Ted that were among the possessions he was storing in his wife's garage. This discovery widened the wedge between the couple, and now, reportedly, Ted was no longer welcome even as a visitor to his family's house. He was still staying at the Dansons' Santa Monica retreat. As a stopgap measure, a perplexed Ted rented a house just a few blocks from where Casey and the kids lived in Malibu and just a few miles from Whoopi's current home.

Again, Ted attempted to reconcile with his family and to diminish his ties to Whoopi. Then, one day in late May 1993, Goldberg found herself doubled over in pain. It was Ted who rushed her to the emergency room of a Santa Monica hospital. After two hours of lab tests, the hospital doctors sent her home to rest from the attack of hypertension.

By June 3, 1993, the die had been cast. Cassandra "Casey" Danson filed for divorce in Santa Monica Superior Court. The agreement on the division of assets was sealed by the presiding judge. They had resolved to have joint custody of their daughters: Katherine, thirteen, and Alexis, eight. Even at this point, when the whole messy situation seemed to be public knowledge, Goldberg and Danson still chose not to air their personal feelings in public. Professionally they were talking about making a sequel to *Made in America* and/or to star in *Pink Vodka Blues*. The latter was to be filmed in Chicago and would feature the couple as two alcoholic escapees from a rehab center. Neither project came to be.

In early July 1993 it was revealed in the *Star* that Danson was again seeing a therapist, repeating a procedure that had begun thirteen years earlier when his then wife, Casey, suffered a paralyzing stroke. Ted said, "I have a lot of rage in me. Rage is usually about stuff that happened when you were a kid that didn't get resolved and got buried. . . . And when you have rage and you're nice, then you're [actually] hostile. There's a lot of hostility in me that people can't see." He stated that the therapy sessions now included his parents and his older sister.

As to his ongoing acquaintanceship with Goldberg, he allowed: "She's quite remarkable. She makes the worst puns known to man. We can be funny together, we can be bad, and we can be serious. And that's fun, because I like to be serious, too. . . . So it's fun, and the rest is private."

By the fall of 1993, the media had successfully overdosed the public with "facts," rumors, and speculations regarding the extent of the romance between America's most famous interracial couple. If most people, including the pair themselves, could not forecast their future together, celebrity predictor Jeanne Dixon had no such qualms. She insisted: "The next two years will be traumatic for Ted Danson and Whoopi Goldberg as they analyze their commitments to marry. There will be times in the next six months when they won't be speaking to each other—then find their love renewed."

By the time Dixon's prognostications were published in the *Star,* Goldberg and Danson had become embroiled in the infamous Friars Club roast of October 8, 1993. The ruckus that occurred thereafter made the previous hubbub over the status of their romance seem mild by comparison.

If formerly there had been ugly racial slurs voiced aloud about Whoopi's being with Danson, matters escalated out of hand now. On Saturday, October 16, 1993, Danson awoke to find a six-foot Ku Klux Klan–style cross erected on his front lawn. He was so shaken by the sight and the threatening phone calls he'd been receiving that he panicked. He drove off in his $40,000 1992 Lexus car in such a highly emotional state that he promptly had an accident, totaled his car, and had to receive medical treatment at a nearby hospital. Interestingly, it was his estranged wife he called to take him home. Supposedly, on the drive together, he told Casey he was willing to come back to her *if* she agreed to his continuing to see Whoopi. Mrs. Danson, not unexpectedly, found that proposal totally unacceptable.

Thereafter, the Danson-Goldberg relationship sputtered out. On November 5, 1993, following in the wake of the Friars Club roast, the couple issued a joint statement that they had ended their eighteen-month romance and parted as friends. The public message read: "We look forward to working together again in the future and hope that we may do so without the kind of media scrutiny we have been subject to over the past year. . . . Although we had hoped, perhaps naively, that we could keep our private lives private, it has become increasingly apparent that this is not possible." A few days later, Danson's publicist said, in an understatement: "They've never been exposed to anything like it individually. Never."

In the coming months, it became clear that, on her part, Whoopi had grown tired of waiting for Ted to make up his mind whether to stay with or leave his wife. She said, "I was nuts about the guy. But once I started talking marriage, he ran." On Danson's part, the controversy that his interracial romance with Goldberg created was more than he had bargained for, and, reportedly, the realization of how he had alienated much of the public with his Friars Club shenanigans was the final blow to his already-long-faltering attachment to Whoopi.

Goldberg offered her own postmortems of the high-voltage affair. She insisted that her love match with Ted Danson did not become scandalous because of the race issue: "I don't think people jumped us because we were an interracial couple." She further told *Newsday*, "They jumped us for all the other reasons. It was the big, rich, very sexy man from *Cheers* and Whoopi, who was, like, considered asexual for, you know, the first nine years in Hollywood."

Whoopi also went on record as saying that the Danson amour "truly broke my heart. It was devastating. . . . It is a painful thing to be rejected by someone you think you want to spend a great deal of your time with." What also bothered her was that she and Danson were no longer pals. "The loss of this friendship hurts a great deal. We can never go and have a soda, anywhere. . . . I'm friends with almost every man I've gone out with except for this man."

The complex Goldberg-Danson "scandal" ended with an ironic twist. During the peak of their relationship, Whoopi came across a property that she thought was an ideal screen vehicle for Danson. She put the proper parties in touch with one another, and eventually *Pontiac Moon* was scheduled to go into production. However, professional obligations and personal concerns made Whoopi drop out of the running to costar in this low-keyed vehicle. It dealt with an eccentric dad taking his eleven-year-old son on a bonding trip at the time of the *Apollo 11* moon landing in mid-1969. Instead of Goldberg, Mary Steenburgen was cast to play Danson's phobia-suffering on-screen wife.

During the *Pontiac Moon* shoot, Danson and Steenburgen, the former wife of actor Malcolm McDowell, fell in love. Once Danson's divorce from Casey was final, he and Mary wed.

CHAPTER THIRTY-ONE

A Family Closure

I've learned to take time for myself and to treat
myself with a great deal of love and a great deal of
respect 'cause I like me. I really do. I think I'm kind
of cool.

—WHOOPI GOLDBERG, SEPTEMBER 1992

An old maxim claims: "Time Heals All Wounds." But as late as 1993, that was not the case for thirty-eight-year-old Whoopi and her long-absent father, Robert James Johnson.

Johnson had disappeared a few months after Whoopi's birth, in 1955. Then Caryn Johnson, Goldberg grew up in a New York City housing project and saw how difficult life was for her single parent. Her mother, Emma Johnson, had to work a demanding day job to support her two children and also had the burden of taking care of the household itself. Her mother's sacrifices over the years—most of which could be traced to her father's abandonment of the family—led to a feeling of hatred on Whoopi's part of her absentee dad.

As the years passed, Whoopi's emotional reaction to people's questions regarding her father—whatever happened to him?—made her emotionally freeze and grow silent until the subject was changed. Even when Goldberg became a big-name movie star and the media wanted more details about her childhood and family, she had little to say about her missing parent. When she did comment, it was to mention with bitterness that he had deserted his family and she had never really forgiven him.

In the years after Johnson abandoned his wife and two children, his life apparently spiraled downward. Rev. Wyatt Tee Walker, of the Canaan Baptist Church of Christ in Harlem, first came into contact with Johnson around 1977, when he started to attend services there.

Like many traditional African-American houses of worship in New York City, the Canaan Baptist Church of Christ catered to a nucleus of parishioners who themselves, or their relatives, had migrated northward from a particular area of the South. The Canaan Baptist Church of Christ had long-standing ties with members who had moved to New York from South Carolina, where Johnson's family came from, which explains why he was drawn to this particular place of worship.

According to the Reverend Walker's recollection, Robert Johnson gave the impression that he had been living from hand-to-mouth on the streets for a long time. It is Walker's remembrance that drugs had probably played a major role in Johnson's poverty-level existence.

As Reverend Walker got to know Johnson better, he encouraged the man to participate more fully in church activities. This led Whoopi's father to join the choir at the church. With the passing of time, it became evident to the clergyman that Robert wanted to turn his life around, and Walker fully supported him. Walker said, "When he became serious about following Jesus Christ, he made a choice. He was a new creature in Jesus Christ."

Sometime later, Johnson confided to Reverend Walker that he wanted to enter the clergy. As part of the process, Johnson gave a trial sermon at the church. This led to other test preaching and eventually to Johnson's embarking on a study course at the New York Theological Seminary. He became a licensed preacher in 1978 and was ordained in 1982. Thereafter, Whoopi's father, now Reverend Johnson, participated more heavily in preaching and other pulpit work at the Canaan Baptist Church of Christ.

Years passed, and by the mid-1980s, Whoopi had become famous for her outstanding Broadway, film, and TV work. With her high visibility, the facts of her background, as told to the media, must certainly have come to Johnson's attention. It must have been a strange feeling for the father to discover how the daughter he had ignored had overcome a dead-end life on the street and her affinity for substance abuse.

It was in 1988 that Robert Johnson announced to Reverend Walker that he was "retiring" and that he was moving to Los Angeles, where his daughter, the famous Whoopi Goldberg, would support him. Obviously, this was interesting and surprising news to the spiritual leader. The minister would periodically hear from or about Johnson.

The scene shifts to the San Fernando Valley, part of greater Los Angeles. Both Bernice Wynn, an administrative assistant, and Sandra Levy, also employed there, recall working with Robert Johnson in the psychiatric emergency room and holding section of Olive View Hospital in Van Nuys. A nursing attendant working the night shift, Johnson would bring newly admitted patients to the wards and perform other support functions during his shift.

Shortly after becoming a full-time nursing attendant at Olive View, Johnson mentioned to Bernice Wynn, Sandra Levy, and other facility staff members that he was the father of Whoopi Goldberg. At first, his statement about his celebrity relative was not fully believed. One day he brought in a glossy picture of Whoopi the movie star, and it was obvious that there was a great resemblance between the faces of Johnson and Goldberg, especially from the nose down to the chin. Levy also recalls that Johnson participated in a Los Angeles local game show—something akin to *To Tell the Truth*—in which he was introduced as the father of a major celebrity. In later chats with Levy, Johnson confided that his daughter had never forgiven him for deserting the family but that he fully understood her resentment. He mentioned wistfully that he attended *all* of his offspring's movies.

Within a short period, Johnson proved himself an able, dependable worker at the hospital, and he was well liked by the staff. Generally, he was quite sociable, but he could be quiet and self-contained. When chatting with fellow staff members, he sometimes talked enthusiastically of repairing his old car, shared the dirty jokes he had recently heard, and frequently talked about the latest activity of his celebrity child. Johnson never mentioned his wife, Emma, and very little, if anything, about his son, Clyde. There is also no confirmation that Johnson and Whoopi ever met face-to-face in Los Angeles or that, as he suggested over the years, she supported him.

If the Olive View staff thought they knew Johnson to a degree, they were surprised one late evening when he came out of the men's room dressed in a preacher's garb. He then explained that he was sermonizing at a small church in the South Central district of Los Angeles.

After several months of working at Olive View, Johnson announced that he was quitting his nursing attendant's job because he was tired of it. He planned to devote all his time to his congregation and the little cultural museum he intended to open as part of the church. (According to Reverend Walker, Johnson's church in the South Central area never really developed a strong congregation.)

It was sometime in July 1992 that Reverend Johnson moved to the small town of Sumter, South Carolina, about forty miles east of Columbia, the state capital. By then, he knew he had stomach cancer and that the surgery he had undergone at a Brooklyn hospital earlier in the year could not stop the now-terminal disease. He had returned to South Carolina to live out his final days. He worked as an associate minister at the Jehovah Missionary Baptist Church in Sumter and lived in low-income housing in town.

One Sumter neighbor who got to know Johnson says: "Bob was one of the sweetest men I have ever met in my life. He was kind and giving. But there was also a side to him that was very reserved. He didn't like to speak about his past very much. . . . He especially never liked to talk about his family, but once in a while, when he was feeling nostalgic, he would talk about them and how much he loved them." As the cancer spread, Johnson rarely left his home.

One church member said: "Reverend Johnson didn't talk much about his life before arriving in Sumter, but we all knew he was Whoopi Goldberg's father. . . . I remember how he told us that 'a very special friend' had sent him on a luxury cruise. We all knew that it was Whoopi, but he didn't want to make a big thing out of it. I guess he felt bad about having abandoned the family so many years ago."

As it developed, when Whoopi learned from mutual acquaintances that her father was undergoing cancer surgery in New York in 1992, she quietly flew into the city to see him and to ensure that he was being treated properly at the hospital. The two remained in touch by phone or letter thereafter, for it was Goldberg who told her dad in early 1993 that she would pay for a trip for him—wherever he wanted to go. He chose to go on a Caribbean cruise.

On May 25, 1993, Robert James Johnson, sixty-three years old, died at home. The only person with him at the time was his health-care worker. Sumter County coroner Verna Moore, who signed Johnson's death certificate, stated: "The primary cause of death was listed as stomach cancer—secondary cause, HIV. Apparently, Reverend Johnson knew that he had cancer for a year. It wasn't revealed to me how Mr. Johnson contracted HIV, but it is listed as the secondary cause of death." That

Johnson had died of an AIDS-related disease was much discussed in the tabloids at the time of his demise.

Before he passed away, Johnson had planned the full details of his funeral. Rev. Thomas Johnson, a cousin, who lived in the New York City area stated: "About a month ago, Bob called me and asked me to come down and help him handle a few things. I came down, and we went to the undertaker together to pick out a casket. He headed straight over to a black and silver casket, looked at it closely, turned around, and said, 'This is me.' . . . I swear I nearly broke down, but Bob was ready to die; he had made his peace."

About 250 people attended Reverend Johnson's funeral, including Whoopi's brother, Clyde. Johnson was buried in the local Hillside Memorial Park, an all-black cemetery. Goldberg did not go to the services, although she sent a huge bouquet of flowers. Later, an acquaintance of the deceased would remark, "I think it would have meant a lot to Bob if his daughter had shown up. But I guess she just couldn't make peace with him. She will regret this the rest of her life. It's not something she'll ever be able to take back."

In early 1993, while Goldberg's dad was in his final months of life, Whoopi was recuperating from a severe bout of pneumonia at her West Cornwall, Connecticut, home and was busy wrapping up what would prove to be the final installments of her TV talk show. She was also coping with the endless ramifications of her on-again, off-again interracial romance with the married Ted Danson.

In mid-February 1993, Whoopi was seen in an extended interview segment on TV's *60 Minutes,* which found reporter Ed Bradley talking with her at her Connecticut farm retreat. In the course of the profile, viewers who might have thought Goldberg did not enjoy the fine life were in for a surprise. The interior of her well-appointed home was decidedly upscale and boasted artworks by Picasso, Toulouse-Lautrec, and Herzfeld. She told Bradley that upstairs, next to her bed; "I have Wise butter popcorn, a Fun Saver flash camera just in case I get, you know, some visitors or something, and—and these really weird jelly candles that I love. And I have my gun. . . . My shotgun. . . . Yeah. You know, I'm out here, and I'm by myself. Come on to the property . . . I want to know who you are."

On February 17, 1993, thirty-seven-year-old Whoopi was named

Woman of the Year by Harvard University's Hasty Pudding Theatricals, the nation's oldest undergraduate dramatic organization. She attended the parade held in her honor in Cambridge's Harvard Square. She later told the assemblage: "It's quite something to come from the projects to the hallowed halls of Harvard. This is very, very cool." In March, the National Association of Theater Owners presented Whoopi with their Female Star of the Year Award. The recognition was bestowed on her at the group's annual ShoWest convention in Las Vegas. Before the end of March, Goldberg was back in Los Angeles to attend the Academy Awards, wearing a rather outlandish—by some people's standards—outfit: a green-and-grape-colored gown whose skirt's slit allowed the wearer to reveal that she was wearing purple full-length capri pants underneath. Finishing off the ensemble, Whoopi wore aubergine-colored lipstick.

As for her personal life, Whoopi announced, "I'm feeling pretty good. . . . I've worked hard in the field that I love . . . and I've turned out to be a fairly decent person, you know, and a fairly intelligent person, which I like. And I have a lot of fun. I do a lot of reading. I laugh a lot. And I cry a lot. And the idea that I can wake up every morning is pretty remarkable. You know, every time I wake up, I'm really happy. I don't like driving very much. That makes me very unhappy, because I scream a lot in the car, but other than that, life is actually pretty good."

As to the price of fame, the star confided: "The press has made it impossible to have friends outside of my house. I used to be able to go out with, you know, married friends of mine, go and have dinner or something. Can't do it anymore, you know? No matter how strong your friendship with somebody is, those papers wear you down. . . . But you know, I have made myself a wonderful home. The people who want to come see me can and do, and we hang out there in private, where we don't have to be worried about what we say or do. None of that becomes fodder for a newspaper, because it's in the privacy of my own home. And that's where I'm happiest."

It is amazing what a difference a lot of money can make, especially in Hollywood. A little more than a year earlier, Goldberg and the Disney Studios had been at loggerheads over the making of *Sister Act*. Now that it had grossed millions in the United States and abroad, Disney was eager to repeat the formula with a sequel. To lure a somewhat disinterested Whoopi back and into her nun's habit, the studio offered her a whopping salary, rumored to be between $6.5 and $7.5 million. It made her the highest-paid actor in Hollywood, which prompted nationally syndicated columnist Liz Smith to exclaim, "This is an almost unheard of figure for a female star in today's La La Land of economic recession. And for a black woman functioning within the white, male power structure, it is an incredible triumph."

Goldberg's take on her new status: "Right now I'm the highest-paid woman in Hollywood. I can say that because [a reporter] just told me that. But you catch a lot of hell; you hear a lot of 'Who do you think you are?' Everyone may not like everything I've done, but it's all gone into expanding who I am. It has to do with how you view yourself, what your stamina is when you swim against the tide."

This led some people to ask why Goldberg didn't make more movies involving black talent, whether in front of or behind the camera. Her response was that the likes of directors Spike Lee, never her friend, and John Singleton never asked her to be in their pictures, nor was she ever invited to play with black stars like Eddie Murphy or Denzel Washington. "They've never viewed me as the type Denzel would go out with [in a movie]."

Sister Act 2: Back in the Habit began production in late May 1993 with its ever-changing script still not finalized. Because director Emile Ardolino was dying of AIDS (he passed away in November 1993), a new director had to be found for the sequel. In an act of political correctness, Disney selected African-American actor Bill Duke, who had directed such features as *A Rage in Harlem* and *Deep Cover*. Also wooed back into the fold were Kathy Najimy, Wendy Makkena, Mary Wickes, and Maggie Smith. This time, added into the big-screen mix, were three priests, played by Barnard Hughes, Michael Jeter, and Brad Sullivan. Also in the cast were director Duke in a bit role and Goldberg's daughter, Alexandrea. Billed as Alex Martin, she played one of the classroom children at St. Francis High, where Whoopi's Deloris Van Cartier (a.k.a. Sister Mary Clarence) is sent to restore spirit and discipline as well as to help find a financial solution to prevent the beleaguered school from closing.

During the making of this follow-up feature, Whoopi had to cope with several personal matters that she could not escape at the studio. There was the snowballing affects of her hugely publicized romance with Ted Danson. He was frequently on the set of *Sister Act 2* during its filming. However, by midsummer, when he was on location in San Francisco making *Getting Even With Dad* with Macauley Culkin, the relationship was dying. Goldberg was seldom seen visiting Ted on the soundstages. As for Whoopi's daughter, Alex, being in *Sister Act 2,* Goldberg claimed it was her daughter's idea to appear in the film and that seeing the complex pressures of making a movie firsthand did a great deal to improve the strained relationship of mother and daughter.

When asked to describe *Sister Act 2,* Goldberg said: "Deloris is back. The nuns are back. We got some priests. We got some intense kids. It's an all-singing, all-dancing, all-acting kind of thing." Unfortunately, the studio insisted that the new movie be a mix of inner-city-school turmoil, á la *Blackboard Jungle, The Teacher, The Principal,* and the youth-musical genre inspired by *Fame.* All the joys of Goldberg's original feisty character were downplayed in the heavy-handed plot line which had the trio of boring priests given expanded footage and the delicious nuns of the original film being reduced to almost walk-on roles. The tough classroom kids of *Sister Act 2* emerged as mere cardboard stereotypes involved in a trip to Los Angeles and the crucial singing-group playoff competition. The songs worked into the production, under the guidance of returning music supervisor Marc Shaiman, were neither jubilant nor memorable. The sole exception was the film's opening medley, which featured a flying nun, Goldberg, and a Las Vegas casino chorus doing an extended medley of 1970s songs. Whoopi contributed to the creation of one of the film's songs, "Wake Up and Pay Attention."

When released in late 1993, *Sister Act 2* won few plaudits. Jack Mathews confirmed in *Newsday* that the film "decided to accentuate the negative and eliminate the positive from *Sister Act.* . . . *Sister Act* [2] is far too silly a concept to support heavy subplots, and the efforts are painfully protracted." Caryn James wrote in the *New York Times:* "The sequel suffers from a lame, saccharine premise and a fatally earnest manner." James also suggested: "Whoopi Goldberg must have an evil twin. The bad twin is the one who can't stay out of the tabloids. . . . She may be tasteless but at least she's interesting. It's the good twin who surfaces in *Sister Act 2: Back in the Habit,* and she's pretty much a snooze."

Sister Act 2: Back in the Habit grossed a disappointing $56.9 million in domestic ticket sales in the United States and Canada. Its artistic and financial "failure" brought to a seeming close the *Sister Act* franchise for both Disney and Whoopi Goldberg.

———————————

If Goldberg was through—at least for the time being—with playing nuns on-camera, she did not say no to performing as another on-screen domestic in *Corrina, Corrina*. The role in question was that of a college-educated, youngish black woman in the 1950s who, when she can find no work matching her qualifications, is forced—with sublimated rage— to accept the job of housekeeper to a widowed jingle writer and his young daughter. The girl is traumatized over the death of her mother, and it is the maid who becomes her friend and surrogate mother, snapping the child out of her withdrawal. Meanwhile, the domestic and her employer develop an emotional rapport that could verge into love despite their realization that an interracial romance would cause havoc. The gently conceived story was a semiautobiographical account by Jessie Nelson, who both wrote and directed this feature. In the original draft of the screenplay, the lead character, a seventy-year-old maid, was based on the woman who had tended Nelson after the death of her own mother.

When it was announced that Whoopi would star in New Line Pictures' *Corrina, Corrina*, there were outcries from segments of the black community who felt that Whoopi, once again, was betraying them by playing another on-camera maid. Taking offense at such criticism, Goldberg said her detractors were not understanding the positive aspect of her new screen character. "I say pay homage to these women who cleaned other people's houses to put their children through college and make them professors and the great men and women they became." At another time, she reasoned, "Who are we to disparage those women who had college educations and could not get any other work except for being maids, who worked and put their children through college."

In shaping her performance as Corrina Washington, Whoopi said, "I've done the noble maid thing, and I can do it, but I wanted more for her. I wanted people to say, 'Yeah, I could fall in love with her. She's smart, she's funny, she's sexy, she's pretty . . . and she happens to do this for a job' as opposed to 'that's what she *should* be doing.' "

Promoted with the tag line "They needed a family. What they got was magic," the ad campaign for *Corrina, Corrina* deliberately avoided suggesting that it contained any potential romance—let alone a kiss— between the black maid and her white Jewish employer. It also indicated that the widower was Semitic only by inference. Such fence-sitting did not go unnoticed. *Rolling Stone* magazine said: "Here's something new and unwelcome: a timid tear-jerker." The publication also pointed out that "Goldberg strains hard to compensate [for the film's deficiencies]. Her 'What's up girl?' sass has sparked many a movie and it sure livens up this one. But it's decades ahead of the script's time period, as is Corrina's hip psychobabble."

Beth Coleman suggested in the *Village Voice* that *Corrina, Corrina* "provides the next [screen] opportunity for Whoopi Goldberg to play comic-romantic lead opposite a white guy who couldn't survive without her." An exasperated Coleman noted, "Using the period [atmosphere] and the [story-line] mourning as camouflage, *Corrina* drags its tale getting to the good stuff, the adult romance. Because, frankly, what else are we here for? To see Whoopi finally get laid, *sans doute*. Don't hold your breath." Owen Gleiberman in *Entertainment Weekly* rated the film only a "C" and termed it "*The Sound of Music* remade as an AT&T commercial."

Made at a cost of nearly $11 million, *Corrina, Corrina* grossed $20.1 million in ticket sales at U.S. and Canadian theaters. Dismissed as somewhat improbable period fluff by some, it does contain a solid, multilayered performance by Goldberg. Unfortunately, her work is undermined by the undernourished, tentative script and the fact that there is little to no romantic chemistry between herself and her white employer, Ray Liotta. Best known for playing snarly-lipped Italian-American gangsters, as in *GoodFellas,* Liotta had hoped this film would soften and change his well-chiseled screen image. It did not.

Contrary to most critics and to the public, *Corrina, Corrina* justifiably remains a favorite with Whoopi. "I think this is a great movie. I think it's really sweet. Corrina looked good, dressed well, and was smart. She's articulate, a real person. She could be any of our mothers." As to the special dimensions of this screen role, she observed, "It's been the most romance I've had on-screen. This has less to do with my concept than with the powers-that-be's concept of what is sensual, beautiful, and acceptable. Those barriers are changing. There are more women out there that look like me than there were ten years ago. I guess [because] I was involved in real life with several men, people said, 'Oh, okay, I get it, it's possible.' "

In retrospect, *Corrina, Corrina* is remembered in screen history for one reason: It was the final motion-picture appearance of screen veteran and Oscar winner Don Ameche, who died, at eighty-five, on December 5,

1993, of prostate cancer, just a few days after completing his role in this movie as Grandpa Harry.

In Whoopi's personal history, *Corrina, Corrina* is particularly important because while making this picture, she met her third husband-to-be.

CHAPTER THIRTY-TWO

Down the Wedding Aisle—Again

The plan is to eventually marry this person, because
he's the one who asked. But as I've learned, anything
can happen. Things change, and they change rapidly.
They can either keep you in your bed with your arm
over your eyes, or you can get up and go on.
                    —WHOOPI GOLDBERG, AUGUST 1994

The infamous Friars Club roast of October 8, 1993, marked the end
of the sputtering romance between Whoopi Goldberg and fellow
actor Ted Danson. By the time they released a joint statement the
next month confirming the end of their amorous relationship, Goldberg
had found a new companion. He was her thirty-two-year-old Beverly
Hills orthodontist, Dr. Jeffrey Cohen. This clean-cut dentist, who was
treating her overbite and spreading teeth, filled the void left by the end of
her turbulent affair with Danson.

A lot of attention was paid to Goldberg's newest escort when she
flew to Washington on October 29, 1993, to prepare for her hosting of *A
Gala for the President at Ford's Theatre,* which would air over ABC-TV a
month later. Dr. Cohen accompanied Whoopi, and they had, so the press
was quick to point out, adjacent suites, nos. 708 and 710, at the Willard
Inter-Continental Hotel.

When questioned about her new "romance," Whoopi responded,
"We've been out to dinner and the movies. Our trip to Washington was
the third time." She also insisted, "We are not having an affair. He's my

friend, that's all. My friendship with Jeff has nothing to do with my friendship with Ted Danson. I'm still friends with Ted." Of course, the inevitable "insider" told the tabloids of the alleged new lovebirds: "They talk for hours. They both love old movies and Italian food. And Jeff is a true romantic. . . . When they had dinner together, Jeff showed up with flowers. He knows she loves white orchids, and he made sure to include one in the floral arrangement. . . . He's head over heels for her, and she's coming to feel the same way."

However, what the press did not report, and what the public at large did not know, was that by the time of her Washington trek, Whoopi's romance with Danson was irretrievably over. In addition, the Dr. Cohen association was far more casual than anyone was acknowledging; Goldberg already had met the new man in her life. Like Cohen, Danson, and many of the others, this newcomer was white. Like some of her past beaus, including Dr. Cohen and Eddie Gold, he was Jewish.

The man in question was thirty-eight-year-old Lyle Trachtenberg, who had been previously married and divorced. A former teacher at John Burroughs Junior High School in Los Angeles, Lyle had become a labor organizer for the International Alliance of Theatrical Stage Employees (IATSE), the movie and TV technicians' union. He quickly rose in the ranks, gaining the respect of union officials in the process. Carmine Palazzo, vice president of the IATSE, would say of Lyle: "He's a great organizer, and he has a great love for the labor movement."

Whoopi first met Lyle when he came onto the set of *Corrina, Corrina* in October 1993. His purpose was to persuade the film's producers to sign off on basic union conditions for the movie, then under way. In the process of getting the filmmakers' signatures, he had met Whoopi on the soundstages. She later said of their initial encounter: "I don't know if there were sparks, but he definitely had my attention." What caught her interest was not only that he was tall and good-looking but he bore a striking resemblance to Ted Danson. She also liked the fact that Lyle's blue earring matched the color of his car and that he was a man who worked behind the scenes in his profession. He also happened to be a nonsmoker and a vegetarian, very much a health-food enthusaist. Lyle was quickly impressed by Whoopi's efforts to convince the film's producers to talk with him and complete the necessary union paperwork.

To repay Goldberg for her on-the-set kindness, Lyle decided that the union should take her to dinner. By the time of the "date," according to Lyle, "it eventually narrowed down to just me taking her out." The couple went to a small restaurant in Santa Monica—not far from where he was then living—and that was the start of their romance. Before long, they were seen out on the town together. Sometimes the occasion was very "proletarian," like the time she went with him to a political rally at Johnny Carson Park in Burbank. She was even a speaker at the rally held by Lyle's union, the IATSE. On November 5, the day that Whoopi and Ted made the joint announcement that they were dissolving their partnership. Goldberg went to a play in Los Angeles with Trachtenberg. A few days later, Whoopi invited not only Lyle, but his mother as well, to her thirty-eighth birthday party.

By March, Whoopi and Lyle had become such a steady duo on the social circuit that it was assumed they were very serious about one another. That same month, during the Los Angeles Marathon, the two became engaged. Whoopi recalls: "Lyle was running in it, and I met him at the halfway point, but before I could hand him his water, he handed me an engagement ring and asked me to marry him. When I said okay, he started running again."

Goldberg and Trachtenberg—they called themselves "Berg and Berg"—managed to keep their engagement quiet for a few weeks. Then, on April 29, 1994, she was a guest on CNN's *Larry King Live*. On this interview show she told King about her new man: "Lyle's a real normal guy. He's got a regular nine-to-five job. This is kind of a first for me." She also said, "He has his own life, and I'm allowed to have my life, too." She then confided to King (and his cable-TV audience) that she was engaged to him. When King prodded Goldberg for the proposed wedding date, all she would say was "Soon." She then added, "Maybe '95."

Meanwhile, Lyle was sharing Goldberg's Pacific Palisades home, which she had been renting, having purchased it in mid-1993 for approximately $2.5 million. She admitted that her favorite TV show was *X-Files*; his was *Melrose Place*. This brought up another topic with the media—togetherness. "Sharing is a big one," Whoopi said. "It's not like a kid, where you just know by blood, you have to share, you know, you have to share with your child. It's different. He's really pretty cool, though, I have to say."

On October 1, 1994—a year after they first met—the couple planned to celebrate their engagement with a big party in Los Angeles. Thinking ahead to marriage, Whoopi registered her wedding-gift wishes at Geary's, an exclusive Beverly Hills china-and-crystal shop. Her want list included sterling silver at $560 a setting and a $400-per-setting china pattern, among other items.

In the weeks before Labor Day, Goldberg sent out notices to her friends that she was planning to wed and would provide the exact date and place. It was already known by the couple's intimate friends that the bride-to-be and her lawyers had worked out a prenuptial agreement with Lyle. When asked anew what attracted her to Trachtenberg, Whoopi explained, "Fortunately, I've found someone who doesn't give a damn about money. . . . He spends what he can afford to spend, and that's the end of it. . . . What I like about Lyle is that he's got a job, he's got a life, he's secure with himself, and he's a nice man."

By late September, when Whoopi was in Toronto filming *Moonlight and Valentino,* Kim Ironmonger, a dressmaker there, let it be known that she was completing a silk-and-lace wedding gown for the star. By now, simple white wedding invitations had gone out to those on Goldberg and Trachtenberg's guest list for an afternoon ceremony to be held at her Pacific Palisades home, with a party to follow there. The date was now set for Saturday, October 1.

The day of the wedding, the media was in full fury to cover the much-anticipated event. Several helicopters, filled with reporters and paparazzi, hovered noisily over Goldberg's hillside estate, hoping to catch glimpses of the arriving celebrity guests and to record the outdoor wedding ceremony. However, to circumvent the media circus as much as possible, Goldberg had attached to the roof of her house a bunch of big white helium balloons secured on long twine. This ruse prevented the helicopters from flying too close to her backyard. Meanwhile, to let the invading press know just what she thought of their hovering overhead uninvited, she had painted on the roof of her home in bright red "F——— You."

Among the 350 celebrity guests who passed through the black-tented security checkpoints were Quincy Jones and Nastassja Kinski; Dr. Jeffrey Cohen, her onetime companion; Harry Hamlin, whom Whoopi once supposedly dated; Timothy Dalton, whom Whoopi had dated; and Ray Liotta, LeVar Burton, Jon Voight, Natalie Cole, ex–Disney Studios chief Jeffrey Katzenberg, Melanie Griffith, Steven Spielberg, Lisa Niemi, Jay Leno, Matthew Modine, Sam Elliott, Shari Belafonte, Robin Williams and his wife, Marsha, Neil Patrick Harris, Steve Lawrence and Edie Gorme, and many others. Reportedly, Ted Danson was invited to the service but sent his last minute regrets.

The wedding was scheduled to start at 3:00 P.M. but was delayed twenty-five minutes to await the arrival of wheelchair-bound Richard Pryor, who was suffering from multiple sclerosis. Finally, the wedding procession began, with Whoopi walking down a path in her backyard formed by rose petals. She wore an antique-lace white gown that cost $5,000, with satin Mary Janes shoes, which she later substituted for more comfortable sneakers. The bride's hair was fashioned in her traditional dreadlocks, topped by a crown of roses. She carried a bouquet of off-white roses. The groom wore a traditional tuxedo and snakeskin cowboy boots and sported a thin, western-style tie. Whoopi's mother, Emma, and the bride's daughter, Alexandrea, wore gowns designed by Sandra Johnson. Emma, along with Goldberg's eighty-year-old Aunt Ruth, served as attendants. Whoopi's granddaughter, Amarah, was the flower girl.

The wedding ceremony was conducted by a Hawaiian preacher named Kalai, who had been recommended by LeVar Burton. The clergyman wore a flowing blue robe emblazoned with a lion and sported an orange headband. He opened the ceremony with a chant in Hawaiian and then conducted the service largely in English. He also blessed the couple, whom he called "precious beings," with a rectangular hunk of polished green jade, which, he said, had special powers to maintain a strong marriage. When the preacher asked Goldberg if she would cherish her new husband for the rest of her life, she quipped, "Maybe!" Later, when Kalai inquired if they truly agreed to unite, Whoopi said, "Yes! Yes!" After a long kiss, the newlyweds strolled into the house and posed for wedding pictures.

Celebrity chef Wolfgang Puck catered the postnuptial party, and a twelve-piece band played Whoopi's favorite song, "Wonderful! Wonderful!" The celebration lasted until after 8:00 P.M., by which time the guests left through the security checkpoints. Each guest was given an ivory-colored gift bag. It contained a white chocolate swan tied with a ribbon that read "Whoopi and Lyle." Each packet also had four handmade chocolate bonbons. One candy was etched with an impression of Whoopi and Lyle on their wedding day. Another bore the inscription "Today I married my friend and you were here. Whoopi and Lyle."

As a wedding token, Whoopi gave her new husband a $15,000 watch and a $350,000 four-seater plane. He, in turn, presented her with a heart-shaped diamond ring. They spent the next day, Sunday, on their private honeymoon. In the early part of the following week, they returned to their respective professions.

Given Goldberg's past romantic track record, the media kept a sharp watch over the newlyweds in the weeks to come. When not grilling her about her career plans, the press kept asking her how it felt to be married: At one point, she replied, "You know, I get those moments where it's, like, I don't care, and I'm [saying], 'Why have you left foam all over the bathroom?' . . . So—so many things to know. But it's great, I'm happy, you know, and . . . it's hard, it's hard."

On another occasion when discussing her marital state, Goldberg insisted: "I'm a diva. . . . Diva still has to pick her socks up off the floor, you know . . . Diva still has to, like 'If you're not going to be in by one, let me know so I don't worry,' you know. . . . So it's—it's a lot about give-and-take as opposed to, you know, take." She also admitted that it was "nice to be proved wrong" about her past statements that she would never marry again: "It was a combination of saying it was okay to say, 'It would be good to be with someone,' and not be embarrassed about it and finding a really nice man, a kind person who let me go through the changes I needed to go through."

In an even more reflective moment, Whoopi discussed the ramifications of her man's having a celebrity wife: "For him, it's a choice when he goes out with me, you know. He chooses to go out with Whoopi Goldberg, and he chooses to accept that part of going out with her means he may be completely, totally, ignored by the rest of the world. He doesn't care, because he knows that tomorrow he's going to get people's pension and health benefits straightened out or he's going to make sure that people are getting what they're supposed to get in their check and making sure that working conditions are right. So it's really quite wonderful."

Overall, decided Goldberg, life with Lyle was fine: "Yeah, he makes the world better, you know. He makes the world better. People are better off because of what my husband does, and to me that's very exciting. I think I—I might have hit on a—a big old diamond."

There were recurring rumors from those who claimed to be in the know that Whoopi had never gotten over the loss of Ted Danson and that Lyle was just not the complete substitute she needed. Then, too, cause for speculation about the couple's future together was raised when it was discovered that Trachtenberg still maintained his Santa Monica apartment, where neighbors saw him frequently checking for mail and watering his left-behind plants.

By August 1995 the ever-busy Whoopi was filming a new comedy, *Eddie,* in North Carolina. By this time the bloom had faded from her marriage. As was her custom, she had already fastened her attention on a new potential "special" friend, her movie costar, Frank Langella. Like Goldberg, he was very much married. Meanwhile, while his wife was off moviemaking, Lyle and his good buddy Fabio, the hulking blond model, were seen frequently in Los Angeles, partying with assorted attractive females.

Later, when Fabio was said to have led his gym buddy, Lyle, astray, the heavily accented romance-novel cover guy reportedly told a friend, who told the tabloids: "I never would do anything to hurt Whoopi intentionally. I feel so bad her marriage ended. But in the end, I guess they just weren't meant to be with each other."

Although it was not discovered by the press until early December 1995, Whoopi actually filed for divorce from Lyle on October 26, 1995. Her petition in Los Angeles had gone unnoticed because she used her given name, Caryn Johnson.

When reflecting back on her third failed marriage, Whoopi explained, "I met a guy and got married and then realized I had made a mistake and said, 'I've made a mistake. I'm really sorry,' and was in the process of getting out of that when I met Frank [Langella]."

Left unsaid was that Goldberg's marriage to Lyle Trachtenberg had been motivated in part by her desire to "get back" at Ted Danson for leaving her and ending their romance.

CHAPTER THIRTY-THREE

Ladies and Gentlemen, Your Host Tonight Is . . .

I've always had this ability [to be controversial], it's just that nobody paid attention before. . . . There's always been [stuff] going on in my life, always. Suddenly, the big ol' magnifying glass was on me. Two months before me, it was Burt Reynolds; now it's on Michael [Jackson]. . . . The sadness about it is that it's so vicious—and based in untruth, a great much of it.

—WHOOPI GOLDBERG, DECEMBER 1996

As Whoopi looked back on 1993, she had to have mixed feelings. On the plus side, she had maneuvered herself into becoming Hollywood's highest-paid female movie star. It was a hard-won title that she relished all the more because it allowed her to thumb her nose at those negative film-industry powerbrokers who had insisted that a black woman of a certain age (i.e., over thirty) and an unconventional look (i.e., that hair, that profile, that skin color!) could not be a leading lady in films.

On the downside, Whoopi's ongoing dalliance with Ted Danson had placed her under an uncomfortable microscope with the supermarket tabloids in particular and the rest of the media in general. If that ongoing holier-than-thou scrutiny was not pressure enough, worse was yet to come. The October 1993 Friars Club mess had earned her and

Danson the scorn of many in America for being guilty of bad taste, crudity, and political incorrectness.

The public uproar and extended debate on the overheated subjects of racial discrimination, interracial romance, and loyalty to the black community led a surprised and then angry Whoopi to vow, "No, I won't allow anyone to intimidate me to being politically correct. Political correctness is a lie. Politically correct means I am going to lie to you and tell you things I don't believe. That has never been my way. The other piss-off is that I have been doing the same stuff and saying the same stuff for ten years. This is not new. The whole Friars Club thing is quite indicative of my humor. I don't know why people just went berserk."

As for the criticisms of Spike Lee and other black men who objected strongly and loudly to the fact that Goldberg was dating outside her race, her response was equally bold and confrontational: "Well, where are those cards and letters, my brothers? I mean, my phone's not ringing off the hook!"

Then, to cap off the tumultuous year, there was the infamous affair of the cookbook. The good citizens in that part of Connecticut where Whoopi had one of her homes published an anthology cookbook, *Cooking in Litchfield Hills*. The proceeds from this book of recipes was slated for the Pratt Center, the local environmental education organization. The editors of the project had requested Whoopi to supply a recipe for the book. Other celebrities who offered favorite recipes were Tom Brokaw (good and fruity granola), Nancy Kissinger (salade niçoise), Diane Sawyer (potato skins), Eartha Kitt (zucchini soup), and Bill Blass (meat loaf). Goldberg's contribution was Jewish-American Princess Fried Chicken. Her directions included: "Send chauffeur to your favorite butcher shop for the chicken. . . . Have cook prepare the rest of the meal while you touch up your makeup."

When the cookbook appeared in November 1993, it sparked a nationwide furor. Abraham Foxman, national director of the Anti-Defamation League, complained, "I don't think it's funny. It's totally insensitive because it raises all the ugly anti-Semitic stereotypes. In fact, it's sad." That outcry was sufficient to trigger an explosive and heated debate about Goldberg's latest supposed faux pas.

Whoopi was taken aback by the uproar over what had been meant as a joke: "The recipe has been around since 1981. We have sent this recipe out to hundreds of places." When the matter got out of hand and refused to die in the country's press, a now-aggravated Goldberg told reporter Chantal on ABC-TV's *Good Morning America*: "Well, you know, if you want to kick my butt about something, I'm more than happy to listen. But don't kick my butt about something stupid like a chicken recipe that's been around since '81. . . . But there is this idea that it's okay to blurt things out at people, like anti-Semite or bigot, you know, and write anonymous quotes. . . . You want to call me a bigot? . . . Identify yourself and get to know the facts. Then you can talk to me. But if you're not going to be knowledgeable and you want to waste my time, you can kiss my ass. I'm not interested."

Rising to Whoopi's defense, Cathy Setterlin, executive director of the Pratt Center, which was the beneficiary of the cookbook's sales, said, "There have been a couple of people who have not appreciated the recipe. But we haven't received more than just two complaints and we've sold more than three thousand books. My personal feeling is that it suits her humor. It's typical Whoopi Goldberg. We're not in the business of offending people."

Eventually, the furor over the recipe evaporated.

In its February 1994 issue *Ebony* magazine observed politely but pointedly, "Last year was a bad public relations year for Goldberg, and her many fans hope that 1994 will bring more positive headlines." That proved to be a hope fulfilled.

A major piece of good news for the harassed Goldberg in early 1994 was the announcement that the board of governors of the Academy of Motion Picture Arts and Sciences had selected her to be the solo hostess of the Academy Awards that year. This was a tremendous coup for Whoopi, for it was the first time that a black person had been chosen to be the emcee of the Oscars and the first time that a woman had been picked for the prestigious assignment. (Goldberg was already a seasoned hand at hosting a major televised award show. She had been the emcee of the 34th Annual Grammy Awards in February 1992.)

Selecting Whoopi reflected a great deal of bravery on the governors's part, for one never knew when the highly spontaneous, opinionated Goldberg might deviate from the agreed-upon script for the awards show and launch into a barrage of potentially explosive remarks. After all, it was Whoopi herself who had told the theater audience—including President and Mrs. Clinton—when she hosted the televised *Presidential Gala at Ford's Theatre* in November 1993: "I'll bet you're nervous, and I don't blame you, because you all know that I am truly politically incorrect." On another occasion, when she cohosted *Comic Relief VI*, which aired over HBO, she sounded off—with obscenity-filled sentences— against the type of people who had publicly criticized every facet of her life in recent months.

However, it might just have been Goldberg's entrenched reputation for controversy that appealed to the Oscar producers. She certainly had the knack for creating great public anticipation as to what over-the-edge remark she might make next in a live performance. Audience interest in whether she would say something outrageous could easily translate into higher viewer ratings for the forthcoming Academy Award ceremonies.

The announcement that Goldberg would host the 66th Annual Academy Awards was made on Sunday, February 7, 1994. A few weeks earlier, Billy Crystal, who had hosted the last four Oscar telecasts, claimed he needed to "lighten my workload" and had declined to emcee the coming year's edition. (Some observers insisted that Crystal had grown stale in the emcee role and new blood was badly needed for the hosting chore.) This led the academy into a mad scramble to find a suitable replacement—one generally chosen from the ranks of nationally known stand-up comics. Among those who were considered were Johnny Carson, David Letterman, Robin Williams, Eddie Murphy, Tom Hanks, Jerry Seinfeld, and of course, Whoopi. Academy President Arthur Hiller insisted that Goldberg, had always been among the contenders for the honor but that her hectic film schedule had prevented her from taking on the assignment in past years.

In selecting Whoopi, Hiller explained the academy's position: "She has humor, wit, and an ability to quickly tie into what's going on. And, obviously, she is a very charming lady. She has dignity, which is very important on the show." Gilbert Cates, producer of this world-famous annual event, concurred. "Whoopi Goldberg has all the qualities of a great Oscar host. She is a major movie star with millions of fans, and she is also one of the funniest, most talented performers working today. Watching the Oscars is a great annual tradition for movie lovers around the world, and with Whoopi Goldberg as host, it will be fun as well."

Late-night TV-talk-show host David Letterman had his own take on the Oscar host situation: "Congratulations to Whoopi, although this does take some of the suspense out of who's going to win for best makeup this year."

As for Goldberg, the chance to host the Oscars was a dream come true. "I'm thrilled about my date with Oscar. To go from watching to winning to hosting in one lifetime is major." To help promote further interest in the upcoming event, Whoopi's publicity squad announced, "It's too early to say what she'll do. I'm sure that everyone would want that to be a surprise."

Once the bloom of being chosen passed, Whoopi would reflect: "I like the idea that the academy came to me. It's a bit of an honor. It's a pain in the butt, but it's an honor."

What made the situation so arduous for Goldberg was that at the time she was preparing and rehearsing for the Oscar telecast, she was also in the midst of location work—in Arizona—on a new film, *Boys on the Side*. It meant she had to juggle her shooting schedule to allow time, periodically, to fly back to Los Angeles for Oscar business (dress fittings; script conferences) or for meetings on location with awards producer Gilbert Cates and others.

As the time grew closer to the Oscars, the hype increased about what Whoopi could or might say during the show. Buzz Kohan, one of the Oscar writers, said, in true understatement, "If she maintains the unpredictability for which she's famous and doesn't dip her toes in the waters of controversy, we'll all get to shore safely and get to sail again." In a *TV Guide* feature article, interviewer Dennis McDouglas reported that all over Hollywood "insiders have been making book for more than a month now on the precise moment Oscar host Whoopi Goldberg will step on her own tongue. . . . It isn't that the first woman ever to host the Academy Awards solo would intentionally be rude or vulgar. . . . It's just that Whoopi is Whoopi, and even she doesn't always know what will come out when she opens her mouth."

Further heating up the waters of controversy, Goldberg began hinting that she already had in mind some blunt Whoopi-isms to air on the Oscar telecast, especially in the realm of politics. "What better time to let people know that you're concerned about them and to say something. The world should know that we're not just these fluff pigs you read about. We do think about more than just our hair and our salaries." (All of this was in reference to the prior year's Academy Awards when actors Susan Sarandon, Tim Robbins, and Richard Gere used their role as presenters to advance political causes. It had infuriated Oscar producer Gilbert Cates, who fumed: "I would not invite such a person to my home, and I would not invite them back on any show I do.")

Finally, Monday, March 23, 1994, arrived, and the celebrity crowds converged on the Dorothy Chandler Pavilion in Los Angeles. The previous year, Goldberg had been scorned by some for her startling emerald-green outfit that she'd worn to the Oscars. This year, she—and the show's producer—took no chances. She wore a far more traditional brown velvet gown, albeit with major cleavage and a sweeping train, designed by famed costumer Ray Aghayan. (Said Goldberg, "Normally I don't do trains, but this is the Oscars!") To ensure that she would look her physical best, Whoopi had dieted away fifteen pounds and looked quite svelte.

At 6:00 P.M., West Coast time, the festivities began. After a dreary introductory speech by academy president Arthur Hiller, Goldberg made her first appearance on the huge stage. She stepped front and center with her arms wide open as the house orchestra played the "Triumphal March" from Verdi's opera *Aida*. Once the audience applause died down, she launched into her opening monologue: "So, they gave me a live microphone for three hours. There haven't been this many show-biz executives so nervous sweating over one woman since Heidi Fleiss, honey." A few moments later, she zinged: "I want to put a rumor to rest. I did *not* get this gig because I'm Sidney Poitier's daughter. I got it because I seem to cross so many ethnic and political lines. I'm an equal-opportunity offender." Next, Goldberg launched into a shopping list of political, environmental, and other causes that were the hot issues of the day. It prompted her to say, "I think I took care of everything . . . including my career."

Warming up to her chore and enjoying the fact that she could say or do most anything she wanted, she took a potshot at the *Los Angeles Times's* Calendar section, which had raked her over the coals in a recent Sunday profile, suggesting that the newspaper section could better be used to hold animal droppings. Now, quite relaxed, Goldberg looked out into the audience, spotted singer-actor Whitney Houston, and said, "Hey, girl! We don't have a statue for you tonight." Then Whoopi began to sing—facial gestures, gesticulations, and all—Houston's trademark song from her movie *The Bodyguard*.

During one of her periods offstage and while others were presenting awards, Goldberg did a speedy costume change. When she reemerged onstage, she was now wearing a Giorgio Armani tuxedo, complete with a white ruffled shirt. In response to the audience's oohs and ahs, Whoopi quipped, "Come on! You didn't think I was gonna spend the whole night in that dress, did you? Nah! I got tired of trying to catch that train. Besides, this is Armani."

Finally, some three-hours-plus later, all the Oscars had been handed out, including one to Paul Newman for the Hersholt Humanitarian Award and a Best Supporting Actress prize to young, tongue-tied Anna Paquin for *The Piano*. It was now time to bid the theater audience and millions of TV viewers around the world goodbye. And how did she do that? "Well, that's Oscars sixty-six, baby." With that a visibly relaxed Goldberg exited the stage, and as she did so, she pumped her arm upward in a victory salute and said, almost to herself, "Yeah!"

Afterward, a much-relieved Goldberg, wearing khaki slacks, a white jersey shirt, blue blazer, and white sneakers, made the round of fashionable post-Oscar parties. She thought she had done a good job with the exception of an Oliver Stone conspiracy-based joke that noticeably flopped. However, she soon was to find out differently. In the next several days, the media would review the Oscar telecast and in particular Whoopi's performance. The "Newsmakers" column of *Newsweek* summed up the general consensus: "Even those who normally wring drama dress-watching found the evening drab. . . . The only excitement, really, was keeping tabs on the post-Oscar parties." In discussing the postshow festivities, the same column discussed Elton John's popular post–Academy Awards bash and noted: "Emcee Whoopi Goldberg also made the scene. Maybe she was funnier there."

Whoopi was stunned and badly hurt by the critical response to her handling of the Oscar chores. She would later say, "I was just me. I was me for the little kids watching TV that might have been awake; I was me for the people who expected me to have a little bit of elegance. I wasn't the *Comic Relief* here's-Whoopi-up-your nose me, because that's not what's called for. It wasn't my show; it's called the Oscars, not the Whoopis. . . . I thought I was good. I felt I was funny, a little nervous in the beginning, but you should be: a billion people! A billion goddamn people!"

A few months later, the Emmy nominations were announced for the 1993–94 season. Whoopi recalls: "The day before, I said, 'They'll never nominate me. There's no way.' I took a lot of grief for that show. I had to read reviews that said how dreadfully boring it was. At least they said I looked nice, which was kind of a backhanded compliment: 'The show sucked, but she looked nice.' For some reason, people assumed that I was going to be tactless. I have never, ever, been tactless on network television. I save that for HBO." To her surprise and pleasure, Goldberg *was* nominated for her hosting chores on the Oscars. It prompted her to say about the Emmy bid: "It was very nice that somebody said, 'You know what? Whoopi did a good job. She came into a tough gig and stood up to the fire.' And, you know, I want those pats on the back. I want to know that I'm doing a good job. I've taken all the heat I'm going to take for the next couple of years."

Although Whoopi did not win an Emmy Award, she felt redeemed by the nomination. When asked whether she would consider hosting the Oscars another time, she said, "I'd do it again, but they haven't asked me." And they didn't. The next year, David Letterman was chosen to emcee the 67th Annual Academy Awards. At the time, Ted Harbert, president of ABC Entertainment, the network that presented the Oscars worldwide, said that he hoped the selection of Letterman would be the "long-term solution" of who would host the key program. "If Dave likes the experience, this could be a great answer for the show, just the way [Johnny] Carson did the show for many years." Harbert added about Letterman: "That was the name to me that was really the home run. Dave's name has magic to it now." Confirming what many had begun to suspect as to why Whoopi had been ultimately chosen for the March 1994 Oscar show over odds-on-favorite Letterman, Robert Morton, Dave's executive producer, told the press: "Last year the timing was wrong. This year Dave feels he's ready."

As the host of the March 1995 Oscars, comedian David Letterman bombed from start to finish. His nervous, uninspired performance, as well as his on-camera attitude of condescension, made the telecast one of the most boring in recent decades. There was no question he would not be asked back again.

When it was time to prepare for the 68th Annual Academy Awards, Gilbert Cates was no longer producing the elaborate program. Instead, Quincy Jones was in charge. Jones had a long association with Whoopi Goldberg—going back to *The Color Purple*. He suggested that she emcee the event. When Whoopi heard this startling news, she said, "I started laughing and said, 'Do they know you are asking me?'" She also recalls: "I thought if he felt that strongly about it, it was a good idea. Also, I feel like I am a little bit vindicated for whatever reason. I don't know if my ego is just very big— How did I feel about not being asked [last year]? I was so full of work last year that it didn't have a lot of time to sink in."

Having agreed to accept the challenge again, she explained why the

Oscar-hosting task was so difficult: "It's a tough room because nobody is there to see you. It's like opening for the biggest rock-'n'-roll band in the world. People don't care. They don't want to see you; they want to see the band. That is kind of what you have to know going in." She also pointed out: "The hardest thing about it is the hype before[hand]. You can only hype the [nominated] movies so much, because nobody knows who's going to win, so the focus then falls on the host. 'What are you going to wear?' 'Are you going to be irreverent?' 'Why did they choose you? You're not that funny.' "

The media, of course, wanted to know if she would do anything different onstage for the coming awards. Goldberg answered, "I will try to get to it a little bit quicker, but there's not much you can do because you got to open the show and you have to make the introductions. So you got to be as witty as you can in a moment's notice or deal with something that's happened and, if you're fast enough, to comment on it and move on." Naturally, she was asked if she had seen her predecessor, David Letterman, perform on the Oscars last year. She diplomatically replied, "I didn't even see it, because I was in transit from one job to another. . . . You don't want to sit in judgment because you know how hard it is."

Despite the pressure of fulfilling everyone's expectations, Goldberg admitted of her Oscar coup: "I'm back and I'm thrilled, honey. Thank you, Quincy." She also acknowledged: "Everyone should have to do it twice, because the first time, you're just all adrenaline; there's nothing you can do about it. . . . And the second time, you have a much easier time of it. Fortunately, we had a new regime, so Quincy, understanding how my very strange mind works, gave me some leeway that I didn't have the first time."

Later on, she would confide: "I had to do it a second time because I got such bad reviews the first time. I couldn't believe how badly I was talked about. I heard people on TV saying things like 'She was too fat for the dress!'. . . . Then they got Letterman to host the next year because they said I was 'too busy.' Know what? They never even asked me."

As the night of the Oscars came around once again, Goldberg pledged: "I am trustworthy, and I do have a modicum of grace and style and class, and that is how I will carry myself." She also had developed the confidence of an experienced Oscar emcee and spoke of a few lessons the 1994 episode had taught her: "Well, I learned it's not about the host. It's about 'Welcome to the Academy Awards. Here's what happened during the year in movies, and here's the first winner.' One billion people around the world want those answers, and they want to see what everybody's wearing. And I learned that you have to respect the people in the audience who are sitting there quite uncomfortably with lots on their minds. People think that a gaudy audience is not a good audience. They're a great audience; they're just preoccupied."

Once again it was zero hour: 6:00 P.M., Monday, March 25, 1996. Backstage in the wings, Whoopi put her hands across her face and transformed herself into a "go" mode. Walking onstage, she gained immediate approval for wearing a chic black velvet dress, designed by Donna Karan, accented with an array of expensive diamonds. Reaching the podium, she slyly asked, "So, did you miss me? Yeah?" That broke the ice, and the audience and the evening were hers!

Entertainment Weekly's Ken Tucker would say of Whoopi's opening salvo at the 1996 Oscars: "Goldberg's greeting was also an instant reassurance to the show-business audience . . . that nothing untoward was going to occur for the next few hours. This has always been Goldberg's paradoxical formula for success: to come on with a Baby-I'm-too-hip-for-the-room attitude while acquiescing in anything anyone in the room might want of her."

She proved to be in rare, relaxed form right from the start: "I am your host, Whoopi Goldberg, or as I am known in certain circles, the mighty Afro deity, especially this year." Then she deftly acknowledged— and took a swipe at—the overdone, often self serving tradition of presenters wearing lapel ribbons signifying their favorite humanitarian causes. Goldberg announced, "I want to say something to all the people who sent me ribbons to wear: You don't ask a black woman to buy an expensive dress and then cover it with ribbons."

This led into her rapid-fire monologue: "I got a red ribbon for AIDS awareness. Done. I got a purple ribbon for breast cancer. Done. I got a yellow ribbon for the troops in Bosnia. Done. I got a green ribbon to free the Chinese dissidents. Done. I got a milky white ribbon for mad-cow disease. Done. I got a rainbow ribbon for gay-rights disease. Done. Done. Done again. A fake-fur ribbon for animals rights. Done. A wet white ribbon to end whitewater. Done. . . . A plaid ribbon that Mel Gibson wore instead of pants in *Braveheart*. Done. And a blue ribbon that someone swiped off Babe [the movie pig]. Done. Enough with the ribbons. It's done."

But Goldberg was not finished. She then dealt with a political matter that had made the Oscar-show producers nervous for weeks. Rev.

Jesse Jackson and some of his followers were picketing the Academy Awards at ABC-TV's Los Angeles studio because, in their estimation, an insufficient number of blacks had been nominated for Oscars. The subtext of the complaint was that not enough African Americans were being hired to work in front of or behind the cameras in Hollywood. Goldberg told the audience: "Jesse Jackson asked me to wear a ribbon, and I got it, but I had something I wanted to say to Jesse right here, but he's not watching. So why bother." The audience cheered at this solvo.

Some of the evening's highlights occurred when Goldberg did a sharp imitation of Oscar-winning British actor-screenwriter Emma Thompson. An amused Thompson came out on stage, curtseyed to the host, and said, "Thank you, oh, great one." Later, manic Robin Williams sauntered onstage and began to dance with Whoopi. Among her choicer wisecracks were "Why do supermodels always get that look on their faces. They're getting ten grand an hour and they still look p——d off?" As to Republican presidential nominee Bob Dole, Goldberg zinged: "Oscar's sixty-eight—younger than Bob Dole." When referencing the number of actors who had been nominated this year for playing prostitutes on-screen, Goldberg zapped: "How many times did Charlie Sheen vote?" This was in reference to the actor's alleged expensive and frequent tastes in paid companions which had been made public during the court hearings of accused Los Angeles madam Heidi Fleiss.

As the evening wound down—highlighted by a surprise appearance by wheelchair-bound actor Christopher Reeve and a speech by stroke-impaired Kirk Douglas—Whoopi summed up, "Well, we've stomped our way through another Oscar show once again. A special good-night to all you kids out there who are dreaming of being here someday. You have the power. Ladies and gentlemen—thank you and good night." With that she swished her gown and sashayed triumphantly offstage.

This time, Goldberg received much better reviews for her hosting chores than before. Lynn Elbert of the Associated Press wrote, "After last year's disappointing turn by [David] Letterman, Goldberg redeemed the emcee's role Monday with a confident performance that cast a charming, breezy spell over a long evening. . . . Goldberg sailed through the Academy Awards ceremony with ease and sassiness to spare, teasing her famous guests at the Dorothy Chandler Pavilion and those who were absent."

There was, however, a backlash from some black groups who felt that Whoopi had been disrespectful to the cause of Rev. Jesse Jackson. To that charge, she said, "I saw him [i.e., Jesse Jackson] at a party after the Oscars, and he said, 'Whoopi, let's be buddies.' I said, 'Why didn't you call us before you talked to the press?' . . . There's been a lot of us fighting these [discrimination] battles for a long time in Hollywood. There's me, Danny Glover, Angela Bassett, Quincy Jones, Harry Belafonte. I told Jesse that to come and bomb us and walk away wasn't the right thing to do."

Still later, Goldberg would explain, "I was ready to rip . . . [Jesse Jackson] a new behind. But Quincy said that he didn't want me to do anything. . . . Quincy has been fighting this [discrimination in show business] battle for forty-five, fifty years. Harry Belafonte has been fighting it for sixty years. Sidney Poitier for years and years. So I just had to quietly deal with it. A lot of people were very angry. They thought I insulted Jackson."

Criticism also came at Whoopi from another quarter. In *GQ* (September 1996), an article appeared entitled "The 1996 Overrated List" that detailed "certain people, places and things who enjoy reputations not justified by social usefulness. . . . Not all are bad per se . . . but none deserve their current high regard." Among those listed were "Whoopi Goldberg's performance at this year's Oscars." Despite these carpings comments, Whoopi was again nominated for an Emmy for hosting the Oscars. However, again she failed to win the trophy.

By that fall, she was already being asked if she would consider hosting the Oscars yet again. Her answer: "Absolutely not. I did it twice very, very well. I told them Rosie O'Donnell would be great next year. I just did it [a second time] to show them that I could do it. I did it, and now I'm moving on."

As it turned out, Billy Crystal would again host the Academy Awards in March 1997.

PART VI

Superstar—"Super" Life

CHAPTER THIRTY-FOUR

Boys on the Side
and More

First it was my name, now it's my age. I don't care
because you can't tell because I'm not gonna wrinkle.
I have no qualms about aging—I'm really excited to
turn forty—because I was never a leading lady. So I
can still have boyfriends and loves and husbands in
movies, and I can be somebody's mother or best
friend and that's cool.

—WHOOPI GOLDBERG, MARCH 1995

etween 1994 and 1996, Whoopi Goldberg hosted the Oscars twice.
She got married and divorced and found new love yet again. She
became a grandmother for the second time. She cohosted *Comic
Relief VI* and *VII* and raised funds for sixty other charities! She was a
recipient of the 33rd Annual Golden Plate Awards given by the American
Academy of Achievement in Las Vegas, Nevada, in June 1994 for inspiring "youth with new dreams of achievement in a world of boundless
opportunity." These were just *some* of Whoopi's varied activities in this
period, which also included, besides making movies, recording the au-
dio-book version of *Having Our Say: The Delany Sisters' First 100 Years*.

Back in 1993, Whoopi was set to appear in the docudrama *And the Band
Played On*, a history of the early years and spread of the AIDS epidemic.
She had been cast as Dr. Selma Dritz, the assistant director of the Bureau

of Communicable Disease Control for San Francisco's Department of Health. At the last minute, Whoopi dropped out of the project due to illness. (Later, she redefined the reason for canceling: her overcrowded work schedule.) She was replaced in the HBO project by Lily Tomlin. In 1995, Goldberg *did* participate in a 1996 documentary on the history of the treatment of gays in Hollywood movies, *The Celluloid Closet.* She was one of many celebrities interviewed on-camera for this screen study, which received mixed reviews.

In the novel *The Color Purple,* Celie was a lesbian. However, that aspect of her character was severely downplayed in Steven Spielberg's film adaptation. A decade later, in 1995, Whoopi had another opportunity to try a gay film role—this time in *Boys on the Side.* Goldberg played Jane DeLuca, a singer in a third-rate New York bar who is dumped by her girlfriend. To change her luck, she relocates to California. She shares a cross-country car ride with Robin—played by Mary-Louise Parker—a repressed real estate agent who is returning home to San Diego. They stop in Pittsburgh, where Jane visits an old friend, the young, frivolous Holly (played by Drew Barrymore). Soon the trio are fleeing the authorities, who are pursuing Holly for the manslaughter killing of her ex-boyfriend, a drug dealer. Later, the women settle in Tucson. There Jane transforms her growing physical attraction for Robin—who has AIDS from a one-night stand with a guy—into a genuine regard for her dying pal.

In discussing this demanding acting assignment, Whoopi said, "I got to play a sort of different character, a little more contemporary, not quite as dizzy as Deloris in *Sister Act* but not quite as biting as the woman from *The Player*." She stated that although this screen role had not been written especially for her, "it felt like a glove." As to playing a gay woman, Goldberg explained, "It allowed me to pay homage to a lot of the women that I know, you know, by not looking like everyone's stereotypical idea of what lesbians look like, you know, because it's time to get beyond all of that." Whoopi said that her biggest concern was to make her character real and original. "Having gone through that early in my career—being a victim of stereotyping—I wanted to just play my character for what she was: a human being who loved women. . . . There was no need to 'butch' it [up] to make it acceptable visually. She's a woman who's soft, but she's got edges. And that's been my experience of gay women."

Another reason Goldberg made *Boys on the Side* was that it allowed her to sing three songs on-camera: "Piece of My Heart," "Superstar," and "You Got It."

The R-rated *Boys on the Side* was released in February 1995. Many critics failed to appreciate its understated virtues, especially the ensemble performances by its three leads. Lisa Schwarzbaum of *Entertainment Weekly* rated it a "B–" and compared it unfavorably to the landmark genre piece *Thelma & Louise*. She insisted, "*Boys on the Side* is a fake. These three amigas would never be together; these three Lifestyle Scenarios would never end up in a lesbian-friendly Southwestern bar." In contrast, Schwarzbaum approved of Goldberg's screen work: "Her performance here is contained, modulated, dignified without cushioning the Whoopi edge that makes her work so interesting and uncategorizable."

People's Leah Rozen, likewise, had no affinity for this "draggy, mawkish affair," but she pointed out that, "Goldberg manages to be both cuttingly funny and restrained as a lesbian in love with a straight friend."

Boys on the Side was not a commercial winner. It grossed only a moderate $23.9 million in ticket sales at U.S. and Canadian box offices in its first twelve weeks of release. Nevertheless, it enhanced Whoopi's reputation as a versatile actor-technician.

Moonlight and Valentino, Whoopi's next movie in 1995, was another female-bonding picture. It focused on a college teacher who tragically loses her husband and relies heavily on the women in her life to help her through the difficult healing process. Whoopi was on hand as an eccentric pottery maker who thinks her own marriage is going to pieces. As such, she is too self-absorbed to comfort her needy friend. When asked why she accepted such a small, unchallenging role, Goldberg replied, "I need the work."

If all this activity wasn't enough for a successful, wealthy movie star turned forty years old, the next year, 1996, would be even more frantic with professional activity. On the personal front, Alexandrea, who had been married since 1993 and hoped to develop a singing career, would give birth to her second child, Jerzey, in early 1996. And three-times-divorced Whoopi would find the next new love of her life.

CHAPTER THIRTY-FIVE

Whirling Through Life

If your last twenty movies made $200 million, you
have power in Hollywood. Other than that, you're a
hired hand. I never saw *Nell* [1994—with Jodie
Foster] or *The River Wild*, 1994—with Meryl Streep]
. . . or *Death and the Maiden* [1994—with Sigourney
Weaver]. You know, I never saw any of those scripts.
So there's power, and then there's power. You can't
equate the fact that you make money as an actor
with the fact that you have power. . . . And . . . I
have one thing that keeps a lot of scripts away from
[me]. I happen to be black, and it still affects people.
— WHOOPI GOLDBERG, MARCH 1995

In mid-March 1995, Goldberg signed an approximately $20 million,
two-film deal with Hollywood Pictures, a division of Disney Studios,
her old nemesis from *Sister Act*). Again Whoopi was in the forefront of
female Hollywood stars in general and of such African-American leading
ladies as Whitney Houston and Angela Bassett in particular. In the struggle to be at the top of the pyramid, Goldberg, who had turned forty, once
again proved she still had it.

While completing and promoting her assorted film releases, Goldberg kept busy on other fronts. As a high-income celebrity, she diversi-
fied her assets not only by collecting rare artworks and antique furniture;
she also had become a business investor, joining with Steven Seagal and
other notables in backing the Hollywood restaurant, Eclipse. Later that
year, Tribeca Productions, under the guidance of its founders, Robert De
Niro and Jane Rosenthal, announced the development of a new half-hour

series with Goldberg. It was to be called *Whoopi's World* and would be based loosely on her early years growing up in New York City's Chelsea projects. Goldberg herself would appear occasionally as a homeless person. However, the show never came to be. Meanwhile, Whoopi matched wits once again with Robin Williams and Billy Crystal when they cohosted *Comic Relief VIII* at the Universal Amphitheater in California, which was also shown on HBO.

On a personal level, in 1995, Whoopi had improved her relationship with Alexandrea, the latter now wed and soon to be the mother of a second child. In the March 1995 issue of *McCall's* magazine, Goldberg told writer Michele Willens, "I'm a better friend than I am a parent, and that just doesn't work. I didn't feel I was ready to take on all the responsibilities a parent has to take on—and this was after my daughter was, like, ten! But I'm lucky I got a second chance. I dig being a mother at this time, and of course, as a grandmother I just run amok."

As for her other family members, Whoopi was taking good care of her mother, having bought her a brownstone in New York not far from the old neighborhood where Goldberg had grown up. Whoopi's brother, Clyde, now worked as a personal driver for his sister on her string of new movies.

Adding to her real-estate portfolio, the very wealthy Goldberg purchased, for just over $1 million, a ranch house and spread near Santa Barbara in May 1995. The property boasted its own stream and spring as well as an adobe-style house with four bedrooms and walls two-feet thick. Also on the estate was a two-bedroom guest house and a caretaker's cottage. The trio of dwellings was surrounded by a lush miniforest of oak trees. (In the spring of 1997, having invested $700,000 in remodeling the Santa Barbara ranch, she sold the 180-acre spread for nearly its $1.7 million asking price.) Despite her growing inventory of homes on both sides of the United States, Whoopi still resided primarily in her Pacific Palisades, California, home that she had acquired nearly two years before at a cost of about $2.5 million.

How was Whoopi Goldberg faring as she crossed over into her forties? She admitted, "Number one, I cannot cook. I've never been able to cook. Now I have a professional chef who does that, and it's great. But if I feel like I've gotten way big—like I was in *The Player*—I'll start to think, What can I do? But quit smoking for a while, and that puts weight on, and I also have an underactive thyroid, so I tend to go boom. The smoking's not under control, but the thyroid thing is happening."

Although her responses were often more geared to her impulsive feelings of the moment, Goldberg generally had an answer for any question the media thrust at her. When asked why she churned out so many movies, she told Larry King: "Because I like them. I like to be able to go and live someone else's life. It's magic to me." She also acknowledged, "You can't guarantee that they will [do well], but you can always guarantee that you will do your best. And sometimes they work and sometimes they don't, but you keep on going. But we live in a strange little sort of enclave where you make movies because it is about box office often."

Perhaps Goldberg's seemingly let's give it a try attitude about non-stop filmmaking—whether said for real or for momentary effect on her listeners—explained why she got herself involved in *Theodore Rex* (a.k.a. *T. Rex*). Sometime in the fall of 1992, Whoopi had impulsively agreed to star in a new live-action movie with a very bizarre premise: She would be a police officer teamed with a dinosaur! She would be paid a $5 million fee plus a percentage of the net profit. Originally the project was set to go into production in February 1993. However, because she was then preoccupied with her failing TV talk show and, soon thereafter, with *Sister Act 2: Back in the Habit,* she negotiated, reportedly, a new starting date of September 1993 for this strange buddy-cop movie. Then, allegedly, in February 1993, Goldberg and her representatives informed the producers of the projected new movie that she no longer wished to be involved in the venture, to be directed by Jonathan Betuel from his own script. One of the reasons that Whoopi had lost interest in the project, besides her complex work schedule, was that supposedly the filmmakers had tried to renegotiate—downward—her verbally agreed upon compensation package for starring in the movie.

In early March 1993, the principals involved with T. Rex Productions filed suit in Los Angeles Superior Court against Whoopi Goldberg, asking for compensatory damages of at least $4 million. Claiming that Goldberg was obligated to appear in the film, they requested an injunction to stop her from appearing in any other entertainment programming after October 15, 1993, until principal photography on *Theodore Rex* had been completed. The production company stated that the needed $30 million in financing had been arranged for the project. Meanwhile, Goldberg and her representatives filed a cross-suit alleging that the plaintiff did not have a written agreement with her to make the film and was thus not entitled to damages and that, besides, she had been "defrauded" into believing that the producers actually had solidified the $30 million financing.

Meanwhile, another Hollywood star, Kim Basinger was involved in a $8.9 million lawsuit with a production company that claimed she had made an oral agreement to star in the movie *Boxing Helena* and reneged on the deal. Two weeks before the Goldberg–*Theodore Rex* legal skirmish began, the court decided against Basinger and ordered her to pay damages to the plaintiff. Although the Basinger suit would go through damages-reduction proceedings and appeals, it seemingly set a legal precedent that worked *against* Goldberg's cause in court.

As Whoopi's case dragged on into May 1993, the presiding judge ordered her to complete her stalled deposition for the opposing party. The other side claimed that Whoopi had failed to complete the required deposition when she allegedly learned that the production company claimed to have a tape of a conversation in which she had agreed to do the picture. The court ordered that Goldberg's deposition was to be completed by the end of June 1993 and that the plaintiff was to turn over a copy of the alleged "oral contract" tape to Whoopi's lawyers.

By the end of August 1993, Whoopi lost her bid for dismissal of the lawsuit. A few weeks later, on September 17, 1993, both sides issued a brief statement saying that the parties had "settled their dispute and are going to make the movie." Part of the final agreement, settled in the chambers of Judge Stephen Lachs, was that both sides agreed to delay production of *Theodore Rex* until the fall of 1994.

Forced to comply, Goldberg begrudgingly made the picture. The plot is set in the near future, when the world's atmosphere no longer supports most animals and vegetation. However, genetic scientists have been able to reconstitute prehistoric beasts and provide them with vocal chords, education and even athletic shoes. As punishment, wisecracking, antiauthority cop Whoopi is assigned to be partnered with the not-so-bright Teddy, an eight-foot-tall dinosaur, the first of its kind to become a detective, as they track down the killer of a fellow dinosaur.

Not only was the premise flimsy, but the script was ridiculous, and the pacing was lethargic. During filming, Goldberg and the director were at loggerheads as to how she should interpret her character—as a boisterous law enforcer or a taciturn type similar to Clint Eastwood's Dirty Harry movie character. Worst of all, in a filmmaking era in which Steven Spielberg's *Jurassic Park* had set the new high-tech, special-effects standards for on-camera monsters, the makers of the unsophisticated *Theodore Rex* settled for a man in a monster suit to play the three-ton title figure. Completed in early 1995, the film sat on the shelf for several months, occasionally being dragged out for a test screening as well as a brief release abroad. The distributor, New Line Cinema, eventually gave up on a theatrical release in the United States and shipped it directly to video stores for rentals and sales in the summer of 1996.

Leonard Klady (*Daily Variety*) took occasion to review the videocassette of *Theodore Rex*. He wrote: "What's on view is a bloated youth appeal picture with disappointing effects and a very thin story. . . . It has the feel of a direct-to-video title perfect for baby-sitting duties. . . . Writer-director Jonathan Betuel goes for the cute and cuddly. That chafes badly with the flip Goldberg (looking very constrained in a leather jumpsuit) and Armin Mueller-Stahl as the urbane mad scientist who turns the clock and is scheming to create a new ice age." As a Thanksgiving 1996 treat, *Theodore Rex* made its television-cable debut in prime time. The sloppy film was quickly branded a creative "turkey" by critics and TV viewers alike.

Whoopi's other five 1996 film releases were almost all near disasters. In *Eddie* she was a limousine chauffeur who turns her superenthusiasm for the New York Knicks into a new career when she becomes the faltering team's new coach. For *Tales From the Crypt Presents Bordello of Blood*, an R-rated, campy and gory entry, stand-up comic Dennis Miller was a smart-mouthed private eye. Goldberg had a cameo as a hospital patient. *Bogus*, filmed in Las Vegas, Nevada, Newark, New Jersey, and Toronto, Canada, had Goldberg again caring for an emotionally distressed youngster. A no-nonsense businessperson, she has great difficulty in relating to the child, a situation finally remedied by the boy's guardian angel (Gerard Depardieu). The poorly received *Bogus*, which cost an estimated $32 million to make, earned only a disastrous $4.4 million in ticket sales from U.S. and Canadian distribution. It was Goldberg's worst flop since *The Telephone* and *Homer & Eddie*.

By now Whoopi's movies were jumping off the Hollywood assembly line so fast that they tumbled over one another, making her a too familiar face on the big screen. Her fifth and typical release of 1996 (if one counts the direct-to-video *Theodore Rex*) was *The Associate*, the second of her two-film, $20-million pact with Hollywood Pictures. For that price, one might have thought they would have found Goldberg fresh material. Instead, they chose to remake a 1979 French movie, *L'Associe*, which itself was at least the third screen adaptation of Jenaro Prieto's 1928 book *El Socio*. In all the various movie versions, the part now assigned to Whoopi had been written for a man.

When asked to describe her new picture, Goldberg replied, "It's a film about the 'isms.' Racism. Sexism. Nepotism. It's about how the system is warped." As a study of discrimination against women, it dealt with workplace sexism, often called the "glass ceiling." For Whoopi, exposing this unfair treatment of females in the office environment played an important role in her doing the project. Then, too, *The Associate* was also a female-empowerment picture in the same vein as *The First Wives Club*. Yet another aspect of the film, to which Goldberg could relate, was the perils of being a celebrity under the relentless scrutiny of the media.

Within *The Associate*, Whoopi's character, Laurel Ayres, is a dedicated, ambitious broker in a Wall Street firm. When she sees her fine work passed over in favor of a smarmy, lazy associate, who gets ahead in the company because he is a man, Laurel quits. She is soon joined by Sally (two-time Oscar winner Dianne Wiest), a longtime secretary in the firm, who has also left the brokerage house because of its sexist policies. Thereafter, Laurel and Sally start their own firm. In short order, the two women discover that the powerbrokers dealing in Wall Street selling and buying will not listen to Laurel's intelligent proposals because they come from a female. To remedy the situation, Laurel creates Robert Cutty, a fictitious associate at her firm. He soon becomes the darling of the financial sector for his brilliant strategies. Eventually, important customers of Laurel's demand to meet this Wall Street wizard, and she must bring the nonentity to life.

The buildup to seeing Goldberg's character transformed into a raspy-voiced, eccentric-looking man is the main suspense maker of *The Associate*. In white-face makeup, a ponytail, and a stomach paunch, the nonexistent Robert Cutty that Laurel becomes is almost a dead ringer for today's aged, vastly overweight Marlon Brando, with a dash of George Washington thrown in. That Goldberg's screen makeover verges on the ludicrous and unbelievable is, unfortunately, one of the film's several misjudgments.

The advertising tag line for *The Associate* read: "Behind every great man is a woman . . . wishing he'd get the hell out of her way." The PG-rated feature opened in late October 1996. *USA Today* alerted its readers: "*The Associate* at least keeps its dopey gimmick at bay for a while. The usually bolder Goldberg tones it down as a whiz with figures who isn't smart enough to suspect a weaselly co-worker of wrongdoings until he steals her rightful promotion."

Roger Ebert wrote in the *Chicago Sun-Times*: "Maybe Goldberg wanted to play a white man just to prove a point, but if she'd made Cutty a black man, she could have made a more provocative point and probably looked more convincing at the same time."

In six weeks of national distribution *The Associate* tallied only $12.3 million in ticket sales at U.S. and Canadian theaters. It was yet another box-office defeat for Whoopi. As had been the case increasingly in recent years, there were rumors that Goldberg was being demanding on the set. In a recent issue of *Buzz* magazine, an article entitled "Inside the Screen Factory," by Catherine Seipp, listed the ten-biggest "screamers" in the film business. Among those included, besides several big-shot film executives, was Whoopi. The account pointed out that although Goldberg the actor is "generally well liked, she nevertheless is known for public-humiliation-style screaming at colleagues and self-righteous tantrums when she feels others are unprepared. Favorite phrase: 'Do your fucking job.' "

After so many inconsequential films—many of which floundered in distribution—it is little wonder that Whoopi chose to join the cast of the prestigious drama *Ghosts of Mississippi*. It allowed her to portray a real-life, living person for the first time on-screen. The individual in question was the much-revered Myrlie Evers, the widow of slain civil-rights leader Medgar Evers. After his death, she went on to become chairperson of the NAACP while crusading for decades to bring her husband's accused killer to justice. Making *Ghosts of Mississippi* appealed to Whoopi's sense of irony because it allowed her to work with director Rob Reiner, who had dismissed her request to be considered for the leading role of his comedy film *The Princess Bride* a decade earlier.

In tackling this role, Goldberg acknowledges her recollections of the slaying, which occurred five months before the assassination of President John F. Kennedy: "I was a kid when Medgar Evers was shot, but I remember the pictures in *Life* magazine and hearing adults talk about him. It wasn't until we started making this movie, though, that I realized how important he was to the civil rights movement. Evers's death turned media attention to the South, and that led eventually to Martin Luther King becoming prominent a few years later. When I hear people talking about that era, I think, Wait a minute. A whole lot of things wouldn't have happened the way they did had Evers not been assassinated. The cooker might not have been turned up as high."

In evolving the screen character of Myrlie Evers for the movie, director Rob Reiner said, "We sent her [Evers] every draft of the script and she gave us feedback and notes that I tried to incorporate as much as I could. Virtually everything that Whoopi says in the movie is something that Myrlie told us she'd said."

Goldberg adds, "I sat with Myrlie [Evers] quite a bit in Mississippi [where the movie was shot], and we talked extensively about Medgar and their life together. I didn't attempt to do an imitation of her—I'm not Rich Little—but I tried to re-create her essence as best I could."

Furthermore, said the performer, "Myrlie Evers is definitely powerful. She has a huge presence when she enters a room, much like other incredible women, like Shirley Chisholm or Coretta King. . . . One of the things Myrlie instilled in me was that she and her children celebrated Medgar. They kept him alive by celebration. People only die if you forget them. She loved her husband with every fiber of her being, and she is able in the film to pass the idea that justice is real to Bobby DeLaughter [the white assistant district attorney who spearheaded the retrial of her husband's accused killer]. When Myrlie talks to me about Bobby in real life, she glows. They really changed the judicial system in Mississippi."

Getting inside her real-life character was not easy for Goldberg: "Myrlie and I are from two separate eras. Her cadence and her manner are so vastly different from mine, I had to get into her from the sixties forward as an adult, as I was a kid in the sixties. Playing a real character as opposed to a fictional one carries with it a responsibility, and luckily for many of us on the film, our characters were set visitors."

After the picture was completed, director Rob Reiner would comment, "It was a very tough part for Whoopi to play, and I think she felt an enormous pressure carrying the mantle of Myrlie Evers. But Whoopi wanted so badly to play her and to make her contribution to this story, and I think she did a great job."

Many of the film's scenes, including the graphic gunning down of Evers, were shot on actual locations in Hinds County, Mississippi. In the movie, Byron De La Beckwith shoots Medgar Evers as the latter enters his house one evening in 1963. Although there is substantial evidence that De La Beckwith, a racist, committed the crime, two Mississippi juries, all white and all male, cannot decide on his guilt, and they each declare a mistrial. Determined to vindicate her husband's death by having his killer found guilty in court, Myrlie persists year after year in pressuring the local district attorney's office to reopen the much-publicized homicide case.

Finally, new evidence of jury tampering in the earlier trials is discovered, and assistant district attorney Bobby DeLaughter (Alec Baldwin) is put in charge of bringing De La Beckwith, now seventy-three, to trial once again. Guided more by a desire for legal truth than for racial equality, DeLaughter overcomes each obstacle in the pending trial. Buoyed by Myrlie's determination and conviction, he sees the case through to ultimate victory. De La Beckwith is found guilty and is sentenced to serve a life sentence.

Ghosts of Mississippi debuted a few days before Christmas, 1996, to qualify for Academy Award consideration. Even before it opened, there were rumblings that this well-intentioned feature might not be the testament to the real-life story that it claimed to be. From Oregon, where she now lived, Myrlie Evers was quoted as saying, "I have often described myself and my children as damaged goods, and in a sense we are. The wound is so deep it never really healed. I *wish* that could have been shown in the movie, what we went through. It was a living hell. . . . I wanted to be involved, and Rob [Reiner] was very generous with his time in listening to my suggestions and recommendations. But I know he felt he had to do it his way."

Ms. Evers was referring to the fact that the film, directed and packaged by a mostly white team, told very little of the life of Medgar Evers and that the bulk of screen time was focused on the white southern attorney handling the case and his personal battle with himself when he realizes he has lived a life frequently blinded by inbred racism and false values.

As to the actor who was portraying her on-screen, Ms. Evers noted, somewhat ambiguously: "Whoopi Goldberg is a superb actor. I'm being very tactful. I don't want to cast any aspersions."

However, reviewers were unhappy with the end result. No mention was made by the press regarding the fact that Whoopi had put on weight—more than was becoming. Writing in the *Los Angeles Weekly*, Ella Taylor noted: "With the exception of Whoopi Goldberg as Evers' wife, Myrlie, and several members of the Evers family in cameos as themselves, hardly a black face crosses the screen." Taylor argued, "The only character with anything like a complex personality is De La Beckwith, played under several tons of makeup by James Woods."

Kenneth Turan, of the *Los Angeles Times,* criticized the righteous movie because "the filmmakers have taken the drama out of what should be a riveting scenario, leaving nothing for an audience to become involved with. And it's made its characters so predictable we half expect to see halos over the heroes and the villain twirling a waxed mustache." As to Goldberg's performance, Turan wrote: "Normally warm and funny, Goldberg gives the kind of preserved-in-amber performance as Evers' widow you would expect from an authorized film biography of Mother Teresa. Its embalmed, worshipful quality does credit neither to her nor to Myrlie Evers."

Regarding Whoopi, Robert Ebert of the *Chicago Sun-Times* concluded: "The emotional center of the film should probably be Myrlie Evers (Whoopi Goldberg), who cradled her bleeding husband as he died that night, her weeping and frightened children around her. But the role is underwritten to such a degree that Myrlie never really emerges except as an emblem, and Goldberg plays her like the guest of honor at a testimonial banquet. There's no juice. . . . That's partly Goldberg's fault . . . but mostly the fault of the filmmakers, who see their material through white eyes and use the Myrlie character as a convenient conscience."

With such adverse critical response, *Ghosts of Mississippi* struggled through seven weeks of major national release, toting up a meager $12.7 million in ticket sales at U.S. and Canadian theaters. Initially, there had been hype that *both* Goldberg and James Woods would certainly be nominated for Academy Awards for their performances. In fact, the movie's distributor, Castle Rock, campaigned for an Oscar in the Best Supporting Actress category for Whoopi, but no nomination was forthcoming. In contrast, James Woods was nominated for his uncanny portrayal of the aged, unrepentant murderer. At the March 1997 Oscar ceremonies it was Cuba Gooding Jr. (*Jerry McGuire*) who won the Best Supporting Actor Academy Award, not Woods or any of the other three male contenders in that classification.

In the aftermath of the film's discouragingly poor reception, Goldberg insisted that the critics were not being practical when they chastised the filmmakers for devoting so much screen time to the white characters. It was Whoopi's theory that this feature had positively stretched Hollywood's boundaries of bringing black subject matter onto the big screen. According to Goldberg's theory, sometime in the future the *full* story of Medgar Evers's life could and would be told on film. In her typical confrontational fashion, Whoopi had practical advice for anyone who faulted *Ghosts of Mississippi*: "If someone feels that strongly that something is missing, then let them make a film about it."

To be noted in the cast of *Ghosts of Mississippi* were Yolanda King, daughter of slain Rev. Dr. Martin Luther King Jr. She portrayed Medgar Evers's daughter, Reena, while Evers's real-life sons, Darrell and James, were cast as themselves.

CHAPTER THIRTY-SIX

Divorce—
The Hollywood Way

Well, girl, please, this isn't the end of an M-G-M
movie [musical]. It's as good as it is.
—WHOOPI GOLDBERG, MARCH 1995

In Whoopi's world, romances and marriages typically never last very
long. Usually, by the second year of intimacy she and her beau have
drifted apart and pursued other interests. A rare exception was
Whoopi's early 1980s rapport with Berkeley playwright–performance artist David Schein, which lasted over three years. However, Goldberg's
marriage to husband number three, Lyle Trachtenberg, the labor-union
official, was no such exception.

By the summer of 1995, nearly a year after they wed, it must have
been clear to Lyle that he would always be "Mr. Goldberg" in their household. He had to realize also that with his wife's life so focused on her
nonstop career ventures, her family, her entourage, and of course, her
charity activities, there was not that much room left in her daily schedule
or thoughts for him. It certainly must not have helped their marriage to
hear her tell interviewers over and over again how Ted Danson had
broken her heart and how painful the recovery had been and still was. It
may have finally dawned on Trachtenberg that Whoopi had married him
on the rebound. That he still maintained, after several months of marriage, his Santa Monica, California, apartment while living with his wife
at her Pacific Palisades home was a clear indication that he was keeping
all his options open.

325

In August 1995, Whoopi left Los Angeles for extended location filming in North Carolina for her new movie *Eddie*. Lyle remained behind to attend to his own work with the IATSE union. Pretty soon gossip items in Los Angeles publications were mentioning that Trachtenberg and his gym buddy Fabio were seen out on the town with various pretty women.

Meanwhile, in North Carolina, Whoopi was becoming very friendly with her leading man, Frank Langella. He had been cast as Wild Bill Donovan, the crafty Texas entrepreneur who becomes the latest owner of the New York Knicks basketball team. As such, he hires superfan Whoopi to replace the existing team coach (Dennis Farina) and, unbeknownst to her, manipulates her to convert the basketball squad into a winning team so he can sell the franchise to the highest bidder. As a result, he and Goldberg's Eddie battle throughout much of the screen comedy. In real life it was far different. He had literally swept *Eddie*'s star off her feet.

Frank Langella was born on January 1, 1940, in Bayonne, New Jersey, where his father, Frank senior, was the president of the Bayonne Barrel and Drum Company, which manufactured containers of assorted sizes. More interested in the theater than in corporate business, Frank junior gained his first acting notices in the sixth grade portraying a ninety-five-year-old man in an Abraham Lincoln pageant. After graduating from Syracuse University, he played guitar and sang with a folksinging group as they toured Europe. Back in New York, he made his off-Broadway debut in 1963 in a revival of *The Immoralist*. The rest of the decade was spent appearing off- and on Broadway as well as in regional repertory theater. He made his movie debut in Mel Brooks's *The Twelve Chairs*, followed by such films as *The Wrath of God* (with Robert Mitchum and Rita Hayworth). He first appeared on Broadway playing a lizard in Edward Albee's *Seascape*, for which he won a Tony. He gained great acclaim in the New York stage revival of *Dracula* and repeated the title role of the legendary vampire in Universal's screen version of the Gothic romance in 1979.

Over subsequent years, Frank continued alternating between directing, producing, and acting off- and on Broadway and in regional theater while making additional movies. Summing up his acting credo and career choices over the years, he once said, "I would rather have a sixty-year span as a good, fine actor than have five hot years as a superstar, become rich, and then disappear. My work is my life, and I want my work to last the length of my lifetime."

Beyond a fancy acting fee, what compelled six-foot-four Langella to accept a stock catalyst's role in the rather mundane *Eddie* was his high regard for Goldberg as a talent. She would later recall their first meeting on the set when she asked him, "Why are you doing this movie?" He said gallantly, "This is probably the only way we'll ever get to work together." For her part, she had long been aware of Frank and was tremendously impressed with his acting talent and credentials.

Whoopi says, "This was somebody that I always wanted to know. . . . I always believed that I would know Frank from the time that I was a very young woman. . . . My only experience with Frank had been from the cinema. I was fourteen the first time I saw him in *Twelve Chairs*. And then, the following week, I saw *Diary of a Mad Housewife*." Later, Goldberg would add, "When we finally met, I made my mother clarify and stamp the fact that I have always believed I would know him. And my mother said to him, 'Oh, yeah, since she was fourteen you have been a focal point for her.'"

After filming began on *Eddie*, romantic sparks began to fly between Whoopi and Frank. Apparently, it did not seem to matter that, at the time, she was married to Lyle Trachtenberg. As for Langella, he had been wed since 1979 to Ruth Weil, the former editorial director of *House Beautiful*. Ruth was the mother of their two children, age fourteen and twelve.

Goldberg recalled the night they first had dinner together. "'Can I be your friend? I'll be your friend,' I said. 'I'll be a good friend. . . . I'm somebody who you will be all right with. I won't let anything fuck with you, because I think you're the greatest and have always felt that.' . . . And I didn't know why, but I knew it fluidly, I knew it body fluidly. I knew it heartwise, I knew that he would be there sometime. . . ." She also remembers that "he hugged me, and it was overwhelming, and I thought, I can't explain to you how much I need you in my life."

Before long, on- and off-set chatting and flirting between Whoopi and Frank turned into a serious romance, and they became inseparable. Word of the liaison soon reached Lyle in Los Angeles. Reportedly, he flew to the North Carolina filming site to confront his wife. Supposedly, no sooner did he check into the local hotel where Goldberg and Langella were ensconced than Frank checked out. Thereafter, Mr. and Mrs. Trachtenberg engaged in several long talks.

By the time *Eddie* wrapped and Goldberg was back in Los Angeles, she and Lyle were married in name only. As of October 17, 1995, the Trachtenbergs were officially separated, and soon thereafter he moved out of their home. On October 26, 1995, Whoopi filed for divorce in Los Angeles. The news remained hidden for well over a month because she had brought her court action under her given name Caryn Johnson. Meanwhile, proving he was serious about his growing romance with Whoopi, Frank and his wife separated. On November 7, 1995, one day after their eighteenth wedding anniversary, Ruth Langella filed for divorce. Whoopi was not entirely the catalyst for the Langellas' split. Reportedly, Ruth had started, then dropped, divorce proceedings four years before.

When the *Star* contacted the soon-to-be ex–Mrs. Langella to see if she had any comments, Ruth replied, "This is the wrong route you're taking by talking to me. Ask the other woman." When, in turn, Goldberg was asked how it felt to be labeled "the other woman," she sallied, "That's just so much crap. Nobody can break up a good marriage." On the subject of marriage, the experienced Goldberg confided: "I'll give a man all of me, and all I ask in return is that he be true to me. When he doesn't want that, then I want him to come and tell me. . . . That's the way I work, and that's the way my men have to work."

Having completed *Eddie* and before starting her next two movies (*The Associate; Ghosts of Mississippi*), Whoopi spent a great deal of her "free" time in New York, often seen in the company of silver-haired Langella. Astute New Yorkers could spot the couple strolling along Madison Avenue hand in hand, taking rides in Central Park in a horse-drawn carriage, and disembarking from limousines to sweep into trendy Manhattan restaurants. One evening, they attended a preview of *Patti LuPone on Broadway.* By late 1995, Whoopi and Frank were a steady twosome, seen in and about Manhattan shopping for such domestic items as linens at ABC Carpet & Home. Neither party would say whether marriage was in their future. At about this time, *New York* magazine offered a suggestion to Langella in their column entitled "Making Whoopi, Take Two." It read: "Advice to Frank Langella: steer clear of Friar's [sic] Club Roasts."

There were lots of changes in Whoopi's life in 1996. For one thing, she switched talent agencies, moving from CAA to another powerful institution, the William Morris Agency, where superagent Arnold Rifkin, well known for resuscitating the faltering careers of megastars, became her representative. As a businessperson, she also continued to diversify her holdings. She became one of the owners of Planet Hollywood, a trendy franchise that had such celebrity stockholders-backers as Bruce Willis and Demi Moore, Sylvester Stallone, and Arnold Schwarzenegger.

When not making films—her latest was a Hollywood satire entitled *An Alan Smithee Film*—Whoopi was fund-raising and doing TV commercials. She spent a great deal of her free time with Langella, who remained busy with theater assignments, such as the off-Broadway revival of *The Father*. Sometimes the couple rendezvoused in New York City or at her West Cornwall, Connecticut, estate. At the latter hideaway they were spotted enjoying moonlight horseback rides or having candlelight dinners. A waitress at a West Cornwall restaurant was quoted as saying, "They're more like high school kids who've discovered love for the first time." On other occasions, the duo found time for one another on the West Coast, sometimes staying at Whoopi's Pacific Palisades home and on other occasions at a more centrally located hotel.

For one of their spring 1996 get-togethers at the Beverly Hills Hotel, a hotel source noted, "They've spent more than four thousand dollars on room-service deliveries in just a few weeks. . . . She has had room-service attendants running out to get her and Frank expensive bottles of champagne, expensive orchids, take-out pizza, even sexy lingerie from Frederick's of Hollywood. . . . They didn't leave their room for the entire weekend! . . . They ordered videos from the local Blockbuster and had the hotel concierge pick up a sexy flick from Odyssey Video."

According to this same observer, before they checked into the hotel, Whoopi called ahead and ordered three dozen orchids, two dozen Godiva chocolate-covered strawberries, and plenty of chilled champagne. "And she also told the housekeepers to get rid of all the down pillows because he was allergic to down. Basically, she turned the hotel room into her home."

Now Goldberg was being quoted as saying of her beau: "Frank is mature and knows what he wants. And I know what I want—love and lots of it." There were rumors that she was interested in their marrying in the near future, pushing him for a commitment, so the grapevine said, as she had a few years prior with Ted Danson. On his part, Langella, who had never received so much publicity in his long and productive career, said that the idea of his marrying Whoopi was not new. He acknowledged, tongue in cheek: "I was shaken when Whoopi proposed. Heck, the guy's supposed to do the asking. And we were both still married! . . . Then I thought, Why not? We were getting on like a house on fire. Some weekends we hardly got out of bed. Just lots of champagne and sex. When we weren't making love, we were laughing and kidding each other."

In reviewing her year-long liaison with Langella, Whoopi would tell Larry King on his cable-TV talk show in September 1996 that the chemistry between herself and Frank had been present from day one. As to their being opposites, she acknowledged, "Well, yeah, I guess visually we're a little odd to look at on occasion, but temperamentally I think we're pretty okay and I. . . . You know, you have to want to be with someone who is great. . . . Not just good but great."

When King asked if Langella brings "greatness home," she answered, "Oh, yeah. Yeah, on good days he's great to be around, like me." As to the lopsided degree of fame that each member of the duo brought to the relationship, she explained, "He's been famous longer. . . . He's been famous a long time. So he's very supportive and kind of, very proud, you know? Very proud of me, so there—it's kind of groovy. You know, I don't—I don't know what is going to happen, but we're pretty happy. We laugh a lot, you know, and we try to support each other and be there."

Questioned whether it was because of Langella that she was now so often in Manhattan, she responded, "No, I'm in New York because I want to be here. See, I'm actually a separate person. This is one of the great things about, you know, having a relationship. . . . Some days I do belong to him. Other days, he cannot have me at all. . . . That's how it goes."

By the end of 1996, Whoopi would be saying of "her" Frank: "This man came to me fully formed. He's got his own thing going on. And he's fine." When asked by *Essence* magazine's Bebe Moore Campbell why she had a proclivity to date white men, she reminded the writer: "Listen, I was married to a black man; he is my daughter's father. Before I met Frank, I went out with five different men. And two of them were black.

That didn't make the papers because that's not news. I've always gone out with the people who asked me out."

As to the burden of dating superstar Whoopi Goldberg, the performer allowed: "My life is so chock-full that it takes a lot of adjusting for whomever I bring in[to] it. My relationships haven't always been successful, but when they haven't worked, it's been for a lots of different reasons. Sometimes it's the fame that surrounds me. It takes a lot of work to be a child, a family member, a lover of mine."

As to the changing nature of her association with Langella, Whoopi admitted that at first it "was more about working together. . . . In my mind, I had to come up to his level. He's extraordinary and a really good guy. Which is not to say that the other men in my life haven't been. They were nice men, but somehow there's something extraextraordinary about this one. I'm taking it a day at a time. And by the way, he's cute. I had to add that. He's fine, as my daughter would say."

For his part, Langella was also candid with the media. Now approaching sixty, he acknowledged that he went through a severe crisis years back when he began to lose his youthful good looks: "In my middle forties, as I moved toward my fifties, I struggled with it more than I care to remember. I had a lot of hair. I had *big* hair." The actor claimed that it was his increasing awareness of his own superficiality that actually helped prepare him for meeting Whoopi: "I wouldn't have been ready for the profundity of her persona. I wouldn't have seen it. . . . I wouldn't have been the open flower I was when I met her."

In reviewing their courtship, Frank remembers: "One of the early presents Whoopi gave me was a book by [Rainer Maria] Rilke which I randomly opened to see what I would read and how it would relate to us. It said that the tragedy of people when they fall in love young is that half a person falls in love with half a person. . . . Rilke says, Wait, wait, wait, until you are mature and a whole person falls in love with a whole person." The actor observed: "It has taken me my entire life to be ready to meet someone who is as full as I would like to be."

Chapter Thirty-Seven

Back to Broadway

Once you hit a certain level in the business, you're
expected to always be that person. And I've never
sort of believed that that was a truism for performers.
Performers should always evolve and do things
differently. So it's one of the reasons I haven't been
onstage recently, because I don't want the pressure of
being Whoopi Goldberg to get in the way of the
experiment . . . that I want to do. So I have to find
a way to balance that.

—Whoopi Goldberg, September 1995

By the fall of 1996 it was clear to Whoopi that her movie career was
stagnating. (Before the end of that December, her four starring
movie vehicles for the year would have registered as flops to one
degree or another.) Her television assignments lately—the 1996 Oscar
telecast and *Comic Relief* aside—were mostly unmemorable guest appearances on awards shows or specials. As for her personal life, Goldberg's
daughter, Alexandrea, was settled into her own world of domesticity with
her husband and two children. All in all, there was not that much to keep
Whoopi rooted in the West.

In contrast, the East Coast offered nearly unlimited opportunities to
be with her lover, Frank Langella, who was starring on Broadway in the
hit revival of the Noël Coward comedy *Present Laughter*. Whoopi's
mother, Emma, also spent a great deal of time in New York, and being
there would give Whoopi and her many more opportunities to be together. There was also Goldberg's very comfortable "farm" in West Corn-

wall, Connecticut, and finally, there were opportunities in New York City to get back to her roots—the theater. For years she had hoped to return to the stage, not just in her one-woman showcase but in a legitimate play. She had even considered such vehicles as *Saint Joan* or *The Lion in Winter*. Very recently, Whoopi and Frank had talked of mounting a revival of *Two for the Seesaw,* but their conflicting schedules made the venture impossible.

All in all, from Whoopi's point of view, it made sense to shake up her movie-star existence by relocating to her hometown. There were other less essential reasons as well. As she quipped to her cable-talk-show pal on *Larry King Live* (September 18, 1996) about living in Manhattan: "I think it's easier for me to go and get something to eat there. You can go out the door and go to a deli, you know, you have to get in the car in L.A. You've got to get in the car; you've got to make sure you've got your driver's license. You have to dress; you have to clean up. You can't just go around the corner and say, 'Give me something to eat,' you know?"

With her new career plan in place, Whoopi got her first taste of returning to the New York stage on August 18, 1996. She hosted the Democratic Party's fund-raiser at Radio City Music Hall, which drew a sellout crowd to celebrate President Bill Clinton's fiftieth birthday and to contribute to his election campaign. Then, on October 23, Whoopi reprised her one-woman show for one night at the prestigious Carnegie Hall as a charity event. Mike Nichols, her old mentor, coached her on this venture. More exciting, it had become official that Goldberg was returning to the Broadway stage.

The show in question was *A Funny Thing Happened on the Way to the Forum,* the classic stage musical based on the plays of Plautus, with a new book by Burt Shevelove and Larry Gelbart and music and lyrics by Stephen Sondheim. It had debuted on Broadway on May 1, 1962, and starred the irrepressible Zero Mostel, Jack Gilford, and David Burns. The hit show ran for 964 performances. Four years later, Mostel and Gilford, with the addition of Phil Silvers and Buster Keaton, joined together for the not-so-great screen adaptation of the Broadway smash success. Thereafter, in March 1972, *Forum* had its official Broadway revival with Phil Silvers now in the key role of Pseudolus, the lascivious slave of ancient Rome who craves his freedom above all else. That production lasted 156 performances.

A few decades later, on April 18, 1996, yet another major Broadway revival of *Forum* took place, this time headed by stage and film funny man Nathan Lane. His interpretation of Pseudolus won him a Tony Award, as had the role for both Zero Mostel and Phil Silvers. The revival proved to be extremely popular, and the musical developed into a long-running hit. When Lane let it be known that he planned to leave *Forum* in early 1997, the producers began their search for a likely—and hopefully very commercial—replacement. As it happened, Nathan Lane's talent agent, Jeff Hunter, also represented Whoopi. Hunter came up with the notion that Goldberg replace Lane on Broadway. There were other interrelationships between the *Forum* team and Whoopi. One of the musical's producers had been the executive producer on Goldberg's *Sister Act* (1992). Then, too, Goldberg and Lane—as well as Ernie Sabella, one of the comedic foils in this *Forum* revival—had all provided voices for the animated feature *The Lion King*.

Whoopi liked the wild and crazy idea of taking over the lead in *Forum* and agreed to star in the musical for a limited run. This information was kept secret for a month, until the startling announcement was made public in early October 1996.

When the news was released, there was tremendous excitement about this bold casting coup. The backers of *Forum* got a lot of publicity mileage out of the fact that Goldberg, undeniably black and female, would be taking over a starring role created and traditionally interpreted by a white male performer. As the news spread that Whoopi would be playing the part, Roger Berlind, one of *Forum*'s producers, craftily whetted the public's curiosity by not initially confirming whether Goldberg would play Nathan Lane's male character as a man or woman. Berlind merely said, "We'll decide that when Whoopi starts rehearsals."

Meanwhile, Goldberg admitted, "It's really insane." She hinted that perhaps the sexual orientation of her character would become androgynous when she took over Lane's role. Not to be left out of the promotional fun or the limelight, Nathan Lane, the departing *Forum* star, joined the debate as to how Goldberg would play her new stage assignment: "My subtext for [my stage character of] Pseudolus has always been that I'm a black woman trapped in a white man's body. Whoopi will be brilliant, obviously, as the wily slave."

Summing up the controversial casting situation, the *New York Times* later wrote: "The role in *Forum* is an eyebrow raiser even for a woman who loves to defy convention, who transformed herself from a welfare mother into one of Hollywood's highest-paid actors, and who has taken on a wide range of characters from a fake nun to a computer nerd to a basketball coach."

Now ensconced in a fashionable East Side Manhattan hotel with Langella, Whoopi began preparation for the *Forum* rehearsals. Soon the play's coauthor Larry Gelbart announced that not many of the original lines in the musical would have to be altered to accommodate Goldberg's presence as—now it was revealed—a woman playing a woman. Stephen Sondheim adjusted the lyrics of the song "Free" to better suit the role as now interpreted by Goldberg. Whoopi began working with a vocal coach as well as with director Jerry Zaks, who had staged the Nathan Lane revival. When Frank Langella was not performing in his own starring Broadway comedy, he rehearsed *Forum* dialogue with Goldberg.

Langella repeatedly reassured his concerned girlfriend and the eager press that he was confident Whoopi would do well in the taxing assignment of Pseudolus. Goldberg, conscious that she had put on quite a bit of weight, joked to the media: "They're making my toga [costume for the show] a little longer so my ass won't look like a shelf." Demonstrating that she had lost none of her sense of humor about herself, she added, "I will look like Huggy Bear."

In the weeks that followed, the New York newspapers were filled with rumors and ruminations: whether Goldberg was physically up to the demanding task, that she was being a prima donna during rehearsals with the cast and director, and whether she would do well once the public previews began. One New York City publication's gossip columnist quipped that Goldberg's singing "could augur the decline and fall of the Roman musical comedy."

When Whoopi was asked how she felt she was doing in her preparations, she told the *New York Times*: "It's a big change and I'm excited and I'm scared. It's like trying to walk on water. Sometimes you make it halfway through and then you sink. It's very scary. But I need to be nervous. I need to stretch."

As had been done with all the previous comedy giants who had played Pseudolus, Goldberg was encouraged by the play's creators and director to be as individualistic as possible. Also, in the grand tradition of burlesque—to which this musical owed a great deal—she was urged to be as improvisational as her fertile imagination allowed.

As she warmed up to her new stint on Broadway, Goldberg would become so relaxed onstage that she would frequently stop the show to chastise late-arriving audience members. Then, too, there was the late

April 1997 performance in which she found herself stumbling to remember the words to "Free," one of her first-act songs. She stopped, looked directly at the audience, and said, "Sorry, you all. This is God's way of telling you that you are too old for the perils of live theater." Next, she turned to costar Jim Stanek, who plays Hero, and kiddingly begged him: "Just shoot me." In response, he drew a small dagger from his toga and pretended to stab her. Thereafter, with help from the show's musical conductor, Goldberg finished singing "Free." For her quick-thinking efforts, Goldberg received a standing ovation at show's end.

On Friday, February 7, Whoopi and the cast performed the revamped show for an invited Broadway audience. Among those attending the run-through were Julie Andrews and Blake Edwards, Eartha Kitt, and Frank Langella. When the performance was over, Goldberg made a curtain speech thanking the cast and orchestra for their help and sending her love to Frank out front. Backstage a double layer cake was being consumed by the cast. It was a gift from Whoopi and had inscribed in frosting on top, "Thank You. Thank You. Thank You. Thank You."

Tuesday, February 11, 1997 was the actual start of the *Forum* previews. Theater critics were asked, and had all agreed, to hold off reviewing Whoopi's performance until the official opening on March 6, 1997. To help the star through her preview debut, Frank Langella took the evening off from his *Present Laughter* chores to be in the audience of the St. James Theatre to cheer her on. Other celebrities that night included Glenn Close and Timothy Dalton. While Goldberg occasionally forgot lines of dialogue and seemed a bit stiff in the proceedings—compared to the majority of the cast, who had been doing the musical for months—she survived the ordeal quite successfully.

Finally, on Thursday, March 6, 1997, Whoopi officially returned to Broadway at the 1,617-seat St. James Theatre; tickets ranged from seventy dollars downward. During the course of the two-act musical, Goldberg was responsible for participating in such show songs as "Comedy Tonight" (which opens and closes the production), "Free," "The House of Marcus Lycus," "Everybody Ought to Have a Maid," "Bring Me My Bride," and "Lovely."

If there was a major concern as to whether Whoopi could satisfy a demanding crowd of Broadway theatergoers out to enjoy a breezy musical filled with low comedy, she erased all worries that crucial evening. Goldberg also got her biggest laugh of the night with her newly devised onstage in-joke: "What am I going to do with that old white man?" she says about one character in the course of the show. Whoopi's Pseudolus answers herself with the tag dialogue: "Hell. I got one at home."

Ben Brantley of the *New York Times* wrote that Whoopi "has marked her claim to the territory . . . like a cat taking over a chair in an unfamiliar apartment. . . . She finds comic fodder not only in her present personal life but in her professional life in Hollywood as well. When a doll representing an infant is flung onto the stage (part of a narrative that establishes the play's back story), she shrieks: 'I don't want that blond baby. That's another movie, honey.' "

According to David Patrick Stearns of *USA Today* in his four-star plaudit, Goldberg "serves the show better than Nathan Lane. . . . Lane attempted to play a character when there's not much to play; Goldberg simply plays her big, lovable, raucous self. . . . Goldberg is such effortless fun, you don't really notice the dramatic gender change." Stearns mentioned that "her only drawback is her lack of physical agility; it slows down what should be a hectic, lightning-paced farce."

While the critical response was an important indicator of Whoopi's Broadway reception, another was the weekly box-office ticket sales at the cavernous St. James Theatre. In the final weeks that Nathan Lane had been *Forum*'s star, tickets sales averaged over 85 percent of capacity. When Whoopi assumed the starring role, *Forum*—by then nearly a year old on Broadway—sales dipped slightly, to around 80 percent. It proved that Goldberg could attract theatergoers on a continuous basis. In fact, she so enjoyed playing the conniving slave onstage that she extended, for another few weeks, her original contract for the daily Broadway stage grind beyond its June 29, 1997, expiration date, ending her run on July 13, 1997. At one point, there were even rumors that her boyfriend, Frank Langella, whose *Present Laughter* had closed in late April 1997, might join her for the show's extended run after he fulfilled a film commitment.

With her successful takeover in *A Funny Thing Happened on the Way to the Forum*, the chameleonlike Goldberg was once again a winner.

CHAPTER THIRTY-EIGHT

Looking to the Future

I feel only the responsibility to be the best person I
can. That, in turn, will speak for any of the things
people need to know, like being a black person or a
woman or a black woman. As soon as you set
yourself up as a role model, you have no leeway for
learning, you have no leeway to make mistakes. I
don't tell anyone to do as I do, but if it works for
you too, great. If it doesn't, try something else and
don't come to me.

—WHOOPI GOLDBERG, MARCH 1995

As the new toast of Broadway, Whoopi used her clout to devote her
offstage energies to various charity pursuits. In the annual Easter
Bonnet Competition among New York shows to raise funds to
fight AIDS, Whoopi headed the *Forum* cast that won the contest by
bringing in a remarkable $226,906 in donor contributions.

But even as Broadway's new darling, Whoopi could not seem to
avoid controversy for long. For example, there was the inauguration-
party contretemps of January 1997. In her years of supporting Bill Clinton's presidential campaigns and hosting presidential galas at the Ford
Theatre, she had become an intimate of the chief executive and his wife,
Hillary. Goldberg had even dined at the White House, and on occasion,
when the president and first lady visited New York, Whoopi would dine
with them. She was proud of the fact that a girl from the housing projects
could rise to such a lofty position in the sociopolitical hierarchy.

When Clinton won reelection to the presidency, Whoopi was

among the hardworking celebrity supporters invited to the Washington festivities to celebrate Clinton's second-term victory. Because she was busy with *Forum* rehearsals and her escort, Frank Langella, had his own Broadway-show schedule, the couple decided to drive from New York City to Washington on Sunday morning, leaving a very small margin of time to arrive in the nation's capital on time. Somehow—and no one wanted to claim "credit" for the fiasco—the "word" went out that Goldberg's car required a police escort from each state through which she was traveling to help the star reach her destination in a timely manner. The "order" did not meet with favor from the New Jersey executive office. Governor Christie Whitman claimed it was inappropriate to provide a police escort for Whoopi's 148-mile turnpike ride within the state's boundary.

Goldberg and Langella did receive a police escort at the Delaware border as the vehicle negotiated the fifteen miles from the Delaware Memorial Bridge to the Maryland state line, where that jurisdiction's state police took over. Goldberg reached Washington in time to fulfill all her commitments.

However, there was an immediate uproar—which led to a nationwide media debate—as to whether a civilian, such as Goldberg, should have requested police escorts for nonofficial business. Both Whoopi and the presidential inaugural committee denied having made the request, but the matter would not die. Finally, to end the fracas, Goldberg wrote out a check for $61.50 to reimburse the Delaware State Police Department for providing her with an official escort.

Then there was the not-so-publicized matter of Goldberg's attempt to purchase an appropriately expansive co-op apartment. She had been searching for a fancy layout in one of several rather staid Manhattan residential buildings. Whoopi had set her sights on a spacious duplex in an address near Seventy-ninth Street and Fifth Avenue. Supposedly, a board member's spouse did not relish the idea of Whoopi, "a single, black, female movie star with a penchant for high-profile romances," as the *New York* magazine described her, moving into the building. However, Goldberg's creative real-estate broker introduced Whoopi to the building's board president, an investment banker, and in short order Whoopi had charmed the man into approving her purchase. Of course, it did not hurt matters that Goldberg was willing to pay $2.9 million, the full asking price, for her latest residence.

In yet another area, Goldberg raised further clouds of controversy—

or, at least, envy. This time it was in the world of publishing. In late 1996, she negotiated an enviable $6 million contract to write a book of observations for the publisher William Morrow in which she would "talk about things I see and think." When asked why—beyond the huge fee—she was doing the book, she quipped, "Because I had nothing else to do and someone asked me." When questioned how big a manuscript the publisher was expecting in late 1997 for such a huge cash layout, she responded, "Sixty-thousand words." To which she added, "How many pages is that? Too many. I am just not that deep, okay."

While Whoopi was regaining her stature as a stage performer, accepting an honorary doctorate degree from Brandeis University, and establishing new roots on the East Coast, her film career remained on hold. (In the realm of TV, she made *Ruby,* a sitcom pilot for the UPN network in the 1997–1998 season, in which she provided her voice as a puppet Hollywood star.) She also placed her footprints and "braid prints" in the cement of the forecourt of Mann's Chinese Theatre in Hollywood. That was some degree of movie-star immortality. But what of her body of film work to date?

In reviewing Goldberg's movie accomplishments, *Entertainment Weekly* pointed out in its November 1, 1996, issue: "She's made an astonishing thirteen movies over the last five years plus had gigs hosting the Oscars and bartending on the *Enterprise.* By statistical happenstance, she's managed to bump into a few hits over the decades (like her *Sister Act* movies), but for the most part she's been utterly indiscriminate in her choices—and it shows. Rather than develop her own projects (after all, there aren't too many scripts out there written for zany black actors), she's churned out one flopped formula comedy after another: *Fatal Beauty, Homer & Eddie, Bogus, Eddie*—and who could forget *Theodore Rex?*"

Earlier, Evie Arup wrote in the *British Weekly Journal* that due to Hollywood casting directors, Goldberg's efforts had backfired on her, especially in the black film community: "Does she have the likes of Spike Lee, John Singleton or the Hughes Brothers beating a path to her door with a juicy part? I don't think so. And that's a shame because it's a sure bet that if Goldberg worked with any of those guys the end result would be something rather special."

For years Goldberg claimed that she was not offered prime properties because she was black, female, and not conventionally beautiful by Hollywood standards. Later, she would reason: "But I also did some of those movies because I was trying to show that black actors can go after any role; it doesn't have to be specifically black. Hollywood hasn't begun to understand that black people can play roles other than the ones where it says 'for a black actor only.' I want them saying they've got a role—here is a role for a great actor; call up Whoopi Goldberg."

More recently—especially after her string of 1996 box-office duds—Goldberg claimed that the lack of her artistic success in Hollywood during the 1990s was due to filmmakers who were so concerned with box-office grosses that they would rehash anything resembling a past successful formula and not experiment creatively. This has led her to say: "I'm tired of movies because I'm not really sort of doing stuff that my heart is in the way I wanted to be." To some, these grumblings sounded like sour grapes and led some industry observers to suggest that perhaps Goldberg was burning bridges she might well want to recross in years to come.

If Goldberg's film career remains uncertain, she has taken a few steps in the right direction over the past several months. For one, when producer Fred Zollo, with whom Goldberg worked on *Ghosts of Mississippi,* asked her to join the ensemble cast of *In the Gloaming* in the late summer of 1996, Whoopi readily agreed. She did so for several reasons. The prestige project, an hour-long made-for-cable feature, was to be the directorial debut of Christopher Reeve, the movies' ex-Superman who had suffered a near fatal riding accident that had left him paralyzed. Through dint of enormous courage and effort, Reeve recovered sufficiently so that, even wheelchair-bound, he could direct this touching study of a young adult, an AIDS victim, who has come home to die. Before this invalid passes on, he hopes to reconcile with his overprotective mother—played by Glenn Close—and his emotionally repressed father. Goldberg accepted the small but key role of Myrna, the kindly nurse who helps the mother deal realistically with this tragic situation.

When aired on HBO on April 20, 1997, the critics were nearly unanimous in praising this thoughtful drama. Don Heckman reported in the *Los Angeles Times*: "In his ability to inspire and to create the opportunity for outstanding performances from the actors, Reeve's directorial debut has to be considered a significant achievement." Terry Kelleher in *People* rated the production an "A," reasoning: "Credit the sensitivity of Christopher Reeve . . . and an acting ensemble that plays this somber chamber piece flawlessly. . . . And Whoopi Goldberg shows her softer side in the small role of a nurse who does tell the truth, gently."

Perhaps under the guidance of her new talent representative, Arnold Rifkin of the William Morris Agency, known as the "makeover maven," Goldberg will substitute quality for quantity in choosing future roles and learn to say no more often when asked to do cameos, such as those seen in *Tales from the Crypt Presents Bordello of Blood* and *The Little Rascals*.

As to her future with relatively longtime companion Frank Langella, she seems to have moved forward from the we-must-marry state to one of taking it one day at a time and let's see. She admits that her involvement with the actor has surprised many of her friends, even those used to the unexpected from her. Goldberg explains, "People think, How did this happen? because we're the last two people in the world you would picture in a relationship." She confides that their situation has reached such a comfortable stage that, these days, her favorite place to have dinner is not a chic restaurant. Rather, it's "in bed reading a book and looking over and seeing Frank surfing the TV, eating . . . [chicken wings and fried pork chops] and a bag of Wise potato chips."

Looking at her life, from starting as a housing-projects kid to becoming a superstar, Whoopi says: "Do you know what I fear? I fear waking up one morning and finding out it was all for nothing. . . . I believe I'm here for a reason. And I think a little bit of the reason is to throw little torches out to the next step to lead people through the dark." Asked if she were interviewing herself on a talk show, what would be the first thing she would ask herself, Whoopi, an expert in interpreting her past actions in a favorable light, replied, "The first question I would probably ask her is why she does what she does. Why? Why the way that she does it? Why not just take the easy way and just take all the—the downtrodden, sort of 'let's be black women' movies, you know. She would probably answer, 'Because if I did that, that's all I'd be. That's all I'd be.' But in doing it my way, it's just been a wild, strange, and wonderful ride."

Whoopi has no hesitation in saying she owes her success to "my mom and my big brother [who continues to work on Hollywood film crews]. They never, ever, gave me. . . . No one ever gave me the impression there was anything I couldn't do and that if I was willing to work for what I wanted that it was all possible. No one ever, you know, said, 'No, you can't.' And I grew up in a time in this country when the government was supportive of you, you know, that you weren't made to feel like you were sucking the government dry, which is sort of where people are at now. I was raised to believe that I could become part of the fabric of this country no matter what it was I wanted to do, you know? . . . And Mom gave it [this faith] to me, President Kennedy gave it to me, my big brother gave it to me, Harry Belafonte gave it to me—people who went out and did gave it to me."

Once driven, Whoopi insists she is happy with today: "Look, I am probably one of the most gifted observers of life and people, and so, in observing myself, I realize I am one of the luckiest people on the face of the earth. I do what I want. I look the way I want. I sit with people I like, and the ones I don't like I don't have to be with. I have a healthy kid, healthy grandkids. My mom is still with me, and I've got a great brother and a great man in my life and a cat who loves me. You know, it doesn't get any better than that."

Filmography and Other Media Appearances

Feature Films

THE COLOR PURPLE
1985
A Warner Bros. Release

CAST: Danny Glover (*Albert*); Whoopi Goldberg (*Celie*); Margaret Avery (*Shug*); Oprah Winfrey (*Sofia*); Willard Pugh (*Harpo*); Akosua Busia (*Nettie*); Desreta Jackson (*Young Celie*); Adolph Caesar (*Old Mr.*); Rae Dawn Chong (*Squeak*); Dana Ivey (*Miss Millie*); Leonard Jackson (*Pa*); Bennet Guillory (*Grady*); John Patton Jr. (*Preacher*); Carl Anderson (*Reverend Samuel*); Susan Beaubian (*Corrine*); James Tillis (*Buster*); Phillip Strong (*Mayor*); Larry Fishburne (*Swain*); Peto Kinsaka (*Adam*); Lelo Masamba (*Olivia*); Margaret Freeman (*Odessa*); Howard Starr (*Young Harpo*); Daphanie Oliver (*Young Olivia*); Jadili Johnson (*Young Adam*); Lillian Njoki Distefano (*Young Tashi*); Donna Buie (*Daisy*); Leon Rippy (*Store Clerk*); Saunders Sonny Terry Greg Phillinganes, and Roy Gaines (*Jook Joint Musicians*).

CREDITS: Executive producers, Jon Peters and Peter Guber; producers, Steven Spielberg, Kathleen Kennedy, Frank Marshall, and Quincy Jones; director, Spielberg; based on the novel by Alice Walker; screenplay, Menno Meyjes; production designer, J. Michael Riva; art director, Robert W. Welch; set decorator, Linda DeScenna; costumes, Aggie Guerard Rodgers; music, Jones; choreography, Claude Thompson; sound, Willis Burton; special effects, Matt Sweeney; camera, Allen Daviau; editor, Michael Kahn; rating, PG-13; running time, 155 min.

JUMPIN' JACK FLASH
1986
A Twentieth Century–Fox Release

CAST: Whoopi Goldberg (*Terry Doolittle*); Stephen Collins (*Marty Phillips*); John Wood (*Jeremy Talbot*); Carol Kane (*Cynthia*); Annie Potts (*Liz Carlson*); Peter Michael Goetz (*Mr. Page*); Roscoe Lee Browne (*Archer Lincoln*); Sara Botsford (*Lady Sarah Billings*); Jeroen Krabbe (*Mark Van Meter*); Vyto Ruginis (*Carl*); Jonathan Pryce (*Jack*); Tony Hedra (*Hunter*); Jon Lovitz (*Doug*); Phil E. Hartman (*Fred*); Lynne Marie Stewart (*Karen*); Ren Woods (*Jackie*); Tracy Reiner (*Page's Secretary*); Chino Fats Williams (*Larry, the Heavyset Guard*); Jim Belushi (*Sperry Repairman*); Paxton Whitehead (*Lord Malcolm Billings*); June Chadwick (*Gillian*); Tracey Ullman (*Fiona*); Jeffrey Joseph (*African Embassy Guest*); Caroline Ducroco (*French Embassy Guest*); Julie Payne (*Receptionist at Elizabeth Arden*); Kellie Martin (*Kristi Carlson*); Benjji Gregory (*Harry Carlson Jr.*); Garry K. Marshall (*Detective*).

CREDITS: Producers, Lawrence Gordon and Joel Silver; associate producers, Richard Marks, George Bowers, and Elaine K. Thompson; director, Penny Marshall; story, David H. Franzoni; screenplay, Franzoni, J. W. Melville, Patricia Irving, and Christopher Thompson; production designer, Robert Boyle; art director, Frank Richwood; set designers, Henry Alberti, Richard McKenzie, and Richard Pitman; costumes, Susan Becker; music, Thomas Newman; sound, Jerry Jost; special effects, Thomas Ryba; camera, Matthew F. Leonetti; editor, Mark Goldbatt; rating, R; running time, 100 min.

BURGLAR
1987
A Warner Bros. Release

CAST: Whoopi Goldberg (*Bernice Rhodenbarr*); Bob Goldthwait (*Carl Hefler*); G. W. Bailey (*Ray Kirschman*); Lesley Ann Warren (*Dr. Cynthia Sledrake*); James Handy (*Carson Verrill*); Anne DeSalvo (*Detective Todras*); John Goodman (*Detective Nyswander*); Elizabeth Ruscio (*Frankie*); Vyto Ruginis (*Graybow*); Larry Mintz (*Knobby*); Michael Nesmith (*Cabbie*); Thomas Bray, Hugh Wilson (*Bits*).

CREDITS: Producers, Kevin McCormick and Michael Hirsh; associate producer, Michael Green; coproducers, Joseph Loeb III and Matthew Weisman; director, Hugh Wilson; based on novels by Lawrence Block; screenplay, Loeb III, Weisman, and Wilson; production designer Todd Hallowell; art director, Michael Corenblith; set director, Daniel Loren May; set designer, Dan Maltese; costumes, Susan Becker; music, Sylvester Levay; sound, Dari Knight; special effects, Stan

Parks; camera, William A. Fraker; editors, Frederic Steinkamp and William Steinkamp; rating, R; running time, 102 min.

FATAL BEAUTY
1987
An M-G-M Release

CAST: Whoopi Goldberg (*Rita Rizzoli*); Sam Elliott (*Mike Marshak*); Ruben Blades (*Carl Jimenez*); Harris Yulin (*Conrad Kroll*); John P. Ryan (*Lieutenant Kellerman*); Jennifer Warren (*Cecile Jaeger*); Brad Dourif (*Leo Nova*); Mike Jolly (*Earl Skinner*); Charles Hallahan (*Deputy Getz*); David Harris (*Raphael*); James LeGros (*Zack Jaeger*); Neill Barry (*Denny Miflin*); Mark Pellegrino (*Frankenstein*); Clayton Landey (*Jimmy Silver*); Fred Asparagus (*Delgadillo*); Catherine Blore (*Charlene*); Cheech Marin (*Bartender*); Michael DeLorenzo (*Falco*); Carlos Cervantes (*Basqual*); Ebbie Roe Smith (*Marty*); M. C. Gainey (*Barndoller*); Price Hughes (*Big Bubba*).

CREDITS: Producer, Leonard Kroll; associate producer, Art Schaefer; director, Tom Holland; story, Bill Svanoe; screenplay, Hilary Henkin and Dean Riesner; production designer, James William Newport; set decorator, Rick Simpson; set designer, E. C. Chen; music, Harold Faltermeyer; sound, William Nelson, Julies Strasser, and Mychal Smith; special effects, Kenneth D. Pepiot, Grant Burdette; camera, David M. Wals; editor, Don Zimmerman; rating, R; running time, 104 min.

THE TELEPHONE
1988
A New World Release

CAST: Whoopi Goldberg (*Vashti Blue*); Severn Darden (*Max*); Amy Wright (*Honey Boxe/Irate Neighbor/Jennifer's Voice*); Elliott Gould (*Rodney*); John Heard (*Telephone Man*); Ronald J. Stallings (*Saxophone Player*); John Hattan, Lina Chu (*Sidewalk Vendors*); Don Blakely Robin Menken, James Victor, and Herve Villechaize (*Voices on the Freeway*); Danae Torn (*Voice of Crying Woman/Midge's Voice*); Don Blakely (*Larry's Voice*); James Victor (*Big Ray's Voice*).

CREDITS: Producers, Robert Katz and Moctesuma Esparza; associate producer, Joel Glickman; director, Rip Torn; screenplay, Harry Nilsson and Terry Southern; art director, John Pohl; set decorator, Antonia Vincent; music adapter, Christopher Young; visual consultant, David Myers; camera, David Claessen; editor, Sandra Adair; rating, R; running time, 82 min.

CLARA'S HEART
1988
A Warner Bros. Release

CAST: Whoopi Goldberg (*Clara Mayfield*); Michael Ontkean (*Bill Hart*); Kathleen Quinlan (*Leona Hart*); Neil Patrick Harris (*David Hart*); Spalding Gray (*Peter Epstein*); Beverly Todd (*Dora*); Hattie Winston (*Blanche Loudon*); Jason Downs (*Alan Lipsky*); Caitlin Thompson (*Celeste*); Maria Broom (*Felicia*); Wanda Cyristine (*Lydia*); Maryce Carter (*Bobs*); Angel Harper (*Rita*); Fred Strother (*Bundy*); Father Joseph Muth (*Father Joe*); Warren Long (*Leo*); Kathryn Dowling (*Deena*); Mark Medoff (*Dr. Stevens*); Joy Green (*Duty Nurse*); Forry Buckingham (*Coach Stillson*).

CREDITS: Executive producer, Marianne Moloney; producer, Martin Elfand; director, Robert Mulligan; based on the novel by Joseph Olshan; screenplay, Mark Medoff; production designer, Jeffrey Howard; art director, Stephen Walker; set decorator, Anne H. Abrens; costumes, Bambi Breakstone; music, Dave Grusin; sound, Bill Nelson; camera, Freddie Francis; editor, Sidney Levin; rating, PG-13; running time, 108 min.

KISS SHOT
1989
CBS-TV

CAST: Whoopi Goldberg (*Sarah Collins*); Dennis Franz (*Max Fleischer*); Tasha Scott (*Jenny Collins*); David Marciano (*Rick Powell*); Teddy Wilson (*Billy Tatum*); Dorian Harewood (*Kevin Merrick*); Adilah Barnes (*Amanda Gilbert*); and Charles Branklyn, Phyllis Coates, Richard Dupell, Bob Ernst, Eva Gholson, Michael Halton, Chuck L. Hilbert, Kathryn Keats, Joe Lerer, Drew Letchworth, Thomas McCrory, Ivar Mikelson, Michael Orcena, Angelo Pagan, Jeff Richmond, Blaine Souza, Howard Swain, Maud Winchester, Billy Woodruff, and Sigrid Wurschmidt.

CREDITS: Executive producer, Jerry London; producers, Mel A. Bishop and Salli Newman; associate producers, Chad Cooperman and Abra Edelman; director, London; teleplay, Carl Kleinschmitt; production designer, Tom Wells; art director, Jack Wiley; set decorator, Luana Speelman; costumes, Gayle Evans; music, Steve Dorff; technical adviser, Jerry Briesath; sound, James Pilcher; camera, Chuy Elizondo; editor, Michael Brown; not rated; running time, 89 min.

BEVERLY HILLS BRATS
1989
A Taurus Release

CAST: Burt Young (*Clive*); Martin Sheen (*Jeffrey Miller*); Terry Moore (*Veronica Miller*); Peter Billingsley (*Scooter*); Ramón Sheen (*Sterling*); Whoopi Goldberg (*Woman in Red Car*).

CREDITS: Executive producer, Rupert A. L. Perrin; producers, Terry Moore and Jerry Rivers; associate producers, Grant Kramer and Janet Sheen; director, Dimitri Sotirakis; story, Moore and Rivers; screenplay, Linda Silverthorn; production designer, George Costello; art director, Jay Burkhardt; set decorator, Maria Caso; music, Barry Goldberg; camera, Harry Mathias; editor, Jerry Frizell; rating, PG-13; running time, 91 min.

GHOST
1990
A Paramount Release

CAST: Patrick Swayze (*Sam Wheat*); Demi Moore (*Molly Jensen*); Whoopi Goldberg (*Oda Mae Brown*); Tony Goldwyn (*Carl Bruner*); Stanley Lawrence and Christopher J. Keene (*Elevator Men*); Susan Breslau (*Susan*); Martina Degnan (*Rose*); Richard Kleber and Macka Fole (*Movers*); Rick Aviles (*Willie Lopez*); Phil Leeds (*Emergency-Room Ghost*); John Hugh (*Surgeon*); Sam Tsoutsouvas (*Minister*); Sharon Breslau Cornell (*Cemetery Ghost*); Vincent Schiavelli (*Subway Ghost*); Angelina Estrada (*Rosa Santiago*); Armelia McQueen (*Clara Brown*); Gail Boggs (*Louise Brown*); Thom Curley (*Loft Workman*); Stephen Root (*Police Sergeant*); Laura Drake (*Policewoman*); Augie Blunt (*Orlando*); Alma Beltran and J. Christopher Sullivan (*Ghosts*); Sondra Rubin and Faye Brenner (*Nurses*); Charlotte Zucker (*Bank Officer*).

CREDITS: Executive producer, Steven Charles Jaffe; producer, Lisa Weinstein; associate producer, Bruce Joel Rubin; director, Jerry Zucker; screenplay, Rubin; production designer, Jane Musky; art director, Mark Mansbridge; set decorator, Joe D. Mitchell; costumes, Ruth Morley; music, Maurice Jarre; sound, Jeff Wexler; special-effects supervisors, John Van Vliet and Kathy Kean; visual-effects supervisor, Bruce Nicholson; camera, Adam Greenberg; editor, Walter Murch; rating PG-13; running time, 127 min.

THE LONG WALK HOME
1990
A Miramax Release

CAST: Sissy Spacek (*Miriam Thompson*); Whoopi Goldberg (*Odessa Cotter*); Dwight Schultz (*Norman Thompson*); Ving Rhames (*Herbert Cotter*); Erika Alexander (*Selma Cotter*); Lexi Faith Randall (*Mary Catherine Thompson*); Richard Habersham (*Theodore Cotter*); Jason Weaver (*Franklin Cotter*); Cherene Snow (*Claudia*); Dan E. Butler (*Charlie*); Phil Sterling (*Winston*); Schuyler Elizabeth Fisk (*Judy—Girl in Oak Park*); Nancy M. Atchison (*Anne—Girl in Oak Park*); Haynes Brooke (*Policeman at Oak Park*); Jim Aycock (*Roger*); Rebecca Wackler (*Lucille*); Charles Hubbard (*Mr. Cooper*); Harriet Summer (*Mrs. Cooper*); Gleaves Azar (*Grandma Thompson*); Norman Matlock (*Preacher*); Dr. T. Clifford Bibb (*Choir Leader*); Dorothy Love Coates (*Lead Singer at Car Lot*); Mary Steenburgen (*Narrator*).

CREDITS: Executive producers, Taylor Hackford and Stuart Benjamin; producers, Howard W. Koch Jr. and Dave Bell; associate producer, Edwin C. Atkins; director, Richard Pearce; screenplay, John Cork; production designer, Blake Russell; set decorator, Gretchen Rau; costumes, Shay Cunliffe; music, George Fenton; camera, Roger Deakins; editor, Bill Yahraus; rating, PG; running time, 97 min.

HOMER & EDDIE
1990
A Cineplex Odion/Kings Road Release

CAST: James Belushi (*Homer Lanza*); Whoopi Goldberg (*Edwina "Eddie" Cervi*); Karen Black (*Belle*); Nancy Parsons (*Maid*); Anne Ramsey (*Edna*); Beah Richards (*Linda Cervi*); Vincent Schiavelli (*Priest*); Tracey Walter (*Tommy Dearly*); Ernestine McClendon (*Esther*); Angelyne (*Blonde*); John Waters (*Robber*); and Robert Glaudini, Wayne Grace, Andy Jarrell, Jim Mapp, James Thiel, and Jeffrey Thiel (*Bits*).

CREDITS: Producers, Moritz Borman and James Cady; director, Andrei Konchalovsky; screenplay, Patrick Cirillo; production designer, Michel Levesque; art director, P. Michael Johnson; costumes, Katherine Kady Dover; music director, David Chackler; camera, Lajos Koltai; editor, Henry Richardson; rating, R; running time, 99 min.

SOAPDISH
1991
A Paramount Release

CAST: Sally Field (*Celeste Talbert*); Kevin Kline (*Jeffrey Anderson*); Robert Downey Jr. (*David Barnes*); Whoopi Goldberg (*Rose Schwartz*); Cathy Moriarty (*Montana Moorehead*); Elisabeth Shue (*Lori Craven*); Carrie Fisher (*Betsy Faye Sharon*);

Garry Marshall (*Edmund Edwards*); Teri Hatcher (*Ariel Maloney*); Arne Nannestad (*Burton White*); Kathy Najimy (*Tawny Miller*); Paul Johansson (*Bob Brennan*); Costas Mandylor (*Mark*); Sheila Kelley (*Fran*); Tim Choate (*Assistant Director*); Phil Leeds (*Old Man*); Herta Ware and Dorothy Patterson (*Old Women*); Cornelia Kiss (*Receptionist*); Robert Camiletti (*Actor*); Michael Berkowitz (*Young Autograph Seeker*); Leeza Gibbons, John Tesh and Stephen Nichols (*Themselves*); Clive Rosengren (*Doorman*); Gino Lucci (*Bus Driver*).

CREDITS: Executive producer, Herbert Ross; producers, Aaron Spelling and Alan Greisman; coproducers, Victoria White and Joel Freeman; director, Michael Hoffman; story, Robert Harling; screenplay, Harling and Andrew Bergman; production designer, Eugenio Zanetti; art director, Jim Dultz; set decorator, Lee Poll; costumes, Nolan Miller; music, Alan Silvestri; sound, Peter Hliddal; special-effects coordinator, Tony Van Den Ecker; camera, Ueli Steiger; editor, Garth Craven; rating, PG-13; running time, 95 min.

HOUSE PARTY 2
1991
A New Line Release

CAST: Christopher Reid (*Kid*); Christopher Martin (*Play*); Martin Lawrence (*Bilal*); Tisha Campbell (*Sidney*); Brian George (*Zilla*); Lucien George (*Pee-Wee*); Paul Anthony George (*Stab*); Queen Latifah (*Zora*); Iman (*Sheila*); Kamron (*Jamai*); D. Christopher Judge (*Miles*); Tony Burton (*Mr. Lee*); Louie Louie (*Rick*); William Schallert (*Dean Kramer*); Eugene Allen (*Groove*); George Anthony Bell (*Reverend Simms*); Barry Diamond (*Policeman*); Randy Harris (*Hubert, the Humping Man*); Caryl M. Mitchell (*Chill*); William S. Murray (*Yuppie*); Whoopi Goldberg (*Devilish Professor*).

CREDITS: Executive producer, Janet Grillo; producers, Doug McHenry and George Jackson; coproducer, Suzanne Broderick; directors, McHenry and Jackson; screenplay, Rusty Cundieff and Daryl G. Nickens; production designer, Michelle Minch; costumes, Ruth E. Carter; music, Vassal Benford; executive music supervisor, Louil Silas Jr.; camera, Francis Kenny; editor, Joel Goodman; rating, R; running time, 94 min.

THE PLAYER
1992
A Fine Line Release

CAST: Tim Robbins (*Griffin Mill*); Greta Scacchi (*June Gudmundsdottir*); Fred Ward (*Walter Stuckel*); Whoopi Goldberg (*Det. Susan Avery*); Peter Gallagher

(*Larry Levy*); Brion James (*Joel Levison*); Cynthia Stevenson (*Bonnie Sherow*); Vincent D'Onofrio (*David Kahane*); Dean Stockwell (*Andy Civella*); Richard E. Grant (*Tom Oakley*); Sydney Pollack (*Dick Mellen*); Lyle Lovett (*Detective DeLongpre*); Dina Merrill (*Celia*); Angela Hall (*Jan*); Leah Ayres (*Sandy*); Paul Hewitt (*Jimmy Chase*); Mike E. Kaplan (*Marty Grossman*); Susan Emshwiller (*Detective Broom*); Michael Tolk (*Eric Schecter*); Stephen Tolk (*Carl Schecter*); and Steve Allen, Richard Anderson, René Auberjonais, Harry Belafonte, Shari Belafonte, Karen Black, Michael Bowen, Gary Busey, Robert Carradine, Charles Champlin, Cher, James Coburn, Cathy Lee Crosby, John Cusack, Brad Davis, Paul Dooley, Theresa Ellis, Peter Falk, Felicia Farr, Kasia Figura, Louise Fletcher, Dennis Franz, Teri Garr, Leeza Gibbons, Scott Glenn, Jeff Goldblum, Elliott Gould, Joel Grey, David Alan Grier, Buck Henry, Anjelica Huston, Kathy Ireland, Steve James, Maxine John-James, Sally Kellerman, Sally Kirkland, Jack Lemmon, Andie MacDowell, Marlee Matlin, Malcolm McDowell, Jayne Meadows, Martin Mull, Jennifer Nash, Nick Nolte, Alexandra Powers, Bert Remsen, Guy Remsen, Patricia Resnick, Burt Reynolds, Jack Riley, Julia Roberts, Mimi Rogers, Annie Ross, Alan Rudolph, Susan Sarandon, Adam Simon, Jill St. John, Rod Steiger, Joan Tewkesbury, Brian Tochi, Lily Tomlin, Robert Wagner, Ray Walston, Bruce Willis and Marvin Young (*Themselves*).

CREDITS: Executive producer, Cary Brokaw; co–executive producer, William S. Gilmore; producers, David Brown, Michael Tolkin and Nick Wechsler; associate producer, David Levy; based on the novel by Tolkin; screenplay, Tolkin; production designer, Stephen Altman; art director, Jerry Fleming; set decorator, Susan Emshwiller; costumes, Alexander Julian; music, Thomas Newman; sound, John Pritchett; camera, Jean Lepine; editor, Geraldine Peroni; rating, R; running time, 123 min.

SISTER ACT
1992
A Touchstone Release

CAST: Whoopi Goldberg (*Deloris Van Cartier [a.k.a. Sister Mary Clarence]*); Maggie Smith (*Mother Superior*); Kathy Najimy (*Sister Mary Patrick*); Wendy Makkena (*Sister Mary Robert*); Mary Wickes (*Sister Mary Lazarus*); Harvey Keitel (*Vince LaRocca*); Bill Nunn (*Eddie Southern*); Robert Miranda (*Joey*); Ellen Albertini Dow, Carmen Zapata, Pat Crawford Brown, Prudence Wright Holmes, Georgia Creighton, Susan Johnson, Ruth Kobart, Susan Browning, Darlene Kolderhoven, Sheri Izzard, Edith Diaz and Beth Flower (*Choir Nuns*); Rose Parenti (*Sister Alma*); Jospeh Maher (*Bishop*); Jim Beaver (*Clarkson*); Jenifer Lewis (*Michelle*); Charlotte Crossley (*Tina*); Lois De Banzie (*Immaculata*); Robert Jimenez (*News Reporter*); Mike Jolly, Jeremy Roberts (*Bikers*).

CREDITS: Executive producer, Scott Rudin; producer, Teri Schwartz; coproducer, Mario Iscovich; associate producer, Cindy Gilmore; director, Emile Ardolino; screenplay, Joseph Howard; production designer, Jackson DeGovia; set decorator, Thomas L. Roysden; set designers, Robert M. Beall and Ann Harris; costumes, Molly Maginnis; music/music adapter, Marc Shaiman; choreography, Lester Wilson; technical advisers, Sister Ada Geraghty and Rev. Martin Greenlaw; sound, Darin Knight; special effects, Rocky Gehr; camera, Adam Greenberg; editor, Richard Halsey; rating, PG; running time, 99 min.

WISECRACKS
1992
An Alliance Release

CAST: Phyllis Diller, Whoopi Goldberg, the Clichettes, Faking It Three, Geri Jewell, Jenny Jones, Ellen DeGeneres, The Alexander Sisters, JoAnne Astrow, Joy Behar, Maria Callous, Dreenagh Darrell, Dorothy Hart, Maxine Lapiduss, Jenny Lecoat, Emily Levine, Paula Poundstone, Sandra Shamus, Carrie Snow, Pam Stone, Deborah Theaker, Robin Tyler, Kim Wayans and Lotus Weinstock (*Interviewees*).

CREDITS: Executive producers, Rina Fraticelli, Ginny Stikeman and Susan Cavan; producers, Gail Singer and Signe Johannson; director, Singer; camera, Zoe Dirse, Bob Fresco; editor, Gordon McClellan; no rating; running time, 90 min.

THE MAGICAL WORLD OF CHUCK JONES
1992
A Warner Bros. Release

CAST: Steven Spielberg, Whoopi Goldberg, Ron Howard, Matt Groening, Leonard Maltin, Joe Dante, George Lucas, Steve Guttenberg, Chris Connelly, Danny Elfman, Gary Rydstrom, Fritz Freleng, Roddy McDowall, June Foray, Kathleen Helppie-Shipley, Maurice Noble, Roger Mayer, Linda Jones Claugh, Marian Jones Valerie Kausen and Chuck Jones (*Interviewees*).

CREDITS: Producers, David Ka, Lik Wong and George Daugherty; director/screenplay, Daugherty; music, Cameron Patrick; camera, Peter Bonilla; editors, Peter E. Berger and Rick Trader; rating, PG; running time, 100 min.

SARAFINA!
1992
A Hollywood Pictures Release

CAST: Leleti Khumalo (*Sarafina*); Whoopi Goldberg (*Mary Masembuko*); Miriam Makeba (*Angelina*); John Kani (*School Principal*); Dumisani Diamini (*Crocodile*); Mbongeni Ngema (*Sabela*); Sipho Kunene (*Guitar*); Tertius Meintjes (*Lieutenant Bloem*); Robert Whithead (*Interrogator*); Somizi "Whacko" Mhlongo (*Fire*); Nhlanhai Ngema (*Stimela*); Faca Kulu (*Eddie*); Wendy Mseleku (*China*); Mary Twala (*Sarafina's Grandmother*); James Mthoba (*Sarafina's Uncle*); Greg Latter and Gideon De Wet (*Policemen*); Nicky Rebelo and James Whyle (*Soldiers*); Xolani Diamini, Siya Ngcobe (*Sarafina's Brothers*); Sam Ngakane (*Guitar's father*); Dominic Skosana and Ishmael Boikanyo (*Prison Guards*); Thulani Didi, Vincent Ngobese, Vukani "Marko" Diamini (*Crocodiles' Gang Members*).

CREDITS: Executive producers, Kirk D'Amico, Sudhir Pragjee, Helena Spring, Sanjeev Singh; producers, Anant Singh, David Thompson; line producer, Tania Jenkins; director, Darrell James Roodt; based on the play by Mbongeni Ngema; screenplay, William Nicholson; production designer, David Barham; music, Stanley Myers; choreography, Michael Peters, Ngema; sound, Henry Prentice; camera, Mark Vicente; editors, Peter Hollywood, Sarah Thomas, David Heitner; rating, PG-13; running time, 100 min.

NATIONAL LAMPOON'S LOADED WEAPON 1
1993
A New Line Release

CAST: Emilio Estevez (*Jack Colt*); Samuel L. Jackson (*Wes Luger*); Jon Lovitz (*Becker*); Tim Curry (*Jigsaw*); Kathy Ireland (*Destiny Demeanor*); Frank McRae (*Captain Doyle*); William Shatner (*General Mortars*); Dhiru Shah (*Translator*); Gokul (*Hindu*); Tom Bruggeman, Danny Castle (*Mini Mart Punks*); Lance Kinsey (*Irv*); Bill Nunn (*Police Photographer*); Dr. Joyce Brothers (*Coroner*); Lin Shaye (*Witness*); Vito Scotti (*Tailor*); Ken Ober (*Dooley*); Richard Moll (*Prison Attendant*); F. Murray Abraham (*Harold Leacher*); Charlie Sheen (*Valet*); Denis Leary (*Mike McCracken*); Corey Feldman (*Young Cop*); Phil Hartman (*Comic Cop*); J. T. Walsh (*Desk Clerk*); Michael Castner, Erik Estrada and Larry Wilcox (*Themselves*); Paul Gleason (*FBI Agent*); Allyce Beasley (*Spinach Destiny*); Charles Napier, Charles Cyphers (*Interrogators*); Whoopi Goldberg (*Sergeant York*); Bruce Willis (*Man Whose House Is Attacked*).

CREDITS: Executive producers, Michel Roy, Howard Klein and Erwin Stoff; co–executive producer, Michael DeLuca; producers, Suzanne Todd and David Willis; director, Gene Quintano; story, Don Holley and Tori Tellem; screenplay Holley and Quintano; production designer, Jaymes Hinkle; art director, Alan E. Muraoka; set decorator, Sarah B. Stone; costumes, Jacki Arthur; music, Robert Folk; sound, Martin Raymond Bolger; special effects, Jim Doyle and Richard L.

Thompson; camera, Peter Deming; editor, Christopher Greenbury; rating, PG-13, running time, 83 min.

MADE IN AMERICA
1993
A Warner Bros. Release

CAST: Whoopi Goldberg (*Sarah Matthews*); Ted Danson (*Hal Jackson*); Will Smith (*Tea Cake Walters*); Nia Long (*Zora Mathews*); Paul Rodriguez (*Jose*); Jennifer Tilly (*Josie*); Peggy Rea (*Stacy*); Clyde Kusatsu (*Bob Takashima*); David Bowe (*Teddy*); Jeffrey Joseph (*James*); Rawley Valverde (*Diego*); Fred Mancuso (*Bruce*); Charlene Fernetz (*Paula*); Shawn Levy (*Dwayne*); Lu Leonard (*Clinic Nurse*); Joe Lerer (*Hospital Doctor*); Janice Edwards (*Hospital Nurse*); Michael McFall (*Hospital Intern*); Phyllis Avery, Frances Bergen (*Caucasian Women in Store*); O'Neal Compton (*Rocky*); Michael Halton (*Stew*); Mel Stewart (*Principal Rockwell*); Jim Cranna (*Person at Car Lot*); Akihide "Bo" Fujiyama (*Sushi Chef*).

CREDITS: Executive producers, Nadine Schiff and Marcia Brandwynne; co–executive producer, Steven Reuther; producers, Arnon Milchan, Michael Douglas and Rick Bieber; coproducer, Patrick Palmer; director, Richard Benjamin; story, Brandwynne, Schiff and Holly Goldberg Sloan; screenplay, Sloan; production designer, Evelyn Sakash; costumes, Elizabeth McBride; music, Mark Isham; choreography, Lester Wilson; sound, Richard Lightstone; camera, Ralk Bode; editor, Jacqueline Cambas; rating PG-13, running time, 111 min.

SISTER ACT 2: BACK IN THE HABIT
1993
A Touchstone Release

CAST: Whoopi Goldberg (*Deloris Van Cartier [a.k.a. Sister Mary Clarence]*); Kathy Najimy (*Sister Mary Patrick*); Barnard Hughes (*Father Maurice*); Mary Wickes (*Sister Mary Lazarus*); James Coburn (*Mr. Crisp*); Michael Jeter (*Father Ignatius*); Wendy Makkena (*Sister Mary Robert*); Sheryl Lee Ralph (*Florence Watson*); Robert Pastorelli (*Joey Bustamente*); Thomas Gottschalk (*Father Wolfgang*); Maggie Smith (*Mother Superior*); Lauryn Hill (*Rita Watson*); Brad Sullivan (*Father Thomas*); Alanna Ubach (*Maria*); Ryan Toby (*Ahymal*); Ron Johnson (*Sketch*); Jennifer "Love" Hewitt (*Margart*); Devin Kamin (*Frankie*); Christian Fitzharris (*Tyler Chase*); Tanya Blount (*Tanya*); Mehran Marcos Sedghi (*Marcos*); Valeria Andrews, Dionna Brooks-Jackson, Monica Calhoun, Martha Gonzales, Deondray Gossett, Frank Howard, David Kater, Kimberlee Kramer, Deedee Magno, Patrick Malone, Alex[andrea] Martin, Jermaine Montell, Sacha Thomas, and Ashley Thompson

(*Classroom Kids*); Bill Duke (*Mr. Johnson*); William D. Hall (*Chapman Choir Leader*).

CREDITS: Executive producers, Laurence Mark and Mario Iscovich; coexecutive producer, Christopher Meledandri; producers, Dawn Steel and Scott Rudin; director, Bill Duke; screenplay, James Orr, Jim Cruickshank and Judi Ann Mason; production designer, John DeCuir Jr.; art director, Louis M. Mann; set decorator, Bruce Gibeson; set designers, Lauren Cory and Sandy Getzler; costumes, Francine Jamison Tanchuck; music, Miles Goodman; music supervisor, Marc Shaiman; sound, Jim Webb; special-effects supervisor, James Karl Fredburg; camera, Oliver Wood; editors, John Carter, Pem Herring, and Stuart Pappe; rating, PG; running time, 106 min.

NAKED IN NEW YORK
1994
A Fine Line Release

CAST: Eric Stoltz (*Jake Briggs*); Mary-Louise Parker (*Joanne White*); Ralph Macchio (*Chris*); Jill Clayburgh (*Shirley Briggs*); Tony Curtis (*Carl Fisher*); Timothy Dalton (*Elliot Price*); Lynne Thigpen (*Helen*); Kathleen Turner (*Dana Coles*); Roscoe Lee Browne (*Mr. Reid*); Whoopi Goldberg (*Tragedy Mask*); Jude Ciccelela (*Dump Truck Driver*); John Vennema (*Neighbor*); Paul Guilfoyle (*Román*); Bobo Lewis (*Bubba Sera*); Vacek C. Simek (*Willie*); Michael Stahl, Steve Stahl, Alexa Knapp, and Ariel Knapp (*Alternate Baby Jakes*); Leo Charles (*Jake at Age 8*); Stephen Piemonte II (*Jake at Age 13*); Arabella Field (*Jenny Taylor*); Olek Krupa (*Drama Professor*); Richard Price, Ariel Dorfman, Bruce Fierstein, Marsha Norman, William Styron, Gael Love, Eric Bogosian, Quentin Crisp, Karen Duff, Tommy Page, and Arthur Penn (*Themselves*); David Johanssen (*Orangutan Voice*); Rocco Sisto (*Comedy Mask*); Griffin Dunne, Luis Guzman, and Colleen Camp (*Auditioners*); Chris Noth (*Jason Brett*).

CREDITS: Executive producer, Martin Scorsese; producer, Frederick Zollo; coproducer, Carol Cuddy; director, Dan Algrant; screenplay, Algrant and John Warren; production designer, Kalina Ivanov; costumes, Julie Weiss; music, Angelo Badalamenti; camera, Joey Forsyte; editor, Bill Pankow; rating, R; running time, 91 min.

THE LION KING
1994
A Walt Disney Studios Release

CAST (Voices): Rowan Atkinson (*Zazu*); Matthew Broderick (*Adult Simba*); Niketa

Calame (*Young Nala*); Jim Cummings (*Ed*); Whoopi Goldberg (*Shenzi*); Robert Guillaume (*Rafiki*); Jeremy Irons (*Scar*); James Earl Jones (*Mufasa*); Moira Kelly (*Adult Nala*); Nathan Lane (*Timon*); Cheech Marin (*Banzai*); Ernie Sabella (*Pumbaa*); Madge Sinclair (*Sarabi*); Jonathan Taylor Thomas (*Young Simba*); Carmen Twillie (*"Circle of Life" Solo Singer*); Sally Dworsky (*Adult Nala Singing Voice*); Jason Weaver (*Young Simba Singing Voice*); Joseph Williams (*Adult Simba Singing Voice*); Laura Williams (*Young Nala Singing Voice*).

CREDITS: Executive producers, Thomas Schumacher and Sarah McArthur; producer, Don Hahn; associate producer, Alice Dewey; directors, Roger Allers and Rob Minkoff; screenplay, Irene Mecchi, Jonathan Roberts, and Linda Woolverton; production designer, Chris Sanders; art director, Andy Gaskill; music/music arranger, Hans Zimmer; visual effects, Scott Santoro; editors, Tom Finan and John Carnochan; rating, G, running time, 87 min.

THE LITTLE RASCALS
1994
A Universal Release

CAST: Travis Tedford (*Spanky*); Bug Hall (*Alfalfa*); Brittany Ashton Holmes (*Darla*); Kevin Jamal Woods (*Stymie*); Zachary Mabry (*Porky*); Ross Elliott Bagley (*Buckwheat*); Sam Saletta (*Butch*); Blake Jeremy Collins (*Woim*); Blake McIver Ewing (*Waldo*); Jordan Warkol (*Froggy*); Courtland Mead (*Uh-Huh*); Juliette Brewer (*Mary Ann*); Heather Karasek (*Jane*); Mel Brooks (*Mr. Welling*); Whoopi Goldberg (*Buckwheat's Mom*); Daryl Hannah (*Miss Crabtree*); Reba McEntire (*A. J. Ferguson*); Ashley Olsen and Mary-Kate Olsen (*Twins*); Raven-Symone (*Stymie's Girlfriend*); Lea Thompson (*Ms. Roberts*); Donald Trump (*Waldo's Dad*); George Wendt (*Lumberyard Clerk*); E. G. Daily (*Froggy's Voice*).

CREDITS: Executive producers, Gerald R. Molen, Deborah Jelin Newmyer, and Roger King; producers, Michael King, Bill Oakes; coproducer, Mark Allan; director, Penelope Spheeris; story, Penelope Spheeris, Robert Wolterstorff, Mike Scott, Paul Guay, Stephen Mazur; screenplay Guay, and Mazur, and Penelope Spheeris; production designer, Larry Fulton; art director, Gae Buckley; set decorator, Linda Spheeris; costumes, Jami Burrows; music, William Ross; sound, Susumu Tokunow; camera, Richard Bowen; editor, Ross Albert; rating, PG; running time, 82 min.

CORINA, CORINA
1994
A New Line Release

CAST: Whoopi Goldberg (*Corrina Washington*); Ray Liotta (*Manny Singer*); Tina Marjorino (*Molly Singer*); Wendy Crewson (*Jenny Davis*); Larry Miller (*Sid*); Erica John (*Grandma Eva*); Jenifer Lewis (*Jevina*); Joan Cusack (*Jonesy*); Harold Sylvester (*Frank*); Steven Williams (*Anthony T. Williams*); Patrika Darbo (*Wilma*); Lucy Webb (*Shirl*); Courtland Mead (*Howard*); Asher Metchik (*Lewis*); Don Ameche (*Grandpa Harry*); Noreen Hennessey (*High Heels*); June C. Ellis (*Miss O'Herlihy*); Mimi Lieber (*Rita Lang*); Karen Leigh Hopkins (*Liala Sheffield*); Lin Shaye (*Repeat Nanny*); Pearl Huang (*Mrs. Wang*); Marcus Toji (*Tommy*); Brent Spiner (*Brent Witherspoon*); Curtis Williams (*Percy*); Ashley Taylor Walls (*Mavis*); Bryan A. Robinson (*Chubby Boy*).

CREDITS: Executive producers, Ruth Vitale and Bernie Goldmann; producers, Paul Mazur, Steve Tisch, and Jessie Nelson; associate producer, Joseph Fineman; line producer, Eric McLeod; director/screenplay, Nelson; production designer, Jeannine Claudia Oppewall; art director, Dina Lipton; set designer, Louisa Bonnie; set decorator, Lauren M. Gabor; costumes, Francine Jamison-Tanchuck and John Hayley; music, Rick Cox, Thomas Newman; sound, David Kelson; camera, Bruce Surtees; editor, Lee Percy; rating, PG, running time, 114 min.

STAR TREK GENERATIONS
1994
A Paramount Release

CAST: Patrick Stewart (*Captain Jean-Luc Picard*); Jonathan Frakes (*Comdr. William Riker*); Brent Spiner (*Lieutenant Commander Data*); LeVar Burton (*Lt. Comdr. Geordi La Forge*); Michael Dorn (*Lieutenant Commander Worf*); Gates McFadden (*Dr. Beverly Crusher*); Marina Sirtis (*Counselor Deanna Troi*); Malcolm McDowell (*Dr. Soran*); James Doolan (*Montgomery "Scotty" Scott*); Walter Koenig (*Comdr. Pavel Chekov*); William Shatner (*Capt. James T. Kirk*); Whoopi Goldberg (*Guinan*); Alan Ruck (*Captain Harriman*); Jacqueline Kim (*Demora*); Jenette Goldstein (*Science Officer*); Thomas Kopache (*Commanding Officer*); Glenn Morshwer (*Navigator*); Tim Russ (*Lieutenant*); Tommy Hinkley, John Putch, and Christine Jansen (*Journalists*); Michael Mack (*Ensign Hayes*); Dendrie Taylor (*Lieutenant Farrell*); Pati Yasutake (*Nurse Ogawa*); Granville Ames (*Transporter Chief*); Henry Marshall (*Security Officer*); Brittany Parkyn (*Girl With Teddy Bear*); Majel Barrett (*Computer Voice*); Rif Hutton (*Klingon Guard*); Kim Braden (*Picard's Wife*); Matthew Collins, Mimi Collins, Thomas Alexander Dekker, Madison Eginton, and Olivia Hack (*Picard's Kids*); Christopher James Miller (*Picard's Nephew*).

CREDITS: Executive producer, Bernie Williams; producer, Rick Berman; co-producer, Peter Lauritson; based upon the TV series *Star Trek* created by Gene

Roddenberry; director, David Carson; story, Berman, Ronald D. Moore, and Brannon Braga; screenplay, Moore and Braga; production designer, Herman Zimmerman; art director, Sandy Veneziano; set decorator, John M. Dwyer; set designers, Robert Fechtman, Ron Wilkinson, and Dianne Wager; costumes, Robert Blackman; music, Dennis McCarthy; special visual effects, Industrial Light & Magic and John Knoll; special-makeup-effects designer-supervisor, Michael Westmore; sound, Thomas D. Causey; camera, John A. Alonzo; editor, Peter E. Berger; rating, PG; running time, 118 min.

THE PAGEMASTER
1994
A Twentieth Century–Fox Release

CAST: Macaulay Culkin (*Richard Tyler*); Christopher Lloyd (*Mr. Dewey/Pagemaster*); Ed Begley Jr. (*Alan Tyler*); Mel Harris (*Claire Tyler*); voices of Patrick Stewart (*Adventure*); Whoopi Goldberg (*Fantasy*); Frank Welker (*Horror*); Leonard Nimoy (*Dr. Jekyll & Mr. Hyde*); George Hearn (*Captain Ahab*); Dorian Harewood (*Jamaican Pirates*); Ed Gilbert (*George Merry*); Phil Hartman (*Tom Morgan*); Jim Cunnings (*Long John Silver*); B. J. Ward (*Queen of Hearts*); Dick Erdman, Fernando Escandon, and Robert Piccardo (*Pirates*).

CREDITS: Producers, David Kirschner and Paul Getz; live-action-scenes producer, Michael R. Joyce; animation coproducers, David J. Steinberg and Barry Weiss; associate producers, Claire Gidden and Roxy Novotny Steven; animation director, Maurice Hunt; live-action director, Joe Johnston; animation-sequence director, Glenn Chaika; story, David Kirschner, David Casci; screenplay, Casci and Kirschner; live-action production designer, Roy Forge Smith; set decorator, Ronald Reiss; animation production designers, Gay Lawrence and Valerio Ventura; animation art director, Pixote; music, James Horner; sound, Steve Nelson; special-effects coordinator, Robbie Knott; camera, Alexander Gruszynski; editor, Kaja Fehr; rating G; running time, 75 min.

LIBERATION
1994
A Simon Wiesenthal Center Film

NARRATORS: Ben Kingsley, Whoopi Goldberg, Patrick Stewart, Miriam Margolyes, and Jean Boht.

CREDITS: Executive producer, Richard Trank; producers, Marvin Hier, Arnold Schwartzman; associate producer, Isolde Schwartzman; director, Arnold Schwartzman; screenplay, Martin Gilbert, Hier, Arnold Schwartzman; production designer, Arnold Schwartzman; music, Carl Davis; sound, Mark Friedman; editors, David Dresher, Steve Nielson; no rating; running time, 98 min.

BOYS ON THE SIDE
1995
A Warner Bros. Release

CAST: Whoopi Goldberg (*Jane DeLuca*); Mary-Louise Parker (*Robin Nickerson*); Drew Barrymore (*Holly*); Matthew McConaughey (*Abe Lincoln*); James Remar (*Alex*); Billy Wirth (*Nick*); Anita Gillette (*Elaine Nickerson*); Dennis Boutsikaris (*Massarelli*); Estelle Parsons (*Louise*): Amy Aquino (*Anna*); Stan Egi (*Henry*); Stephen Gevedon (*Johnny Figgis*); Amy Ray and Emily Saliers (*Indigo Girls*); Jude Ciccolella (*Jerry*); Gede Watanabe (*Steve*); Jonathan Seda (*Pete*); Mimi Toro (*Carrie*); Lori Alan (*Girl With Attitude*); Mary Ann McGarry (*Dr. Newbauer*); Michael Storm (*Tommy*); Danielle Shuman (*Young Robin*); Ted Zerkowski (*Drug Buyer*); Marine Crossen (*Nurse*); Aaron Lustig (*Judge*); Adria Contreras (*Mary Todd at 5 Months*); Malika Edwards (*Mary Todd at 10 Months*).

CREDITS: Executive producers, Don Roos and Patricia Karlan; producers, Arnon Milchan, Steven Reuther and Herbert Ross; coproducer, Patrick McCormick; director, Ross; screenplay, Roos; production designer, Ken Adams; art director, William F. O'Brien; set designers, James Bayliss, Jann K. Engel, and Stephen Berger; set decorator, Rick Simpson; costumes, Gloria Gresham; music, David Newman; sound, Jim Webb; camera, Donald E. Thorin; editor, Michael R. Miller; rating, R; running time, 115 min.

MOONLIGHT AND VALENTINO
1995
A Gramercy Release

CAST: Elizabeth Perkins (*Rebecca Trager Lott*); Gwyneth Paltrow (*Lucy Trager*); Kathleen Turner (*Alberta Russell*); Whoopi Goldberg (*Sylvie Morrow*); Jon Bon Jovi (*Painter*); Jeremy Sisto (*Steven*); Josef Sommer (*Thomas Trager*); Shadia Simmons (*Jenny Morrow*); Erica Luttrell (*Drew Morrow*); Matthew Koller (*Alex Morrow*); Scott Wickware (*Policeman*); Kelli Fox (*Nurse*); Harrison Liu (*Mr. Wong*); Wayne Lam (*Mr. Wong's Son*); Ken Wong (*Mr. Wong's Father*); Carlton Watson (*Henrik*); Alan Clifton (*Street Vendor*); Judah Katz (*Marc*); Peter Coyote (*Paul Morrow*).

CREDITS: Producers, Alison Owen, Eric Fellner, and Tim Bevan; coproducer, Mary McLaglen; associate producer, Liza Chasin; director, David Anspaugh; based on the play by Ellen Simon; screenplay, Simon; production designer, Robb Wilson

King; art director, David Ferguson; set decorator, Carol Lavoie; costumes, Denise Cronenberg; music, Howard Shore; sound, Bruce Carwardine; special effects coordinator, Michael Kavanagh; camera, Julio Macat; editor, David Rosenbloom; rating, R; running time, 103 min.

THE CELLULOID CLOSET
January 30, 1996
HBO

CAST: Lily Tomlin (*Narrator*); Jay Presson Allen, Susie Bright, Quentin Crisp, Mart Crowley, Tony Curtis, Antonio Fargas, Harvey Fierstein, Whoopi Goldberg, Farley Granger, Harry Hamlin, Tom Hanks, Arthur Laurents, Shirley MacLaine, Armistead Maupin, Daniel Melnick, Ron Nyswaner, Jan Oxenberg, Paul Rudnick, Barry Sandler, Susan Sarandon, John Schlesinger, and Gore Vidal (*Interviewees*).

CREDITS: Executive producers, Bernie Brillstein, Brad Grey, Howard Rosenman, and Sheila Nevins; co–executive producer, Lily Tomlin; producers, Robert Epstein and Jeffrey Friedman; coproducer, Michael Lumpkin; associate producers, Wendy Braitman, Michael Ehrenzweig, and Caryn Mendez; director, Robert Epstein; based on the book by Vito Russo; screenplay, Epstein, Friedman, and Sharon Wood; narration writer, Armistead Maupin; production designer, Scott Chambliss; art director and music, Carter Burwell; sound, Lauretta Molitor, Peggy Names; camera, Nancy Schreiber; editors, Friedman and Arnold Glassman; rating, R (when released by Sony Pictures Classic); running time, 102 min.

TALES FROM THE CRYPT PRESENTS BORDELLO OF BLOOD
1996
A Universal Release

CAST: John Kassir (*Voice of the Crypt Keeper*); Dennis Miller (*Rafe Guttman*); Erika Eleniak (*Katherine Verdoux*); Angie Everhart (*Lilith*); Chris Sarandon (*Reverend Current*); Corey Feldman (*Caleb Verdoux*); Aubrey Morris (*McCutcheon*); Phil Fondacaro (*Vincent Prather*); William Sadler (*Mummy*); Ciara Hunter (*Tamara*); Leslie Ann Phillips (*Patrice*); Juliet Reagh (*Tallulah*); Eli Gabay (*Miguel*); Matt Hill (*Reggie*); Eric Keenleyside (*Noonan*); Kim Kondrashoff (*Jenkins*); Robert Paul Munic (*Zeke*); Gary Starr (*Jed*); Robin Douglas (*Jonas*); Ravinder Toor (*Bartender*); Robert Rozen (*Rabbi Goldman*); Whoopi Goldberg (*Hospital Patient*); Heather Hanson (*Babe*); Sheila Mills (*Bride of Frankenstein*); Korrine St. Onge, Claire Marie Harvey, Lyne Hachey, Sheena Galloway, Kikka Ferguson, and Melody Cherpaw (*Bordello Vampires*).

CREDITS: Executive producers Richard Donner, David Giler, Walter Hill, Joel Silver, and Robert Zemeckis; producer, Gilbert Adler; coproducers, Al Katz and Alexander Collett; associate producers, Dan Craccholo, Richard Mirsch, and Scott Nimerfro; director, Adler; based on *Tales from the Crypt* comic books, originally published by William M. Gaines; story, Bob Gale and Zemeckis; screenplay, Katz and Adler; director, Adler; production designer, Gregory Melton; costumes, Trish Keating; music, Chris Boardman; *Tales from the Crypt* theme, Danny Elfman; sound, Paul Rodriguez; camera, Tom Priestley; editor, Stephen Lovejoy; rating, R; running time, 87 min.

EDDIE
1996
A Hollywood Pictures Release

CAST: Whoopi Goldberg (*Eddie*); Frank Langella (*Wild Bill Burgess*); Dennis Farina (*Coach Bailey*); Richard Jenkins (*Assistant Coach Zimmer*); Lisa Ann Walter (*Claudine*); John Benjamin Hickey (*Joe Nader*); Troy Beyer (*Beth Hastings*); John Salley (*Nate Wilson*); Rick Fox (*Terry Hastings*); Malik Sealy (*Stacy Patton*); Mark Jackson (*Darren Taylor*); Dwayne Schintzius (*Ivan Radovadovitch*); Greg Ostertag (*Joe Sparks*); Vernel Singleton (*Jamal Duncan*); Marv Albert, Chris Berman, Fabio, Walt Frazier, Mayor Rudolph Giuliani, Sirajul Islam, Mujibur Rahman, Dennis Rodman, and Donald Trump (*Themselves*); Aasif Mandvi (*Mohammed*); Johnny Williams (*Big Al*); Albert Pisarenkov (*Mischa*); Edward Koch (*Former Mayor of New York City*); Gene Anthony Ray (*Dancer*).

CREDITS: Executive producers, Ron Bozman, Steve Zacharias, and Jeff Buhai; producers, David Permut and Mark Burg; coproducer, Andrew Gunn; director, Steve Rash; story, Zacharias, Buhai, Jon Connolly, David Loucka; screenplay, Connolly, Loucka, Eric Champnella, Keith Mitchell, Zacharias, Buhai; production designer, Richard Halsey; art director, Robert K. Shaw Jr.; set decorator, Roberta J. Holinko; costumes, Molly Maginnis; music, Stanley Clarke; choreography, Eartha D. Robinson; basketball consultant, Glenn "Doc" Rivers; sound, James E. Webb; camera, Victor Kemper; editor, Richard Halsey; rating, PG-13; running time, 100 min.

THEODORE REX (alternate release title: *T. Rex*)
1996
A New Line Release

CAST: Whoopi Goldberg (*Kate Coltrane*); Armin Mueller-Stahl (*Elijar Kane*); Juliet Landau (*Dr. Shade*); Bud Cort (*Splinter*); Stephen McHattie (*Edge*); George Newbern (*Voice of Theodore Rex*); Carol Kane (*Voice of Molly Rex*); Richard Roundtree

(*Commander Lynch*); Jack Riley (*Alaric*); Peter MacKenzie (*Alex Summers*); Joe Dallesandro (*Rogan*); Toy T. Johnson (*Sebastian*); Susie Coelho (*Dr. Armitrof*); Peter K. Wong (*Toymaker*); Robert Martin Robinson (*Knife*); Edith Diaz (*Ella*); Queen Kong (*Meanest Woman Truck Driver*); William Boyett (*Desk Sergeant*); Moon Orsatte (*Adam*); Marius Mazomanian (*Burglar*); Jan Rabson (*Voice of Tina Rex*); Pons Maar (*Theodore Rex Suit Performer*); Tony Sabin Prince (*Molly Rex Suit Performer*); Hayward O. Coleman (*Oliver Rex Suit Performer*); Jennifer Darling, Anne Lockhart, and Jan Rabson (*Voices*).

CREDITS: Executive producers, Stefano Ferrari and Jonathan R. Betuel; producers, Richard Gilbert Abramson and Sue Baden-Powell; line producers, Cathy Mickel Gibson and Maria Dylan; director/screenplay, Betuel; production designer, Walter P. Martishius; costumes, Mary E. Vogt; music, Robert Folk; camera, David Tattersall; editors, Rick Shaine and Steve Mirkovich; rating, PG; running time, 90 min.

BOGUS
1996
A Warner Bros. Release

CAST: Whoopi Goldberg (*Harriet Franklin*); Gerard Depardieu (*Bogus*); Haley Joel Osment (*Albert*); Denis Mercier (*Mr. Antoine*); Andrea Martin (*Penny*); Nancy Travis (*Lorraine*); Ute Lemper (*Babette*); Sheryl Lee Ralph (*Ruth Clark*); Barbara Hamilton (*Mrs. Partridge*); Kevin Jackson (*Bob Morrison*); Al Waxman (*Principal*); Fiona Reid (*Teacher*); Don Francks (*Dr. Surprise*); Elizabeth Harper (*Ellen*); Richard Portnoy (*M. Clay Thrasher*); Mo Gaffney (*Traveler's Aide—New Jersey*); Sara Peery (*Traveler's Aide—Las Vegas*); Cynthia Mace (*Flight Lieutenant*); Justine Johnston (*Woman in Plane*); Frank Medrano (*Man in Plane*); Doug Gilmore (*Surprise Guest*).

CREDITS: Executive producers, Michael Nathanson, Patrick Markey, and Gayle Fraser-Baigelman; producers, Norman Jewison, Arnon Michan, and Jeff Rothberg; director, Jewison; story, Rothberg and McCarthy; screenplay, Alvin Sargent; production designer, Ken Adam; art director, Alicia Keywan; set designers, Neil Morfitt, and Gord White; set decorator, Hilton Rosenmarin; costumes, Ruth Myers; music, Marc Shaiman; choreography, Walter Painter; sound, Bruce Carwardine; camera, David Watkin; editor, Stephen Rivkin; rating, PG, running time, 111 min.

THE ASSOCIATE
1996
A Hollywood Pictures Release

CAST: Whoopi Goldberg (*Laurel Ayres*); Dianne Wiest (*Sally*); Eli Wallach (*Fallon*); Tim Daly (*Frank*); Bebe Neuwirth (*Camille*); Austin Pendleton (*Aesop*); Lainie Kazan (*Cindy Mason*); George Martin (*Manchester*); Kenny Kerr (*Charlie*); Lee Wilkof (*Bissel*); Helen Hanft (*Mrs. Cupchick*); George Morforgen (*Plaza Manager*); Zeljko Ivanek (*SEC Agent Thompkins*); Miles Chapin (*Harry*); Jean De Baer (*Loan Officer*); Louis Turenne (*Peabody Club Concierge*); William Hill (*Detective Templeton*); Colleen Camp Wilson (*Detective Jones*); Brian Tarantina (*Eddie*); Jerry Hardin (*Harley Mason*); John Short and Thomas Wagner (*Harley Mason's Associates*); Johnny Miller, Donald J Trump, and Sally Jessy Raphael (*Themselves*); Peter McRobbie, Daryl Edwards (*Executives at Strip Club*); Socorro Santiago (*Syntonex Worker*).

CREDITS: Executive producers, Ted Field, Scott Kroopf, Robert W. Cort, and David Madden; coproducers, René Gainville and Michael A. Helfant; producers, Frederic Golchan, Patrick Markey and Adam Leipzig; director, Donald Petrie; based on the novel *El Socio* by Jenaro Prieto; screenplay, Nick Thiel; production designer, Andrew Jackness; art director, Phil Messina; set decorator, Jessica Lainer; costumes, April Ferry; music, Christopher Tyng; music supervisor, Barkle K. Griggs; sound, Rosa Howell-Thornhill; camera, Alex Nepomniaschy; editor, Bonnie Koehler; rating, PG-13; running time, 113 min.

GHOSTS OF MISSISSIPPI
1996
A Castle Rock Release

CAST: Alec Baldwin (*Bobby DeLaughter*); Whoopi Goldberg (*Myrlie Evers*); James Woods (*Byron De La Beckwith*); Craig T. Nelson (*Ed Peters*); William H. Macy (*Charlie Crisco*); Susanna Thompson (*Peggy Lloyd DeLaughter*); Michael O'Keefe (*Merrida Coxwell*); Bill Smithrovich (*Jim Kitchens*); Wayne Rogers (*Morris Dees*); Diane Ladd (*Caroline Moore*); Virginia Madsen (*Dixie Moore DeLaughter*); Yolanda King (*Reena Evers*); Darrell Evers, and James Evers (*Themselves*); Lucas Black (*Burt DeLaughter*); Bill Cobbs (*Charlie Evers*); James Pickens Jr. (*Medgar Evers*);

CREDITS: Executive producers, Jeffrey Stott and Charles Newirth; producers, Rob Reiner, Frederick Zollo, Nicholas Paleologos, and Andrew Scheinman; coproducer, Frank Capra III; director, Reiner; screenplay, Lewis Colick; production designer, Lilly Kilvert; art director, Christopher Burian-Mohr; set decorators, Alan S. Kaye and Karen O'Hara; costumes, Gloria Gresham; music, Marc Shaiman; sound, Robert Grieve; camera, John Seale; editor, Robert Leighton; rating, PG-13; running time, 120 min.

In the Gloaming
April 20, 1997
HBO

CAST: Glenn Close (*Janet*); Bridge Fonda (*Anne*); Whoopi Goldberg (*Myrna*); Robert Sean Leonard (*Danny*); David Strathairn (*Martin*); Annie Starke (*Young Anne*); Will Reeve (*Young Danny*).

CREDITS: Executive producers, Frederick Zollo, Nicholas Paleologos, and Michael Fuchs; producer, Nellie Nugiel; coproducer, Bonne Timmerman; director, Christopher Reeve; based on the short story by Alice Elliott Dark; teleplay, Will Scheffer; production designer, Andy Jackness; art director, David Stein; set decorator, Catherine Davis; costumes, Jane Greenwood; music, Dave Grusin; sound, Chris Newman; camera, Fred Elmes; editor, David Ray; no rating; running time, 60 min.

An Alan Smithee Film
1997 (in post production)
Cinergi Productions

CAST: Eric Idle, Whoopi Goldberg, Sylvester Stallone, Robert Evans, Robert Shapiro, Larry King, Ryan O'Neal, Jackie Chan, Naomi Campbell, MC Lytle, Chuck D, Coolio, Dr. Joyce Brothers, Lt. Gov. Gray Davis, Troy Aikman, Dan Martino, John Elway, Richard Jeni, Anthony Pellicano, Shane Black, and Sandra Bernhard.

CREDITS: Executive producer, Andy Vajna; producers, Ben Myron and Joe Eszterhas; coproducer, Fred Caruso; director, Arthur Hiller; screenplay, Eszterhas; production designer, David L. Snyder; costumes, Laura Cunningham; camera, Reynaldo Villabos; editor, Jim Langlois.

Television Series

Star Trek: The Next Generation
(Syndicated, 1987–94), 60 min.

CAST: Patrick Stewart (*Capt. Jean-Luc Picard*); Jonathan Frakes (*Comdr. William Riker*); LeVar Burton (*Lt. Geordi La Forge*); Denise Crosby (*Lt. Tasha Yar [1987–88]*); Michael Dorn (*Lieutenant Worf*); Gates McFadden (*Dr. Beverly Crusher [1987–88; 1989–94]*); Marina Sirtis (*Counselor Deanna Troi*); Brent Spiner (*Lieutenant Commander Data*); Wil Wheaton (*Wesley Crusher [1987–90]*); Colm Meaney (*Transporter Chief Miles O'Brien [1987–93]*); Diana Muldaur (*Dr. Kather-*

ine Pulaski [1988–89]); Whoopi Goldberg (*Guinan [1988–93]*); Rosalind Chao (*Keiko O'Brien [1991–93]*); Brian Bonsall (*Alexander Roshensko [1992–94]*); Michele Forbes (*Ensign Ro Laren [1991–92]*); Patti Yasutake (*Dr. Elissa Ogawa [1993–94]*).

BAGDAD CAFÉ
(CBS-TV, 1990–91), 30 min.

CAST: Whoopi Goldberg (*Brenda*); Jean Stapleton (*Jasmine Zweibel*); Scott Lawrence (*Juney*); Monica Calhoun (*Debbie*); James Gammon (*Rudy*); Cleavon Little (*Sal*); Sam Whipple (*Dewey Kunkle*).

CAPTAIN PLANET AND THE PLANETEERS
(TNT-Cable/Syndicated, 1990–95), 30 min.

CAST (Voices): David Coburn (*Captain Planet*); Whoopi Goldberg (*Gaia [1990–93]*); Margot Kidder (*Gaia [1993–95]*); LeVar Burton (*Kwame*); Joey Dedio (*Wheeler*); Kath Soucie (*Linka*); Janice Kawaye (*Gi*); Scott Menville (*Ma-Ti*); Frank Welker (*Such*).

THE WHOOPI GOLDBERG SHOW
(Syndicated, 1992–93), 30 min.

HOST: Whoopi Goldberg

Broadway

WHOOPI GOLDBERG
Lyceum Theatre, New York City, October 24, 1984, 150 performances.

CAST: Whoopi Goldberg.

Presenters, Mike Nichols, Emanuel Azenberg, and the Shubert Organization; production supervisor, Nichols; sketches by Goldberg; visual consultant, Tony Walton; lighting designer, Jennifer Tipton; sound designer, Otis Munderloh. Original cast album: Geffen Records GHS 24065.

A FUNNY THING HAPPENED ON THE WAY TO THE FORUM
St. James Theatre, New York City, March 6, 1997.

CAST: Whoopi Goldberg (*Prologue Actor/Pseudolus*); Brad Aspel, Cory English and Ray Roderick (*The Proteans*); Jim Stanek (*Hero*); Jessica Boevers (*Philia*); Dick Latessa (*Senex*); Mary Testa (*Domina, Wife of Senex*); Ross Lehman (*Hysterium*); Ernie Sabella (*Lycus*); Pamela Everett (*Tintinabula*); Holly Cruikshank (*Panacea*); Tara Nichole, Kristin Willits (*The Geminae*); Pascale Faye (*Vibrta*); Kena Tangi Dorsey (*Gymnasia*); William Duell (*Erronius*); Cris Groenendaal (*Miles Gloriosus*).

Presenters, Jujamcyn Theaters, Scott Rudin/Paramount Pictures, the Viertel-Baruch-Frankel Group, Roger Berlind, Dodger Productions; director, Jerry Zaks; based on the plays of Plautus; book, Burt Shevelove, Larry Gelbart; set-costume designer, Tony Walker; music-lyrics, Stephen Sondheim; orchestrator, Jonathan Tunick; music supervisor, Edward Strauss; dance/music arranger, David Chase; choreography, Rob Marshall; lighting designer, Paul Gallo; sound designer, Tony Meola.

This revival production began its initial Broadway run on April 18, 1996 with Nathan Lane originally in the role of Pseudolus.

Partial List of Sources

Of the several libraries and research centers utilized for this book, particularly helpful were those collections and reference shelves found at the Academy of Motion Picture Arts and Sciences, the Beverly Hills Public Library, the Hollywood Public Library, the Museum of Television and Radio and the New York Public Library at Lincoln Center (the Billy Rose Theater Collection).

Of great assistance were all those individuals who took the time to talk with me—both on and off the record—about their working and/or social relationships over the years with Ms. Whoopi Goldberg.

Sources of Chapter Opening Quotes

1. Tom Provenzano, "Whoopi Goldberg," *Drama-Logue*, December 9, 1993, p. 16.
2. "Blacks Fail to See Humor in Ted Danson's Blackface Tribute to Whoopi Goldberg," *Jet*, November; 1993, pp. 56–59.
3. David Rensin, "Whoopi Goldberg," *Playboy*, June 1987, pp. 51–57, 154–57.
4. Dotson Radner, "I Knew What I Wanted to Be," *Parade*, November 11, 1992, pp. 4–6.
5. Angela Bonavoglia ed., *The Choices We Made*, (New York: Random House, 1991, pp. 115–23).
6. David Rensin, "Whoopi Goldberg," *Playboy*, June 1987, pp. 51–57, 154–57.
7. Ibid.
8. Darrah Meeley, "Close Up: Whoopi Goldberg," *Screen Actor* fall 1988, pp. 16–19.
9. Rensin, "Goldberg."
10. Interview by Carolyn Wendt, *City Area Monthly* Oct. 1992.
11. Janet Coleman, "Making Whoopi," *Vanity Fair*, July 1984, pp. 36–38, 108–9.
12. Rensin, "Goldberg."

13. Edward Guthmann, "A Comic's Uncanny Replay of Moms Mabley," *San Francisco Sunday Examiner & Chronicle,* Datebook section pp. 23–24.

14. "Whoopi Goldberg," *Interview,* December 1984, pp. 75–76.

15. Rensin, "Goldberg."

16. Edward Guthmann, "Doing It Her Way, Whoopi's a Smash," *San Francisco Chronicle,* December 16, 1984, Datebook section, pp. 34–36.

17. Rader, "I Knew What I Wanted to Be."

18. Laura B. Randolph, "The Whoopi Goldberg Nobody Knows," *Ebony,* March 1991, pp. 110–15.

19. *Fatal Beauty* press kit.

20. David Rensin, "Goldberg."

21. Newspaper clip (unmarked) dated October 30, 1987.

22. Ian Spelling, "Classic 'Trek' Inspired Goldberg," "Inside Trek" column, *Los Angeles Times,* August 1993.

23. Darrah Meeley, "Close Up: Whoopi Goldberg," *Screen Actor,* fall 1988, pp. 16–19.

24. Rod Lurie, "Remaking Whoopi," *West Side Spirit,* August 21, 1990, pp. 1, 3, 8, 23.

25. Transcript, *Oprah Winfrey Show,* May 1, 1989.

26. Mark Morrison, "Remakin' Whoopi," *Cable Guide,* February 1990, pp. 25–27.

27. Rod Lurie, "Remaking Whoopi," *West Side Spirit,* August 21, 1990, pp. 1, 3, 8, 23.

28. David Rensin, "Goldberg," *US,* October 1992, pp. 67–74.

29. Elisa Leonellli, "Love and the Single Parent," *Venice,* June 1993, pp. 40–43.

30. Ibid.

31. Transcript, *Saturday Today,* NBC-TV, September 1, 1992, interviewer Wendy Hobbs.

32. Jill Nelson, "The World According to Whoopi," *USA Weekend,* August 5, 1994, pp. 4–5 (in *New York Daily News*).

33. Bob Strauss, "Whoopi's Words," *Los Angeles Daily News,* December 10, 1996, LA Life Weekend section, pp. 6–7.

34. Michele Willens, "Whoopi—Hollywood Big Wheel," *McCall's,* March 1995 pp. 94–98.

35. Transcript, *Good Morning America,* ABC-TV, January 30, 1995, interviewer Chantal.

36. Michele Willens, "Hollywood Big Wheel."

37. Transcript, *Good Morning America,* ABC-TV, September 5, 1996, interviewer Charles Gibson.

38. Michele Willens, "Hollywood Big Wheel."

Books

Adams, Mary Agnes. *Whoopi Goldberg: From Street to Stardom*. New York: Dillon Press, 1993.

Barth, Jack. *Roadside Hollywood*. Chicago: Contemporary Books, 1991.

Blue, Rose and Corinne J. Naden. *Whoopi Goldberg: Entertainer*. New York: Chelsea House, 1995.

Bogle, Donald. *Blacks in American Films and Television*. New York: Garland Publishing, 1988.

———. *Toms, Coons, Mulattoes, Mammies and Bucks*. (revised ed.), New York: Continuum Publishing, 1992.

Bonavoglia, Angela, ed. *The Choices We Made*. New York: Random House, 1991, pp. 115-23.

Brode, Douglas. *The Films of Steven Spielberg*. Secaucus, N.J.: Citadel Press, 1995.

Farrand, Phil. *The Nitpicker's Guide for Next Generation Trekkers*. New York: Dell Publishing, 1993.

Gordon, William A. *Shot on This Site*. Secaucus, N.J.: Citadel Press, 1995.

Katz, Sandor. *Whoopi Goldberg: Performer With a Heart*. New York: Chelsea House, 1997.

Lance, Steven. *Written Out of Television*. Lanham, Md.: Madison Books, 1996.

Leab, Daniel J. *From Sambo to Superspade*. Boston: Houghton Mifflin Co., 1976.

Nemecek, Larry. *The Star Trek Next Generation Companion*. New York: Pocket Books, 1995.

Null, Gary. *Black Hollywood: From 1970 to Today*. Secaucus, N.J.: Citadel Press, 1993.

Parish, James R. *Let's Talk! America's Favorite Talk Show Hosts*. Las Vegas: Pioneer Paperbacks, 1993.

———. *Today's Black Hollywood*. New York: Pinnacle Books, 1995.

Parish, James R., and Don Stanke. *Hollywood Baby Boomers*. New York: Garland, 1992.

Taylor, Philip M. *Steven Spielberg*. New York: Continuum, 1992.

Terrace, Vincent. *Experimental Television, Test Films, Pilots, and Trial Series*. Jefferson, N.C.:McFarland, 1997.

Walker, Alice. *The Color Purple*. New York: Pocket Books, 1982.

———. *The Same River Twice: Honoring the Difficult*. New York: Pocket Books, 1996.

Warren, Roz, ed. *Revolutionary Laughter: The World of Women Comics*. Freedom, Calif.: Crossing Press, 1995.

Magazine, Newspapers, and Other Periodicals

Alexander Ron. "*Soapdish* Dresses in *Dynasty* Style." *New York Times,* May 28, 1991.

Archerd, Army. "Just for Variety" column. *Daily Variety,* October 10, 1986.

———. "Just for Variety" column, *Daily Variety,* April 27, 1987.

Arup, Evie. "Is This Sister Acting Up." *British Weekly Journal,* January 5, 1995.

Bandler, Michael J. "Whoopi Goldberg." *Arts & Entertainment,* July 1993, pp. 23–24.

Berlin, Joey. "Ted and Whoopi Aren't Talking." *New York Post,* May 22, 1993, p. 11.

Bishop Katherine. "Whoopi Goldberg's Role, From Sidekick to Star." *New York Times,* August 26, 1986.

"Bitter Whoopi: Ted Danson Broke My Heart." *Star,* August 30, 1994, p. 21.

"Blacks Fail to See Humor in Ted Danson's Blackface Tribute to Whoopi Goldberg." *Jet,* November 1, 1993, pp. 56–59.

Brennan, Steve. "Whoopi Needs Clean Sweeps." *Hollywood Reporter,* October 26, 1992, pp. 3, 23.

Broeske, Pat. H. "The Crash, the Burn, the Return . . . John Travolta's Talking about a Comeback." *Newsday,* September 8, 1989, p. II–12.

———. "Whoopi Wises Up." Los Angeles Times, April 22, 1990, Calendar section, pp. 3, 88-90.

California, Letters to Editor section, March 1985.

Campbell, Bebe Moore. "Whoopi Talks B(l)ack." *Essence,* January 1997, pp. 56–58, 100–2.

Chambers, Veronica. "Sisters Are Doin' It for Themselves." *Premiere,* special issue, 1993, pp. 90–94.

"*Cheers* Hunk Ted Danson Steps Out With Costar Whoopi." *Star,* October 13, 1992, pp. 36–37.

Coates, Julia. "Ted Danson & Whoopi Rekindle Romance at D.C. Concert." *National Enquirer,* February 2, 1993, p. 34.

———. "Ted Danson in Horrifying Car Crash." *National Enquirer,* November 9, 1993, p. 20.

Coates, Julia, and Patricia Towle. "Whoopi Dumps Ted." *National Enquirer,* November 16, 1993.

Coleman, Janet. "Making Whoopi." *Vanity Fair,* July 1984, pp. 36–38, 108–109.

Collier, Aldore. "Whoopi Goldberg: Tough and Tender in New Film Drama, *Clara's Heart.*" *Jet,* October 24, 1988, pp. 30–32.

Dworkin, Susan. "The Making of *Color Purple.*" *MS,* December 1985, pp. 66–70, 94–95.

Ebert, Roger. "Goldberg's Ghosts." *New York Daily News,* March 10, 1991, City Lights section.

"The $8 Million Woman." *Ladies Home Journal,* June 1993, p. 52.

Erickson, Steve. "Whoopi Goldberg." *Rolling Stone,* August 8, 1996, pp. 39–42, 90, 92, 94.

Freilich, Leon, and Steve Tinney. "Whoopi's Mr. Romance. He's Taught Her to Love Again With Candlelight and Cuddles." *Star,* April 2, 1996, p. 24.

"Friend of Labor." *People,* May 16, 1994, p. 52.

Furse, Jane. "Whoopi's Recipe for Laughs." *New York Daily News,* December 1, 1993.

Garchik, Leah. "Whoopi and Other Characters." *San Francisco Chronicle,* February 6, 1983, Datebook section, pp. 3–7.

"Ghosts of Mississippi." *Jet,* December 30, 1996, pp. 56–61.

Gittelson, Natalie. "Whoopi & Jean Rap." *McCall's,* November 1990, pp. 110–14.

Gould, Martin. "I Was Whoopi Goldberg's First Hubby." *Star,* August 31, 1993.

Guthmann, Edward. "A Comic's Uncanny Replay of Moms Mabley." *San Francisco Sunday Examiner and Chronicle,* May 27, 1984, Datebook section, pp. 23–24.

―――. "Doing It Her Way, Whoopi's a Smash." *San Francisco Chronicle,* December 15, 1984, Datebook section, pp. 34–36.

Harper, Hilliard, "S.D. Version of Bertolt Brecht Play Has American Setting." *Los Angeles Times,* June 15, 1981, pp. F6–F7.

Haun, Harry. "The Making of a Whoopi." *Playbill* l, November 1984, pp. 44–46.

―――. "Whoopee! Whoopi's on Broadway." *New York Daily News,* October 21, 1984, Leisure section, p. 3.

Honeycutt, Kirk. "Host Goldberg Thrilled by 'My Date With Oscar.' " *Hollywood Reporter,* February 7, 1994, pp. 1, 16.

Hutchings, David. "Whoopi's Hideaway." *In Style,* August 1994, pp. 50–59.

Janusonis Michael. "First Cher. Then Tina. Now Whoopi." *Long Beach Press-Telegram,* May 31, 1987.

Kahn, Alice. "That's Not Funny." *San Francisco Express,* March 25, 1983, pp. 1, 9–11.

Kearney, Jill. "Color Her Anything." *American Film,* December 1985, pp. 25–27.

Kempley, Rita. "Whoopi Goldberg." *US,* November 14, 1988, pp. 34–39.

Key, Melissa. "Whoopi Goldberg's Dad Dies of AIDS." *Star,* June 15, 1993, p. 5.

King, Susan. "Whoopi and the Oscars: The Sequel." *Los Angeles Times,* March 25 1996, Calendar section, pp. F1, F5.

Kogan, Rick. "Her *Chaos* Will Hit the Boards in Chicago." *Chicago Tribune,* May 16, 1988, section 2, p. 3.

Leonelli, Elisa. "Love and the Single Parent." *Venice,* June 1993, pp. 40–43.

Levitt, Shelley, and Kristina Johnson. "Changing Partner" column. *People,* November 22, 1993.

Lieberman, Jane. "Starlight Foundation Honors Goldberg Charity Work." *Los Angeles Times,* March 15, 1989.

Lurie, Rod. "Openers." *Los Angeles Times,* May 1993, p. 16.

———. "Remaking Whoopi." *West Side Spirit,* August 21, 1990, pp. 1, 3, 8, 23.

"Making Whoopi!" *Globe,* October 31, 1995, p. 29.

"Marriage Addict Whoopi at It Again." *Globe,* September 17, 1996, p. 38.

McDougal, Dennis. "Whoopi Takes on Hollywood." *TV Guide,* March 19, 1994, pp. 26–37.

Meeley, Darrah. "Close Up: Whoopi Goldberg." *Screen Actor,* fall 1988, pp. 16–19.

Michaelson, Judith. "Finally, the Band Will Play." *Los Angeles Times,* March 21, 1993, Calendar section, pp. 5, 74–77.

Mitchell, Sean. "Waking the Ghosts." *Los Angeles Times,* December 15, 1996, Calendar section, pp. 5, 34–39.

Modine, Matthew. "Whoopi Goldberg." *Interview,* June, 1992, pp. 88–90, 117.

Morrison, Mark. "Remakin' Whoopi." *Cable Guide,* February 1990, pp. 25–27.

Nelson, Jill. "The World According to Whoopi." *New York Daily News,* August 5, 1994, USA Weekend section, pp. 4–5.

Norville, Deborah. "Girl Talk With Whoopi Goldberg." *McCall's,* June 1993, pp. 118–21, 162.

Pearlman, Cindy. "The Movie that Made a Man Out of Whoopi." *UpTown,* November 12, 1996, pp. 6–7.

Pickle, Betsy. "Could It Be Love?" *Scripps Howard Syndicate,* June 2, 1993.

Provenzano, Tom. "Whoopi Goldberg." *Drama-Logue,* December 9, 1993, p. 16.

Radner, Dotson. "I Knew What I Wanted to Be." *Parade,* November 1, 1993, pp. 4–6.

Rensin, David. "Whoopi Goldberg." *Playboy,* June 1987, pp. 51–57,154–57.

Rodack, Jeffrey. "Revealed! Fabio Ruined Whoopi's Marriage." *National Enquirer,* December 10, 1996, p. 2.

Roush, Matt. "A Wounded Whoopi on Ted's Turnaround." *USA Today,* September 5, 1994, p. 2.

Russo, Vito. "Goldberg: A Matter of Heart." *Advocate,* November 21, 1988, pp. 43–45.

Sales, Nancy Jo. "Whoopi, Frankly." *New York,* February 17, 1997, pp. 4–14.

Shapiro, Marc. "Fantasy Medium." *Starlog,* November 1990, pp. 9–12.

Sheff, David. "Whoopi Goldberg." *Playboy,* January 1977, pp. 51–58, 178–80.

Siegel, Greg. "Taking Pride and Paying Homage." *Entertainment Weekly,* August 25, 1994, p. 3.

Siegel, Scott and Barbara Siegel. "Whoopi Goldberg: the 'In' Girl." *Drama-Logue,* September 19, 1996, p. 5.

Silverman, Stephen M. "Whoopi's Cushion." *New York Post,* October 27, 1987, p. 33.

Skow, John. "The Joy of Being Whoopi." *Time*, September 21, 1992, pp. 58–60.

Spelling, Ian. "Classic *Trek* Inspired Goldberg." *Los Angeles Times*, August 15, 1993.

Stanton, Ali. "Enthusiastic Applause and Hoopla for Whoopi Goldberg." *New York Amsterdam News*, February 25, 1994, p. 28.

Stimac, Elias. "Whoopi Goldberg." *Drama-Logue*, May 27, 1993, pp. 4–6.

Strauss, Bob. "Whoopi's Words." *Los Angeles Daily News*, December 10, 1996, LA Life Weekend section, pp. 6–7.

Swarns, Rachel L. "Someone Familiar . . . Stages a Homecoming." *New York Times*, February 9 1997, p. H–4.

"Ted Woos Whoopi With Wine, in $900-a-Night Hideaway." *Star*, December 1, 1992, pp. 36–37.

Thomas, Bob. "Whoopi Goldberg Takes Acting Seriously." *Associated Press Syndicate*, October 29, 1986.

"The Transom" column. *New York Observer*, October 18, 1993.

Turan, Kenneth. "Whoopi's Two Films Lift Her Cannes Spirits." *Los Angeles Times*, May 12, 1992, pp. F1, F4.

Van Gelder, Lindsay. "I'm Whoopi and You're Not." *New York Daily News*, December 22, 1995, Magazine section, pp. 5, 12–13.

Weiner, Bernard. "Whoopi's *Moms* Returns in Style." *San Francisco Chronicle*, May 27, 1984, Datebook section, p. 37.

Wendt, Carolyn. "Whoopi Goldberg." San Francisco *City Area Monthly*, October 1992.

Wenner, Jan S. "This Sister's Act." *US*, April 1994, pp. 59–64, 88.

"Whoopi and Ted Sizzle." *Star*, February 9, 1993, pp. 2–3.

"Whoopi Goldberg." *Aquarian Weekly*, November 14, 1985, pp. 9, 55.

"Whoopi Goldberg." *Interview*, December 1984, pp. 75–76

"Whoopi Goldberg." *Jet*, November 30, 1989, p. 22.

"Whoopi Goldberg." *Jet*, August 29, 1994, pp. 32–35.

"Whoopi Goldberg." *Luxury Lifestyles*, September 1993, p. 11.

"Whoopi Goldberg." *People*, December 23, 1985, pp. 99–103.

"Whoopi Goldberg." *San Francisco Focus*, June 1992.

"Whoopi Goldberg: I Turned My Back on My Daughter Because I Wanted to Be a Big Star." *Star*, June 2, 1992, p. 31.

"Whoopi Goldberg Plans to Play Lead in *Forum*." *New York Times*, October 10, 1996.

"Whoopi Pledges New TV Talker Won't Be Pushy." *Hollywood Reporter*, June 12, 1992.

"Whoopi's Making Whoopi." *Star*, April 30 1996.

"Whoopi, Ted Danson, Issue Joint Statement." *Jet*, November 22, 1993, p. 16.

Willens, Michele. "Whoopi—Hollywood Big Wheel." *McCall's*, March 1995, pp. 94–98.

Winer-Bernheimer, Linda. "I've Taken All the Heat I'm Going to." *Newsday,* August 7, 1994, Fanfare section, p 4.

———. "Whoopi: Bruised But Unbowed. *Los Angeles Times,* August 8, 1994, pp. F1, F5.

Winn, Steve. "How Homages Do and Don't Work." *San Francisco Chronicle,* June 10, 1984.

Wolf, Jeanne. "I Stole My Name from a Cushion." *New York Daily News,* October 20, 1996.

Wuntch, Philip. "Celebrity Status Makes Whoopi a Little Uneasy." *Chicago Tribune,* December 21, 1985.

Zook, Kristal Brent. "Maid in America." *Los Angeles Weekly,* August 12, 1994, p. 33.

Television Program Transcripts

Bill Boggs' Corner Table (TV Food Network):
April 27, 1997

CBS This Morning (CBS-TV)
March 29, 1990
January 15, 1991
March 26, 1991
February 25, 1992
June 3, 1992
May 28, 1993
August 24, 1994
February 7, 1995
September 6, 1996

The Charlie Rose Show (PBS-TV)
December 30, 1996

Geraldo (Syndicated-TV)
October 29, 1993

Good Morning America (ABC-TV)
August 20, 1991
September 8, 1992
February 16, 1993
December 7, 1993
December 30, 1993

March 21, 1994
July 24, 1994
August 25, 1994
January 30, 1995
November 10, 1995
May 29, 1996
September 5, 1996

Larry King Live (CNN)
October 8, 1992
April 29, 1994
February 9, 1995
September 18, 1996

NBC Saturday Today (NBC-TV)
September 19, 1992
August 27, 1994

NBC Today (NBC-TV)
May 9, 1990
June 3, 1991
May 29, 1992
May 27, 1993
October 11, 1993
October 24, 1996

Oprah Winfrey Show (Syndicated TV)
May 1, 1990
April 5, 1991

Showbiz Today (CNN)
April 3, 1990
May 26, 1993
August 10, 1994

60 Minutes (CBS-TV)
February 14, 1993

Internet Web Sites

Acme Whoopi Home Page: http://www.bestware.net/spreng/whoopi/
index.html
All-Movie Guide Database: http://ALLMOVIE.com/amg/
movie_Root.html?86,30
The AVI Mall Entertainment Archives: http://avimall.com/entertain/index.html
Buzz Online: http://www.buzzmag.com
Eagle-1 Lone Eagle Database: http://www.loneeagle.com/eaglei/index.html
E! Online: http://www.eonline.com
The Internet Movie Database: http://us.imdb.org
Mr. Showbiz: http://www.mrshowbiz.com
Pathfinder: http://www.pathfinder. com
The Whoopi Home Page: http://www.tu-berlin.de/~gruhlke/forum/whoopi

About the Author

JAMES ROBERT PARISH, a unique show business chronicler, is the author of ninety published major books on the performing arts. Considered an authority on the subject, he is often a guest on TV-talk and news shows to discuss Hollywood—past and present.

Born in Cambridge, Massachusetts, Mr. Parish attended the University of Pennsylvania and graduated Phi Beta Kappa with a degree in English. A graduate of the University of Pennsylvania Law School, he is a member of the New York Bar. As president of Entertainment Copyright Research Co., Inc., he headed a major media researching facility. Later he was a reviewer-interviewer for *Variety* and *Motion Picture Daily* trade newspapers as well as an entertainment publicist.

Besides contributing to national magazines on the subject of show business, Mr. Parish is advisor for Greenwood Press' acclaimed series, Bio-Bibliographies in the Performing Arts. He is also a consultant to publishers and data base resources on the entertainment industry.

Mr. Parish resides in Studio City, CA.

Index